The Rights and Wrongs of Children

M. D. A. Freeman

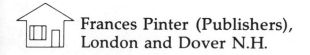
Frances Pinter (Publishers),
London and Dover N.H.

©M. D. A. Freeman 1983

First published in Great Britain in 1983 by
Frances Pinter (Publishers) 5 Dryden St., London WC2E 9NW

ISBN 0 903804 20 4   hardback
ISBN 0 86187 226 6   paperback

First published in the USA in 1983 by
Frances Pinter (Publishers) 51 Washington Street
Dover New Hampshire 03820

Library of Congress Cataloging in Publication Data

Freeman, Michael D. A.
   The rights and wrongs of children.
   Includes bibliographical references.
   1. Children's rights — England.   I. Title.
HQ789.F73   1983   305.2'3'0942   83-124532
ISBN 0-903804-20-4
ISBN 0-86187-226-6 (pbk.)

British Library Cataloguing in Publication Data

Freeman, M. D. A.
   The rights and wrongs of children.
   1. Children's rights — Great Britain
   I. Title
   323.4   HQ789

   ISBN 0-90380-420-4
   ISBN 0-86187-226-6

Typeset in IBM Journal by Folio Photosetting, Bristol
Printed by SRP Ltd, Exeter

CONTENTS

Dedication

To my children Hilary and Jeremy
and my nephews and niece,
Jonathan and Lucy Clein and James Corré

PREFACE

Much has been written on children's rights in the last ten years. There have been a number of collections of essays and several monographs. Much was published to cash in on the International Year of the Child which was 'celebrated' in 1979. The temptation to join that bandwagon has been resisted. This book is offered as a reflection on the status of children a thousand days after IYC has come to an end.

Children's rights are a complex problem, and there are no easy solutions. What is required is a fine balance, so that the personality and autonomy of children are recognised and they are not abandoned to their rights. As a student of the subject for a number of years, I have been struck by the intemperate nature of some of the proposals and by the lack of a coherent structure. Much talk about children's rights has been trite. This is regrettable. The insights exist in moral and legal philosophy, in psychology, in history, in sociology as well as other disciplines but too much writing on the subject has failed to take account of them. This book is an attempt to put these together into a coherent whole.

I have not attempted complete coverage. Writing as a lawyer I have tried to concentrate on areas of children's rights upon which the law can have some impact. I was at first disposed to look at the problems from the perspective of different legal systems but this proved unmanageable. Accordingly, the main focus of attention is on English law, though there are many references to other systems.

In writing the book I have received help from many sources. My ideas have germinated over a long period and have been tested out at conferences. Many people have given of their time and thought. They are too numerous to mention and it would be invidious to single anyone out. The responsibility is anyway mine. I should however like to thank my wife, Vivien, for her help and patience. My gratitude is also extended to the secretarial staff of the Law Faculty of University College London and in particular to Eleanor Maloney, Panna Shah and Ann Watson who have knocked my manuscript and its many drafts into good shape.

PROLOGUE

First, it was blacks, then women and now, in the last decade or so, children and youth. Movements to bring equal opportunities, to root out discrimination, practices such as affirmative action and institutional frameworks like the Commission For Racial Equality and the Equal Opportunities Commission have arrived on the scene: their goal, to obliterate the less than equal treatment of ethnic minorities and women. This is not the place to estimate their impact or success. The move towards children's rights, even children's liberation, seems in perspective inevitable, part of the inexorable progress of mankind. And yet, of course, it takes but a moment's reflection to realise that the position of children is not strictly comparable with that of women or blacks. Children are by definition not adults, even if the dividing line between the two is relatively arbitrary, a historical and shifting social construction. Much depends on what is understood by being an adult, for it is certainly the case that arguments used to deny children and adolescents rights can equally well be produced to deny those of mature years those very same rights.

This is part of the problem. Take, for example, the right to vote. In England this is exercisable at the age of eighteen, the age of majority. But many sixteen-year-olds and doubtless many children of a younger age are politically aware, are capable of making an informed political choice. We do not give them the vote because there is a widely held belief that children in general are incompetent to exercise the responsibilities and discharge the obligations associated with full citizenship. But if competence is the test, a by no means insignificant proportion of children must be granted full political status and a large number of adults would have to be disenfranchised. So what are the arguments adduced to deny children the vote? There is the one which relies on incompetence but this, we have seen, can equally undermine the right of many adults. Another argument cites the child's lack of experience and understanding. It suggests or at least implies that these are gained during the traditional period of childhood. This argument typically adduces the fact, if fact it be, that children lack foresight, that given the capacity to make decisions they will make disastrous ones. But is this not the case with adults too? It cannot really be suggested that none of the

1

policies undertaken by governments of the day is harmful. Many, indeed, of those pursued by the current British Government are injurious not least to children themselves. If experience and/or understanding is the criterion, many children would have the vote and many adults would not. A further argument would justify denying children the franchise in terms of a belief that the decisions of children are not based on rational, that is in the minds of those who put such arguments usually utilitarian, considerations. Thus Scarre, justifying paternalism and not specifically disenfranchisement, argues for intervention in an individual's affairs 'when there is reason to believe his decisions are not based on rational considerations, and that they are likely to result in a diminution of his stock of existing good, or underachievement of his possible stock of good'.[1] To Scarre 'rational actions are those which are directed to maximizing the expected utility of the agent. In addition, actions backed by rational decisions typically manifest themselves as elements of a systematic approach adopted by the agent for maximizing his good.'[2] Scarre's concept of rationality is unduly confined but leaving that aside, can it really be said that adults' actions are always motivated by rational considerations? Indeed, it would not be difficult to find examples of decisions motivated by rational considerations which did not maximise the agent's utility nor were expected to do so.

This debate could be pursued further but at this juncture in the book it serves merely as an illustration and a warning. It is relatively easy to demolish the arguments adduced to support the double standard employed in our treatment of adults and children. It is also not difficult to show that children today occupy a different status from that of the young in earlier centuries and in different cultures. The line between adulthood and minority was not drawn as clearly by earlier generations.[3] There is abundant evidence that children in past centuries participated in adult activities, work, sex and leisure in a way that would surprise and shock most of us. What conclusions are we to draw from this? If moral argument and history appear to be on the side of the enfranchisers and liberators, are we to admit that we are wrong? Should we abandon the distinction between children and adults even if this means, as one commentator astutely put it, 'abandoning children to their rights'?[4]

Few, I think, would go quite this far. Even the most extreme proponents of children's liberation would preserve some protective legislation, though wisely they would look at all claims to protect children with scepticism. But the conclusion is drawn by some that if children worked in earlier societies then today's restrictions on child labour should be removed. Thus, Hoyles can write: 'The crucial separation which modern children suffer is the separation from work.'[5] Note the word 'suffer': when children had the 'right' to work, they certainly suffered.[6] Both Farson [7] and Holt [8] advocate giving children the right to work: to Farson it is part of what he calls the 'right to economic power'. They would go much further than this. They would give the child the right to do, in general, what any adult may legally do. 'In important matters', writes Holt, 'nobody can know better than the child himself.'[9] So central is this to his thought that he italicises the sentence to stress its importance. Surprisingly, Holt also recognises that young children are egocentric. He writes: they are 'animals and sensualists; to them what feels good *is* good. They are self-absorbed and selfish. . . . They are barbarians, primitives.'[10] Farson's manifesto is strikingly similar and so are his arguments. Overriding all 'birthrights', he argues, is the right of self-determination. So, he claims 'children, like adults, should have the right to decide the matters which affect them most directly.'[11] Farson concedes that there will be resistance to his ideas. He foresees opposition from 'those who are closest to the problem: parents, teachers and children themselves.'[12] Presumably, he would explain away children's opposition to their own liberation in terms of false consciousness or in some such similar way.

It is my view that the liberationists' case is politically naive, philosophically faulty and plainly ignores psychological evidence. But it is the case which has attracted most attention. It is grist for the media's mill which, on the whole, would ridicule the whole notion of children's rights, just as it tried with some initial success to uphold the women's movement as committed to trivia such as 'bra-burning'. Because the case presented by Farson, Holt, Friedenberg[13] and a few others is naive, it is easy to dismiss the credibility of the whole argument for children's rights. My aim is to put the case for children's rights without committing myself to a position such as that adopted by proponents of children's liberation.

We have distanced ourselves from children and, in doing so, we have to an extent dehumanised the young. Children are persons, not property. Sentimentality towards children (in John Holt's words, seeing children as 'cute')[14] is no substitute for the recognition of a child's entitlement to the right to equal concern and respect.[15] This does not mean the treatment of children as adults. It requires, however, respect for the competencies of children. It argues for children to be seen as persons, not cases. It demands that children's capacities be acknowledged, that they be given a say in the decision-making processes concerning them whenever this is feasible and they are capable of participating meaningfully. It expects that the interests of children will be taken into account in public policy-making, whether the issue is lead in petrol, taxation, the financing of local government or education. It requires the recognition of a whole gamut of children's rights: protection from abuse and neglect, a fair system of justice for those children who break the law and many others adumbrated in this book. Above all, it necessitates that we provide 'a childhood for every child'[16] and not, as Farson and Holt would, an adulthood for every child.

A dichotomy has been drawn between a nurturance and a self-determination orientation,[17] between, as Farson puts it, protecting children and protecting their rights.[18] I do not see these as polar positions, rather as points on a continuum. We need to do both. I am fully prepared to admit the failures of the protectionist philosophy, exemplified in the child-saving movement.[19] These must be guarded against: we can learn from errors of the past. But protecting children and protecting their rights are not incompatible aims. Rights are linked with autonomy. But interference with a child's liberty is an inescapable consequence of the biological and psychological dependence of children. We must have a criterion against which to measure such interventions. We need a morally neutral theory of the good. It is as unacceptable to make a parent's notion of this count as it would be to make the state's. So where are we to discover this? I argue in Chapter 2 that the key may lie in Rawls's theory of justice.[20] We must look to the original position and to the principles that rationally autonomous people behind the veil of ignorance would choose.[21] The exercise must perforce be hypothetical. We must ask ourselves the question: from what actions and decisions would we wish, as children, to be protected, on the assumption that we would in due course desire to be rationally autonomous, capable of planning our lives and deciding on our own system of ends as rational beings? Looked at in this way, idealised though it is, we can certainly defend much protective legislation. Some form of compulsory education, not necessarily that which currently prevails, can also be justified in these terms.

The goal, however, must ultimately be the child's rational independence. To this end a theory of liberal paternalism, such as that suggested here, imposes duties on parents to prepare children for this eventual independence.[22] This requires them to recognise that critical rationality is acquired gradually and to encourage its emergence and growth. Adolescents in particular must be encouraged to take decisions of their own. Not all decisions can, however, be taken by adolescents. Paternalism, at least the kind of liberal paternalism justified here, can be used to defend the taking of certain decisions on adolescents' behalfs. An example I have in mind is education. It is through this that adolescents acquire the capacity for full autonomy. It is in part a result of this that adolescents are rendered capable of taking decisions in matters which affect them. A morally neutral theory of the good would, I believe, require adolescents to undergo education whether they wished to do so or not. That many would not is a sign that short-term gains rather than lasting benefits were uppermost in their thoughts.

I have used the terms 'children' and 'adolescents' but I have not specified ages. The omission is deliberate. Rigid age stereotypes are unhelpful. It depends on the activity, a fact recognised by legal systems even if their classifications are often suspect, and the individual child and adolescent. Flexibility is more important than certainty. It may be that we need an action for emancipation to be brought by, or on behalf of, an adolescent who can demonstrate himself to be capable of taking major decisions.

The first two chapters of this book spell out concepts and justifications. There is an analysis of the concept of childhood and a framework for analysing rights. A theory of rights based upon liberal paternalism is then adumbrated. Subsequent chapters focus on problem areas. Here I have necessarily been selective. The areas chosen, delinquency, child abuse and neglect, children in care, the divorce decision, parental autonomy in child-rearing and children's autonomy, have been selected for three reasons: (i) they seem to me to be central to the debate; (ii) they are areas which interest me personally and (iii) they are, on the whole, areas where the law has something to say and may be able to achieve something. There are other putative rights such as that 'to responsive design', to 'alternative home improvements' or 'travel', the first advocated by Farson,[23] the third by Holt,[24] which, however desirable, do not, I think, lie within the capacity of law to achieve. The rights I seek for children and adolescents are put forward as a first step towards recognising their personality and individuality. We need to change childhood but this need not mean ignoring its existence.

Notes

1. G. Scarre, 'Children and Paternalism', *Philosophy*, 55 (1980), pp. 117, 123.
2. Idem.
3. See P. Ariès, *Centuries of Childhood*, London, Jonathan Cape, 1962.
4. B. Hafen, 'Puberty, Privacy and Protection: The Risks of Children's Rights', *American Bar Association Journal*, 63 (1977), p. 1383.
5. M. Hoyles, *Changing Childhood*, London, Writers and Readers, 1979, p. 5.
6. See e.g. J. Walvin, *A Child's World: A Social History of English Childhood 1800–1914*, Harmondsworth, Penguin, 1982, ch. 4.
7. Richard Farson, *Birthrights*, Harmondsworth, Penguin, 1978, ch. 10.
8. John Holt, *Escape From Childhood*, Harmondsworth, Penguin, 1975, ch. 18.
9. Ibid., p. 19.
10. Ibid., p. 14.
11. Farson, *Birthrights*, p. 27.
12. Ibid., p. 10.
13. Friedenberg, *The Anti-American Generation*, New Brunswick, New Jersey, Transaction Books, 1971.
14. Holt, *Escape from Childhood*, p. 85.
15. Cf. R. Dworkin, *Taking Rights Seriously*, London, Duckworth, 1977, ch. 6.
16. The phrase is Mark Gerzon's. See *A Childhood For Every Child — Politics of Parenthood*, New York, Outerbridge & Lazard, 1973.
17. See C. Rogers and L. Wrightsman, 'Attitudes Towards Children's Rights: Nurturance or Self-Determination', *Journal of Social Issues*, 34, no. 2 (1978), p. 59.
18. Farson, *Birthrights*, p. 165.
19. See, e.g. A. Platt, *The Child-Savers*, Chicago, University of Chicago Press, 1977, (2nd ed.).
20. See also V. Worsfold, 'A Philosophical Justification For Children's Rights', *Harvard Educational Review*, 44 (1974), p. 142. I used not to think this. See 'The Rights of Children in the International Year of the Child', *Current Legal Problems*, 33 (1980), pp. 1, 19.
21. The terms are John Rawls's. See *A Theory of Justice*, Cambridge, Mass., Harvard University Press, 1972.
22. This is recognised by John Locke, *Two Treatises of Government* (ed. P. Laslett) 1967, pp. 322-35.
23. Farson, *Birthrights*, pp. 63, 42 respectively.
24. Holt, *Escape from Childhood*, p. 149.

1   CHILDREN'S RIGHTS: THE EVOLUTION OF A CONCEPT

'Children's rights' has become something of a 'hurrah' idea. We all claim to be in favour. More than twenty years ago the United Nations passed a Declaration of the Rights of the Child (reproduced in the Appendix). The year 1979 was set aside as the International Year of the Child. There had been international years before this. International Geophysical Year in 1957 was the first. Refugees, mental health, telecommunications, tourists, human rights, freedom from hunger, books, population, women, anti-apartheid and the disabled were to follow. This year, 1983, is the International Year of World Communications. Of all international years, it was IYC, as it became known, that most vividly caught the public imagination. Whether IYC achieved much will be considered in the concluding chapter. Chapters 3 – 7 focus on a number of problem areas and give the reader an opportunity to make his or her own assessment of the success or otherwise of our current concern for children. If concern for children's rights is to be meaningful then every year must be an international year of the child. In this sense IYC has set us a continuing challenge.[1]

The expression 'children's rights' brings together two concepts, both of which are problematic. The concept of rights is considered in the next chapter. We must pause here to consider what we mean by children. It is easy to assume that childhood is a fixed notion determined by biological and psychological facts. But childhood, like adulthood or old age, is to a large extent a social construct. In Britain, indeed in much of the world, childhood ends at eighteen. It is convenient, even imperative, to have a specific dividing line between childhood and adulthood. There is, of course, no magic in the age of eighteen. At different stages of our history ten and twelve may have been the age of majority. In medieval times a distinction was drawn between sons of knights and sons of inferior classes. The former came of age at twenty-one at which time they were deemed strong enough to bear full armour and fight as a knight. The latter, as late as the twelfth century, were regarded as of full age at fourteen or fifteen, when, it was assumed, they were capable of working the land. By the thirteenth century the upper-class standard became the norm for all classes[2] and the age of majority remained twenty-one until 1970.[3] Further, today children come of age for the purpose of acquiring the capacity to participate in different activities at different ages.[4] They can own an air rifle at fourteen,[5] leave school and commence full-time employment at sixteen[6] and buy an alcoholic drink in a public house at eighteen.[7] A ten-year-old may be convicted of a criminal offence.[8] If there is any logic behind these distinctions it is difficult to detect. They are, in fact, the product of historical accidents and responses to particular pressures at particular times. Distinctions also exist between girls and boys: for example, in law boys acquire the capacity for sexual relationships at an earlier age (fourteen) than girls (sixteen).[9] This distinction too is rooted in cultural norms and values rather than biological facts or psychological realities.

There are complex moral problems also in deciding when human personality begins. To what extent do the unborn have rights?[10] Should we treat foetuses as legal persons?[11] Attempts have been made, notably in American judicial decisions, to break up the period of gestation into trimesters. In *Roe* v. *Wade*,[12] the American Supreme Court argued that the state's interest in protecting pre-natal life grew 'substantially as the woman approaches term'. The 'compelling point', as Justice Blackmun described it, is at viability. Of course, as critics are apt to point out, an infant born at full term will not be 'viable' for very long without human intervention and help. Further, as technology enables more and more premature babies to be saved, this test would increasingly reduce the time during which a mother is permitted to have an abortion. In Missouri, viability is statutorily defined as 'that stage of fetal development when the life of the unborn child may be continued indefinitely outside the womb by natural or artificial life-supportive systems.' The Supreme Court has upheld this defini-tion.[13] Abortion is and will remain a controversial problem. In Britain there have been a succession of parliamentary bills which have attempted to tighten up what their sponsors consider to be over-indulgent legislation.[14] A central issue has been and remains the latest time at which abortion is to be permitted. Is a fixed date preferable to a viability test? Viability may vary with each pregnancy.[15] The dilemmas raised by the abortion decision are not unique to the abortion situation. Who, for example, should decide whether defective newborns live? Both of these questions raise issues as to who should make child-rearing decisions. How much parental autonomy should be allowed? Should decisions be left to experts, to medical personnel, child development experts or judges? What say should the child himself have? Who speaks for the child? Who, indeed, speaks for the interests of the unborn foetus? These questions are further considered in Chapter 7.

The question 'what is a child?' is one answered by adults. Adults impose their conceptions of childishness on beings whom they consider to be children. There have been different conceptions of the nature of childhood at different periods of history. There has in the modern period been a tendency to associate children with all sorts of negative qualities, weakness, irrationality, imbecility, prelogicism, primitivism. Adults may have less contact with children now than in medieval times. Our society is marked by greater segregation of ages than earlier societies were. Farson comments with some justification that our ideas about childhood are 'being developed and reinforced not through contact between adults and children, but through lack of it.'[16]

It is not only those whose chronological age is low who are treated differently from adults. Adults too are sometimes treated as children. The American slave, the black in South Africa today, are just two examples of persons regarded by those in authority as children. Like children they are kept in a lowly position and under constant 'paternal' supervision. It is common to refer to them as 'boy' or to address them by their first name alone. The master will often have the right (and certainly the power) to inflict corporal punishment. The whipping of farm labourers is still common in South Africa today.[17] There may be control over the servant's sexual activities or his purchasing abilities. To be a child one does not have to be young.[18] It seems that those in authority determine who is a child. In this sense childhood is a social construct, a man-made phenomenon.

The Invention of Childhood

Childhood must be put into its historical context. Historical evidence is crucial, for history demonstrates both repeated patterns and wide disparities in the way children have been treated and been expected to behave at different periods of time and in different cultural contexts.[19]

The most interesting interpretation of the history of childhood is found in Philippe Ariès's study *Centuries of Childhood*.[20] He argues that our whole concept of childhood today is a modern invention, largely invented in Europe in the seventeenth century. He points out that in the tenth century artists in Europe were unable to depict a child except as a man on a smaller scale. He continues:

> in medieval society, the idea of childhood did not exist; this is not to suggest that children were neglected, forsaken or despised. The idea of childhood is not to be confused with affection for children: it corresponds to an awareness of the particular nature of childhood, that particular nature which distinguishes the child from the adult . . . In medieval society this awareness was lacking.[21]

He sets out to answer the question: 'how did we come from that ignorance of childhood to the centring of the family around the child in the nineteenth century?'[22]

Ariès shows how in medieval times and before childhood was of no consequence. No records were kept of childbirth or of age. The difference between the shapes of children and adults were not recognised throughout the ancient civilisations until the Renaissance, except in Greek Art of the Hellenistic period when the child's physical proportions were realistically portrayed in the shape of little Eroses, mythical creatures with rounded bodies. Even then the child's position in the social structure was ignored. After the Hellenistic period these children disappeared from iconography for many centuries.

In the Middle Ages children were dressed exactly like adults. Once out of swaddling clothes they adopted the dress of their parents. From the seventeenth century, however, the child 'had an outfit reserved for his age group, which set him apart from the adults.'[23] Similarly, in pre-modern times, children played the same games and had the same pastimes as adults. Ariès argues that 'the phenomenon which needs to be emphasized is the abandonment of these games by adults of the upper classes and their survival among both the lower classes and the children of the upper classes . . . . It is important', Ariès claims, 'to note that the old community of games was destroyed at one and the same time between children and adults, between lower and middle class. This coincidence enables us to glimpse already a connection between the idea of childhood and the idea of class.'[24]

Contemporary morality enjoins us to avoid reference to sexual matters in the presence of children. But, says Ariès, 'this notion was entirely foreign to the society of old.'[25] Referring to a diary kept by Henri IV's physician, Ariès argues that 'no other document can give us a better idea of the non-existence of the modern idea of childhood at the beginning of the seventeenth century.'[26] We would be profoundly shocked by the sort of sexual behaviour that took place at that time in the presence of children. Ariès gives two reasons for this attitude to sex. First, children under the age of puberty were believed to be unaware of, or indifferent to, sex so that the behaviour had no sexual significance for them. Secondly, 'the idea did not yet exist that references to sexual matters . . . could soil childish innocence' because 'nobody thought that this innocence really existed.'[27] If innocence was not believed to exist, a corollary was the notion of original sin. Children were tainted with this equally with adults and were in the same danger of hell. Accordingly, to take care of their spiritual welfare children were expected to pray as adults. Just as children played with adults, so also they worked with them. Education was 'carried out by means of apprenticeship.'[28]

One can only speculate as to why the idea of childhood did not exist in medieval society. It may in part have been the result of fear of the infant's bestiality, itself the product of ignorance of, and pain associated with, childbirth. In part too there is an element of indifference (though this can be exaggerated), since infant mortality rates were so high.[29] The historian, J. H. Plumb, quotes Montaigne who is reported as saying 'all mine die', rather as a gardener might talk about his cabbages.[30] Certainly, he spoke with rather less affection than someone today might speak of his pet cats or dogs. But, on the other hand, high infant mortality rates cannot explain why pre-modern society denied the existence of childhood. Apart from anything else the 'invention' of childhood long ante-dates any significant decline in such rates.[31]

Childhood became an important phase in life with profound changes in our civilisation associated with the Renaissance and, more particularly, the Reformation and its aftermath. The emergence of childhood became associated with the ideas of childish innocence and weakness and with the need accordingly to discipline children. 'It reacted at one and the same time against indifference towards childhood, against an excessively affectionate and selfish attitude which turned the child into a plaything for adults and encouraged his caprices and against a reverse of this last feeling, the contempt of the man of reason.'[32] This change emerged first amongst the upper ranks of society, the better educated and the prosperous. The education of children became a linchpin for civilisation. Children were never to be left alone; not to be pampered and to be accustomed to strict discipline early in life; their modesty and decency was to be insisted upon and, 'the old familiarity' had to be 'abandoned and its place taken by great moderation of manners and language.'[33] Ariès notes that the idea of childish innocence resulted in two kinds of attitude and behaviour towards childhood. Special attention had to be given to the upbringing of children to safeguard them 'against pollution by life', particularly by sexuality, and secondly to strengthen their character and reason. Children had to be subjected to 'a special sort of treatment, a sort of quarantine'[34] before they were allowed to join adult society. He comments:

> We may see a contradiction here, for on the one hand childhood is pre-
> served and on the other it is made older than its years, but the contradiction
> exists only for us of the twentieth century. The association of childhood
> with primitivism and irrationalism or prelogicism characterizes our con-
> temporary concept of childhood. This concept made the appearance in
> Rousseau, but it belongs to twentieth-century history . . . the ideas of inno-
> cence and reason were not opposed to one another.[35]

Ariès also shows how childhood lengthened more rapidly for boys than it did for girls. As far as girls were concerned, 'the habits of precocity and a brief childhood remained unchanged from the Middle Ages to the seventeenth century.'[36] Girls could be married and in control of households by the time they were thirteen or fourteen. Ariès notes that even in the seventeenth century 'by the age of ten, girls were already little women.'[37] This differential treatment of the sexes must be understood in terms of the position which women occupied in society.

Ariès provides a wealth of historical material on the evolution of the concept of childhood. He is supported by anthropological evidence.[38] But what he does not do very adequately or very convincingly is explain why the change in attitudes towards children took place. He argues that the beginnings of the idea of childhood as innocence and weakness is to be found in the ideas of 'a small minority of lawyers, priests and moralists. But for their influence', he claims, 'the child would have remained simply the *poupart* or *bambino*, the sweet, funny little creature with whom people played affectionately but with liberty, if not indeed with licence, and without any thought of morality or education.' The change is due to 'moralists and pedagogues of the seventeenth century, heirs of a tradition going back to Gerson . . . . We find the same men . . . at the origins of both the modern concept of childhood and the modern concept of schooling.'[39] The link between childhood and schooling is undoubtedly an important one, but it is questionable whether Ariès is right to concentrate on the ideas of intellectuals rather than on the activities of an emergent bourgeoisie. If the explanation for the recognition of childhood is to be sought in intellectual thought, how are we to account for the differential treatment of boys and girls? Why was a boy's childhood prolonged long before a girl's was? And why was it that childhood emerged first among the prosperous commercial and professional classes? Weber[40] and Tawney[41] have both shown a clear connection between Protestansism and the growth of capitalism, and, even though Ariès is singling out Jesuit thinking as well as later Enlightenment theory, the relationship of thought to economic activity cannot be ignored. Thought is adopted when it serves the needs of significant groups in society.[42] If education was the medium through which childhood was expressed, why was it that an emergent bourgeoisie in the seventeenth century demanded an expansion in education? Indeed, why a hundred years later, when in power, did they wish to restrict it?[43] Ariès's idealistic interpretation of history does not, and cannot, explain these changes.[44] They can in part be explained as a response to changes in the economic organisation of society consequent upon the emergence of capitalism. This had profound effects on the bourgeoisie and nascent professional class. Life was more complex; it demanded greater skills. It required its initiates to undergo more lengthy educational and training processes. It also produced wealth and this required an orderly transmission to a next generation which, having been controlled, could be trusted to use it purposefully. This is why the change in childhood affected boys rather than girls and why its impact was greatest in the middle-class ranks of society rather than amongst the nobility or landowning classes.

The result of the ideological developments described by Ariès was that children no longer regulated themselves. In Coveney's words' 'the child was to be trained out of his childish ways into normal and rational perfection of regulated manhood.'[45] Ariès shows how it was in part the institutionalisation of a systematised method of discipline on the part of adults against children which served to separate children from adults. Not completely though, for adults too were whipped. 'In the fifteenth and sixteenth centuries corporal punishment became widespread at the same time as an authoritarian, hierarchical — in a word, absolutist — concept of society.' But 'among the adults, not all were subjected to corporal punishment: people of quality escaped it, and the way in which discipline was applied helped to distinguish the social classes. On the other hand all children and youths, whatever their rank, were subjected to the same disciplinary system and were liable to be birched.'[46] He also draws attention to the significant fact that adolescents were lumped together with children for disciplinary purposes: 'inside the school world, the adolescent was separated from the adult and confused with the child, with whom he shared the humiliation of corporal punishment, the chastisement meted out to villeins.'[47]

Ariès *Centuries of Childhood* is an important document of cultural history and must be recognised as such. We are never likely to think of children in the uncritical way we did before his study was published. Ariès has proved immensely influential, particularly with the sort of liberationist thought that one associates with John Holt[48] and Richard Farson. But there is a danger in Ariès's findings being taken too uncritically. Thus, for example, he draws extensively upon records[49] about the upbringing of the child later to become Louis XIII. But we must ask how representative this was of the daily life of millions of French children, who were contemporaries of the Dauphin and whose lives have not been documented for posterity. Nor should the fact be overlooked that the records we have are predominantly, if not exclusively, products of male authors. It may well be that fathers who had little contact with children did not see them as very different from adults, but mothers and nurses certainly recognised the differences between them. We have no way of knowing. History is written by predominantly upper-class male adults.

Whether or not Ariès is right, and his evidence is highly suggestive and has not as such been falsified, there is no doubt that children are different from adults, even if the differences may be exaggerated. They do have different needs,[50] different claims, different interests. One feature of childhood is the child's state of dependence. As Tucker notes, 'man is born very much unfinished.'[51] Man is the only species where cerebral growth and development continue well into physical maturity: the human brain at birth is less than one quarter of its eventual size. Some developmental processes are inborn (smiling is an example) but others, like walking and talking, require support, stimulation and the opportunity to practise.[52] Young children think in a different style from older children and adults.[53] Children in medieval society may have dressed as their parents and indulged in the same pastimes. They may have been exposed to sexual activity and allusion. Society may have regarded them as answerable for their wrongs and accordingly bound to pray as an adult would. But a young child's physical needs have always been different, even if an earlier society did not recognise his psychological wants. Ariès to an extent concedes this. He refers to a child belonging to adult society in the medieval world as soon as he 'could live without the constant solicitude of his mother, his nanny or his cradle-rocker.'[54]

Care must be taken over conclusions which may legitimately be drawn from Ariès's research. Writers who work within the children's liberation paradigm are wont to assert that, if at earlier stages of history children were not treated differently from adults, this warrants the conclusion that children today should be treated like adults.[55] This conclusion would not follow even were the premise correct. It would still require reasoned argument. But it is not. Ariès's study is more limited than is often realised. His is a study of the history of family life. It is not a history in the wider sense of relationships between adults and children. These, as the next section shows, did not change as dramatically as those within families. In some cases attitudes to children today are little removed from those of earlier centuries.

Children as Property?

Attitudes to children, however, have changed. Stone has shown how in 1500 parent-child relationships were 'exploitative and authoritarian rather than', as he demonstrates they have become, 'affectionate and nurturant.'[56] Relations were formal and obedience was enforced with brutality. The swaddling of infants,[57] which completely immobilised them, may have been rooted in some form of naive altruism (there was a widespread popular fear that unless restrained an infant might tear off his ears, scratch out his eyes or break his legs), but it was undoubtedly extremely convenient for adults (it slows down an infant's heartbeat, thus inducing far longer sleep and less crying).[58] It also, Stone notes, 'allowed the infant to be moved about like a parcel and left un-attended in odd corners or hung on a peg on a wall without danger to life or limb and without overt protest.'[59]

Stone has accumulated considerable evidence to show how in the period 1540-1660 children were in utter subjection to their parents. Children were not supposed to have a will of their own. In the seventeenth century, he adds, 'the early training of children was directly equated with the bating of hawks or the breaking-in of young horses or hunting dogs.' These were, he comments, 'all animals which were highly valued and cherished . . . and it was only natural that exactly the same principle should be applied to the education of children, especially now that parents began to care more about them.'[60] Whipping was commonplace; so much so that a seventeenth-century moral theologian, wanting to convey a notion of Heaven to children, told them that it was a place where children 'would never be beat any more.'[61] This subordination and discipline was manifested in outside signs of deference which children were expected to pay to their parents: kneeling before parents, 'a symbolic gesture of submission which John Donne believed to be unique in Europe',[62] the language used in conversation and correspondence; as well as in other examples of standardised etiquette.

Stone attributes this subordination and severe upbringing of children in part to the 'drive for moral regeneration' with its 'increasing concern to suppress the sinfulness of children'; 'the only hope of preserving social order was', it was thought, 'to concentrate on the right discipline and education of children.'[63]

One result of this submission to patriarchy, for, despite loose reference to 'parents', that is what it was, is that fathers were able to control their sons' occupations[64] and their children's marriages. Authoritarian control over marriages lasted longest in aristocratic circles 'where the property, power and status stakes were highest'[65] but it exerted considerable influence in the squirarchy too. The lower down the economic scale one went the greater freedom of choice the children enjoyed. Among the propertyless, children even in the sixteenth century were freer to choose a spouse than their class superiors; their parents had no economic leverage and they had probably left home anyway when ten or a little older to become apprentices, domestic servants or living-in labourers in other people's houses.

During most of this period the dominant and certainly the articulated justification for parental control was derived from moral precept. But an argument such as that of Richard Allestree, that 'children are so much the goods, the possessions of their parent, that they cannot, without a kind of theft, give away themselves without the allowance of those that have the right in them,'[66] though written in 1663, that is at the very end of the period under consideration, may have struck the right chord for many. Stone describes Allestree's statement as 'an ingenious attempt to shore up ancient but decaying patterns of authority by using new economic theories, but it was not very convincing.'[67] He does, however, concede that popular attitudes changed with 'glacial slowness'[68] and legacies of such ideologies, indeed, such justifications, intrude even today.[69]

It is Stone's thesis that the period from the Restoration to the French Revolution saw marked changes in attitudes towards children. He describes the growth of a 'maternal, child-oriented, affectionate and permissive mode of child-rearing'[70] though he concedes that this came to prevail largely among the upper ranks of the bourgeoisie and the squirarchy. The period was characterised by greater freedom for children, warmer affective relationships and by the recognition of the child as a special status group. Swaddling was abandoned, and for ideological rather than scientific reasons. Maternal breast-feeding replaced reliance on wet-nursing. Teaching methods were less brutal, psychological manipulation replacing physical coercion.[71] Parent-child relations appear to have been more permissive than previously, in some cases indulgently so. For deference was substituted respect and this change affected such things as modes of address. Stone argues that:

> . . .these changes reflect a general easing of those tensions which justified the iron discipline of the post-Reformation century, and in their turn they helped to produce individuals less suspicious of the world at large, less prone to violence, and now capable of intense personal attachments to other individuals, in particular to their wives and children.[72]

Childhood came 'to be regarded as the best years of one's life, instead of the grim purgatory it had been in the seventeenth century.'[73] Even then, Stone believes, considerable control was exercised over the career choice of sons.

The attitudes described here permeated much of one section of society. It did not affect the aristocracy, many of whom were indifferent to their children, nor the artisan and cottager class where brutality still reigned and children were exploited for their labour. As far as the mass of the very poor were concerned, the available evidence, which is thin,[74] suggests that 'the common behaviour of many parents towards their children was often indifferent, cruel, erratic and unpredictable.'[75] Bad as things were for such children, they were better in 1820[76] than they had been in 1770.

Changes in parent-child relationships have not, then, been uniform. Nor have they been linear. There was a reversal in the permissive trend, just described, which led to a revival in the Victorian period of the authoritarian 'pater familias'. Patterns of child-rearing became repressive once again. Punishments were severe and included sensory deprivation[77] as well as flogging. Supervision of children was more intense and oppressive since it tended to be motivated by extreme religious fervour. The Puritan concept of the innate sinfulness of the child was revived. Hannah More, a middle-class educational reformer of the poor could thus write, early in the nineteenth century, of children 'as beings who bring into the world a corrupt nature and evil dispositions, which it should be the great end of education to rectify.'[78] Once again the wealthy were able to control their children's marriages. There was sexual repression too, symbolised by the extreme lengths, including clitoridectomy, chastity belts, straitjackets, deliberately painful circumcision and the attaching of toothed rings to boys' penises, to which parents went to prevent their children masturbating.[79] Pinchbeck and Hewitt, writing of the status of children at this time, describe children as 'legally the property of their parents'. They 'were used by them', they note, 'as personal or family assets . . . among the poor, the labour of children was exploited; among the rich their marriages were contrived; all to the economic or social advantage of the parents.'[80]

They comment on a 1761 case, in which a woman was given two years' imprisonment for putting out the eyes of young children 'with whom she went begging about the country'.[81] To have done the same to a sheep might have attracted the death penalty. The children were not hers. 'Had it been the eyes of her own children possibly no notice would have been taken of the matter, for parents commonly treated their unhappy offspring as they chose.'[82] The Victorian era was a dark age for children. They were exploited, not least by their parents. Pinchbeck and Hewitt believe that much of the complacency regarding their exploitation 'sprang from the notion, supported by religious sanctions, that in society there was a place for everyone, and everyone should remain in his place. Hence the knowledge that for some that place could be unpleasant was merely confirmation that they belonged to lesser and lower orders of creation.'[83] But, as they rightly note, it was also linked to notions of parental rights. Reformers had to fight the views of parental responsibility and rights which identified patriarchal decision-making with family stability and this with societal cohesion. Nor are the views of the well-known reformers always consistent.

Lord Shaftesbury, the great factory reformer, who wished to safeguard children from exploitation by factory owners, opposed proposals for the compulsory education of children, since, he believed, they infringed the right of a parent to bring up his children as he saw fit.[84] Free school meals were strenuously opposed by a leading welfare agency, the Charity Organisation Society, on the ground that it was better in the interests of the community to allow in cases of undernourished children 'the sins of the parents to be visited on the children, than to impair the principle of the solidarity of the family and run the risk of permanently demoralising large numbers of the population.'[85] Another example is the way in which nineteenth-century feminist movements opposed legislation to outlaw the evil of baby-farming. The National Society for Women's Suffrage published a *Memorial* in which they claimed that the proposed legislation (the Infant Life Protection Act of 1872) 'would interfere in the most mischievous and oppressive way with domestic arrangements.'[86] Similarly, the Committee for Amending the Law in Points where it is Injurious to Women objected to the proposal of the legislation to compel parents only to use nurses with licences.[87]

That the twentieth century has seen reversals in this trend cannot be denied. The dominant pattern of child-rearing in England today is permissive rather than repressive. Stone sees this beginning among the middle classes as early as the 1870s, spreading to the social élite in the 1890s and 'then in the 1920s and more dramatically in the 1960s and 1970s, spreading for the first time to all sections of the population.'[88] Parents no longer control the choice of their children's occupation nor do they select a marriage partner for their offspring. Patriarchal power of father over children has been cut down to a minimum. Where once there was deference, today there is little even of what earlier generations would have recognised as respect.

Children are freer today than they were fifty or a hundred years ago; they even have greater autonomy than in previous permissive ages such as the eighteenth century. At no other time in history could a children's liberation movement[89] have flourished. Yet remnants of earlier philosophies remain and ideas of the child as property rather than person or on the importance of protecting family autonomy are still with us. Mia Kellmer-Pringle is right to have detected an attitude that 'a baby completes a family, rather like a TV set or fridge . . . that a child belongs to his parents like their other possessions over which they may exercise exclusive rights.'[90] One does not have to agree with her approach to eradicating such beliefs, and I do not, to acknowledge the continuing existence of such cultural notions. They led also, until about 1973, to an unwillingness on the part of social workers and others to remove children who had been physically abused from their parents, and to an over-hasty readiness to return such children to their parents.[91] Such attitudes were commented upon critically in reports of enquiries set up after such children died at the hands of their parents. The Maria Colwell case[92] was the most notorious case.[93] An extreme critic like John Howells can even claim that Maria Colwell was killed by a misplaced emphasis on the blood-tie.[94] Where nineteenth-century commentators referred to the natural law, their twentieth-century counterparts used science, or rather pseudo-science. The 'blood-tie' was accordingly used to justify a toddler's transfer from prospective adopters, the only parents he knew, to his middle-aged father, and his wife with whom he had had no contact, because, as Russell L.J. argued, 'if a father (as distinct from a stranger in blood) can bring up his own son as his own son, so much the better for both of them.'[95] The decision was grounded in father's rights rather than a child's welfare.

The other strand referred to, family autonomy, finds its most distinct expression in the writings of the legal-psychoanalytic alliance of Joseph Goldstein, Anna Freud and Albert Solnit, but it is found commonly elsewhere in writings on both sides of the Atlantic.[96] It can lead to Goldstein and his colleagues expressing a view that a non-custodial parent should have no legally enforceable right to visit his child for the decision as to whether such access is desirable should reside with the custodial parent.[97] This view rests on the doubtful assumption[98] that a child cannot respond to two 'psychological' parents at the same time unless they act in consort. It can also lead, as it does in their recent book *Before The Best Interests of The Child*, to a belief in minimal state intervention in child-rearing decisions. They are quite right to point to the difficulties of, and dangers inherent in, intervention in the family but there are problems with non-intervention too. These issues are fully considered in Chapter 7, and are not further considered here. Suffice it to say that the protection of children's rights may depend upon infringing parental autonomy and family privacy. It is notable that children's rights do not figure prominently in the analysis of Goldstein *et al*.

Treatment of children in the period charted by Stone, and beyond, has not been consistent. In Stone's language, it 'has oscillated cyclically between the permissive and the repressive.'[99] Nor has it been uniform. There has, since the emergence of the concept of childhood, been concern for children and this has grown in an almost linear fashion. *Concern* for children has been expressed even when child-rearing practices have been at their most repressive. We must be careful when we come to interpret 'concern'. The 'child-saving' movement[100] of the late nineteenth and early twentieth centuries may have had humanitarian concern for children but it produced a social practice redolent of the rankest repression.[101] Even in eras of repression there have been pockets of permissiveness. Similarly, where as today, the permissive model of child-rearing prevails, there remains a residue of repression. Children are no longer property as they were in the Puritan or Victorian eras. They are, however, not yet fully persons.

Rights, Child-Saving and the Reification of Children

It is with the fullest blossoming yet of permissiveness that children's rights have become much talked about. In part this is a response to an obvious gap between the image and the reality. Children's rights, though, is an idea with a long heritage. The beginnings of a children's rights movement can be traced back to the middle of the nineteenth century. An article published with the title 'The Rights of Children' appeared as early as June 1852.[102] In France, Jean Vallès attempted to establish a league for the protection of the rights of children in the aftermath of the Paris Commune. He dedicated his novel, *L'Enfant*, written in 1879, to all oppressed children.[103] Kate Douglas Wiggins's *Children's Rights*, sub-titled *A Book of Nursery Logic*, was published in 1892.[104] Its theme, that it was possible to build a strong Christian character in children without eliminating childhood pleasures, fitted the ethos of the period well. It did, at least, emphasise what she considered to be the distinct needs of the child.

This was also the period of the child-saving movement[105] and thus of the development of juvenile justice, as well as of the establishment of compulsory education.[106] Society's concern for the child is to be seen very much in terms of the child's usefulness to society.[107] The picture emerges of children as objects of intervention rather than as legal subjects. Distinguishing children from adults, for example, in terms of the way those who break the law are dealt with, becomes a conceptual means of rationalising, controlling, even exploiting children.[108] Children become, and often remain, a convenient focus for public ills. By personalising causes the social reality of trouble can be astutely ignored.[109] Individualisation also has the effect of depoliticising. Blaming the victim is, as Ryan has noted,[110] a common approach to social problems. Of course, under-privileged groups, and children in particular, are a soft touch. Reification involves 'treating a notational device as though it were a substantive term . . . a construct as though it were observational.'[111] Pfuhl argues forcefully that 'the "name" and the meanings assigned to it become the thing to which we react. The thing is symbolised by the name; the name takes on an existence of its own.'[112] This is well illustrated by the end product of the child-saving movement. It produced a tendency to think of children as a 'problem population'.[113] When dealing with youthful behaviour it ignored the fact that society is inherently criminogenic, a contemporary manifestation of which is mass youth unemployment. It is common to blame children for societal ills. Not only can children not be expected to mobilise protest against such definitions, they may even internalise the definitions of themselves put about by ideologues of the child-saving movement and the media.

Talk of children's rights in the twentieth century has predominantly been couched in child-saving language, in terms of 'salvation'.[114] It has usually referred to children's rights but its essential concern has been with protecting children rather than their rights.[115] Children have been subjected to all sorts of treatment in order to further their welfare. There is then, at the very least, a distinction between two approaches to children's rights. Rogers and Wrightsman distinguish the 'nurturance' and the 'self-determination' orientation.[116] The former stresses the provisions by society of supposedly beneficial objects, environments, services, experience, etc. for the child; the latter 'stresses those potential rights which would allow children to exercise control over their environments, to make decisions about what they want, to have autonomous control over various facets of their lives.' The former corresponds broadly to child-saving notions of 'giving children what is good for them'; the latter conforms to the idea propagated by child liberationists who want children to have greater autonomy so that they are given the freedom to decide 'what is good for themselves'.[117]

This distinction is useful in this context in showing the great divide between the earliest notions of children's rights and contemporary treatments of allegedly the same issue. But it over-simplifies the problem, as the next chapter demonstrates.

Recent Developments in Children's Rights

Children's rights first attracted international attention after the First World War. One of the earliest significant documents is the declaration adopted by the Fifth Assembly of the League of Nations in 1924. It reflected a concern with the rights of children afflicted by the devastation of the 'Great War' and its aftermath. The declaration emphasised children's material needs. It proclaimed, for example, that children 'must have' means requisite for their normal development, including food for the hungry, nursing for the sick, help for the handicapped, and shelter and succour for the orphan and waif.[118]

Thirty-five years later, the League's successor, the United Nations adopted a second world declaration. The 1948 Universal Declaration of Human Rights had not specifically mentioned children. The 1959 Declaration of the Rights of Children filled the gap. It is based on the premise that 'mankind owes to the child the best it has to give' (see the Appendix, p. 283). Implicit in this premise is an emphasis on duties to children and hence children's rights in the sense of claims (see Chapter 2). In fact, although the preamble to the declaration refers to rights and freedoms, the ten principles set out in it do not embrace children's liberties (or freedoms) at all.[119] Indeed, the articles of the declaration are deliberately vague, both as to the rights its authors believe children should have and, necessarily, as to who is to bear the correlative duties (see Chapter 2). The Declaration is nothing more than a proclamation of general principles. An International Convention on the Rights of Children is planned[120] but whether the effects of it, if it ever emerges, would be any greater than the current Declaration may be doubted. Certainly, the Declaration, though commonly quoted, has had no real influence on the lives of children throughout the world.

The 1970s witnessed an upsurge in interest in, and awareness of, the significance of children's rights which culminated in the adoption of 1979 as the International Year of the Child. One of the earliest documents was the pamphlet produced by the National Council for Civil Liberties in 1972.[122] In 1974, in the United States, Foster and Freed published their Bill of Rights for Children.[122] This has proved to be highly influential. It contains a rag-bag of ideas, common to documents of the period. These range from 'the right to receive parental love and affection', unenforceable but non-contentious, to the right to be regarded 'as a person' which is so fundamental that it may be said to overarch all others.

In British Columbia the Berger Commission[123] called for the enactment of a Bill of Rights for Children. It advocated that a child whose rights were violated should have a remedy by way of 'judicial declaration' of entitlement to the right. It concentrated on legally enforceable rights and obligations. So did the United States Institute of Judicial Administration and American Bar Association Joint Commission in their report on the *Rights of Minors* as part of their juvenile justice standards project. The report concentrates on such areas as support obligations, medical care, youth employment and minors' contracts.[124]

Both judiciaries and legislatures have been active on the children's rights front in many parts of the world. In the United States there have been a number of landmark decisions. In *Re Gault* in 1967 the Supreme Court affirmed the constitutional standing of children: 'neither the Fourteenth Amendment nor the Bill of Rights is for adults alone', said Justice Fortas.[125] The court held that juveniles accused of delinquency and faced with the possibility of severe State action must be accorded certain basic constitutional protections including notice of the charges, the right to counsel, the privilege against self-incrimination, and the opportunity to confront and cross-examine witnesses. In *Re Winship*[126] the Supreme Court held that due process requires an adjudication of juvenile delinquency to be based on a finding of proof beyond reasonable doubt, the standard applied to adult defendants in criminal trials. In 1969, in *Tinker* v. *Des Moines School District*, the Supreme Court, in holding students to be entitled to the constitutional protection of the First Amendment and thus able to wear black armbands to protest against the Vietnam War, said that 'minors, as well as adults, are protected by the Constitution and possess constitutional rights.'[127] Children are persons under the Constitution: constitutional rights do not mature and come into being magically when the state-defined age of majority is reached. Too much should not be read into these developments. The American Supreme Court has not extended to children all those rights constitutionally guaranteed to adults.[128] Rather, it has extended in a piecemeal fashion, and not always consistently, certain adult rights. Thus, for example, a juvenile has been held not to be entitled to jury trial in a delinquency adjudication[129] and corporal punishment in schools has been said by the Supreme Court to violate neither the constitutional prohibition on cruel and unusual punishment nor the Fourteenth Amendment right to due process.[130]

English developments barely compare with those in the United States. There has been a new offensive on juvenile crime[131] with an emphasis on locking up children.[132] In a sense this reflects the revival of retributivism,[133] but children have not been accorded rights before, during and after trial, to accompany this shift in philosophy and practice. The Children Act of 1975 was hailed at the time as a 'children's charter'.[134] It is difficult to see why it was so regarded; most of its innovatory ideas[135] concentrated on strengthening the substitute family, so that to call it a 'foster parents' charter' might be more apposite.[136] Anyway, much of the Act, more than seven years later, remains unimplemented.

Nevertheless, English judges have on a number of occasions been concerned to emphasise children's rights. Unlike American judges, they do not work within the framework of a written constitution or an entrenched bill of rights: their approach accordingly has been rather different, more tentative and less assertive, pragmatic rather than analytical. In several cases where what they perceive to be children's best interests clashed with those of parents asserting their rights, the English judiciary has laid stress on the importance of according primacy to children's interests. A statutory provision stating that in custody disputes a child's interest is 'first and paramount' has been interpreted liberally with the consequence that the child's welfare determines the course to be followed.[137] Thus, for example, access to a non-custodial parent, long regarded as that parent's right,[138] was proclaimed to be a child's right in 1973.[139] The courts, despite this pronouncement, remain reluctant to deny a parent access, even in cases where such a refusal would not be difficult to justify.[140] The courts have also in the late 1970s rejected the idea that matrimonial misconduct should play a part in the determination of custody disputes. The question is not, said one member of the Court of Appeal in *S(B.D.)* v. *S(D.J.)*, what the 'essential justice of the case' required (in other words, had one parent been 'wronged' by the behaviour of the other), but 'what the best interests of the children' demanded.[141] The resurgence of the wardship jurisdiction of the High Court in which 'the welfare of the child . . . is considered first, last and all the time' is another example of current judicial concern.[142] So is the way in which a child's right to education has been allowed to prevail over his parents' refusal to allow him to attend the local comprehensive school.[143] Yet another is the way in which a child's need for a home has come to prevail over property considerations in matrimonial disputes.[144]

The English judiciary has concerned itself with promoting what it considers to be children's rights. Indeed, one might almost describe it as being in the vanguard of English institutions in so doing. We must be careful, however, when we analyse these decisions. They can be conceptualised as a move towards the recognition of children's rights but it might be better to regard them as a determination to remove certain decision-making processes from parents and give them instead to the state by using, some might say abusing, *parens patriae* notions. The problem is at its acutest where questions relating to neglect are concerned, for, outside an obvious core of agreement, consensus is lacking as to what are the proper standards of parental care. This subject is considered further in Chapter 7.

The most articulate expressions of children's rights have not come from commissions, legislatures or courts but from the pens of a number of libertarian writers. Several monographs and rather more collections of essays on the theme of children's rights have been published in the last decade.[145] Together they form a loose children's rights movement.[146] Prominent amongst this 'school' are the American writers, John Holt and Richard Farson. It is worth pausing to consider the rights that Holt and Farson would confer on children.

Holt[147] argues for the right to equal treatment at the hands of the law (see, further, Chapter 3); the right to vote and take full part in political affairs; the right to be legally responsible for one's life and acts; the right to work, for money (this is considered in Chapter 2): the right to privacy; the right to financial independence and responsibility (for example, the right to own property, establish credit, sign contracts); the right to direct and manage education (see, further, Chapter 2); the right to travel, to live away from home, to choose or make one's own home; the right to receive from the state whatever minimum income it may guarantee to adult citizens; the right to make and enter into, on a basis of mutual consent, quasi-familial relationships, for example, to choose guardians; the right to do, in general, what any adult may legally do.

Farson's 'Bill of Rights'[148] contains many of the same ideas. For him the basic right upon which all the others depend is the right to self-determination. He also argues that children should be given the right to alternative home environments (but who would provide these?); the right to responsive design (he argues that 'society must accommodate itself to children's size and to their need for safe space'); the right to information ordinarily available to adults; the right to design their own education (the implication of this is the abolition of compulsory education); the right to freedom from physical punishment (this is considered in Chapters 4 and 5); the right to sexual freedom ('the right to all sexual activities that are legal among consenting adults'); the right to economic power (do adults have this?); the right to political power (or at least to vote);[149] and the right to justice. Farson describes these as a child's 'birthrights'.

These manifestos are two of the more radical blueprints for childhood. There is a concern which goes wider than these particular authors that, to quote another leading contemporary protagonist of children's liberation, Mark Gerzon, 'the oppression of children by adults has continued after every previous revolution that adults have engineered.'[150] The liberationist school would argue that the legal status of children should not in any way be dependent on the age factor. Just as the civil rights movements and women's movements have argued that a person's legal status should not be made dependent on race or sex, unless there is a highly cogent justification for so doing, so the same considerations are asserted in the case of children. Of course, age is a relevant differentiating factor where race, for example, is not. I can find no argument to support a system that refuses to employ blacks because they are black or indeed one which imposes irrelevant hiring conditions which lead to indirect discrimination:[151] it is easy to assemble convincing arguments for a system which limits the employment opportunities of small children. The assertion of the irrelevance of age does not square with our knowledge of biology, psychology or economics. The flaws in the liberationist argument are further considered in Chapter 2.

Not only has the cudgel been taken up by adults on behalf of children but youth itself has proclaimed its need to be liberated. One of the more articulate of such programmes emanates from a body in Michigan known as Youth Liberation of Ann Arbor.[152] Their fifteen-point programme puts together 'truth about what is wrong with our present situation' and lays out 'changes that must be made.' 'We know', they proclaim, 'there is a basic decision to make: either we stay quiet and become part of a system of oppression, or we seize control of our lives, take risks, and struggle to build something new.' They set out demands to have the power to determine their own destiny; they want an immediate end to 'adult chauvinism' for, they assert, 'age *in itself* deserves no recognition'; they want full civil and human rights; an abolition to compulsory education which is, they say, 'a form of imprisonment'; they want the freedom to form into communal families; an end to male chauvinism and sexism ('Macho must go'); they want also the opportunity to create an authentic culture with institutions of their own making (this entails *inter alia* the legalisation of all drugs); they want sexual self-determination; an end of class antagonism among young people, and the end of racism and colonialism, freedom for all unjustly imprisoned people (juveniles 'did not receive a trial before a jury of their peers, and the society they offended is itself criminal'); they want the right to be economically independent of adults; the right to live in harmony with nature; they want to 'rehumanize existence' and to develop communication and solidarity with the young people of the people of the world 'in our common struggle for freedom and peace'.

This programme, its authors admit, strays from the specific needs of youth. It attacks sexism, bureaucracy and the products of a technocratic society. As such it has much in common with other libertarian movements in contemporary Western society. Like the other two manifestos, it represents a change in the focus of children's rights. The 'self-determination' orientation, long-submerged in child salvation, has broken through at last. Although I am critical of much that is central to the child liberation movement, since I regard many of its proposals as blatantly naive, it has to be conceded that the exponents of child liberation are prepared to treat children as persons. Too many of those in the past who claimed to be in favour of giving children rights treated children as things, as problems, but rarely as human beings with personality and integrity.

Was IYC Significant?

The International Year of the Child (IYC) does not belong to the tradition of child liberation. Its values, its whole ethos, harked back to an earlier era of concern for children. Of course, proponents of child liberation were able to climb on the bandwagon, but they did not have much impact upon the direction it took.

At the end of an opening chapter it would be presumptuous if not foolhardy to estimate the success or otherwise of IYC. A few comments on the impact of IYC, both global and directed to this country, will nevertheless be made.

Almost every country in the world took part in IYC in some way or other. Lip-service at least was paid to the ideal entrenched in the United Nations Declaration. The question must remain as to how deep this commitment went. It is not difficult to issue commemorative postage stamps, but how many countries ploughed the profits from such ventures back into funds designed to further the interests of children? It takes some courage to organise a Young People's Parliament,[153] as happened in the United Kingdom in October 1979: it shows very little to ignore its proposals and demands. Do those in power in Britain today even remember them, if they ever knew them? Many countries which subscribed to the ideals of IYC pay little attention to the rights of its adult citizens and in these taking part in IYC was little more than an elaborate charade. In much of the world child labour[154] is a scandal, and one constantly exposed in 1979, but without the money earned by children the poverty of their families would be even greater than it is. It is difficult to talk of rights when resources are such that basic needs are not being met.

Fifteen million children under the age of five died during IYC. Four hundred million children under the age of six did not have access to health services in 1979. One hundred million children suffered from malnutrition.[155] These children live (or lived, since many are now dead) mainly in the Third World. The Brandt Commission report[156] was published after IYC had ended, but the scant attention given to it by Western governments[157] does not suggest that its publication at an earlier date would have affected their responses, or in any way have furthered redistribution of wealth, so as to provide Third World countries with the resources to satisfy at least some of the basic needs of children in the underprivileged 'South'. The Brandt Commission conveyed some perspective by looking at the resources spent on military expenditure. For example, it noted that the world's military expenditure for only half a day would suffice to finance the whole malaria eradication programme of the World Health Organisation. Forty thousand village pharmacies could be set up with the money currently expended on one jet fighter. One half of one per cent of one year's world military expenditure would pay for all the farm equipment needed to increase food production and approach self-sufficiency in food-deficit, low-income countries by 1990.

Examples like these put the issue of children's rights into wider perspective. But, though less dramatic, examples drawn from Britain also show fundamental denials of children's needs and rights. Half a million children live in families where the family income is below the official poverty level, even though one or both parents go out to work full-time.[158] Almost one million children live in families that have to depend on supplementary benefit because the head of the family is sick or unemployed or elderly or a single parent. Supplementary benefit payments are low.[159] The parent of a ten-year-old child gets £1.25 a day to cover all the child's needs, apart from rent.[160] Not surprisingly, many such children survive on deficient diets and live in continuous insecurity. Many find their way into the care of local authorities or voluntary organisations.[161] Many children still live in households unfit for human habitation or lacking basic amenities; others are homeless or live in bed and breakfast accommodation. Yet child benefit has not been uprated,[162] exceptional need payments to pay for such ordinary needs as shoes have been abolished and the public sector housing programme is currently being cut by 48 per cent over the period from 1980 to 1983.[163]

The Court Report on Child Health Services, which reported in 1976, has not been implemented. It noted that 'children still die in our lifetime for nineteenth-century reasons'.[164] Twice as many children of unskilled workers die in the first year of life as children of professional workers and the gap is widening, not closing. Two and a half times more children die in socioeconomic classes 4 and 5 than in classes 1 and 2 of certain infectious diseases. When a child dies from parental brutality, the public vents its anger. The social work profession is usually pilloried for failing to stop it.[165] But do we really care so much about the health and safety of our children? Compared to our defence budget, how much would implementation of the Court report or the Finer report on one-parent families[166] or the Warnock report on the education of children with special needs cost?[167] Finer's proposal for a guaranteed maintenance allowance for one-parent families was reckoned to cost about the same per year as two miles of motorway: Warnock, now being implemented without additional expenditure,[168] would cost something less than the annual upkeep of Britain's regimental bands.

Our children still grow up exposed to lead pollution in petrol, in paint and through petrol fumes in food.[169] Corporal punishment is still widely practised in schools and community homes. In Tunbridge Wells a boy who had recently lost the sight of one eye was spanked publicly at a school assembly; in Harrow a seven-year-old epileptic was caned by the headmistress;[170] Leicestershire now permits corporal punishment of girls to an extent and of a severity that would not have been permitted in workhouses a hundred years ago.[171] Our immigration laws and their administration (not necessarily the same thing at all) constantly break up families.[172] The Ditta case in Bradford is but one recent and highly publicised example of this policy.[173]

Many more examples could be given. They would show that children are still given low priority in the nation's attention despite certain rhetoric. In subsequent chapters many more examples will be given. Was IYC significant? In a sense, it was. It drew attention to many of these evils. But in reality few policies have changed as a result. Children in 1983 are not better off than they were in 1979. Indeed, as a result of many retrogressive policies they are actually more disadvantaged than they were. Some positive things have emerged from IYC. The establishment in London of a Children's Legal Centre may ultimately prove to be one of these. A rights strategy requires a conscious policy of legal intervention: it requires lawyers to fight for children's rights.

Notes

1.   The title, I note, of the report of the UK Association for the International Year of the Child, written by Judith Stone, published by the IYC Trust, London, 1981.
2.   See F. Pollock and F. W. Maitland, *The History of English Law*, London, Cambridge University Press, 1968 (2nd ed.), vol. II, p. 438-9.
3.   Family Law Reform Act 1969, s.1, operative January 1970, following the report of the Latey Committee on *Age of Majority*, Cmnd. 3342, London, HMSO, 1967.
4.   See M. D. A. Freeman, 'Coming of Age?' *Legal Action Group Bulletin* (1977), p. 137-8 for a thumbnail sketch. See also M. Rae *et al.*, *First Rights*, London, NCCL, 1979.
5.   Firearms Act 1968, s.22(2).
6.   The law is very complicated. See H. K. Bevan, *The Law Relating to Children*, London, Butterworth, 1973, pp. 446-50.
7.   Licensing Act 1964, s. 169.
8.   Children and Young Persons Act 1933, s. 50, as amended by Children and Young Persons Act 1963, s. 16. The Ingleby Committee (1960), Cmnd. 1911, recommended the age of criminal responsibility be raised to twelve.
9.   Sexual intercourse with a girl under sixteen is an unlawful act. Further, care orders are made on promiscuous girls under seventeen on the ground that they are 'in moral danger'.
10.   According to Sir George Baker, then President of the Family Division: 'The foetus cannot, in English law, . . . have any rights of its own at least until it is born and has a separate existence from the mother' (*Paton* v. *Trustees of the British Pregnancy Advisory Service* [1978], 3 WLR 687, 693.
11.   For a balanced account see L. W. Sumner, *Abortion and Moral Theory*, Princeton, Princeton University Press, 1981.
12.   410 US 113 (1973). See, further, J. Mohr, *Abortion in America*, New York, Oxford University Press, 1978, p. 246.
13.   In *Planned Parenthood of Central Missouri* v. *Danforth* 428 US 52 (1976).
14.   The most recent was John Corrie's Abortion (Amendment) Bill, the second reading of which is in *Hansard*, H.C. vol. 970, cols. 891-984, 1806-8.
15.   A point also made in *Planned Parenthood*, op. cit., note 13, p. 64. Lucinda Cisler rejects the viability motion altogether: 'the only event in the sequence of pregnancy that can be assigned a specific time is birth itself . . . . All else is mystique and conjecture' ('Unfinished Business: Birth Control Women's Liberation' in Robin Morgan (ed.), *Sisterhood Is Powerful*, New York, Random House, 1970, p. 274).

16. See Richard Farson, *Birthrights*, Harmondsworth, Penguin, 1978, p. 22.
17. See *The Sunday Times*, London, 5 April 1981.
18. See also Michel Foucault's observation that 'Madness is childhood' (*Madness and Civilization*, translated by Richard Howard, London, Tavistock, 1967, p. 252).
19. As to which see M. Mead and M. Wolfenstein, *Childhood in Contemporary Cultures*, Chicago, University of Chicago Press, 1955. See also M. Mead, 'Early Childhood Experience and Later Education in Complex Cultures' in Murray Wax *et al.* (eds), *Anthropological Perspectives on Education*, New York, Basic Books, 1971.
20. Philippe Ariès, *Centuries of Childhood*, London, Jonathan Cape, 1962 (translated from the French by Robert Baldick).
21. Ibid., p. 128.
22. Ibid., p. 10.
23. Ibid., p. 50.
24. Ibid., p. 99.
25. Ibid., p. 100.
26. Idem.
27. Ibid., p. 106.
28. Ibid., p. 366.
29. See W. Langer, 'Checks on population growth: 1750–1850', *Scientific American*, 226 (Feb. 1972), pp. 93–9.
30. J.H. Plumb, 'Children: The Victims of Time' in *The Light of History*, London, Allen Lane, 1972. See also L. Stone, *The Family, Sex and Marriage in England 1500–1800*, London, Weidenfeld & Nicolson, 1977, p. 105.
31. See Stone, *The Family, Sex and Marriage*, p. 247. See also P. Ariès, *Western Attitudes Towards Death From The Middle Ages to the Present*, Baltimore, Johns Hopkins University Press, 1974.
32. Ariès, *Centuries of Childhood*, p. 114.
33. Ibid., p. 117.
34. Ibid., p. 396.
35. Ibid., p. 119.
36. Ibid., p. 331.
37. Ibid., p. 332.
38. See, generally, the essays in Mead and Wolfenstein, *Childhood in Contemporary Cultures*.
39. Ariès, *Centuries of Childhood*, p. 239. Gerson wrote *De Confessione Mollicei*.
40. See H.H. Gerth and C. Wright Mills (eds), *From Max Weber — Essays in Sociology*, London, Routledge & Kegan Paul, 1948, ch. xii.
41. R.H. Tawney, *Religion and the Rise of Capitalism*, Harmondsworth, Penguin, 1938.
42. See C. Hill, *Intellectual Origins of The English Revolution*, Oxford, Oxford University Press, 1965.
43. Only in the nineteenth century, with the need for more skilled labour, did the move to compulsory education find impetus.
44. Nor, I think, does a purely materialistic interpretation. For agreement, see M. Hoyles, *Changing Childhood*, London, Writers and Readers, 1979, pp. 26–9.
45. Coveney, *The Image of Childhood*, Harmondsworth, Penguin, 1967, p. 40 (previously published as *Poor Monkey*, London, Hutchinson, 1957).
46. Ariès, *Centuries of Childhood*, p. 261.
47. Ibid., p. 262. See also Stone, *The Family, Sex and Marriage*, p. 163.
48. John Holt, *Escape From Childhood*, Harmondsworth, Penguin, 1974.
49. For example, the diary kept by Heroard, Louis XIII's doctor.
50. See Mia Kellmer-Pringle, *The Needs of Children*, London, Hutchinson, 1980 (2nd ed.).
51. N. Tucker, *What Is a Child?*, London, Fontana, 1977, p. 31.
52. See W. Dennis, 'Causes of Retardation Amongst Institutional Children: Iran', *Journal of Genetic Psychology*, 96 (1960), pp. 47–59.
53. See the writings of J. Piaget, notably *The Language and Thought of the Child*, London, Routledge, 1926, and *The Child's Conception of The World*, London, Routledge, 1929.

54.   Ariès, *Centuries of Childhood*, p. 128.
55.   For example, Farson, *Birthrights*; Holt, *Escape from Childhood*; Hoyles, *Changing Childhood*.
56.   Stone, *The Family, Sex and Marriage*, p. 405.
57.   See M.J. Tucker, 'The Child As Beginning and End' in L. de Mause (ed.), *The History of Childhood*, London, Souvenir Press, 1974, pp. 242-2. The practice was common in other countries too.
58.   E.L. Lipton *et al.*, 'Swaddling, A Child Care Practice: Historical, Cultural and Experimental Observations', *Pediatrics*, 35 (1965), p. 521.
59.   Stone, *The Family, Sex and Marriage*, p. 162.
60.   Ibid, p. 163.
61.   J. Janeway, *A Token For Children*, London, 1676, Preface (quoted in Stone, *The Family, Sex and Marriage*, p. 164).
62.   Stone, *The Family, Sex and Marriage*, p. 171.
63.   Ibid., p. 174.
64.   Ibid., p. 179.
65.   Ibid., p. 184.
66.   Richard Allestree, *The Whole Duty of Man*, London, 1663, p. 291.
67.   Stone, *The Family, Sex and Marriage*, p. 180.
68.   Ibid, p. 191.
69.   Generally, and also in relation to marriage.
70.   Stone, *The Family, Sex and Marriage*, p. 405.
71.   Ibid., p. 435.
72.   Ibid., p. 448.
73.   Ibid., p. 449.
74.   There is some evidence in de Mause, *The History of Childhood*.
75.   Ibid., p. 470.
76.   Ibid., p. 477, quoting Francis Place, 'a very well-informed observer of urban poverty in the metropolis'.
77.   Ibid., p. 669.
78.   Quoted ibid., p. 468. Her view on children's rights is worth reproducing. She denounced the rights of man, ridiculed the rights of women and continued: 'It follows, according to the actual progression of human beings, that the next influx of irradiation which our enlighteners are pouring on us, will illuminate the world with the grave descants on the rights of youth, the rights of children, the rights of babies' (Hannah More, *Strictures on the Modern System of Female Education* (1799), vol. 1, pp. 172-3).
79.   Ibid., p. 48.
80.   I. Pinchbeck and M. Hewitt, *Children In English Society*, London, Routledge & Kegan Paul, 1973, vol. II, p. 348.
81.   Ibid., p. 350.
82.   Idem.
83.   Ibid., p. 357.
84.   Quoted ibid.., p. 358.
85.   See E. Cohen, *English Social Services: Methods and Growth*, London, Allen & Unwin, 1949, p. 20.
86.   Pinchbeck and Hewitt, *Children in English Society*, p. 617.
87.   See M. Hewitt, *Wives and Mothers in Victorian Industry*, 1957, p. 172.
88.   Stone, *The Family, Sex and Marriage*, p. 680.
89.   On which see B. Gross and R. Gross, *The Children's Rights Movement*, Garden City, New York, Anchor Books, 1977.
90.   Kellmer-Pringle, *The Needs of Children*, p. 156.
91.   See C. Andrews, 'Is Blood Thicker Than Local Authorities?', *Social Work Today*, 12, no. 1 (1980), p. 19.
92.   See the Field-Cisher report into the *Care and Supervision Provided in Relation to Maria Colwell*, London, HMSO, 1974.
93.   Though far from the only one. See DHSS, *Child Abuse: A Study of Inquiry Reports 1973-1981*, London, HMSO, 1982 (a study of the lessons of eighteen cases).

94. John Howells, *Remember Maria*, London, Butterworth, 1974.
95. See *Re C(MA)* [1966] 1 All E.R. 838.
96. Joseph Goldstein, Anna Freud and Albert Solnit, *Beyond the Best Interests of the Child*, New York, Free Press (revised edition 1979), and *Before the Best Interests of the Child*, New York, Free Press, 1979. See also Chapter 7.
97. Goldstein *et al.*, *Beyond*, p. 38.
98. Cf. J.S. Wallerstein and J.B. Kelly, *Surviving The Breakup: How Children And Parents Cope With Divorce*, New York, Basic Books, 1980.
99. Stone, *The Family, Sex and Marriage*, p. 683.
100. Most graphically portrayed in A. Platt's *The Child Savers: The Invention of Delinquency*, Chicago, University of Chicago Press, 1977 (2nd ed.).
101. See, e.g. L. Taylor *et al.*, *In Whose Best Interests?*, London Mind/Cobden Trust, 1980.
102. Slogvolk, 'The Rights of Children', *Knickerbocker*, no. 36 (1852), pp. 489–90.
103. T. Zeldin, *France 1848–1945*, London, Oxford University Press, 1973, refers to this.
104. Kate Douglas Wiggins, *Children's Rights*, Boston, Houghton Mifflin, 1892. She is, of course, better known as a writer of children's stories.
105. See S. Tiffin, *In Whose Best Interest?: Child Welfare Reform In The Progressive Era*, Westport, Connecticut, Greenwood, 1982.
106. See J. Bowles and H. Gintis, *Schooling In Capitalist America*, London, Routledge & Kegan Paul, 1976.
107. P. B. Meyer refers to the 'investment motive'. See 'The Exploitation of the American Growing Class' in D. Gottlieb (ed.), *Children's Liberation*, Englewood Cliffs, New Jersey, Prentice Hall, 1973, p. 51.
108. P. Sartorius, 'Social-Psychological Concepts and The Rights of Children' in V. Haubrich and M. Apple (eds), *Schooling and the Rights of Children*, Berkeley, California, McCutcheon, 1975.
109. See C. Wright Mills, 'The Professional Ideology of Social Pathologists', *American Journal of Sociology*, **49** (1942), p. 165, and E. Schur, *Labeling Deviant Behaviour*, New York, Harper & Row, 1971.
110. Ryan, *Blaming The Victim*, New York, Vintage Books, 1976 (revised ed.).
111. See A. Kaplan, *The Conduct of Inquiry*, San Francisco, Chandler Publishing, 1964, p. 61.
112. See Pfuhl, *The Deviance Process*, New York, D. Van Nostrand, 1980, p. 28. See, further, P. Berger and T. Luckmann, *The Social Construction of Reality*, New York, Doubleday, 1967.
113. See S. Spitzer, 'Toward a Marxian Theory of Deviance', *Social Problems*, **22** (1975), pp. 638, 642.
114. See C. R. Margolin, 'Salvation Versus Liberation: The Movement for Children's Rights In A Historical Context', *Social Problems*, **22** (1978), p. 441.
115. A distinction drawn by Farson, *Birthrights*, p. 9.
116. C. M. Rogers and L. S. Wrightsman, 'Attitudes Toward Children's Rights: Nurturance or Self-Determination?', *Journal of Social Issues*, **34**, No. 2 (1978), pp. 59, 61.
117. See also V. L. Worsfold, 'A Philosophical Justification For Children's Rights', *Harvard Educational Review*, **44** (1974), p. 142, who distinguishes between the paternalistic view of children and children's rights to fair treatment.
118. For a study of the UN Declaration through its three drafts see Chanlett and Morier, 'Declaration of The Rights of The Child', *International Child Welfare Review*, **5** (1968), p. 22.
119. This point is also made by O. O'Neill and W. Ruddick in *Having Children — Philosophical and Legal Reflections on Parenthood*, New York, Oxford University Press, 1979, p. 111.
120. On the initiative of Poland.
121. *Children Have Rights*, London, NCCL, 1972.
122. 'Bill of Rights For Children', *Family Law Quarterly*, **6** (1972), p. 343.
123. *Report of Royal Commission on Family and Children's Law*, 1975, part III.
124. Institute of Judicial Administration/American Bar Association Juvenile Justice

Standards Project, *Rights of Minors*, Cambridge, Mass., Ballinger, 1977. Another example, which I have not been able to read, is U. Jacobson, *Ett Barns Rattigheter*, Stockholm, Askild & Karnekull, 1978 (there is a useful summary by the author in *Current Sweden*, no. 224 (June 1979)).

125.   387 US 1 (1967).
126.   397 US 358 (1970).
127.   393 US 503 (1969).
128.   See H. Rodham, 'Children Under The Law', *Harvard Educational Review*, 43 (1973), p. 487.
129.   *McKeiver* v. *Pennsylvania*, 403 US 528 (1971).
130.   *Ingraham* v. *Wright*, 430 US 651 (1977).
131.   Characteristic of which is the 'short, sharp shock' policy, on which see M. D. A. Freeman, *N. L. J.*, **130** (1980), p. 28, and N. Tutt, *Short, Sharp Shocks*, London, Justice for Children, 1979. Introduced in 1979, despite the fact that the detention centre itself is a failure (see I. Crow, *The Detention Centre Experiment*, London, NACRO, 1979), it is provided for in the Criminal Justice Act 1982.
132   See Children's Legal Centre, *Locking Up Children*, London, Children's Legal Centre, 1982. There has been limited reform in 1982 (see Criminal Justice Act 1982 s. 25). Note also that a number of juveniles are in adult prisons (on 31 May 1982, 118 juveniles including two fourteen-year-old boys were in adult prisons and a further 260 were locked away in remand centres). Yet the DHSS says that the stock of secure places is sufficient to accommodate all these juveniles in community homes (DHSS, *Offending By Young People: A Survey of Recent Trends*, London, DHSS, 1981).
133.   See, e.g. A. von Hirsch, *Doing Justice: The Choice of Punishment*, New York, Hill & Wang, 1976. I consider some of the problems of retribution in M. A. Stewart (ed.), *Law, Morality and Rights*, Dordrecht, Reidel, 1982 (forthcoming).
134.   See, e.g. J. Rowe, 'A Children's Charter for Happiness?', *Community Care*, 5 November 1975, p. 14.
135.   For example, custodianship (s. 33) and freeing for adoption (s. 14).
136.   See M. D. A. Freeman, *The Children Act 1975*, London, Sweet & Maxwell, 1976. See also J. Tunstill, 'In Defence of Parents', *New Society*, 42, no. 785 (20 October 1977), p. 121.
137.   The provision is the Guardianship of Minors Act 1971 s. 1: the interpretation is that of Lord MacDermott in *J* v. *C* [1970] A.C. 668, 710.
138.   See *S* v. *S and P* [1962] 2 All E.R. 1.
139.   In *M* v. *M* [1973] 2 All E.R. 81, discussed in Chapter 6.
140.   See, e.g. *Re T* (1973) 3 Fam. Law 138.
141.   [1977] Fam. 109, 114.
142.   *Re D* [1977] 3 All E.R. 481.
143.   *Re S* [1978] Q.B. 120.
144.   Most recently in *Richards* v. *Richards* [1983] 1 All E.R. 1017.
145.   Examples are P. Adams *et al.*, *Children's Rights*, London, Elek, 1971: W. Aiken and H. La Follette, *Whose Child?*, Totowa, Littlefield, Adams, 1980; H. Cohen, *Equal Rights For Children*, Totowa, Littlefield, Adams, 1980; L. Cole, *Our Children's Keepers*, New York, Ballentine Books, 1972; E. Boulding, *Children's Rights and The Wheel of Life*, New Brunswick, Transaction Books, 1979, Farson, *Birthrights*, op. cit.; Harvard Educational Review, *The Rights of Children*, Reprint No. 9, Cambridge, Massachusetts, 1974; J. Holt, *Escape From Childhood*, Harmondsworth, Penguin, 1975; A. Schorr, *Children and Decent People*, New York, Basic Books, 1974; D. Gottlieb (ed.), *Children's Liberation*, Englewood Cliffs, Prentice-Hall, 1973; A. E. Wilkerson (ed.), *The Rights of Children*, Philadelphia, Temple University Press, 1973; L. Taylor *et al.*, *In Whose Best Interests?*, London, Cobden Trust/Mind, 1980; A. Morris *et al.*, *Justice For Children*, London, Macmillan, 1980.
146.   The title of a collection edited by B. Gross and R. Gross: *The Children's Rights Movement*, New York, Andover Press, 1977.
147.   See 'Why Not a Bill of Rights For Children?' in Gross and Gross (eds), *The Children's Rights Movement*, p. 319. The rights are set out more fully in chs. 17–26 of Holt *Escape From Childhood*.

148. In Farson, *Birthrights*. See also in Gross and Gross (eds), *The Children's Rights Movement,* p. 325 (from *Ms Magazine*, March 1974).
149. See J. Harris, 'The Political Status of Children' in K. Graham (ed.), *Contemporary Political Philosophy: Radical Studies,* Cambridge, Cambridge University Press, 1982, p. 35; cf. F. Schrag, 'The Child In The Moral Order', *Philosophy* **52** (1977), p. 167.
150. Mark Gerzon, *A Childhood For Every Child: The Politics of Parenthood,* New York, Outerbridge & Lazard, 1973.
151. See R. A. Wasserstrom, 'Racism, Sexism and Preferential Treatment', *UCLA Law Review,* **24** (1977), p. 581. On indirect discrimination see *Griggs v. Duke Power Co.,* 401 US 424 (1971) and Race Relations Act 1976 s. 1(1)(b).
152. In Gross and Gross (eds), *The Children's Rights Movement,* p. 329.
153. It is discussed briefly in the IYC Report by Stone, p. 76. A number of its proposals would disappoint child liberationists (e.g. it was against more democracy in schools, lowering the voting age and the abolition of corporal punishment in schools).
154. See E. Mendelievich (ed.), *Children At Work,* Geneva, International Labour Office, 1979.
155. See, further, S. George, *How The Other Half Dies,* Harmondsworth, Penguin, 1976.
156. *North–South: A Programme for Survival,* London, Pan, 1980.
157. A conference was held in Mexico, but little or nothing seems to have emerged from it.
158. Quoted from IYC publication, *UK Children O.K.?,* published in 1979. The Child Poverty Action Group suggests 2¼ million children in Great Britain living in or on the margins of poverty in 1979, that is 18 per cent of all children in Great Britain. See *Poverty,* No. 52 (August 1982), p. 30. See also *Hansard,* H.C. vol. 28, cols. 144–6 (20 July 1982).
159. The plight of families on supplementary benefit is graphically portrayed in L. Burghes, *Living From Hand To Mouth: A Study of 65 Families Living on Supplementary Benefit,* London, Family Service Unit/Child Poverty Action Group, 1980. See also D. Piachaud, *Children and Poverty,* London, Child Poverty Action Group, 1981.
160. Weekly rate from 23 November 1982. See, further, J. Allberson and J. Douglas, *National Welfare Benefits Handbook,* London, CPAG, 1982 (12th ed.).
161. See R. Holman, *Inequality in Child Care,* London, Family Rights Group/Child Poverty Action Group, 1980 (2nd ed.).
162. Child benefit is worth less in real terms today than the equivalent child support provided by child tax allowances and family allowances in 1955. See A. Walker (ed.), *The Poverty of Taxation: Reforming The Social Security and Tax Systems,* London, Child Poverty Action Group, 1982, p. 36.
163. See, further, C. Whitehead, 'Fiscal Aspects of Housing' in C. Sandford *et al.* (eds), *Taxation and Social Policy,* London, Heinemann, 1980, p. 84.
164. *Fit For The Future,* London, HMSO, 1976, p. 4.
165. This is the case in nearly every report of an inquiry into a child death at the hands of a parent. See DHSS *Child Abuse.*
166. *One-Parent Families,* Cmnd. 5629, London, HMSO, 1974.
167. *Special Educational Needs,* London, HMSO, 1978.
168. See the Education Act 1981.
169. See the Lawther Report, London, DHSS (HMSO), 1980. See also R. Rogers, *Lead Poison,* London, New Statesman (N S Report 7), 1982.
170. Examples quoted in Stone, p. 58.
171. See *Caring For Children?* London, STOPP, 1981, p. 9.
172. On which see L. Grant and I. Martin, *Immigration Law and Practice,* London, Cobden Trust, 1982, p. 148 *et. seq.*
173. *Observer,* 4 January, 1981; and *Guardian,* 13 March 1981.

Hillary Rodham, in an oft-quoted sentence, has described 'children's rights' as 'a slogan in search of a definition'.[1] In a later article, she has stated that 'although that search is still continuing, there has been significant progress in our efforts to define and achieve children's rights.'[2] In this chapter a critical look is taken at some of these efforts. 'Children's rights' is a phrase that continues to be used imprecisely. A number of commentators[3] have pointed out that the phrase is something of a catch-all idea embracing different notions. It is clear that an appropriate definitional analysis of rights is a necessary prelude to an understanding of what having the rights in question entails. When the various rights are laid bare it becomes apparent they are conceptually sub-divided into categories and that they are urged against different persons and have different enforcement problems. Before commencing this analysis an attempt is made to explain why rights are important.

The Importance of Rights

To understand why rights are important, 'valuable commodities', in Wasserstrom's language,[4] it is worthwhile considering a society where rights did not exist. It would be a society in which relationships would approximate to those between a master and his slave. Might would be right. The powerless could make no demands at all. Such a society would be morally impoverished. Rights are important because, as Bandman has put it,[5] they 'enable us to stand with dignity, if necessary to demand what is our due without having to grovel, plead or beg or to express gratitude when we are given our due, and to express indignation when what is our due is not forthcoming.' In this sense rights are important moral coinage. In Joel Feinberg's words,[6] legal rights (that is, claims) are

> indispensably valuable possessions. A world without [them], no matter how full of benevolence and devotion to duty, would suffer an immense moral impoverishment. Persons would no longer hope for decent treatment from others on the ground of desert or rightful claim. Indeed, they would come to

think of themselves as having no special claim to kindness or consideration from others, so that whenever even minimally decent treatment is forthcoming they would think themselves lucky rather than inherently deserving, and their benefactors extraordinarily virtuous and worthy of great gratitude.

Rights, on the other hand, are not mere gifts or favors, motivated by love or pity, for which gratitude is the sole fitting response. A right is something a man can *stand* on, something that can be demanded or insisted upon without embarrassment or shame . . . . A world with claim-rights is one in which all persons, as actual or potential claimants, are dignified objects of respect, both in their own eyes and in the view of others. No amount of love and compassion, or obedience to higher authority, or *noblesse oblige*, can substitute for those values.

Of course, there are other morally significant values, like love, friendship and compassion and it is true, as John Kleinig has intimated,[7] that the absence of these from interpersonal transactions does diminish the moral quality of relationships. It is true, to quote Kleinig, that 'a morality which has as its motivation merely the giving of what is due or what is conducive to the greatest all-round utility, is seriously defective.' It may well be an indictment of contemporary civilisation that rights assume so great an importance. Rights may well reflect the inadequacy or absence of good moral relations. All this may be true. And yet, were society to change overnight, were all these moral imperfections to disappear, rights would still remain important. Rights give their holder dignity and confidence. Benevolence is no substitute.

The enactment of legal rights by itself, though a big step, is not sufficient. Laws which recognise rights are only as good as those who administer them. As Gross and Gross note in their introduction to their collection entitled *The Children's Rights Movement*,[8] 'the rights of children is an abstract, general, legalistic concept. It is an idea, an ideal, at best an affirmation of principle. It does not help children until it is put into practice. If it is ignored, obstructed, or perverted, it does no good; in fact, it may do harm, because many people will take the words for the act and think that because the words have been spoken the condition of children's lives has changed.' The passing of laws is only a beginning. It is a signal that must be taken up by the institutions of society. It requires movement by schools, courts, welfare and social service institutions and by the professions that deal with children. Altering the 'law in the books' achieves nothing if the 'law in action' is not altered as well.[9] Adequate surveillance of institutional practices, therefore, assumes considerable importance. Side-effects of legislation must also be picked up. For example, giving children more rights before the juvenile court may lead to what has been called 'justice without trial'.[10] Further, 'rights without services are meaningless'.[11] Thus, the institution of mandatory reporting laws on child abuse in the United States or registers in this country without more does little to protect (indeed, the reverse may be true) children ill-treated by their parents (see Chapter 4). As Monrad Paulsen noted, 'no law can be better than its implementation, and implementation can be no better than resources permit.'[12]

A further point needs to be made about rights and their importance. Rights can easily backfire. Reform movements intended to enhance children's rights and the concomitant development of professional structures to implement such reforms often generate their own sets of problems and ultimately have deleterious effects on children's rights. It is all too easy with hindsight to say that this is a reflection on the particular reform movements themselves. We can be over-cynical about children's rights movements of the past, such as the child-saving movement which emerged at the conclusion of the nineteenth century. The reforms of one era are apt to become the problems of the next. This should be borne in mind when we construct an agenda for improving a child's place in society. A few examples from the past will confirm the point. Intelligence tests were introduced as a result of Alfred Binet's work in 1907 as a benevolent measure by which an objective test was substituted for the injustice of the subjective method then used for placing children in institutions. Today we associate, and rightly so, the benevolence of 1907 with the stigma of labelling.[13] The juvenile court system was created to separate children from adult institutions and to create procedures which, it was believed, would help children in trouble rather than punishing them as adults would be punished. Today, we appreciate that the introduction of the juvenile court and associated processes has led to a wholesale diminution of the rights of juveniles (see Chapter 3). Other examples which span the century could be given. But, lest it be thought that the process to which reference is being made necessarily has a long gestation period, one further example demonstrates that the temporal gap can sometimes be all too short. The Children and Young Persons Act 1969 sanctioned the practice of police cautioning of juveniles as a way of diverting children from the juvenile court. But this measure has had the opposite effect completely. Cautioning has been found to inflate the number of children brought before the court.[14] One effect of this was to allow police cautions to be cited in court rather as previous findings of guilt by a court are.[15]

Rights: a Framework

Rights are to be found within normative orders. To say that someone has a right is a proposition which belongs to the class of what has been called 'institutional facts'.[16] There are different types of rights. Many are derived from laws or other institutional regulations. It is also common to assert that someone has a moral right to something when it is known that there are no laws and/or regulations conferring such a right. Such assertions are legitimate and make sense; a theory of rights must take account of them. Indeed, one which does not may be said to be defective. One may not agree that the right asserted is legitimate but this does not affect the moral validity of the right in question. Rights usage belongs to normative discourse; it prescribes conduct according to rules. Such language must be distinguished from descriptive statements. Rights do not belong in the world of 'brute facts'. They exist even if they are infringed.[17]

The view expressed here about the existence of moral rights is a contentious one. Bentham, for example, thought that the only rights were positive rights. In *Anarchical Fallacies* he wrote that rights were children of the law: 'from the law of nature come imaginary rights — a bastard brood of monsters.'[18] Of 'natural and imprescriptable rights' he wrote, in one of his ringing phrases, that they were 'nonsense upon stilts'. To write in this way confuses normative and descriptive discourse and is to be avoided. There are rights that exist prior to, or independently of, any legal or institutional rules.

Feinberg has shown[19] that the expression 'moral right' takes in a number of usages which themselves have little in common except that they are not, necessarily, legal or institutional in origin. He subdivides moral rights into conventional rights (rights derived from established custom and expectations, though not recognised by law); ideal rights (rights that ought to be a positive institutional or conventional right and would be so in an ideal legal system or conventional code); conscientious rights (claims 'the recognition of which as valid [are] called for, not necessarily by actual or ideal rules or conventions, but rather by the exercise of an enlightened individual conscience';[20] and exercise rights which, he explains, are not rights at all but moral justifications used in the exercise of a right of some other kind. There is a tendency to use these ideas interchangeably and so ambiguously.

When we talk of children's rights we are often not talking of legal or institutional rights at all. We are referring most often to moral rights, usually in the sense of ideal rights, but sometimes also in the sense of conscientious rights. When we say of a posited right for children that it is an ideal right, we are asserting that children have a claim against those who make society's rules, usually that is the legislature, to convert their moral right into a positive legal one. For example, we might argue that the age of consent to sexual intercourse be lowered or abolished or that children be allowed to take up remunerative employment without the current protective restrictions or that they be free from corporal punishment in schools and other institutions. (None of these are rights *sensu stricto* as will be seen shortly but this does not detract from the general argument.) Conscientious rights are rather different. These are actual claims against individuals for a certain kind of treatment and they are claims that hold true now, if they hold true at all, whatever the positive law may say. Many of these claims will be against educationalists, social workers, juvenile court magistrates and other personnel concerned with children and youth. Others will be directed against parents and will range from the relatively trivial, such as the time to go to bed or the clothes to wear, to such serious matters as whether a girl can seek contraceptive advice without her parents' consent.

What then is the relationship between a right and a claim? The two are often identified.[21] Claiming is 'an elaborate sort of rule-governed activity'.[22] Claims can clearly be distinguished from demands. Bank robbers make demands for money: what tax inspectors may call demands or even 'final demands' are in fact claims. Claims presuppose legitimate entitlements even if they are not recognised, while demands do not necessarily do so. Claims are founded on right: demands can be grounded on might. Feinberg distinguishes three uses of the 'claiming' vocabulary: 'making claim to . . .'; 'claiming that . . .'; and 'having a claim'.[23] He points out that 'only the person who has a title or has qualified for it, or someone speaking in his name, can make claim to something as a matter of right.' Anyone, on the other hand, can claim that, for example, a particular piece of property belongs to Smith. 'One major difference between *making legal claim to* and *claiming that* is that the former is a legal performance with direct legal consequences, whereas the latter is often a mere piece of descriptive commentary with no legal force.' Feinberg argues that '*having a claim consists in being in a position to claim in the performative sense*, that is, *to make claim to*.' This analysis is important because it enables someone to have a claim without even claiming that to which he is entitled or without even knowing that he has the claim.

It has been suggested above that claim and entitlement are integrally linked. This is supported by Feinberg. He identifies right with a 'valid claim'. He shows why it is wrong to identify rights with claims without more. 'All claims are put forward as justified', he argues, 'whether they are justified in fact or not. A claim conceded even by its maker to have no validity is not a claim at all, but a mere demand.' He instances the highwayman. He invokes 'validity', in the same way as I put forward 'entitlement'; both arguments seek justification within a system of rules. Of course, as Feinberg recognises, 'if having a valid claim is not redundant . . . there must be such a thing as having a claim that is not valid.'[24] He argues most persuasively in this way:

> one might accumulate just enough evidence to argue with relevance and cogency that one has a right (or right to be granted a right), although one's case might not be overwhelmingly conclusive. The argument might be strong enough to entitle one to a hearing and fair consideration. When one is in this position, it might be said that one 'has a claim' that deserves to be weighed carefully. Nevertheless, the balance of reasons may turn out to militate against recognition of the claim, so that the claim is not a valid claim or right. Having a claim to X is not (yet) the same as having a right to X, but is rather having a case, consisting of relevant reasons of at least minimal plausibility, that one has a right to X. The case establishes a right, not to X, but to a fair hearing and consideration. Claims so conceived, differ in degree: some are stronger than others. Rights, on the other hand, do not differ in degree; no one right is more of a right than another.

As he rightly says, that is the main difference between rights and claims. In this sense many putative 'rights' for children, when weighed and assessed, may be found to be claims. In time the argument in their favour may become stronger and they may ripen into rights.

What, then, are we to say about fundamental or human rights, the sort of basic rights conceded to be a prerequisite of civilised society? For example, it is a truism that all children everywhere need adequate nourishment if they are to survive and mature. Does this give them a right to food and, if so, who has the duty to provide it? The question becomes significant in environments where food is in short supply. There is a school of thought, of which Feinberg is a proponent or at least a sympathiser, which identifies needs or at least the most basic of needs with human rights. This commits them, as Feinberg notes, 'to the conception of a right which is an entitlement *to* some good, but not a valid claim *against* any particular individual.'[25] As he concedes: 'in conditions of scarcity there may be no determinate individuals who can plausibly be said to have a duty to provide the missing goods to those in need.' The children's rights literature and its documentation commonly employ this special 'manifesto' sense of right. Many references to children's rights turn out on inspection to be aspirations for the accomplishment of particular social or moral goals.[26] The writings of the child liberation movement are replete with such references.[27] Even a document such as the United Nations Declaration of 1959 uses language of this sort. Thus, Principle 4 states, in part: 'the child shall have the right to adequate nutrition, housing, recreation and medical services.' No one would deny this. But who in Bangladesh or Uganda is to bear the duty of providing these services? It is notable that the United Nations document itself couches the obligation in the widest and vaguest terms: 'mankind', it states in the preamble to the Declaration, 'owes to the child the best it has to give.'

Feinberg appears to be suggesting that, although the need of a 'manifesto' rightholder cannot be met, he has a right because he is in a situation that ought to give rise to a valid claim if circumstances allowed for its satisfaction. This comes close to reducing rights to needs and that cannot be right. First, it is logically fallacious: a need cannot constitute a right. Secondly, the reducibility thesis may be censured on the policy grounds that it might provide a recipe for anarchy. Critics of the 'manifesto' conception of rights, however, go too far. Gerber, for example, argues that 'the need for heroin or a cigarette does not constitute a right to it.'[28] Of course, it does not. But this *reductio ad absurdum* does not get us very far. A baby's need for milk is in a different category. We know as an objective biological fact that babies need milk. To talk of need of heroin or a cigarette in similar terms is to misuse the notion of need. Gerber may desire a cigarette but he does not need one. A cigarette may enhance his pleasure (in the short term anyway) but it is not a *sine qua non* of his continued existence. I would not be in breach of any duty if I refused to give someone a cigarette when that person said he needed one and could not get one anywhere else. But I would be in flagrant disregard of my moral duty were I not to supply milk to a starving baby.

What this, I think, draws attention to is that much talk about rights is really talk about obligations and that perhaps it might be better if the sort of discussion found in the 'manifesto' literature were couched in terms of duties rather than by reference to rights.[29] It is not only discussion about 'manifesto' rights that might be improved by talking about obligations instead. Talk about the morality of abortion, often expressed in terms of the foetus's 'right to life',[30] may be more meaningful if expressed in terms of the obligation not to kill. Equally, to talk of rights inherent in those who are incapable of exercising them, the severely retarded child, the animal,[31] the tree[32] is less meaningful than to state our obligations towards them. But what obligations are there, for example, to supply milk to babies, in an environment where milk is scarce or non-existent? It seems to me that, if it is possible to argue for rights (in a 'manifesto' sense) when the situation is such that something ought to be recognised as a valid claim if circumstances permitted its satisfaction, as Feinberg does, then it can equally be argued that if circumstances changed a duty would also come into operation. The duty is conditional but it is better expressed as such than as a 'manifesto' right.

Within the genus of 'rights' it is possible to distinguish a number of different kinds of rights. It was the American jurist, Wesley Hohfeld,[33] who provided us with an analysis of different kinds of legal relations and showed us that common, including legal, usage often confused these different senses. Some legal relations were aptly characterised as rights with correlative duties but other so-called 'rights' were, he demonstrated, 'privileges' or freedoms[34] (the privilege-holder's acts in pursuits of his privileges do not constitute a breach of duty), and still others were 'powers' and 'immunities'. Hohfeld's scheme is neither definitive nor beyond criticism.[35] A detailed discussion of it would be out of place in this context. Undoubtedly, Hohfeld has provided insight into rights and clarified what was rampant confusion. But in his enthusiasm to separate the 'true' meaning of right (which he identifies with a claim)[36] from inaccurate accretions, Hohfeld made a basic error: he insisted that the different relations (right-duty; privilege-no right; power-liability; immunity-disability) had nothing in common sufficient to justify calling them all 'rights' or even species of the genus 'right'. Despite Hohfeld, there is no doubt that 'right' is a unitary concept.

Neil MacCormick has suggested[37] that there are

> common features shared by all that we call 'rights': normative orders can afford to individuals security in the enjoyment of what are normally goods for individuals; that someone has a right to (a) implies that x or freedom or discretion in relation to x is a good, and (b) is true if in one mode or another the individual fulfils the conditions for having some appropriate form of normative security over x or freedom or discretion in relation to x

What Hohfeld clarified were the different ways in which 'normative security' could be achieved. The maximisation of children's rights depends first upon political will[38] and only then involves conceptual analysis. Once the political decision has been taken, the philosopher and jurist are in a position to indicate the appropriate mode of normative security for the right in question within a particular legal system. To achieve some rights, to establish institutional structures or complexes, an amalgam of modes may be necessary. For example, it is common to talk of 'the right to privacy'[39] and 'the right to work'. It is clear that both of these 'rights' could be turned into legal rights if the political will to do so were there. It is also clear that the mechanics of enactment would involve the use of aggregations of different legal relations depicted by Hohfeld as well as of modes of normative protection not perceived by him. Further, there are likely to be different routes to the same end.

Many putative rights for children are, in Hohfeld's terminology, 'privileges'. They depend on being normatively free to do x and this in its turn depends, as Raz has pointed out,[40] on an implied normative permission to do whatever it is not wrong to do (that is, in that normative order). Others depend upon having the power to bring something about and thus on the existence of norms which confer powers. At present a child's capacity to contract is circumscribed by a number of rules: for example, he can buy necessaries but not luxuries.[41] To give children full contractual capacity would involve conferring upon them a complex of powers and at the same time removing from them certain existing immunities. A third species of rights depends heavily on duties. To bestow upon a child the right not to be subjected to corporal punishment would require the imposition of duties on parents, school teachers and others in a position of authority over children not to use physical chastisement.[42] MacCormick shows how a number of levels of normative protection exist in such cases:[43]

> the first level . . . is . . . the existence of norms against infringement of the rights; norms whereby it is a duty not to assault . . . . The second level of protection is the existence of norms whereby wrong-doers in such cases are required to desist from further infringement and to make reparation for harm already done. The third level of protection in legal and other institutionalised systems is that courts etc. are empowered to order desistence by . . . injunctions and to order reparation in cash . . .

The fourth mode depends on the existence of clear limitations on powers to change the permissions or norms under which in the other three ways goods are secured to individuals. Hohfeld characterised such limitations as disabilities with the 'right-holder' correlatively possessing immunities. These distinctions are valuable and should be borne in mind in any analysis of children's rights. Unfortunately, they are often neglected or glossed over with the result that too little attention is given to questions of how to enact and how to enforce the 'rights' supposed to be important.

Children's Rights: a Classification

As was indicated in the first chapter, one obvious way to break down children's rights is into those concerned with the protection of children and those the recognition of which would be geared towards a child's self-determination or autonomy. This distinction can be put into the pithy language of Farson by describing one approach as protecting children, the other as protecting their rights.[44] The distinction is, however, both over-simplistic and deceptive. A study of the wide range of varied claims made on behalf of children, and sometimes by them, reveals that these claims are of a number of different categories. It is important to recognise these differences. Different rights have different problems, both of formulation and enforcement. But it is not surprising that proponents have conflated the different categories of rights. It may be that each is seeking support by appearing to broaden the appeal.

It may be suggested that under the general heading of children's rights there are rights of four categories.[45] The first category are generalised claims on behalf of all children. They can be described as welfare rights. Others may conceptualise them as human rights. The second category is principally concerned with protection. It demands that children be protected from inadequate care, from abuse and neglect by parents, from exploitation by employers or potential employers, and from other forms of danger in their environment. The third demand is grounded in social justice. It is a claim that rights which adults have should be extended to children as well. Those who put this case argue that there is no good reason to treat children differently from adults. This is a claim which has had much prominence in the United States where the existence of a written constitution and a bill of rights makes it relatively clear what rights citizens are accorded. The claim is no less important in this country. The fourth type of claim demands more freedom from control for children, greater recognition of their capacity to choose from alternatives, more autonomy over their lives. It stresses their right to act independently. At one level it demands that children be free to choose the length of their hair, what they eat or when they go to bed: at another level it is expressed as a 'right to alternative home environments'[46] or to seek an abortion without parental consent or notice.

In the next sections of this chapter these different categories of rights are considered separately.

Rights to Welfare

The clearest statement of children's rights in the sense of rights to welfare is to be found in the United Nations Declaration of the Rights of The Child. It is a reaffirmation of faith in 'fundamental human rights and in the dignity and worth of the human person'.[47] The goal is expressed to be 'a happy childhood'.[48] There follow ten principles. These may be summarised as: (i) the enjoyment of the rights in the Declaration regardless of race, colour, sex, language, religion, political or other opinion, national or social origin, property, birth or other status; (ii) special protection, opportunities and facilities to enable the child to develop in a healthy and normal manner, in conditions of freedom and dignity; the best interests of the child to be the paramount consideration in the enactment of laws to this end; (iii) entitlement to a name and nationality; (iv) the benefits of social security, including the right to adequate nutrition, housing, recreation and medical services; (v) special treatment, education and care if physically, mentally or socially handicapped; (vi) the need for love and under-standing and an atmosphere of affection and security; wherever possible the child should grow up in the care and under the responsibility of his parents; (vii) entitlement to free education and equal opportunity to develop abilities, individual judgment, and a sense of moral and social responsibility; (viii) priority in protection and relief in times of disaster; (ix) protection against all forms of neglect, cruelty and exploitation; and (x) protection from any form of racial, religious or other discrimination, and an upbringing in a spirit of understanding, tolerance, peace and universal brotherhood.

Very few of these rights are contentious. One, perhaps, which is today is the special treatment of the handicapped. In the generation since the United Nations Declaration we have come to understand the special educational needs of handi-capped children rather better and their integration within a normal schooling environment is rightly regarded as the goal, wherever possible.[49] This apart, it is difficult to think that there is much opposition, in theory at least, to the rights spelt out in the UN Declaration. By expressing the rights it sets out as 'human rights' the United Nations was not saying that children ought to have these rights but, since children are undoubtedly human beings, that they already have them. This is a matter of some political importance for it is possible as a result to indict certain countries which deny children their entitlements.

Many of the rights in the UN Declaration and similar manifestos contain what must be regarded as the most fundamental of children's rights. It stands to reason that without nutrition and medical care, to take just two of the more obvious examples, few of the other putative rights would be of much value. A child who is under-nourished, denied medical attention or the most basic educa-tion is not in any position to become sufficiently rationally autonomous to exercise self-determination of any sort. As Wald expresses it, 'they are at the heart of a child's well-being.'[50]

It would be noted that the rights in question are not easily formulated as rights against anyone. Rather they are rights against everyone. Where, therefore, they do not exist the complaint needs to be addressed to governments and to legislatures, in some cases to local government. It is a question in each case of deciding on whom the duty falls and who is failing to carry it out. It may be that a particular local authority is failing to implement or obstructing government legislation. It may also be the case that children are being denied their rights by central government initiative. A recent English example concerns the provision of school meals. The Education Act 1944[51] imposed a duty on local education authorities to provide school meals. In 1980 legislation was passed to give authorities a discretion: an LEA 'may provide . . . milk, meals or other refreshment.'[52] The results is that a number of authorities no longer provide school meals as a matter of course,[53] despite an official finding that lack of proper nourishment can prevent children from taking full advantage of the education provided for them.[54] If Article 4 of the UN Declaration can be interpreted to include the provision of school meals, then it is possible to argue that, measured against it, the current English policies, central and local, deny children their valid claims. This is not an area where courts can achieve very much. If change is to come about it must come from a change of legislative policy. Wald puts this well:

> These claims generally are not for things traditionally thought of as legal 'rights', i.e. entitlements enforceable by court order. Courts cannot order that the world be free of poverty or that all children have adequate health care.[55]

But he goes on to say that the legislature cannot guarantee a 'right' to them. This is not correct. What it cannot do is ensure that practice is up to the standards of the rights laid down. And it is here that the courts may have a useful part to play, provided, of course, someone or some institution is failing to comply with standards imposed upon him or it and someone questions it.

The main problem with all these 'rights against the world' is that they are vague. What is 'adequate nutrition', 'education', 'recreation', 'relief'? Some attempt is made by the United Nations to spell out the principles in more detail but vagueness remains. Thus, for example, the right to education is to that which will promote 'general culture', and terms like 'moral and social responsibility' are used. There is a tendency in formulating rights of this nature to be deliberately vague. Different societies have different knowledge and economic resources. They have a different understanding of 'adequate nutrition' and variable abilities to meet such a goal. The same applies to medical services. In England today all children have the right to be vaccinated against polio: those that need it presumably also have the right to use dialysis machines, receive 'hole in the heart' operations or bone marrow transplants. But is it meaningful to talk in this way? We can provide vaccinations: we cannot, it seems, provide adequately for the advanced techniques just mentioned. It is possible that we could if we readjusted our priorities, but that is another matter. It is because of problems like this that rights of the 'human rights' type tend to be expressed generally and so vaguely. There is a tendency to regress to the lowest common denominator. It is dubious, as a result, how valuable a list of such rights are, other than as a series of moral or social goals.

One thing is not in doubt. The rights in question are very different from those to be found in the writings of the child liberation school. The UN document is not conceived as an exercise in children's liberation. It is essentially a protectionist statement. It is a list of the protections that children need and it may be best to conceive of them as protections rather than rights. This is not to underestimate their importance or to denigrate them. If all countries adopted the letter and the spirit of the UN Declaration, the world would be a better place for children. Farson, Holt and others who are similarly inclined would no doubt respond that, as far as children are concerned, it would still be an adult world and children would still occupy an inferior status. And protectionist intentions can backfire: there is abundant evidence of this.

Children and Protection

The first category, just discussed, is conceived in terms of rights, even if the essential ideology is one of protecting the welfare of children. The second category is overtly concerned with protection. It stresses the vulnerability of children, particularly babies and the very youngest children, and it imposes a caretaker role upon parents. When rights are spoken of in this context, it is to inject more responsibility into the parental role. This approach to children's rights is the oldest and the most firmly entrenched. It is the concept which is to the fore every time a tragedy occurs and a child dies or is seriously injured as a result of parental ill-treatment. It is a concept which enables us to believe that most children, unlike those we hear about in sad stories like those concerned with Maria Colwell,[56] Steven Meurs[57] or Maria Mehmedagi,[58] are treated well and so have nothing to complain about. This is the view against which those who espouse children's liberation react with hostility. The distinction between normal and abusive treatment can be drawn too sharply. As I argue in the fourth chapter, our normal treatment of children is in part the explanation of child abuse. Furthermore, the very concept of intervention itself is problematic. Whom does it protect and against what? To a large extent recent tragedies have provoked a moral panic. Where once social workers were reluctant to remove children from parents, now they may do so too hastily. This theme is developed further in Chapter 4.

When rights are spoken of within this framework the attention is on certain freedoms that we believe children should have: freedom from abuse and neglect can also be looked at in terms of a parent's lack of rights (Hohfeld[59] used the infelicitous but accurate expression 'no-right'). The claim that children need these 'rights', or arguably 'more rights', is based on the premise that children are unable to care for themselves and so need adult protection, care and guidance. In our society it falls to parents to undertake these primary responsibilities. Other responsibilities, such as education, are assumed by the state. It is a matter of some controversy today as to how much autonomy parents should be allowed in raising their children. This issue is debated in Chapter 7.

All states set some standards for parental conduct. They are usually pitched minimally. The norm is parental autonomy, rather than state intervention. Recent events have, however, led to an increased state monitoring of the adequacy of parental care. Children's rights advocates are divided on the appropriate role of parents and the state in child-rearing. Some believe that less, rather than more, state intervention in the affairs of families is the best way to protect children. Others disagree. What is agreed is that, short of the implementation of Plato's ideal,[60] the state cannot take over the role of parents.

The claims to protection made on behalf of children are very different from the assertion that children should have more independence or autonomy. As Wald argues:

> They do not change the status of children. The intervention advocated entails substituting one adult decision-maker for another, rather than giving children the choice of deciding whether they like the conditions in which they find themselves.[61]

He also notes, quite rightly, that the intervention process is usually invoked by adults, not children, though older children do sometimes initiate abuse proceedings. There is some evidence that this happens, for example, in the Netherlands, where medical referees are sometimes appraised of cases by children themselves.[62]

Protection as rights is, of course, a highly paternalistic notion. We do not ask children whether they wish to be protected. I do not think it would occur to the average social worker to ask a child, even an older child, whether he wanted to remain with parents who physically ill-treated him. Even when children have lawyers to represent them, the latter will invariably see their role as deciding what is best for the child, rather than representing the child's opinions to the court. It may be fanciful to question whether a child's views should be elicited when abuse or neglect is in issue, but advocates of a child's rights to protection go beyond these rudimentary protections. Thus, for example, the issue is commonly debated as to whether children should be exposed to violence on television or in the cinema, whether their toys and games should pander to their tastes for machismo and violence (guns, war games etc.), whether their food should be regulated so as to avoid their eating harmful substances such as sugar. We do not ask children what they think. Of course, were the state to intervene in these ways, it would give children less rather than more rights. But in doing so it would be following established precedents. After all, we stop children smoking cigarettes (in theory at least), we limit their consumption of alcohol, and it is drugs that they use rather than those used by middle-aged housewives which the law proscribes, even if the evidence suggests the latter are at least as addictive and dangerous as the former.[63]

Whatever may be the public feeling on children's rights generally, there can be no doubt as to the strength of the sentiment supporting child protection. An instructive example is the passage of the Protection of Children Act 1978.[64] In the summer of 1977 the English media published a number of scare stories about the exploitation of children for pornographic purposes in America; 'kiddie porn' it was called. There was no evidence of any similar phenomenon in England. A much-publicised report of an eight-year-old Manchester girl on a list of children available for unlawful sexual activities was later shown to be wholly misleading. The Act was virtually the result of a one-woman campaign, the moral entrepreneur being Mary Whitehouse. She described child 'porn' as 'like an outbreak of rabies', a menace against which legislative action had to be taken. That there was public support for the measure is indicated by the letters from the public which reached both media and Members of Parliament. The Bill was virtually unopposed and became law.[65] It has probably had little effect on the pornography industry or on children. It has also not affected the lives of those who supported the measure: the greater recognition of children's autonomy, of course, would.

Treating Children Like Adults

Is age a suspect classification? Can we justify a double standard in our treatment of adults and children? These are the questions which contemporary advocates of children's rights ask. Double standards are not necessarily unjustifiable. Things which are apparently similar may not, on further reflection, actually be alike. But often they are and the double standards are but a reflection of privilege. Thus, for most of our history we have applied different standards to women from those we apply to men. So we denied women the vote (for a time we even distinguished women under thirty from those over that age) and we imposed numerous incapacities on married women particularly. No one today could put up a rational argument for these distinctions, deeply embedded though they were in our culture and social practices. Can a rational argument be adduced for withholding privileges from children?

On the whole the special treatment of children has been justified on the basis of the child's incapacity or lack of maturity or because of the special protections bestowed upon children. It is not difficult to show that children are younger than adults, and this is a material difference, but it must be accepted that the cut-off point is arbitrary. As Cohen puts it: 'Is there really a significant difference . . . between someone who is eighteen years old, and someone who is seventeen years and 364 days old?'[66] If we accept, as we must do, that the distinction is arbitrary, there are three strategies that can be adopted.

The simplest is to accept the inevitability of some distinction, however arbitrary, and merely to reassess current restrictions in terms of their assumptions. This has to an extent been done already in the recent past: the age of majority was lowered by three years in 1970.[67] Secondly, one could, as Farson[68]

and Holt[69] believe one should, argue for the abolition of all age-related disabilities. To do this would be to fly in the face of evidence from developmental
psychology. Thirdly, it might be possible to make decisions on a case-by-case
basis. My own preference is for this strategy. Wald, I note, is critical. He says
such a determination of capacity is only viable if there are 'objective ways to
measure capacity'.[70] Otherwise he fears discrimination. He sees cost as a further
objection. Cost cannot be a serious objection where rights are at stake. Discrimination, abuse of power, is always troublesome and potentially exists
wherever there is discretion. But this is not an argument for eliminating
discretion which may be valuable, but rather one for confining it and controlling
any possible political or racial biases. These are not objective ways to measure
capacity if by 'objective' we mean metre bars in Paris to measure metres, but
there are ways of measuring it. We could employ a notion of rationality which
enabled us to develop a neutral theory of the good. That constructed by Rawls
in his *Theory of Justice*[71] comes closest to what I have in mind. This idea is
developed further later in the chapter.

Whether we allow a case-by-case determination or not, it is surely important
that age limits are constantly re-examined. Many of them are very old and have
little to commend them but history. We have to ask ourselves whether their
rationales remain valid. Children mature more quickly today than in past ages.
They may be exposed less to the world of work but television and travel have
broadened their horizons. We have more evidence on which to rely with the
growth of developmental psychology. Psychological theories of personality and
moral development which reflect universal developmental assumptions[72] may be
readily challenged as ignoring socio-cultural history and not squaring with
anthropological evidence,[73] but they do show that a child matures through a
succession of stages and gradually increases his competences, cognitive abilities
and moral capacities. Research[74] shows, contrary to what child liberationists
assert, that children under ten to twelve years old lack the cognitive abilities and
skills of judgment which are necessary for them to be able to make decisions
about major events which could severely affect their lives (for example,
decisions about education, work, sexual relations) or the lives of others (for
example, voting for a government). The evidence about older children is not so
clear. It seems, however, that in both moral and cognitive development, many
reach adult levels between twelve and fourteen,[75] though the ability to reason
improves quite obviously throughout adolescence. We expect adolescents to be
criminally responsible at the age of fourteen (indeed, we are prepared to impose
responsibility on them at ten),[76] but we are less willing to accept correla-
tivity of responsibility and rights. Fourteen-year-olds not only have few rights,
they have few rights in the criminal justice process. This, as is argued in Chapter
3, is extremely difficult to justify.

One ingenious attempt to deal with the incapacities of the young is made by
Howard Cohen in his recent book, *Equal Rights For Children*. He notes that all

of us rely upon the capacities of others. We use doctors, lawyers, stockbrokers, etc. Why then, he argues, should not children? His view is that 'any rights currently enjoyed by adults which children could exercise with the aid of agents are rights which children should have' and he adds that this applies to 'all children'.[77] He argues that the 'role of the child's agent would be to supply information in terms which the child could understand, to make the consequences of the various courses of action a child might take clear to the child, and to do what is necessary to see that the right in question is actually exercised.'[78] He gives as a concrete example a child who is approximately twelve years old, is unhappy at home and wishes to live elsewhere. He adds that the parents have done nothing that legally could be described as child abuse or neglect, but they are apparently 'strict disciplinarians'.[79] What could the child agent do? Cohen argues

> [He] could certainly inform the child of the advantages and the importance of continuity, just as the agent could see whether the proposed alternative home was likely to be better or worse than the child's present one. While it is true that an agent . . . could not absolutely prevent a child from making a particular choice which rested within the rightful range, this possibly should not be blown out of proportion. Agents would be trusted advisors, and their views are likely to be respected by children. Furthermore, we are speaking of children who are at least old enough to articulate the desire to change homes, and so are presumably old enough to comprehend something of what would be involved in the move — as long as the agent expressed the situation in an appropriate way.
>
> There is no very good reason to think that children would not be able to exercise this right meaningfully once we have specified an adult whose obligation it is to assess the relative merits of the child's alternatives, to help the child articulate his or her proper interests, and to lay the groundwork for the child's subsequent action.[80]

What is not clear is quite what function the child agent is supposed to fulfil. By calling him an agent Cohen seems to imply that he has his only authority delegated to him by his principal (the child), so that his function would involve the execution of the child's will and nothing more. But if that were to be his only function there would be little point in complicating the decision-making process by adding another stage to it. From the example I have quoted Cohen clearly envisages something more than mere agency. His child agent is a counsellor, a bit like a careers advisor or moral tutor. Cohen seems to want the child to make his own decision but he does not trust him to decide on his own. Is the child (in Cohen's terms) capable of deciding whether he leaves home or not? If he is capable, why does he need an agent? If he is incapable of taking such a serious decision by himself, is he capable of appointing an agent to advise him? It seems as if Cohen, who wants children to be able to exercise the same powers as adults, cannot bear the consequences of this. The child agent looks suspiciously like a parent-substitutue or guardian, albeit a somewhat unusual one because he appears to possess authority but no responsibility.[81] So who are to be child agents? Here Cohen to an extent sits on the fence. He cautions against professional agents yet he expects the agent to possess a number of special skills such that 'some training'[82] would make them more effective. He seems to think that personnel within the social services will be called on but concludes that 'teachers, social workers, day care workers, public health nurses, youth workers, Big Brothers and Sisters, and so on, have the skills of a child agent to a great extent.'[83] So long as we stick to social work-type personnel, all we are doing is giving the state another say in family matters: once we reach siblings we are surely on a course for disaster. Cohen's thesis is a brave attempt to circumvent the limited capacities of children but I do not think it works. He believes the problems of institutionalising child agents, though substantial, can be overcome. I doubt the viability of the concept itself: some of Cohen's analysis suggests to me that he is not as confident as he would like to be.

Rights Against Parents

Cohen's example of the child who wants to leave home[84] takes us to a fourth category of children's rights. This is the claim that children should be free to act independently of their parents before they reach the age of majority. Decision-making can range from the relatively trivial (what to eat, the length of a child's hair, what television programmes to watch) to major steps such as leaving home or having an abortion. There is no doubt that some children do suffer from oppressive, even harmful, parental control. But most are inherently dependent on someone. As Uviller puts it: 'To liberate them from their parents is simply to assign them to another, potentially more oppressive protection.'[85] There is the suspicion that the problem is greater today than in earlier times. Children are exposed to a wider range of ideas with greater scope for conflict with parents. In Britain one well-recognised example of conflict is between parents and children in immigrant families, where the parents cling to the culture of their homeland and their children quest for the lifestyle of their English peers, reject the constraints of their parents' culture and parental discipline.[86]

When rights are spoken of in this area the debate tends to take one of two forms. To some, giving children rights against parents means allowing a child the freedom to act independently. A variant requires the child to seek approval for his or her action, or to challenge the parental decision, in a court or, possibly, before some other agency. The debate has been fought most fiercely in the United States over the question of a girl's right to seek contraceptive advice, use contraceptives and seek an abortion. The question is discussed in relation to these issues in Chapter 7.

Wald summarises the factors to be considered as (i) whether the child can make such decisions adequately; (ii) if not, whether other decision-makers, or decision-making processes, are likely to arrive at better decisions than the parents; (iii) whether the state can really remove the decision-making power from the parents; (iv) the costs of removing the decision from the parents in terms of family autonomy and family privacy (which he says, and we must agree, are cherished values in our society); and (v) the costs of not giving the decision to the child.[87] It is, as he says, unrealistic to treat certain of the rights that tend to be claimed as legally enforceable rights. Children in families can no more enjoy total autonomy over their lives than their parents or adult siblings can. It would be alien to family living to suppose otherwise. More significantly, even if Parliament were to give children the right to decide on their bed-times, for example, there would be enormous enforcement problems. Wald puts it thus: 'If a parent orders a child to bed and the child refuses, can a court order the parent to let the child stay up? If the parents do not follow the court order, will they be sent to jail?'[88] Looked at in this way these claims are not only patently absurd but costly and ineffective as well.

Most, however, would not subscribe to the Farson or Holt line and focus their attention instead on (a) adolescents and (b) major decision-making: abortion and contraception, medical care and possibly issues such as drugs and alcohol. General arguments can be adduced for giving adolescent children rights against parents within these areas. Older children are likely to exercise them anyway. It would not place burdens on courts, as, judging from recent American experience, it now does. Further, the failure to accord older children such rights may actually be deleterious to their welfare: a girl may be psychologically harmed by having to undergo a pregnancy that she wished to terminate. The question may also be investigated by considering the arguments adduced to deny adolescents rights on these matters. Take, for example, an adolescent girl's right to use contraceptives. The arguments put to counter any autonomy for her are usually either moralistic or paternalistic (or a combination of the two). The paternalistic ones are especially weak for, of all groups, it is adolescents who are usually unmarried and experimenting, whose interests are most furthered by contraception. Unwanted motherhood may be exceptionally burdensome for an adolescent. The moralistic arguments are hardly any stronger. If it is not immoral for adults to use contraception to regulate the consequences of their sexual activities, it is difficult to see how the same action can be immoral when undertaken by adolescents. It may be possible to raise objections on both moralistic and paternalistic grounds to sexual behaviour by adolescents but that is another matter.

There is another difference between these major decisions and minor decisions of everyday living, referred to above. They would not entail the active intervention of courts or other state agencies. The rights, if given to adolescents, could be exercised without parental knowledge. Whether rights, such as those relating to medical care, contraception, abortions, drugs and such like, should be legally recognised must ultimately depend upon whether adolescents possess the skills and understanding to make such decisions. We can rely for this on the findings of developmental psychology, references to which have been made earlier in this chapter. On the basis of these there would certainly be a strong moral argument for recognising the capacities of those of fourteen and above to take decisions.

But this does not mean that we should necessarily allow them to do so. For a start, the evidence that fourteen-year-olds have reached adult levels of cognitive development is a generalised finding and may not apply to all adolescents of that age. The riposte that not all adults have reached such levels is, however, difficult to resist. Secondly, it may be argued that giving adolescents decision-making powers may create conflict within the family and that this may be to their detriment. On the other hand, the conflict may be there already or may be instigated by adolescents who are resentful of what they consider to be oppressive parental decision-making. Those, like Goldstein, Freud and Solnit (whose views are fully considered in Chapter 7), who say that giving adolescents decision-making powers threatens the family system, do not fully explain why. Further, it seems to be assumed that, if adolescents had the sort of rights conferred upon them that we are discussing here, they would exercise them. In making such an assumption, which is common, we are attributing to the legislator greater powers than he has. The evidence suggests that in 'expressive'[89] areas of life such as the family, the capacity of the law to change behaviour and attitudes is limited.[90] Why should it be any greater in this most sensitive of matters?

Thus far we have considered the claim that autonomy ought to be given to children, at least those of certain levels of maturity and cognitive ability. The variant of this must also be given some attention. If there is a disagreement between parents and an adolescent on some matter of importance, the final decision could be left to neither of them but referred instead to a court or possibly some other agency for it to resolve the disagreement. As will be seen from the discussion in Chapter 7, this approach has commended itself to the American Supreme Court.[91] As Wald notes, this 'option' is 'attractive' to many legislators'.[92] Wald himself does not find it attractive. He reasons that 'disputes between parents and children cannot be settled by any existing statutes or principles of law. Instead, they involve making value judgments about appropriate family relationships.'[93] He believes these decisions will reflect personal values and biases of the decision-maker. I would concede that this can happen (and has happened). We could construct a legal principle easily enough. The 'best interests' doctrine (the idea that the child's long-term interests are the first and paramount consideration) is an obvious candidate.[94] The Goldstein, Freud and Solnit suggestion that we should look to the 'least detrimental alternative' solution in cases of dispute (though, of course, not this type of dispute) is another.[95] Whatever standard is adopted the possibility of values intruding remains, even if not as overtly as in *Painter* v. *Bannister*,[96] the example Wald gives and which I discuss in Chapter 6. He is equally sceptical about leaving decisions to other professionals since 'there is no scientific method for determining a child's best interest'[97] and he believes value judgments would play as large a role as in the decisions of judges.

A second reason why Wald, for one, does not find the solution of leaving decisions to courts or other agencies attractive is that 'courts, doctors, lawyers and other professionals frequently just drop in and then drop out of the child's life. Yet the child's problems may be ongoing.'[98] This argument has considerable merit and would have more if we could be convinced that parents were able to bear the burden of helping adolescents through the sorts of crisis that Wald envisages (a teenage girl having an abortion, for example). But I am dubious whether most can. Many will not even try, and many will use professional assistance.

His third reason concerns the broader implications for the family as such if, as he puts it, 'courts or experts become the ultimate decision-makers.'[99] This is a major problem, graphically portrayed by Lasch,[100] Donzelot[101] and others, and it is one of which we must be extremely wary. But in this context it can be over-played. First, because disputes between parents and adolescents over major issues are the exception rather than the rule. Secondly, because whether decisions are imposed by outside professionals or not, whether we like it or not, the family is now very much within the grip of the 'therapeutic state'. We may deplore it: we may resist its extension. But the phenomenon is here to stay.

My concern is with children's rights and how best these can be promoted. Where there is a difference of opinion between an adolescent and a parent, we cannot pretend it does not exist. There are difficulties in relying on the 'best interests' doctrine and the use of outside professionals is far from satisfactory. What is the solution? My tentative solution is to see the parents' role in part as one of representation, representing their children's interests. Where they agree with their children's views, there is no problem. Where they do not agree, what are the parents to represent? We are dealing with persons who will in due course become competent and have full decision-making capacity. What, therefore, are parents to do? Gerald Dworkin puts forward what I find a most helpful suggestion. He says that parents

> ought to choose for [children], not as they might want, but in terms of maximizing those interests that will make it possible for them to develop life plans of their own. We ought to preserve their share of what Rawls calls 'primary goods'; that is, such goods as liberty, health, and opportunity, which any rational person would want to pursue whatever particular life plan he chooses.[102]

The value of this is that it provides a reasonably objective test. Despite notions like 'liberty', 'health' and 'opportunity', none of which is value-free, I believe in most of the difficult 'test-cases', the sort described in Chapter 7, the test would provide a solution. More importantly it provides a normative standard which thrusts children's rights to the forefront.

The problems occur when parents will not see their role in this way. The answer seems to lie in holding that representation ceases at the point where parental decision-making is not geared towards a maximisation of the sort of primary social goods which Rawls describes.[103] At this point an outside agency must come in: my own preference would be a court. What I am suggesting provides for children's views to be recognised. It acknowledges that parents usually represent those views. It allows parents to be overriden where it can be shown that they are not representing a child's views and those views if implemented would maximise the child's primary social goods. It is less likely that an outside agency will hear of two other cases: namely, representation of a child's views which hinder the development of life plans based on a rational theory of good; and   decisions taken by a parent, which can be impugned in the way described, on which the child has no opinion. If such cases come into the open, courts have a role to play, as was shown in the recent 'Sotos Syndrome' case of *Re D.*[104]

My plan employs both parents and courts. It circumvents the problems listed by Wald. Parents' views are to be governed by a child's long-term interests and this is defined as neutrally as possible in terms of a maximisation of primary social goods. Courts have a limited role and are governed by the same standard. I believe this scheme, though set out here as little more than an idealised model, could be put into operation. I think the effect would be to recognise the importance of a child's views but it would also provide a workable criterion for over-ruling them in certain cases. Examples are given in Chapter 7. It will be apparent that what I defend here is quasi-paternalistic. In the next two sections of this chapter, I look accordingly at paternalism and its defects and I construct a theory of liberal paternalism to justify children's rights. Paternalism in its classical form does not acknowledge the existence of children's rights. Liberal paternalism, I believe, compels their recognition.

Paternalism and Children

Paternalism is a doctrine which justifies 'interference with a person's liberty of action . . . by reasons, referring exclusively to the welfare, good, happiness, needs, interests or values of the person being coerced.'[105] It can be traced back to Plato[106] and Aristotle[107] but I do not intend to do so.[108] Instead, I look at three leading English philosophers who in different ways defended the paternalistic treatment of children. The most extreme position is taken by Thomas Hobbes. In *Leviathan* he put forward the view that children occupied a position of complete dependence. 'Like the imbecile, the crazed and the beasts, over . . . children . . . there is no law.'[109] He argued that fathers had the power of life and death over children and 'every man is supposed to promise obedience to him in whose power it is to save or destroy him.'[110] The father was the sovereign. The child had neither natural rights nor rights by social contract: he could not have the latter since he lacked the ability to make covenants. How then he was supposed to 'promise obedience' is not explained by Hobbes. Hobbes's underlying assumption was that from the father the child got protection, and obedience was accordingly the child's obligation. From this logic it followed that children had no rights.

Locke's argument was somewhat different. It rejects the sexism of Hobbes (and of Filmer,[111] of course, but that does not concern us here): so it is parental authority that Locke discusses. Secondly, Locke wants to constrain parental dominance. It is, he tells us, a 'temporary Government, which terminates with the minority of the Child';[112] 'the bonds of this subjection are like the Swadling Cloths.'[113] Unlike Hobbes, Locke did not believe that parents had 'an authority to make laws and dispose as they please of their lives and liberties.'[114] Children, like adults, had natural rights which needed to be protected. Parents had to prepare children for their freedom, because that was God's will. Locke argued:

> To supply the Defects of this Imperfect state, till the Improvement of Growth and Age hath removed them, Adam and Eve, and after them all Parents were, by the Law of Nature, under an obligation to preserve, nourish and educate the children they had begotten, not as their own Workmanship, but the Workmanship of their own Maker, the Almighty, to whom they were to be accountable for them.[115]

Children in these terms were not their parents' property but God's property, destined to take their place in the moral and social order as individuals, not merely elements in the smaller social unit of the family. Children 'are not born in a full state of Equality, though they are born to it.'[116] Parents must bring their children to a state where they are capable of independence.

Locke's paternalism is attenuated. I see his thinking as a bridge towards what may be called 'liberal' paternalism.[117] But his emphasis is nevertheless on 'parental power'. Further, he cannot accept that there could possibly be any conflict between parents and children. The child's good was identified with the parents' wishes. As Worsfold puts it, 'parental benevolence is sufficient to ensure the fulfilment of children's rights.'[118] Locke does not question the age of majority (then twenty-one): to him babies and twenty-year-olds are children and parental power is to be exercised seemingly indiscriminately over both. To argue that he could not have predicted the development of what we call adolescence is rather besides the point. Children in the England of Locke's day married at ages as young as twelve for girls and fourteen for boys. They worked, and they fought in wars. These facts cannot have escaped Locke's notice: their implications seem to have done.

John Stuart Mill is best remembered for one sentence in his *On Liberty*. This contains 'one very simple principle': 'the only purpose for which power can be rightfully exercised over any member of civilised community, against his will, is to prevent harm to others.'[119] Mill continues: 'He cannot rightfully be compelled to do or forbear because it will be better for him to do so, because it will make him happier, because, in the opinion of others, to do so would be wise, or even right.'[120] This statement, without more, would give children complete freedom of choice. It is a statement with which neither Farson nor Holt would quarrel. Mill, however, makes his principle subject to this explicit qualification. 'We are not speaking of children, or of young persons below the age which the law may fix as that of manhood or womanhood.'[121] Far from it, for Mill argues that 'society' has 'absolute power' over children: 'the existing generation is master both of the training and the entire circumstances of the generation to come.'[122]

Mill's justification of paternalism in the case of children is twofold. It part it stems from the need to protect children. In his view freedom to make claims was dependent on the capacity for self-improvement as the result of rational discussion. He also summons in support utilitarianism. He is concerned that if children were allowed to interpret their own good they would act in ways which were not for the public good. 'The uncultivated', he writes, 'cannot be competent judges of cultivation. Those who most need to be made wiser and better usually desire it least, and if they desired it, would be incapable of finding the way to it by their own lights.'[123]

The perspective of these three philosophers is not the same. Their justifications are different. Their attitudes to children are by no means similar. In Locke and Mill they are characterised by benevolence: there is no such sentiment in Hobbes's harsh doctrine. Only in Locke are there really any hints of children's rights and these are muted. Yet within Locke are the seeds of a liberal paternalism which I believe can be used to justify children's rights.

Liberal Paternalism, Rights and Autonomy

The general justification of children's rights lies within an over-arching theory of human rights.[124] A theory of human rights requires the treatment of persons as equals. It expresses a normative attitude of respect for individual autonomy. It is not dependent on actual autonomy, rather on the capacity for it. As Richards puts it in a recent article: 'The central mark of ethics is not respect for what people currently are or for particular ends. Rather, respect is expressed for an idealized capacity which, if appropriately treated, people can realize, namely, the capacity to take responsibility as a free and rational agent for one's system of ends.'[125] To deny a person rights is to fail to recognise his capacity for autonomy. Locke comes close to articulating this: he argued for 'that equal Right that every Man hath, to his Natural Freedom, without being subjected to the Will or Authority of any other Man.'[126]

Of all moral theories, and whatever its defects[127] (a discussion of which lies outside the remit of this book), it is Rawls's notion of equality at the stage of a hypothetical social contract[128] which comes closest to expressing the idea of treating persons as equals with respect to their capacity for autonomy. The principles of justice which Rawls believes we would choose in the 'original position'[129] behind a 'veil of ignorance'[130] are equal liberty and opportunity and an arrangement of social and economic inequalities so that they are both to the greatest benefit of the least advantaged and attached to offices and positions open to all under conditions of fair equality of opportunity.[131] Expressed as a general conception these principles entail 'all social primary goods – liberty and opportunity, income and wealth, and the bases of self-respect – . . . to be distributed equally unless an unequal distribution of any or all of these goods is to the advantage of the least favoured.'[132] The legal system has a part to play in ensuring fair equality of opportunity (through race relations and equal opportunities legislation, for example). Other institutions also play a part: schools, media and family can all help to promote capacities to assist young people to shape their lives according to rational goals. Nor can the part which the political and economic systems play be underestimated.

This brings us to paternalism. The principles of justice delineated in the previous paragraph confine paternalism, without totally eliminating it. Parties to the hypothetical social contract would know that some human beings are less capable than others: they would know about variations in intelligence and strength and they would know of the very limited capacities of small children and rather fuller, if not complete, capacities of older children and adolescents. These are matters that they would take into account in constructing principles to govern institutions in society. They would bear in mind in particular how the actions of those with limited capacities now might thwart their autonomy in time to come when their incapacities are no longer.

These considerations would lead to an acceptance of intervention in people's lives to protect them against irrational actions. Richards suggests three constraints on the scope of such paternalism. First, 'the standard of irrationality cannot itself violate the constraints of morality.'[133] His concern, with which I concur, is that subjective values do not intrude. Rather, as he puts it, 'the notion of irrationality must be defined in terms of a neutral theory that can accommodate the many visions of the good life that are compatible with moral constraints.'[134] He would regard as irrational acts those only that frustrated the individual's system of ends. This may be a satisfactory test to apply to adults, though it is not entirely appropriate in the case of children. We may not wish to prevent an adult committing suicide but we should intervene when an adolescent decides he wishes to throw himself in front of a express train, whether he does so because he wants to die or because he believes, perhaps having read Anna Karenina,[135] that it is an aesthetic experience.

The second constraint catalogued by Richards requires the irrationality to be 'severe and systematic, perhaps due to undeveloped or impaired capacities, or lack of opportunities to exercise such capacities, *and* a severe and permanent impairment of interests is in prospect.'[136] We must, in other words, tolerate mistakes. There is a difference, well described by Ronald Dworkin, between having a right to do something and doing the right thing: 'someone may have the right to do something that is wrong for him to do . . ..'[137] Dworkin gives the example of gambling. If we accept the moral precept of treating persons as equals, we must also respect their capacity to take risks and make mistakes.

Thirdly, 'within the already specified bounds of permissible paternalism, intervention is justified only to the extent necessary to obviate the immediate harm or to develop the capacities of rational choice by which the individual may have a fair chance to avoid such harms on her or his own.'[138] Liberal paternalism rejects the need for permanent dependence, save in rare cases where there is continuing need. The corollary of this is that parents and teachers have a duty to help the development of a young person's independent rationality.

What are the implications of this for children? Do children fit into Rawls's scheme of justice and, if so, how? I used to be rather sceptical[139] but I believe now that we can think about children within his framework.[140] In Rawls's theory, children are participants in the formation of the initial social contract to the extent that they are capable. This is defined rather obliquely in terms of 'the age of reason'.[141] The age is neither defined nor linked to a particular conception of rationality. Worsfold believes that Rawls is implying that 'as children's competencies develop, their participation should increase.'[142] Rawls states that:

> the minimal requirements defining moral personality refer to a capacity and not to the realization of it. A being that has this capacity, whether or not it is yet developed, is to receive the full protection of the principles of justice . . . . Regarding the potentiality as sufficient accords with the hypothetical nature of the original position, and with the idea that as far as possible the choice of principles should not be influenced by arbitrary contingencies. Therefore it is reasonable to say that those who could not take part in the initial agreement, were it not for fortuitous circumstances, are assured equal justice.[143]

Some will not be convinced by this. If children cannot participate fully in generating the principles necessary for a just society, they will argue, they should not be accorded rights.

Those who espouse the 'will theory' of rights are likely to be unhappy with Rawls's explanation. The most influential statement of this position is by H.L.A. Hart. 'If common usage sanctions talk of the rights of animals or babies,' he wrote in 'Are There Any Natural Rights?', 'it makes an idle use of the expression "a right", which will confuse the situation with other different moral situations where the expression "a right" has a specific force and cannot be replaced by other moral expressions.'[144] Hart's point is that being a right-holder presupposes capacities for choice not possessed by animals and babies.[145] I have argued in this chapter that a child has rights whether or not he is capable of exercising any autonomy. But Rawls's point is that it is more reasonable to assume that children can participate in formulating principles than to risk the alternative which denies them the possibility of pursuing their own just ends. Worsfold believes that 'Rawls wants to take account of our intuitive sense that even quite young children *do* know what they want, and are capable of weighing alternatives and of acting on the decisions they make – precisely the kind of deliberation required of those choosing the original principles.'[146] Even if they lack this, they certainly have a capacity for autonomy. To deny the appropriateness of 'rights language', as Hart does, is to fail to accept this idealised capacity.

To bring children to a capacity where they are able to take full responsibility as free, rational agents for their own system of ends, in Kant's language,[147] for them to be sovereigns in the kingdom of ends, children must be accorded two types of right. The right to equal opportunity demands that their needs as children be met: good parenting, good teaching, particularly directed towards self-critical awareness, etc. Though the ingredients of this right are much the most important, it is not necessary to spell them out in this context.[148] The right to liberal paternalism is more controversial and must be described.

It has been indicated already that intervention in another's conduct is justified if he lacks rational capacities and the irrational conduct is likely to lead to a severe and permanent weakening of his capacity to achieve his own ends. What notion of irrationality can we apply to a child, particularly a young child who lacks the capacity for 'reflective self-evaluation',[149] who has no coherent system of ends against which to judge issues of rationality? We could use a standard selected by parents. We could use a notion employed by the state, like the 'best interests' of the child. There are dangers in selecting standards of rationality in either of these ways. What we are looking for is something more value-free and independent of the participants. It can be found once again by appealing to Rawls's hypothetical social contract.[150]

The question we should ask ourselves is: what sorts of action or conduct would we wish, as children, to be shielded against on the assumption that we would want to mature to a rationally autonomous adulthood and be capable of deciding on our own system of ends as free and rational beings? We would choose principles that would enable children to mature to independent adulthood. Our definition of irrationality would be such as to preclude action and conduct which would frustrate such a goal; within the constraints of such a definition we would defend a version of paternalism. It is not paternalism in its classical sense. Furthermore, it is a two-edged sword in that since the goal is rational independence those who exercise constraints must do so in such a way as to enable children to develop their capacities.

What is the child to be protected against? Protection against actions which may lead to his death or serious physical injury or mental disability may be readily justified. So may an insistence upon a system of compulsory education. The education provided needs to be somewhat broader and more liberal than that conventionally offered. Richards encapsulates what is meant by this. He writes that such education is

> marked not only by its concern with the basic education of all persons, but by the content the education must take, namely, the development of the general capacities which any person would want in order to determine self-critically and rationally her or his vision of the good life; development of the emotional and other capacities required for autonomous self-determination; and the development of the capacity to live independently with servile and nonconsensual dependence reduced to only the necessary and tolerable minimum.[151]

What is required is education in its broadest sense (and not just though the educational system but the arts and media generally) and not indoctrination. In Britain at the moment it must be difficult to justify education to teenagers for whom there are no job prospects. The justification of education is thus to an extent dependent on economic policies which provide opportunities for school leavers. We must create an environment[152] in which education is meaningful.

Paternalistic restrictions require justification. Many exist, of course, and not all can be justified by showing the behaviour in question to be irrational as tested, as we have done above, by a neutral theory of the good. The important moral limitation on the exercise of paternalism is provided by the notion of the child 'eventually coming to see the correctness of his parent's interventions.'[153] We must have in mind, what has been called, 'future-oriented consent'.[154] When he reaches adulthood he may disagree with decisions taken for him. That cannot be helped. All we can do is test our interventions in terms of what we might expect persons in the 'original position' to approve.

If we do this certain current restrictions will need to be re-examined. In particular it is necessary to question the rather arbitrary 'coming of age'[155] provisions that exist. It is difficult to understand why we allow a fourteen-year-old to own a shotgun[156] but impose restrictions on drinking in public houses on those under eighteen,[157] why a sixteen-year-old can live in a brothel[158] but has to be one year older before he can enter a betting shop[159] (he cannot bet until he is eighteen).[160] This list of anomalies could be multiplied. A re-examination of these restrictions would lead to some being removed. It might also lead to some further restrictions. The case for raising the age at which children may own a rifle or shotgun is easily put, if we apply the criteria adumbrated above of the risk of serious injury (to others in this case as well as the adolescent himself). Given the number of fatal accidents and serious injuries, thought might also be given to raising the age, currently sixteen, at which an adolescent may drive a tractor, even if this restricts farm employment opportunities.[161] But rather more age restrictions are likely to be reduced.

It is, however, in the area of more general restrictions that justifications must be sought. The problems may arise particularly in parent-child relationships. Should adolescents require parental permission to use contraception? Should an adolescent girl need her parents' consent as a pre-requisite to her terminating a pregnancy? The legislature recognised fourteen years ago that sixteen-year-olds could make these decisions for themselves.[162] But what of those younger than sixteen? Of what significance is the fact the law also recognises sixteen as the age of consent to sexual intercourse by girls?[163] There are two principles at stake here. They must be balanced: each must be delimited by reference to the other. The principles are: (i) Equal respect and concern for persons. Applying this, and short of situations of exploitation,[164] it would be difficult to justify either restrictions on sexual behaviour by adolescents or contraception or abortion. (ii) Liberal paternalism legitimating intervention directed at conduct that is irrational judged by a neutral theory of the good. There is room for debate on this but, as I would interpret the principle, it would discourage sexual activity and experimentation by the young whilst encouraging the practice of contraception and giving the girl, rather than her parents, the final say in abortion decisions. This combines protection and autonomy. Protection can be justified because sexual maturity is not necessarily intellectual maturity. An adolescent may find it difficult to defer gratification. This is a defect in practical rationality. It is encumbent on us to supply the rationality that is missing. This can best be done within a framework of education and counselling, rather than compulsion. The age of consent has no real meaning and I would abolish the concept totally. The criminal law has no place in regulating the sexual activities of the young, any more than it should interfere in sexual relationships of adults. But there is scope for autonomy too. The arguments used to restrict the use of contraceptives or abortion services by adolescents do not take account of this. They do not appreciate the importance of allowing persons, whether minor or adult, to decide on matters that will affect the way their lives are planned and organised. The arguments for allowing adolescents the rights to regulate their sexual activity in these ways are, if anything, stronger than those which apply to adults.

These principles and arguments can be used in other areas of life as well. The most obvious is the work situation. Liberationists[165] would give children the right to undertake gainful employment. But can this be justified? Many adolescents would prefer to be 'out in the world' earning a living than at school.

Maximisation of their subjective satisfactions must be a consideration, if we are to have respect for them as persons. But growth to rationally autonomous adulthood is dependent partly on education. It need not be the system of education that we have presently. It may well be that a combination of education and work experience would be beneficial to many adolescents. But robbed of education at, say, thirteen (the age at which English law currently allows minimal gainful employment like 'paper rounds'),[166] the adolescent would be less prepared to become a rationally autonomous person.

The distinction between protecting children and protecting their rights[167] has thus been drawn too broadly. Like many dualisms[168] it is deceptive. The two strategies are integrally linked. This has to be recognised if we are to have respect for the personality of children. Which is to the fore will be heavily dependent on the age of the child and his level of cognitive development.

Notes

1. H. Rodham, 'Children Under The Law', *Harvard Educational Review*, 43 (1973), p. 487.
2. H. Rodham, 'Children's Rights: A Legal Perspective' in P. A. Vardin and I. L. Brody (eds), *Children's Rights: Contemporary Perspectives*, New York, The Teacher's College Press, 1979, p. 21.
3. For example, R. Geiser, 'The Rights of Children', *Hastings Law Journal*, 28 (1977), p. 1027; C. Beck *et al.*, 'Rights of Children: A Trust Model', *Fordham Law Review*, 40 (1978), p. 669; A. Landever, 'The Rights of Children In America — The Differing Perceptions', *Poly Law Review*, 5 (1979), p. 19; M. Wald, 'Children's Rights: A Framework For Analysis', *University of California, Davis Law Review*, 12 (1979), p. 255.
4. R. A. Wasserstrom, 'Rights, Human Rights and Racial Discrimination', *Journal of Philosophy*, 61 (1964), pp. 628, 629.
5. Bandman, 'Do Children Have Any Natural Rights?', *Proceedings of 29th Annual Meeting of Philosophy of Education Society*, (1973), pp. 234, 236.
6. J. Feinberg, 'Duties, Rights and Claims', *American Philosophical Quarterly*, no. 2, 3 (1966), p. 1 at p. 8.
7. J. Kleinig, 'Mill, Children and Rights', *Educational Philosophy and Theory*, 8 (1976), p. 14.
8. B. Gross and R. Gross (eds), *The Children's Rights Movement*, New York, Andover Press, 1977, p. 7.
9. The distinction between the two is derived from the American sociological jurist, Roscoe Pound, and his realist compatriots such as Karl Llewellyn. The dichotomy may be a deceptively false one. See D. McBarnet, 'False Dichotomies in Criminal Justice Research' in J. Baldwin and A. K. Bottomley (eds), *Criminal Justice*, London, Martin Robertson, 1978, p. 23.
10. By Jerome Skilnick, *Justice Without Trial*, New York, Wiley, 1966, though not in this context.
11. By M. Paulsen in 'Child Abuse Reporting Laws: The Shape of The Legislation', *Columbia Law Review*, 67 (1967), p. 1.
12. M. Paulsen, 'Legal Protection Against Child Abuse', *Children*, 13 (1966), p. 48.
13. See J. R. Mercer, 'A Policy Statement on Assessment Procedures and the Rights of Children', *Harvard Educational Review*, 44 (1974), pp. 125–41.
14. See D. Farrington and T. Bennett, 'Police Cautioning of Juveniles in London', *British Journal of Criminology*, 21 (1981), p. 123.

15. See Home Office circular 49/1978.
16. By D. N. MacCormick, 'Law As Institutional Fact', *Law Quarterly Review,* **90** (1974), p. 102.
17. For the distinction between 'brute facts' and 'institutional facts' see J. Searle, *Speech Acts,* Cambridge, Cambridge University Press, 1966, pp. 50–3.
18. J. Bentham, *Works* (Bowring edition, Edinburgh 1838–43), vol. II, p. 501–2. See, further, H. L. A. Hart, *Essays on Bentham: Studies In Jurisprudence and Political Theory,* Oxford, Clarendon Press, 1982, ch. IV.
19. J. Feinberg, *Social Philosophy,* Englewood Cliffs, N.J., Prentice-Hall, 1973, p. 84.
20. Ibid., p. 85.
21. See, e.g. H. J. McCloskey, 'Rights', *Philosophical Quarterly,* **15** (1965), p. 115; W. N. Hohfeld, *Fundamental Legal Conceptions As Applied In Judicial Reasoning,* New Haven, Yale University Press, 1919, p. 38; R. Pound, *Jurisprudence,* vol. 4, St. Paul, Minnesota, West, 1959, pp. 69–71. For a discussion see A. R. White, 'Rights and Claims', *Law and Philosophy,* **1** (1982), p. 315.
22. J. Feinberg, 'The Nature and Value of Rights' in *Rights, Justice and The Bounds of Liberty,* Princeton, Princeton University Press, 1980, p. 149.
23. Ibid., pp. 149–51.
24. Ibid., p. 152.
25. Ibid., p. 153.
26. Cf. F. Michelman, 'In Pursuit of Constitutional Welfare Rights: One View of Rawls' Theory of Justice', *University of Pennsylvania Law Review,* **121** (1973), p. 962.
27. See R. Farson, *Birthrights,* Harmondsworth, Penguin, 1978, or J. Holt, *Escape From Childhood,* Harmondsworth, Penguin, 1975.
28. 'Rights', *Archiv für Rechts-und sozial philosophie,* **62** (1976), p. 329 at p. 345. See also C. Fried, *Right and Wrong,* Cambridge, Mass., Harvard University Press, 1978, pp. 119–24.
29. See P. Montague, 'Two Concepts of Rights', *Philosophy and Public Affairs,* **9** (1980), p. 372.
30. See M. Tooley, 'Abortion and Infanticide', *Philosophy and Public Affairs,* **2** (1972), p. 37; M. A. Warren, 'On The Moral and Legal Status of Abortion' in T. Beauchamp and LeRoy Walters (eds), *Contemporary Issues In Bioethics,* Encino, Calif., Dickenson, 1978.
31. See T. Regan, 'Utilitarianism, Vegetarianism, and Animal Rights', *Philosophy and Public Affairs,* **9** (1980), p. 305.
32. See Christopher Stone, *Should Trees Have Standing?: Towards Legal Rights For Natural Objects,* Los Altos, Calif., William Kaufmann, 1974.
33. W. Hohfeld, *Fundamental Legal Conceptions as Applied in Judicial Reasoning,* New Haven, Conn., Yale University Press, 1919, p. 35 *et seq.*
34. Others have used the term 'liberties': e.g. Glanville Williams, 'The Concept of Legal Liberty' in R. S. Summers (ed.), *Essays In Legal Philosophy,* Oxford, Blackwell, p. 121.
35. For example, W. J. Kamba, 'Legal Theory and Hohfeld's Analysis of A Legal Right', *Juridicial Review* (1974), pp. 249–62, and J. Finnis, 'Some Professorial Fallacies About Rights', *Adelaide Law Review,* **4** (1972), p. 377.
36. Hohfeld, *Fundamental Legal Conceptions,* p. 38.
37. D. N. MacCormick, 'Rights, Claims and Remedies', *Law and Philosophy,* **1** (1982), pp. 337, 346.
38. For the distinction between political decisions and conceptual analysis, see ibid., p. 349.
39. See D. N. MacCormick, 'A Note Upon Privacy', *Law Quarterly Review,* **89** (1973), pp. 23–7; 'Privacy: A Problem of Definition', *British Journal of Law and Society,* **1** (1974), p. 75–8.
40. Raz, *Practical Reason and Norms,* London, Hutchinson, 1975, pp. 85–97.
41. See Alderson B. in *Chapple* v. *Cooper* (1843) *M & W,* **13** pp. 252, 258.
42. At present they are free (they have a privilege, a liberty) to punish, provided it is reasonable and moderate.
43. MacCormick, 'Rights, Claims and Remedies', p. 344.
44. R. Farson, *Birthrights,* Harmondsworth, Penguin, 1978, p. 9.

45.   The analysis that follows is based in part on Wald, 'Children's Rights'.
46.   See Farson, *Birthrights,* p. 42.
47.   See the Preamble in Appendix, p. 283.
48.   Ibid.
49.   See Warnock Report on *Special Educational Needs,* London, HMSO, 1978 and Education Act 1981. American legislation (the Education of All Handicapped Children Act 1975) goes rather further. See F. P. Connor and D. M. Connors, 'Children's Rights and the Mainstreaming of The Handicapped', in Vardin and Brody, *Children's Rights: Contemporary Perspectives,* p. 67.
50.   Wald, 'Children's Rights', p. 260.
51.   In section 49. The 1906 Education (Provision of Meals) Act provided a permissive power to assist in the cost of providing meals for elementary school children who 'are unable by reason of lack of food to take full advantage of the education provided for them.'
52.   In section 22.
53.   See, further, L. Bissett and J. Coussins, *Badge of Poverty,* London, Child Poverty Action Group, 1982. See also D. Bull, *What Price 'Free' Education?,* London, Child Poverty Action Group, 1980, ch. 4.
54.   DES, *Catering In Schools* (Hudson Report), London, HMSO, 1975, para. 79.
55.   Wald, 'Children's Rights', p. 261.
56.   See the Field-Fisher report, London, HMSO, 1974.
57.   See *Report of Review Body Appointed to Inquire into the Death of Steven Meurs,* Norwich, Norfolk Social Services Dept., 1975.
58.   *Maria Mehmedagi: Report of An Independent Inquiry,* London, London Borough of Southwark, 1981.
59.   Hohfeld, *Fundamental Legal Conceptions. . .,* p. 39.
60.   In *The Republic.*
61.   Wald, 'Children's Rights', p. 263.
62.   See M. D. A. Freeman, 'Child Battering — the Dutch Approach', *Family Law,* 7 (1977), p. 53.
63.   Cf. T. Duster, *The Legislation of Morality,* New York, Free Press, 1970.
64.   See B. Roshier and H. Teff, *Law and Society In England,* London, Tavistock, 1980, p. 46.
65.   See P. Lennon, 'How One Woman Routs Forces of Darkness', *Sunday Times,* 12 February 1978.
66.   H. Cohen, *Equal Rights For Children,* Totowa, N.J., Littlefield, Adams, 1980, p. 49.
67.   Family Law Reform Act 1969, s.1, operative January 1970.
68.   Farson, *Birthrights.*
69.   Holt, *Escape From Childhood.*
70.   Wald, 'Children's Rights', p. 270.
71.   J. Rawls, *Theory of Justice,* Cambridge, Mass., Harvard University Press, 1971.
72.   For example, those of Jean Piaget (see *The Moral Judgment of The Child,* London, Routledge & Kegan Paul (1932)).
73.   See A. Skolnick, *Rethinking Childhood,* Boston, Little, Brown, 1976, and P. J. Sartorius, 'Social-Psychological Concepts and the Rights of Children' in V. F. Haubrich and M. W. Apple (eds), *Schooling and The Rights of Children,* Berkeley, California, McCutchan, 1975, p. 64.
74.   See, e.g. W. Damon, *The Social World of The Child,* San Francisco, Jossey-Bass, 1977; J. J. Conger, *Adolescence and Youth: Psychological Development In a Changing World,* New York, Harper & Row, 1973; E. Douvan and J. Adelson, *The Adolescent Experience,* New York, Wiley, 1966.
75.   See, e.g. Piaget, *The Moral Judgment of The Child.*
76.   See J. C. Smith and B. Hogan, *Criminal Law,* London, Butterworth, 1978 (4th ed.), p. 155.
77.   Cohen, *Equal Rights For Children,* p. 60.
78.   Ibid.
79.   Ibid., p. 66.

80. Ibid., p. 69.
81. A similar point is made by F. Schrag in a book review of Cohen, *Law and Philosophy*, 1 (198)2, p. 158.
82. Cohen, *Equal Rights For Children*, p. 85.
83. Ibid., p. 86.
84. Cf. *Re Snyder* 532 P. 2d 278 (1975).
85. Uviller, 'Children Versus Parents: Perplexing Policy Questions For The ACLU', in O. O'Neill and W. Ruddick (eds), *Having Children: Philosophical and Legal Reflections on Parenthood*, New York, Oxford University Press, 1979, p. 214 at p. 215.
86. See K. Fitzherbert, *West Indian Children In London*, London, Bell, 1967.
87. Wald, 'Children's Rights', p. 271.
88. Ibid., p. 272.
89. See Y. Dror, 'Law and Social Change', *Thulane Law Review*, 33 (1959), p. 787. See also G. Massell, 'Law As An Instrument of Revolutionary Change', *Law and Social Review*, 2 (1968), p. 179.
90. See, further, M. D. A. Freeman, *The Legal Structure*, Harlow, Longman, 1974, pp. 54–69.
91. For example, *Bellotti v. Baird* 428 U.S. 132 (1976).
92. Wald, 'Children's Rights', p. 278.
93. Ibid., pp. 278–9.
94. This is considered fully in ch. 6.
95. J. Goldstein, A. Freud and A. Solnit, *Beyond The Best Interests of The Child*, New York, Free Press, 1979 (2nd ed.), p. 53.
96. 140 N.W. 2d 152 (1966).
97. Wald, 'Children's Rights', p. 279.
98. Idem.
99. Ibid., p. 280.
100. C. Lasch, *Haven In A Heartless World*, New York, Basic Books, 1977.
101. J. Donzelot, *The Policing of Families*, New York, Random House, 1979.
102. G. Dworkin, 'Consent, Representation and Proxy Consent', in W. Gaylin and R. Macklin (eds), *Who Speaks For The Child*, New York, Plenum Press, 1982, pp. 191, 205.
103. In Rawls, *A Theory of Justice*, p. 62.
104. [1976] 1 All E.R. 326.
105. See G. Dworkin, 'Paternalism', in R. A. Wasserstrom (ed.), *Morality And The Law*, Belmont, Calif., Wadsworth Publishing Co., 1971, p. 107 at p. 108.
106. Plato, *The Republic*, book III.
107. Aristotle, *Politics*.
108. The Greeks developed neither a concept that all human beings had the capacity for autonomy, nor the language of human rights. See A. Adkins, *Moral Values and Political Behaviour In Ancient Greece*, London, Chatto & Windus, 1972.
109. T. Hobbes, *Leviathan* (ed. C. B. Macpherson), Harmondsworth, Penguin, 1968 (originally published in 1651).
110. Ibid.
111. In his *Patriarcha* (London, 1680).
112. J. Locke, *Two Treatises of Government* (ed. P. Laslett), London, Cambridge University Press, 1960, para. 67 (originally published in 1690).
113. Ibid., para. 55.
114. Ibid., para. 66.
115. Ibid., para. 56.
116. Ibid., para. 55.
117. See, further, D. A. J. Richards, 'The Individual, the Family and the Constitution: A Jurisprudential Perspective', *New York University Law Review*, 55 (1980), p. 1.
118. V. Worsfold, 'A Philosophical Justification For Children's Rights', *Harvard Educational Review*, 44 (1974), pp. 142, 146.
119. John Stuart Mill, *On Liberty*, London, J. M. Dent (Everyman Edition, 1910), pp. 72–3.
120. Idem.

121. Ibid., see also p. 137.
122. Ibid., p. 139.
123. Quoted in Dworkin, 'Paternalism', op. cit., p. 116. There is an excellent appraisal of Mill's paternalism in C. L. Ten, *Mill On Liberty*, Oxford, Clarendon Press, 1980, ch.7.
124. As to which, see E. Kamenka and A. E.-S. Tay, *Human Rights*, London, Edward Arnold, 1978.
125. D. A. J. Richards, 'Rights and Autonomy', *Ethics*, **92** (1981), pp. 13, 16.
126. Locke, *Two Treatises. . .,*
127. But see N. Daniels (ed.), *Reading Rawls,* Oxford, Blackwell, 1975, an excellent collection of critical essays.
128. See Rawls, *A Theory of Justice.*
129. Ibid., p. 17.
130. Ibid., p. 136.
131. Ibid., p. 302.
132. Ibid., p. 303.
133. Richards, 'The Individual, the Family and the Constitution . . .', p. 18.
134. Ibid., p. 19.
135. L. Tolstoy, *Anna Karenina.*
136. Richards, 'The Individual, the Family and the Constitution . . .', p. 19.
137. R. Dworkin, *Taking Rights Seriously*, London, Duckworth, 1977, pp. 188–9.
138. Richards, 'The Individual, the Family and the Constitution . . .', pp. 19-20.
139. Freeman, 'The Rights of Children in IYC', *Current Legal Problems,* **33** (1980), pp. 1, 19.
140. See also Worsfold, 'A Philosophical Justification. . .', p. 151 *et seq.*
141. Rawls, *Theory of Justice*, p. 209.
142. Worsfold, 'A Philosophical Justification . . .', p. 153.
143. Rawls, *Theory of Justice*, p. 509.
144. H. L. A. Hart, 'Are There *Any* Natural Rights?', *Philosophical Review*, **LXIV** (1955), pp. 175–91 at p. 181.
145. An excellent critique of the 'will theory' is Neil Mac Cormick, *Legal Right and Social Democracy*, Oxford, Clarendon Press, 1982, ch. 8. See also D. Lyons, 'Rights, Claimants and Beneficiaries', *American Philosophical Quarterly*, **VI** (1969), pp. 173–85.
146. Worsfold, 'A Philosophical Justification. . .', pp. 153–4.
147. See Jeffrie G. Murphy, *Kant: The Philosophy of Right*, London, Macmillan, 1970.
148. Richards, 'The Individual, the Family . . .', does (see pp. 20–3).
149. The phrase is Harry Frankfurt's. See 'Freedom of the Will and the Concept of a Person', *Journal of Philosophy*, **68** (1971), pp. 5–20 at p. 7.
150. Rawls, *Theory of Justice.*
151. D. A. J. Richards, 'Human Rights and Moral Ideals: An Essay On The Moral Theory of Liberalism', in *Social Theory and Practice,* **5** (1980), pp. 461, 484. With Martin Golding we can say that children have the mandatory right to education. It is a 'welfare-right'. See 'Towards a Theory of Human Rights', *The Monist,* **52** (1968), p. 546.
152. If lead poisoning affects learning, as it is thought to do, policies to eliminate lead in petrol, paint, etc. wherever possible should also be pursued.
153. Dworkin, 'Paternalism', p. 119.
154. By Dworkin, ibid.
155. See M. D. A. Freeman, 'Coming of Age', *Legal Action Group Bulletin,* (1977), pp. 137-8.
156. Firearms Act 1968 s.22(2).
157. Licensing Act 1974 s.169.
158. Children and Young Persons Act 1933 s.3.
159. Betting, Gaming and Lotteries Act 1963 Schedule 4, para. 2. On gaming see Gaming Act 1968 s.17.
160. Betting, Gaming and Lotteries Act 1963, s.21.
161. Road Traffic (Drivers' Ages and Hours of Work) Act 1976 s.1.
162. Family Law Reform Act 1969 s.8.
163. Sexual Offences Act 1956 s.6.
164. Such as incest and paedophilia.

165. Farson, Holt, etc. There is a good assessment of the different arguments in R. Mnookin, *Child, Family and State*, Boston, Little, Brown, 1978, pp. 654 *et seq.*
166. Children and Young Persons Act 1933 s.18 and Children Act 1972 s.1.
167. See Farson, *Birthrights.*
168. For example, 'law in books' and 'law in action'. See McBarnett, 'False Dichotomies in Criminal Justice Research'.

A Historical Perspective

Current policies and practices regarding children who do 'wrong' have to be located within a historical perspective. The beginnings of the movement to treat such children differently from adult offenders can be traced back at least to the 1830s. Children (that is, those over seven years of age, for it had long been established that those under seven were presumed incapable of committing a crime) had for a considerable time been treated more leniently than adults. In 1838 the first prison set aside for boys, Parkhurst, was established.[1] This experiment lasted only until 1864.[2] The idea also evolved of trying juvenile offenders differently. The 1847 Larceny Act empowered justices to deal summarily with offenders under fourteen charged with stealing. This was extended to sixteen in 1850, and in 1879 magistrates were given powers to deal summarily with children under twelve for all indictable offences and with those under sixteen for larceny and embezzlement.

In the 1850s Quaker initiative[3] led to the establishment first of reformatory schools and then industrial schools.[4] The 1854 Act, which established reformatory schools, required that a child must spend fourteen days in prison before going to a reformatory. Parsloe comments: 'this is a nice illustration of how the criminal justice approach, which demanded punishment for wrongdoing, was balanced against the child's need for training and reform.'[5] Conflicts and ambiguities which beset the juvenile justice system today have, it seems, a long heritage. The distinction between those eligible to be sent to reformatories and those suitable for industrial schools followed the separation made by Mary Carpenter who distinguished 'the perishing classes' from 'the dangerous classes'. The former had not yet fallen into actual crime but were destined by reason of their deprived circumstances to do so: the latter had 'already received the prison brand' or were 'notoriously living by plunder'.[6] The deprived-depraved dichotomy originates with this separation.

The regimes in both reformatories and industrial schools were harsh and only a minority of juvenile offenders were sent to them (some younger offenders were committed to industrial schools). The majority of children convicted of criminal offences were still incarcerated in prisons. It was coming to be recognised that prevention of crime or further crime was more important than its punishment. To an extent the industrial schools were built upon this precept. So too was the notion of probation which began to emerge in the last decade of the nineteenth century. The initiative here came from the Church of England Temperance Society which sent missionaries into magistrates' courts in London. Parliament recognised the value of probation in 1907.[7] Probation was designed to reinforce parental control over children with the assistance of welfare agencies: supervision was provided by the Temperance missionaries and later, of course, by the probation service. Probation was necessary, so it was argued, to avoid branding an offender whom the court wished to help. The Gladstone Committee in 1895 had also talked of the need to 'help' children. Rhetoric, which has come to dominate twentieth-century thought, was already firmly established.

The culmination of this early history was the abolition of imprisonment for children, the first of many such attempts,[8] and the establishment of juvenile courts in 1908. Some places, such as Birmingham, already had them. The object, said the Lord Advocate, was 'to treat . . . children not by way of punishing them, which is no remedy, but with a view to their reformation.'[9] The link between criminal behaviour and social deprivation was by then firmly established. The juvenile courts were accordingly given the jurisdiction to deal with children in need of care because of the conditions in which they were living. Such children could be committed to an industrial school. By 1927 a Departmental Committee on the Treatment of Young Offenders was arguing that the distinction between deprived and depraved children was wrong.[10] Neglect, it was argued, led to delinquency. The Children and Young Persons Act of 1933 embodied this ideology. It provided for children in need of care and protection to be brought before the juvenile court. The intention of the juvenile justice system, still in essence the same today, was stated in section 44 of the Act: every court in dealing with a child or young person who is brought before it either as an offender or otherwise, shall have regard to the welfare of the child or young person and shall in proper cases take steps for removing him from undesirable surroundings and for securing that proper provision is made for his education and training.' The juvenile court was there to help, not punish.

The 1933 Act also abolished the distinction between reformatories and industrial schools: thenceforth, both institutions were to be called 'approved schools'. The Home Office spokesman admitted that 'some people feel it is unwise, and perhaps unfair, to mix up in the same school those who are there as punishment for an offence and those who are merely there for their own protection.'[11] But he reassured them that 'the distinction between the two is largely accidental. The neglected child may only just have been lucky enough not to have been caught in an offence.' He did not believe that either would suffer from being in the same school.

There were ambiguities then as now. The juvenile court, in spite of thera-peutic rhetoric, remained in essence a criminal court. The institutions failed to keep pace with the changes and many continued to employ a regime associated with the reformatory. The Curtis Committee in 1946[12] exposed the conditions prevailing in the institutions and stimulated the Labour government to take action. This it did on a number of fronts. It passed legislation imposing a duty on local authorities to receive into their voluntary care children without parents or guardians and those whose parents could not provide for them, where such intervention was necessary in the interests of the welfare of the child.[13] Con-temporaneously, the government was increasing the penal element in the treatment of delinquent children by introducing detention centres, attendance centres and remand centres.[14] It did, however, also abolish imprisonment for those under seventeen.[15]

Another committee reported in 1960. Many of the sentiments of the Ingleby report[16] echo comments in the report of 1927. The juvenile courts, the report argued, should move away from their traditional role as courts and become increasingly agencies to decide what help could best be given to a child coming before them. It recommended a new procedure for dealing with children under twelve who were 'in need of protection or discipline'. It stressed the importance of preventing children from coming into the care of the authorities.[17] The Children and Young Persons Act 1963 adopted Ingleby in an attenuated form. Courts and institutions as ever were left with a confusion as to role.

The 1960s was a period of feverish activity. The Longford Group report, *Crime – A Challenge To Us All*,[18] stimulated the Wilson government into pub-lishing a White Paper entitled *The Child, The Family and the Young Offender*.[19] In a sense the ideas developed in these documents were new but in essence they were but a logical extension of the 1933 Act. If neglect and family problems were at the root of delinquency and also demonstrated a need for state inter-vention and care, then courts were inappropriate places to tackle them. The Longford report noted that it was 'a truism that a happy and secure family life is the foundation of a healthy society and the best safeguard against delinquency and anti-social behaviour. Many pay lip-service to this belief: all too little has been done seriously to attempt its realisation.'[20] Longford accordingly proposed a Family Service to look after the child who might need care.

> No understanding parent can contemplate without repugnance the branding of a child in early adolescence as a criminal . . . . If a more serious charge is involved this is, in itself, evidence of the child's need for skilled help and guidance. The parent who can get such help for his child on his own initiative can almost invariably keep the child from court. It is only the children of those not so fortunate who appear in the criminal statistics.[21]

The Longford Group thought the age of criminal responsibility should be the school-leaving age.

Similar ideas were expressed by the Government White Paper. It envisaged the establishment of a local family council and of family courts to deal with those under sixteen. Children should be spared the stigma of criminality, it argued. It advocated the abolition of the juvenile court. Its concern, like Longford, was with getting parents to 'assume more personal responsibility for their children's behaviour'.[22] In Scotland not dissimilar proposals in the Kilbrandon report[23] were accepted and the Social Work (Scotland) Act of 1968 introduced the notion of juvenile panels.[24] *The Child, The Family and The Young Offender* was subjected to a barrage of criticism[25] and withdrawn. It was replaced in 1968 by *Children In Trouble*,[26] which proposed the retention of juvenile courts as the formal mechanism through which delinquents and deprived children were to pass. But *Childen In Trouble* did not break entirely with the interpretations of Longford and the earlier White Paper. The distinction between 'normal' delinquency and that which appeared to be symptomatic of other problems governs the reasoning of the 1968 White Paper as well.[27] Some misbehaviour, it thought, 'is no more than an incident in the pattern of a child's normal development', but other conduct 'is a response to unsatisfactory family or social circumstances, a result of boredom in or out of school, an indication of maladjustment, or immaturity or a symptom of a deviant, damaged or abnormal personality.'[28] To provide for this, it was stipulated that a child should not be brought before a court merely because he had committed an offence: he also had to fall within a number of categories which indicated the need for 'care, protection or control'.[29]

The Children and Young Persons Act 1969 embodies these principles. Though they are a watering-down of the Longford recommendation and the 1965 White Paper and, though many of the most welfare-oriented of the 1969 Act's provisions have not been brought into operation,[30] the Act may be said to represent the statutory high-water mark of a philosophy which puts needs before rights and treatment before punishment. Had it been fully implemented, criminal proceedings for offenders under fourteen would have been prohibited and would only have been possible against children between the ages of fourteen and seventeen after mandatory consultation between the police and social services departments. The minimum age qualification for a borstal offence would have been seventeen and not the age of fifteen. Detention centres and attendance centres would have been phased out. There was a change of government before the Act could be implemented and these features of the 1969 Act have not been put into operation. But the approved school order has been abolished and intermediate treatment established.[31] Care orders and supervision orders may be made, but an offence (or one of the other grounds)[32] *and* the care or control test[33] must first be established. The indeterminate borstal sentence has now gone, replaced by a determinate sentence of youth custody (Criminal Justice Act 1982, s.1.)

Juvenile Crime: What is the Problem?

The practices and policies, the evolution of which has been traced here, are now under attack. Few any longer subscribe to the view that the 1969 Act is 'enlightened and appropriate', as the British Association of Social Workers told the House of Commons Expenditure Committee in 1974 it was.[34] For the BASW all that is wrong could be mended if the Act were properly implemented. A second school of thought, the 'law and order lobby', sees the 1969 Act as fundamentally unsound. In part what it argues is correct, that is, that the law has blurred the distinction between a child in need of care and a juvenile who has committed a criminal offence. The backgrounds of both may be similar but, for whatever reason, their attitudes do appear to differ on such matters as property and authority.[35] Where the law and order school goes wrong, however, is in a number of unwarranted assumptions it makes.

It asserts that we have been going soft on juvenile offenders. This it links with a supposed increase in juvenile crime. It argues that magistrates have one hand tied behind their backs; that they have lost powers to tender-hearted social workers. In fact if magistrates have lost powers, it is to the police that they have lost them. The practice of police cautioning, to which the 1969 Act gave impetus, has had the effect of drawing more juveniles into the criminal justice system than was the case previously.[36] Much discussion of magistrates' powers today is uninformed. It is commonly said that magistrates, hamstrung by the 1969 Act, are forced to hand over juvenile offenders to social workers who then allow them to go home. The reality of magisterial disposals is that care orders account for only some 6 per cent of cases dealt with by juvenile court magistrates. Social workers then place more than three-quarters of offenders committed to their care to residential care establishments. An increasing number are sent to secure or special units and youth treatment centres. Cawson and Martell have noted that 'conflicts between control, punishment and care are as influential in the child care system as in the judicial and penal system.'[37] Their study of a number of secure units found that only a minority of referrals were considered by their care authorities to constitute a risk to the life and safety of others: a quarter displayed violent behaviour and a further 6 per cent dangerous behaviour, such as arson and car theft. A closer look at some of these 'serious' cases reveals that many were either not serious in the sense of endangering life or safety (arsonists, for example, often set fire to empty property), or were at a level for which other offenders received non-custodial sentences. These conclusions are supported in the research of Spencer Millham and his associates: 'it is difficult', they note, 'to identify any distinguishing characteristics for the few who end up in secure conditions, as compared with other high risk children in open C.H.Es.'[38] Social workers who are assumed to be 'going soft' in reality then are locking up a large number of children.

This is but the tip of the iceberg, for penal policy towards juveniles in the period since the implementation of the 1969 Act has seen an escalation in the trend towards incarceration of juvenile offenders. Table 3.1 indicates that the number of young persons sentenced to detention centres and borstals for indictable offences increased at a rate three times that of the increase in indictable offences known to the police, and twice that of the increase in unknown offenders aged between fourteen and sixteen.[39] These statistics show large increases in the number of juveniles sent to borstals and detention centres.

Table 3.1 Young Persons Sentenced to Detention Centres and Borstals, known Offenders (aged 14-16) and Offences Recorded by the Police 1960-81

	Detention Centre		Borstal		Known offenders (caution and guilt findings)	Indictable offences (recorded by police)
	Number	*% of all sentences*	*Number*	*% of all sentences*		
1960	605	1.7	171	0.6	32,350	800,323
1965	952	2.5	151	0.3	45,428	1,243,463
1971	2,061	4.4	1,285	2.4	74,989	1,665,063
1975	4,296	7.1	1,680	2.5	106,871	2,105,631
1978	5,528	8.5	1,860	2.5	116,171	2,395,757
1981	6,000	9.7	1,700	2.7	134,300	2,794,200

Source: Criminal Statistics, England and Wales 1960-1981. Published by HMSO, London. The latest statistics are in Cmnd. 8668 (1982), Table 7.7. The statistics here refer to indictable offences only.

The number sent to attendance centres has also risen. The minority is incarcerated. Magistrates still fine 35 per cent of juvenile offenders and conditionally discharge another 23 per cent. In fact magistrates are returning home some 58 per cent of juvenile offenders whom they convict. There have been some reductions in the last ten years: fewer juveniles are committed to the care of the local authority and the number placed on supervision orders is down by a third.

Because the law and order school perceives these policies to have failed (and they have done, though not because current policies are insufficiently punitive), it now calls for, and has already got, additional strategies to tackle juvenile crime. At the Conservative Party conference in 1979 the Home Secretary, William Whitelaw, was cheered when he described a new 'get tough with young thugs' regime. 'From 6.45 a.m. to lights out at 9.30 p.m. life will be conducted at a brisk tempo. Much greater emphasis will be put on hard and constructive activities, on discipline and on tidiness, on self-respect and respect for those in authority. Offenders will have to earn their limited privileges for good behaviour.'[40] The 'short, sharp shock'[41] has now been introduced into four detention centres.[42] The Criminal Justice Act 1982 has introduced the residential care order.[43] This, it is said, will reduce the reliance of the courts on custodial sanctions. But it is intended that the courts will retain their powers to impose such sentences on young offenders. The original intent (in the 1969 Act) to end the sentencing of juveniles to borstals and detention centres, found in an unimplemented section of the 1969 Act, has been dropped. 'Short, sharp shocks' and residential care orders are indicative of the bankruptcy of thought that represents contemporary penal policy towards juvenile offenders.

Another line of attack on current policies and practices takes issue with both 'child care' supporters of the ideology of the 1969 legislation and with the crime control orientation of the law and order lobby. It will have been noted that, thus far in this discussion of children who do 'wrong', no mention has been made of children's rights. To anyone schooled in United States jurisprudence, this will have come as a profound shock. There, as in this country, juvenile courts were once hailed as the best plan 'for the conservation of human life and happiness ever conceived by civilized man'.[44] But in the United States there is widespread disenchantment with the juvenile courts' informal, non-adversary procedures as well as with the rehabilitation-oriented 'treatment institutions' and the allegedly non-stigmatising terminology of delinquency policies.[45] In the United States the worst excesses were rejected in principle, if not in practice,[46] in the late 1960s. The claim that children should have any rights, when they are alleged to have done acts that powerful adults perceive to be wrong, has for long been submerged in the rhetoric of therapy. It surfaced in the United States more than a decade ago.[47] In Britain what counted for decriminalisation had reached its apogee (or nadir, depending on viewpoint) at roughly the same time with the Social Work (Scotland) Act in 1968 and the Children and Young Persons Act in 1969. It is astonishing in retrospect that nobody in Britain appeared to notice what was happening on the other side of the Atlantic.

The immediate past has seen the growth of a rights movement in Britain in the area of juvenile justice. Leading representatives of this school are the authors of *Justice For Children*[48] and *In Whose Best Interests?*.[49] With this has come extensive criticism of the operation of the juvenile court, the processes which accompany it such as the social enquiry report and observation and assessment centres and the institutions to which offenders and others are sent. This chapter focuses on a number of problem areas and tries to identify where children are wronged and to suggest where rights might assist children to secure justice.

The Meaning of 'Wrong'

The title of this chapter employs three problematic notions: 'rights', 'children' and 'wrong'. In Chapter 1 there was some discussion of the notion of childhood. It was seen that, to a considerable extent, the idea is a social construct. Rights were discussed in Chapter 2. It was argued that to talk of rights of children was essentially ambiguous. 'Rights', it was argued, embraced a number of disparate notions. One, the relevant one in the context of this chapter, is the claim that children should be treated as adults in certain contexts. We must examine the case for treating children differently.

It is when we examine the idea of 'wrong' that we immediately see one area where children are exposed to sanctions by reason only of their age. Even without this problem, the concept of 'wrong' would be troublesome. As the labelling school of criminology[50] has amply demonstrated, misconduct is not merely behaviour but the interpretation of behaviour by 'significant others',[51] who are society's decision-makers. Children not only do not make the rules in society but even the veneer of participating in the democratic process is denied them. When we talk of children doing 'wrong' (and 'wrong' is as neutral a word as I can find) we are not only referring to theft and assault but to being 'beyond control' or 'exposed to moral danger' or not receiving 'efficient full-time education suitable to age, ability and aptitude'.[52] These are not objective conditions. Their existence depends on the entrepreneurial activity of agents of social control, policemen, social workers, education welfare officers, even headteachers and parents. Furthermore, they are 'conditions' to which only the young are prone. An adult cannot be incarcerated for being intractable or promiscuous or workshy (unless, of course, these conditions can be attributed to mental illness, in which case he is treated not unlike a child).

However, even when a child has committed a criminal offence, such as theft, there is reason to believe, and any examination of social enquiry reports[53] reinforces this belief, that in the minds of decision-makers the seriousness of his behaviour (what he has *done*) takes a back seat behind an interpretation of what he and his family *is*. It was John Lofland[54] who noted that 'the *present evil* of current character must be related to *past evil* that can be discovered in biography' and the treatment of juvenile offenders is vivid testimony to his analysis.

Why Children who do 'Wrong' are Treated Differently

Whether juvenile offenders have ever been treated exactly as their adult counterparts remains a matter of some controversy.[55] There is evidence of young children being sentenced to death and even hanged as late as the 1830s but such cases were almost certainly the exception rather than the rule. As Platt puts it, in his momentous study *The Child Savers*, the juvenile court 'did not herald a new system of justice but rather expedited traditional policies which had been informally developing during the nineteenth century.'[56] The juvenile justice system is less a radical concept than is often supposed, for, as noted above, children had long been treated with leniency. Indeed, it may be questioned as to whether the concept of the juvenile court would have been so readily accepted it if had been a totally new departure.

To understand the speed with which the new measures took hold, it is necessary to take into account not merely benevolence towards children but the convenience of an adult society as well. This, the thesis of Rothman's recent study,[57] though based on an analysis of United States developments, rings true in the British context as well. He claims that

> progressive proposals found a favorable response among the administrators of criminal justice . . . – indeed, a much more favorable response than among the public at large. Wardens, district attorneys, judges, mental health superintendents, and directors of child care agencies welcomed the enlargement of their discretionary authority. The innovations brought them numerous practical advantages, enabling them to carry out their daily assignments more easily and efficiently. For operational reasons, they supported the Progressive innovations with enthusiasm.[58]

The child-saving movement may have assisted in the professionalisation of emergent professions: the ability to exercise discretion is, of course, a hallmark of professionalism. But that is not why it emerged. Platt in *The Child Savers* argues that it was not a 'humanistic enterprise'.[59] He suggests that the expansion in the definition of delinquency gives the lie to the humanitarian claims of the movement. He sees the child-saving movement as a punitive, romantic and intrusive effort to control the lives of lower-class urban adolescents and maintain their dependent status. While it is true that the reformers wanted to increase state intervention in the lives of children, in the main of working-class children, this neither establishes some kind of ruling class conspiracy nor is it direct evidence, as it is often supposed to be, of how humane or otherwise were the intentions of the reformers. Because Platt's book seemed to strike the right chord, it has, if anything, impeded research.[60] Even if he is right about Illinois, on which he focuses much of his attention, it would not necessarily follow that his interpretation had any wider application. A lot of work remains to be done to uncover the origins of the juvenile justice system.[61]

Even if we do not know why child-saving via the juvenile justice system emerged, we know the 'official version', why the participants in this process thought it important to treat delinquent children differently from adult offenders. We also know why they did not really distinguish delinquent children from those abused by parents or growing up in deprived environments. In the minds of the reformers there were two main considerations. First, children were seen as not altogether responsible for their behaviour. Secondly, the ancient notion of *parens patriae* legitimised state intervention into the lives of children, for the state had an affirmative duty to help socialise children.[62]

The first of these considerations is readily appreciable. The criminal law has since its earliest days recognised that it is inappropriate to punish those who cannot be regarded as responsible for their behaviour. This is entrenched in the concept of *mens rea* and defences such as insanity, diminished responsibility, duress and drunkenness. For the same reason the criminal prosecution of children under the age of seven has never been countenanced in England.[63] The juvenile court ideal is merely an extension of this link between crime and responsibility. The development of the juvenile court took place at a time when criminology was in its infancy. Proponents of the juvenile court were not agreed on the causes of juvenile wrongdoing. Some of them emphasised environmental conditions; others directed their minds to psychological phenomena; a further group was still wedded to Lombrosan biological determinism.[64] What they were agreed on was that the juvenile malefactor was not responsible for his actions in the same way as an adult was.

The doctrine of *parens patriae* is that the state has an overall parental responsibility towards those of its members who are unable to care for and protect themselves.[67] The doctrine is commonly applied to children, though other groups, notably the mentally ill, also come within its tentacles. The *parens patriae* basis of the juvenile justice system was explained well by Bernard Flexner, writing in 1910. He stated: 'the child . . . henceforth shall be viewed as the ward of the state, to be cared for by it, and not as any enemy of the state, to be punished by it . . . . This principle is not new; on the contrary it is old, and it is found in many of the early English Chancery cases.'[66] This is correct but what it does not disclose is that the Court of Chancery was concerned with protecting neglected or abused children (or often in fact their property), and not with protecting those who had broken the law. The reformers realised this. The legal-historical justification may have been nothing more than a cloak or a way of giving the juvenile court status. In fact, as Ryerson notes, 'the obliteration of distinctions between delinquent children and dependent or neglected children was the explicit aim of the juvenile court movement.'[67]

If the state was to act as a parent, then its duty was to act in what it saw as the best interests of the child. Clearly, it could not do so if it had to comply with the same procedural rules as govern the trial of adult offenders. In the United States what was seen to be a negation of due process was challenged but appellate courts found no difficulty in accepting the logic of the court's jurisdiction and its practices. Thus, in *Commonwealth* v. *Fisher* in 1905 it was said that 'the natural parent needs no [due] process to temporarily deprive his child of his liberty by confining it in its own home, to save it and shield it from the consequences of persistence in a career of waywardness'; so in the same way 'the state, when compelled, as *parens patriae*, to take the place of the father for the same purpose [is not] required to adopt any process as a means of placing its hands upon the child to lead it into one of its courts' for 'the design is not punishment nor the restraint imprisonment, any more than is the wholesome restraint which a parent exercises over his child.'[68] In this country the absence of a written constitution has meant that there was nothing to test developments in juvenile court against. However, had there been, it is thought that, despite Diceyan notions of the rule of law,[69] the response would have been identical.

If juvenile institutions were to care as parents, offenders had to be treated as individuals. There had to be a case-by-case approach. The key to rehabilitation lay, it was thought, in unlocking the facts of the offender's life history. The institutions (courts, social workers etc.) had, of course, to exercise discretion but parents also exercised discretion so the only difference was thought to be the replacement of one (familial) by another (bureaucratic). This at least is the theory. In practice, as Gilbert Smith recently commented, 'in spite of the central position of discretion in the imagery of professional social work, a growing body of evidence indicates that social workers are probably behaving in ways which are very much more highly routinized than is generally acknowledged, certainly by social workers themselves.'[70] Ideally each case may be individual but in practice labels are necessary.[71] Cases tend to be pigeon-holed into categories and remedies linked to the particular universe of case. An example of this may be drawn from the recent research of Giller and Morris.[72] They demonstrate that cases are typified by social workers either as care cases, in which the whole family is seen as the unit of need, or as delinquency cases in which the child himself is viewed as the unit of need. The further a case was placed towards the delinquency end of the continuum the more likely it was that the child would be seen as the unit of need and his removal from home be sought.

Those who established juvenile courts saw the child's offence as symptomatic of wider problems. They employed what is frequently and appositely called the 'medical model' of the causes of crime. This assumes that delinquents are different from non-delinquents; that delinquents are not responsible for their actions; that delinquent behaviour in itself is not the real problem but merely the symptom of some more intractable disorder. The victory of the medical model inevitably meant the elevation of the expert. Christopher Lasch has argued most persuasively that one way of understanding developments of the 'therapeutic state' is to add 'socialization of reproduction' to 'socialization of production' effected by the industrial revolution. 'Socialization of reproduction proletarianized parenthood, by making people unable to provide for their own needs without the supervision of trained experts'.[73] The juvenile court substituted prevention for punishment and close surveillance for judgment. It treated the child's or adolescent's 'crimes' as symptoms of an unhealthy, un-hygienic home environment, thus justifying enquiries into the morality of his family and his removal from his home if this was deemed necessary.

Donzelot describes how in France (the pattern is similar here) parents who called in the police or social workers in the hope that outside intervention would strengthen their authority over a wayward child of theirs found instead that their authority was transferred to an outside professional authority. He writes:

> Instead of the desired admonition, the juvenile judge, after reviewing the results of the social enquiry, decides in favour of an educative assistance that has another purpose altogether, since it brings the adolescent into the sphere of the tutelary complex, leading to his detachment from family authority and transferral to a social authority . . . all in order to prevent him from

contaminating his brothers and sisters and to enable his parents to devote themselves to the younger children.[74]

Similar processes occurred in this country. The therapeutic state leaves the family intact but subjects it to non-stop supervision. In Lasch's words, the family is 'always "justified" in theory and always suspect in practice'.[75]

The British legislation of the late 1960s (the English Act of 1969 and its Scottish counterpart a year earlier) is the culmination of the child-saving, treatment-oriented ethic. The ideology discussed here is rampant in the government documents which spawned the legislation. Thus, the *Children In Trouble* White Paper,[76] the *fons et origo* of the 1969 Act, stressed that delinquency in itself was not the real problem but was rather a symptom of 'maladjustment or immaturity . . . or of a deviant, damaged or abnormal personality.' The question accordingly was whether the child required care which he was unlikely to receive unless he was referred to the court. The fundamental aim was to ensure that he received help and guidance. A range of factors would indicate 'the need for treatment'. One example is persistent truancy. The White Paper did not probe the reason why the child stayed away from school. The treatment model tends to look at behaviour in a one-sided and unproblematic way.

There is a parallel here in the thinking of Lord Kilbrandon, who chaired a committee the adoption of the report of which led to the Social Work (Scotland) Act in 1968. In referring to truancy, he remarked in a published talk that 'persistent truancy' was 'the first sign of serious maladjustment or psychological disorder. If unattended to (like all disease prognosis) it may have repercussions in after life more serious than delinquency itself.'[77]

But there was another side to these reports. Throughout the treatment model has juxtaposed 'care and control'. It may be questioned how compatible the two notions are. One does something *for* children, the other something *to* them.[78] The helping professions very quickly emerged as agents of social control. This conflict is apparent in *Children In Trouble*. It was concerned not just with the best interests of children but also with the need to protect society against the social consequences of delinquency. It thought that the aims of protecting society against juvenile delinquency and of helping children in trouble were 'complementary and not contradictory'.[79] Whether this is so or not, there is undoubtedly a tension between the two, which is reflected in the operation of the 1969 Act.

As already noted, the Act has been incompletely implemented. But even the practice of what has been implemented falls short of the ideal of the implemented legislation itself. The system still appears to deal with children in trouble mainly on the basis of their offence behaviour rather than on assessments of their personal needs.[80] This would be a preferable approach if only it were pursued directly without the intrusion made necessary by an overarching welfare ideology. In understanding these conflicts and failures one must take into account the fact that practice in part reflects the working needs of organisations concerned with its implementation.[81] Thus, for example, the decline in the number of supervision orders in the last decade in part reflects the magistrates' sentencing policy but is also the result of social workers' reluctance to recommend a remedy they consider to be ineffective.[82] There are also conflicting ideologies among groups such as magistrates, police and social workers to consider.[83] Sometimes despite these conflicts the different groups may agree about *what* is to be done: 'consensus as to the appropriate intervention in a particular case can conceal real conflict in ideological positions.'[84] They may not agree as to *why* it should be done. For example, magistrates and social workers may agree that a care order is appropriate, the former for retributive reasons, the latter on the basis of the child's needs.

The Scottish system of children's hearings is a more positive endorsement of the welfare approach than the English system. But the hearings are as much concerned with control and protection of the public as they are with care and welfare of the child. According to Morris, the system

> hoped to abolish delinquency – and all that could remain would be children in need of care. But delinquency cannot be abolished so easily. Society's attitude to children who offend cannot be isolated from society's attitude to offenders in general – they expect something to be done about the delinquent behaviour.[85]

Morris and McIsaac have shown the extent to which decisions are related to the child's social conformity as much as to his needs: 'criteria of "needs" [are] in fact criteria of "social conformity".'[86] They demonstrate a wish to intervene in and control certain types of families. But though in the English system there has been increased reliance on detention centres and borstals as well as secure units and youth treatment centres, in Scotland the number of children in 'List D' schools today is considerably fewer than the number who were in approved schools when the 1968 Act came into operation.[87] Furthermore, fewer children reach the formal social control agencies in the children's hearings system than in the former court system. The number of children referred to reporters, the intake officials, has declined.[88] So has the number of children prosecuted in the sheriff courts. The reporter himself has become an important means of diversion from further formal proceedings and in three-quarters of the cases where he takes no formal action the children are not referred to him again.[89] In that it is keeping a certain number of children out of the formal control system, the Scottish children's hearings system has reduced the ambiguities, dilemmas and inconsistencies inherent in the English system, but they remain.

'Wrongs' Only Children Can Commit

One of the most troublesome features of juvenile justice is what has been called status offences. They are a matter of concern because they legitimise state intervention in the lives of children, rather than the population as a whole, and are thus discriminatory. However, they also exemplify certain procedures and practices which are endemic in the juvenile justice system whether it is dealing with criminal offences or such matters as promiscuity or truancy. For in all juvenile court cases what is in issue is not the act itself, whether this be theft or vandalism or staying out late or running away, but the fact that the act is deemed to be symptomatic of an underlying psychological condition which is believed to be its cause.

It is difficult to justify status offences. Although other justifications may be posited, in general there are two grounds commonly asserted to support the retention of such offences. First, the behaviour in question is supposed to typify more serious problems in the child and thus to allow intervention to solve those problems. Secondly, it is assumed that children who are promiscuous or smoke or truant or whatever are more likely than other children to commit serious delinquent behaviour in the future. For example, Emerson[90] found that truancy often provides evidence to those who judge delinquents that a child is pointed in the direction of 'serious delinquency'. As prevention is better than cure, early intervention is seen as desirable if these children are to be 'saved'. The underlying assumption, though dubious, is that intervention will deter the child from subsequently engaging in 'harmful' or delinquent activities.

Such arguments make a number of claims. Empirical evidence to support them is lacking. Furthermore, intervention causes any number of evils, notably stigmatisation with the attendant problems for employment prospects and self-image and the fact that it is likely to lead to increased police surveillance. It is difficult to see what is being treated and how: 'being an unruly child is not, any more than being an obnoxious adult, a treatable condition.'[91] The goal is said to be rehabilitation but this is to suggest that intervention is justified not for what the child has done but for what it is feared he might do in the future. There is no evidence at all that there is any connexion between suffering from some kind of psychological disorder and committing a status offence. But then no one has established any causal link between any personality disorder and delinquency nor is it likely that anyone will. We are simply asked by those who support status offences to take too much on trust. After all, the arguments used in support could be used to make similar behaviour illegal in the case of adults.

A lot of concern has been expressed recently about truancy. Truancy as such is not a criminal offence, though the Magistrates' Association has recently asked for powers that would amount to criminalising it and police spokesmen, notably former Metropolitan Police Commisioner, Sir David McNee, have asked for powers to pick up children from the street and return them to their school.[72] However, a care order may be made if a child is of compulsory school age and is not receiving 'efficient full-time education suitable to his age, ability and aptitude' if in addition he is in need of care or control which he is unlikely to receive unless an order is made.[93] The number of children going into care on this ground is increasing. There is reason to believe that it is a short cut to a care order as, compared to some of the other grounds, it is easy to prove. Although in truancy cases the child is on trial it is difficult to avoid the conclusion that the school itself is in many cases part of the problem. It is tempting to suggest, as White has done,[94] that many children are absent with cause. No case has decided what is meant by 'efficient' education, but it is questionable whether many truants are being offered this. There is considerable evidence that children's behaviour and attitudes including their attendance patterns are shaped and influenced by their experiences at school, in particular by the qualities of the school as a social institution.[95] It is easy instead to blame victims. Children who absent themselves from school are often labelled 'maladjusted'. But 'labelling often takes no account of the range of problems behind the symptoms.' As Schrag and Divoky note: 'if one can define deviance as sickness, then by inference the norm becomes healthy and its defense merely an invocation of the natural order.'[96] Focusing attention on truants enables attention to be diverted from the schools (from at least some of which teachers are also known to absent themselves) and from the wider social order. The discovery of new diseases like hyper-kinesis[97] and the ascription to children of labels like 'hyperactive'[98] serve much the same function. Public issues become private troubles.[99]

Status offences have been a common object of attack in the United States. Criticism in this country has been more muted. They are said to be vague and over-broad.[100] Indeed, courts have invalidated statutes on this ground for example, where jurisdiction could be assumed over a wayward minor, defined as one who was 'morally depraved or . . . in danger of becoming morally depraved'.[101] They have not always been consistent. Thus, in *Mailliard* v. *Bonzales* the Supreme Court vacated and remanded a three-judge court decision that struck down a Californian statute, since repealed, which conferred jurisdiction over minors leading an 'idle, dissolute, lewd or immoral life'.[102] There is concern also that status offences tend to discriminate in their operation against girls,[103] a concern rightly shared by writers in this country.[104] Eighty-five per cent of those committed to care as being 'in moral danger' are girls. This is not only unjust (how many 'promiscuous' boys have been committed to care because of their sexual activities?) but it also discriminates unfairly against those girls whose 'wrongs' become known to social welfare agencies as a result of their family's involvement with such organisations. Penalising homosexual youth in this way, as happens, is also difficult to defend.

The American Bar Association Juvenile Standards Project (discussed in detail later in this chapter) has proposed the elimination of the general juvenile court jurisdiction over status offences in non-criminal juvenile misbehaviour.[105]

Instead, the standards place primary reliance on 'a system of voluntary referral to service provided outside the juvenile justice system.' They envisage the need for 'some carefully limited official intervention' in emergency situations where there is 'immediate jeopardy' and the standards provide for this. In general the standards reject judicialisation and coercion. The Project submits:

> Removal of the status offense jurisdiction will encourage more people to get more effective help; stimulate the creation and extension of a wider range of voluntary services than is presently available, and the corrosive effects of treating non-criminal youth as though they had committed crimes; and free up a substantial part of the resources of the juvenile justice system to deal with the cases of delinquency and of abused and neglected children that belong to it.

While in general endorsing this proposal, I believe its implications should be considered carefully. The substitution of 'help'; however 'voluntary', looks like a familiar invocation of welfare philosophy. Some adolescents may need advice, befriending or assistance but many will not. Help assumes the existence of a problem: this may amount to nothing more than the interpretation of fairly normal adolescent behaviour by welfare officials for whom the norm is different. There is a very strong case for removing both the education condition and the moral danger condition as grounds for a care order. Coercive intervention in the lives of young people should be limited to those who commit a criminal offence or who are abused or neglected. Children should only be punished for offences for which adults are punished and however we conceptualise them, children see care orders, particularly where this involves removal from home, as punishment. That much is clear from the National Children's Bureau publication *Who Cares?*[106] to which further reference is made in Chapter 5.

Justice Versus Welfare

Penal policy towards children in England has seen the gradual adoption of a welfare model. This model may be contrasted with one which emphasises justice. In practice neither model is even seen in its pure form.[107] The establishment of rights for juveniles who misbehave requires the adoption of a justice-based system, though it does not inevitably follow that no allowance should be made for individual circumstances. A justice-based system can accommodate, for example, a plea of mitigation, must recognise an age below which criminal responsibility cannot attach and must acknowledge the incapacities of the mentally disordered offender.

The welfare approach[108] is predicated upon the following assumptions:

(i)   Delinquent behaviour has antecedent causes.[109] The causes of delinquency are located within the individual and his family. He is disadvantaged in some way. It follows that state intervention should be directed at removing these disadvantages or alleviating their harmful consequences rather than punishing the offender. A deterministic model of man is adopted and individual choice is subservient or non-existent.

(ii)   These causes can be, and have been, discovered. There are any number of research findings which claim to have discovered the causes of delinquency.[110] At best they do no more than postulate factors which correlate closely with delinquency. For example, West and Farrington's study of over 400 boys growing up in an inner city working-class neighbourhood of London found an association between delinquency and low family income, large family size, a parent with a criminal record, unsatisfactory child-rearing of the parents and comparatively low intelligence of the child (each one was associated with delinquency to some extent independently of the other four).[111] There is, however, no evidence of any causal link between the listed factors and delinquency and some evidence that such factors are not necessarily so associated.[112] The correlation between crime and disadvantage may well reflect differential reaction of social control agencies: the inner city is policed more intensively than suburban areas; this uncovers delinquency and legitimates more intensive policing, more arrests and so on.[113]

(iii) Offenders are different from non-offenders. But we know from self-report studies[114] and victimisation studies[115] that crime is far more evenly spread across the social spectrum and more common than the criminal statistics would indicate. Those convicted by a court of a criminal offence represent about a quarter of those who have actually committed an offence.[116] Hood and Sparks argue that 'to commit one or two delinquent acts is "normal behaviour" for boys', though they indicate that persistent misbehaviour is relatively rare.[117]

(iv)   The discovery of the causes of delinquency (see (ii)) has made possible the treatment and so the control of such troublesome behaviour. Delinquency gets worse without this treatment. The treatment is beneficial and has no harmful side-effects. The juvenile's 'illness' has to be diagnosed (hence assessment centres) before it (and he) can be treated. In each case an individual treatment plan must be developed. This will often focus on behaviour not related to the offence in question (e.g. truancy, glue-sniffing). Morris *et al.* comment:

The rapid expansion of observation and assessment centres since the passing of the 1969 Act epitomises the treatment ideology in practice. Assessment centres, in the name of scientific 'problem solving', serve as the prime example of the bureaucratisation of the labelling process. Such descriptions as 'personality disorder', 'psychopath' and 'dangerous' not only stigmatise children but, perforce, create expectations: the process becomes self-fulfilling. In addition, research shows that the language of 'treatment' merely obfuscates the real criteria of assessment: the age, sex and geographical location of the child and the availability of vacancies in institutions.[118]

Norman Tutt has cogently argued that individual treatment is anyway a myth.[119] It presupposes observation and assessment and this in its turn assumes: (i) human behaviour to be a constant whereas a child behaves differently in the centre from at home; (ii) that children in care have 'idiosyncratic problems open to remedial intervention' yet, if West and Farrington are right, the problems inhere in the parents, not the children; and (iii) observation and assessment are 'functional' but absence of resources and a paucity of knowledge mean that they are not. The assumptions upon which assessment is based appear then to be invalid. It may be doubted whether the staff in these centres anyway have the capacity to assess the children: even if one concedes the existence of professional expertise, only 15 per cent are professionally qualified and turnover is rapid.[120]

But once assessed the welfare model requires the delinquent to be treated. The evidence both from the United States[121] and this country[122] suggests that treatment is ineffective. Effectiveness is usually measured in terms of reconviction rates, often using the time scale of two years. Though a questionable criterion of success (it presupposes that the re-offender is caught), it may be suggested that the failure rates of treatment are higher than the statistics on reconviction. These are high. It is estimated that 57 per cent of the offenders who came into care in 1975-6 were reconvicted within two years, that 75 per cent of male juveniles discharged from detention centre in 1976 were reconvicted within two years, and that the proportion of male juveniles discharged from borstal in 1976 who were reconvicted within two years was 84 per cent.[123] More particularly there is the evidence of a controlled trial conducted in a residential institution for delinquent boys which compared two houses, one a therapeutic community, the other using more orthodox approved school training, which seemed to indicate that 'although the methods and policies of the therapeutic community and C House [the traditional house] programmes differed in many respects, their long-term effectiveness in reducing delinquent behaviour was virtually identical.'[124]

It is wise to be sceptical about treatment – first, because there is a suspicion that claims to treat are spurious, that perhaps what is called treatment is rather just 'smooth management'.[125] Indeed, in the United States there have been successful appeals against commitment to mental hospitals and juvenile institutions on the grounds that these commitments were for treatment which the hospitals or institutions were not in fact providing.[126] As Hardiker has noted, ideologies such as that embodied in the treatment model assumption can be 'mediated by the exigencies of practice'.[127] Secondly, if treatment is situated within social work practice, it may be found, as Giller and Morris indeed found, that care orders mark the stage at which the social worker's ability to deal with a child has become exhausted, the treatment plan only emerging after the care order has been made.[128] Thirdly, the model accepts that to be effective the treatment must be voluntary: the delinquent must accept it, want it, wish to be cured. But consent is rarely forthcoming and treatment is regularly enforced upon the recalcitrant for 'their own good'. Furthermore, the delinquent children themselves do not see residential orders as anything other than punitive.[129] They have been 'sent away' as punishment for their offence. The general public probably sees it this way as well: the general image of children in CHEs is one of wrongdoers removed from their homes because of their delinquency. Hence the stigma which attaches to being in care, irrespective of the reason why the particular child is in care.[130]

The justice model may be described more briefly. Essentially it is tied to a view of crime as a matter of individual choice. It stresses the idea of free will. It postulates an individual with the capacity to control his own behaviour. It sees crime as the individual's response to opportunity. Secondly, it argues that if delinquent behaviour is a rational response to certain situations it is reasonable to hold the individual responsible for his actions. Certain persons are excluded from accountability because they are deemed, either by reason of age or mental incapacity, incapable of making rational choice. As far as children are concerned, ten is currently the age of criminal responsibility in England. The choice of ten owes little to the insights of developmental psychology: rather it is arbitrary and the product of historical expediency.

Thirdly, proponents of the justice model argue that the sole justification for intervention is the commission of a criminal offence and the only basis for punishment is proof of guilt in a court of law. As indicated earlier in this chapter, traditionally the juvenile court has had jurisdiction over children's non-criminal misbehaviour: truancy, running away from home, glue-sniffing and so on. This feature of the justice model has a number of consequences of which the most significant is the importance of legal representation. Currently, barely a quarter of juveniles appearing on criminal charges before the juvenile court are legally represented.[131] The practice is variable as the study by Parker, Casburn and Turnbull illustrates.[132] They found that six times as many of juveniles were refused legal aid in Huyton[133] as in neighbouring Liverpool, and this despite the fact that the Huyton court was highly punitive.

Fourthly, what Hart has called the 'doctrine of fair opportunity'[134] requires that we have advance warning of what types of behaviour attract criminal sanctions. Legality demands the outlawing of crimes by analogy:[135] it insists that crimes should be clearly defined. It does not require a warning to be given to those who skate on thin ice as to the exact point on the lake where they might fall in, but it does presuppose that action will not be taken against someone unless he actually falls in. The justice model deprecates preventive action. Of course, new forms of deviant behaviour do emerge from time to time. Glue-sniffing (more accurately solvent-sniffing) is a recent illustration of this.[136] But if it is not an offence, and currently it is not, then according to the justice model it is not an excuse for intervention. However, to pursue this example further, although government spokesmen have said on a number of occasions that the creation of new offences to deal with glue-sniffing is not justified (their line is that persuasion and education are more appropriate)[137], glue-sniffers are prosecuted ostensibly for being intoxicated on the railways, breach of the peace and other similar offences when in reality the focus of concern is glue-sniffing.[138] There is a list of proscribed drugs[139] but the solvents used by teenagers are not within it. But that does not seem to matter to control agencies. Most apposite is Dorn's comment:

> The drug problem, having been fitted into the scenario of 'children in trouble', offers a rationale for the efforts of control agencies to 'cope with' working class youth 'failing' to make the transition to non-existent work in ways that are within the ideological and practical capabilities of the agencies involved[140]

Fifthly, adherence to a justice model demands the rejection of the individual-ised welfare disposition in favour of a determinate sentence, proportional to the offence committed. It also demands that offenders be treated equally. The justice model would cut down on the amount of discretion which the police, welfare agencies and courts currently exercise.[141] Thus, there are enormous discrepancies in cautioning practice[142] and in sentencing patterns. It is difficult to eradicate discretionary decision-making from the penal process (indeed, it may not be desirable to do so) but it can be cut down: as an example, the recommendation of the Parliamentary Penal Affairs Group that all first and second time offenders receive an automatic caution would reduce police discretion.[143] It may be difficult to establish a tariff system but evidence of current practice suggests little relationship between the seriousness of an offence and the disposition made. For example, Giller and Morris show how social workers often use care orders to get control of a problematic family. They quote one social worker thus:

> I really didn't think that the shop-lifting was important. I thought it was much more important that both places where the girl had been living were falling apart and that she couldn't live there. If they had just been shop-lifting offences or she had had some place to live and the shop-lifting offence had come up then I think that care would have to have been looked at much more carefully and we might not have decided to take her into care.[144]

The justice model would not tolerate this arbitrary decision-making. Offenders would be dealt with because of their offences and not because of their family situations.[145]

Rarely, if at all, can either model function in its pure form. One of the ironies of the last decade has been the undoubted dissonance between the liberal reform intentions of the 1969 Act expressed in its welfare orientation and the punitive nature of the actual system in operation during the 1970s and early 1980s. The Act spoke of a move away from institutionalisation and towards welfare-based community programmes, such as intermediate treatment, but it has been 'subverted to produce an unprecedented increase in the use of custodial measures, namely detention centres and borstals.'[146] It is yet another irony that this has happened at a time when a conscious attempt is being made to reduce the prison population. 'Welfare' is said by the law and order lobby to have failed: supporters of 'welfare' say it has not been properly tried. Where once the trend was towards eroding the distinction between deprivation and depravity, today the move is towards the rediscovery of depravity. New penal measures must be found for the determined 'young offender',[147] for those who are 'deliberately depraved'.[148] At least this brings into focus the offence rather than the pathological features of the offender's environment. But is this to expect responsibility without being endowed with rights? What rights does the offender have? What 'due process',[149] if any, do we accord him? It is to these issues that I now turn.

The Juvenile Court and Juveniles' Rights

One of the most unsatisfactory features of juvenile justice is that in reality there is very little justice. Neither pre-trial procedures nor the court processes themselves observe the sort of elementary natural justice requirements that are taken for granted in a court dealing with adult offenders. In part the problem is the product of a confusion of purposes: welfare versus control; assessment of needs or adversary trial. The problem is not easily solved for it is itself fraught with ambivalence. For example, to substitute an adversary model, which many, not least juveniles themselves, clamour for, would actually lead to more cases coming to court and fewer being screened out by welfare diversionary measures.

Two recent cases express these ambiguities well. In *R* v. *K* the court said that a care order imposed upon a conviction for burglary was not a custodial sentence, so that bail pending an appeal was not applicable. The court reasoned that the restrictions placed by the order on the defendant's liberty were 'no greater than those which may be imposed on any minor member of a well conducted family.'[150] The second case (*Humberside C.C.* v. *D.P.R.*) was not brought in respect of a criminal offence, but in the course of care proceedings, the then Lord Chief Justice, Lord Widgery, described such proceedings as 'essentially non-adversary . . . an objective examination of the position of the child . . . . It is an objective enquiry.'[151] Many criticisms have been made of the way in which juvenile courts operate. They have now led to proposals for reform. Some of these are considered here. Rather than attempting a complete catalogue of the problems of the juvenile court I have taken a look at five problem areas: (i) the information used by juvenile courts; (ii) representation of the defendants; (iii) independence of the decision-makers; (iv) indeterminacy of many of the sentences; (v) perceived absence of proportionality between offence and 'sentence'.

(i) Matza has written of individualized justice that it 'results in a frame of relevance so large, so all-inclusive, that any relation between the criteria of judgment and the disposition remains obscure.'[152] The social enquiry report (S.E.R.) is the linchpin of the juvenile court process. It has been described by Anderson aptly as 'the product of an application of social work ideology to the court context.'[153] According to the Streatfield report in 1961, the

> purpose of the social enquiry report should be to furnish the court with information about the social and domestic background of the offender which is relevant to the court's assessment of his culpability . . . . The report is also intended to indicate against this background some corrective measure by laying information about the offender and his surroundings which is relevant to the court's consideration of how his criminal career might be checked and expressing an opinion as to . . . the likely effect on the offender's criminal career of probation or some other specified form of sentence.[154]

S.E.R.s are required unless there is a positive reason for not providing them. The practice nevertheless varies: Priestley *et al.* found in their research that the social services department in Wiltshire wrote proportionately half as many reports as their colleagues in Bristol did.[155]

It is an elementary requirement of natural justice that the child, his legal representative (if he has one) and his parents, whose characters are often assassinated in S.E.R.s, should be given the opportunity of reading the report prior to the hearing. But there is no absolute obligation to furnish even the child's lawyer with a copy of the report in advance of the hearing. Further, there is no necessity that a S.E.R. be shown at any stage to the child or his parents. Practice is variable. In one court described by Anderson, 'reports are read in silence and parents are handed a copy at the same time as the bench . . . . Defendants are not allowed to read the report, and if an attempt is made to look over the shoulder of their parents they are sometimes told to move to another part of the courtroom.'[156] Parents are said to be 'intimidated' (as indeed are the social workers) and defendants 'alienated'. In Anderson's survey of two courts only a small minority of defendants (11 out of 73) were told of their rights to refuse a report.

S.E.R.s are prone to contain value judgments, to make unsubstantiated assertions and often to be based upon assumptions which are unsupported by evidence. Writers of S.E.R.s, who know no more about the causes of mis-behaviour than the rest of us, tend to assemble information which reinforces stereotypes of 'causes of trouble' such as broken homes, a working mother, and often to put it into language loosely drawn from psycho-analytic theory (personality disorder, psychopath, impaired bonding, dependency needs and such like). According to Morris *et al.*, the rapid expansion of observation and assessment centres in the last decade 'epitomises the treatment ideology in practice'.[157] How easy is it for a child or his parents to challenge the contents of an S.E.R., even when he knows them? It is all to easy for magistrates to label a child who tries to do so, or his parents, and in terms of ultimate disposal of the case the difference may well not be great, as having 'authority problems'.

The extent to which S.E.R.s influence decision-making by magistrates is also a cause for concern. Magistrates accept most recommendations made to them by social workers and probation officers. Not surprisingly, they tend to prefer the language, style and attitudes of probation officers. On the other hand, to make a report which is acceptable to magistrates and therefore effective, writers of reports have to tailor them to what magistrates believe. Thus, according to Anderson, 'a recommendation for supervision . . . may be phrased in a number of ways. Thus, . . . a "punitive" magistrate may . . . receive a recommendation for "an added control over his behaviour", while a welfare-oriented magistrate will be advised of "the need for additional support" '.[158] As a result there is created 'a closed looped system of influences',[159] an alliance between magistrates and professionals which caters more for their needs than those of the children who are the avowed objects of concern. Magistrates are more influenced when the S.E.R. contains a recommendation. Indeed, the recent study by Thorpe *et al.* found that it was uncommon for a magistrate to make a care order contrary to the recommendations made in S.E.R.s by the social services department.[160]

(ii) Few defendants in the juvenile court are represented (for example, less than one-fifth of Anderson's sample of two courts were)[161] although the number who are is increasing.[162] This is the result in part of a growing awareness of the ways courts flout principles of natural justice. It is also the product, mainly as a result of the local law centre movement, of great availability of interested lawyers. In some courts now duty solicitors' schemes operate. Morris and Giller found three reasons why parents did not seek legal representation for their children: the offence was perceived to be trivial; it was a first offence; the child was regarded as guilty.[163] To an extent these may be rationalisations. How many of the parents, for example, had 'legal competence'?[164] How many of them knew anything of the criminal law and its processes?

It is important to establish the principle of representation for without it rights tend to go by the board. Those who are not in favour of greater legal participation in juvenile court cases are inclined to see lawyers as nuisances; they obstruct the welfare orientation of the court; they may use legal procedures and technicalities to prevent facts (or statements dressed up as facts) coming to the attention of the magistrates. But justice demands that grounds be proved beyond reasonable doubt before a decision can be taken about what to do with a child, even if those in charge think it would be better for the child to be removed from home or supervised. Hearsay and other inadmissible evidence should no more be used against a child than an adult on trial for a criminal offence.

It is important for children to be represented. For them and their parents a court appearance is a bewildering experience. They may have communication problems. Some will be fearful of participating in the proceedings; others may think, often rightly, that matters are pre-determined and that nothing they can say will influence the outcome. Morris and Giller found that over half of their survey could not correctly identify the magistrates and over half did not know who made the decision in the court.[165] Where matters of fact are in dispute or where there are defences which are not known to parents and children or where it is advisable to call expert evidence to challenge an S.E.R., a lawyer can play a useful role. It is also important that a reasoned and articulate case be put to the court and a lawyer is, or should be, able to do this. Anderson found that attitudes to solicitors reflected prevailing ideologies in different juvenile courts.[166] Not surprisingly, it was the court which acted primarily as an institution of law, rather than that which operated as an agent of social welfare, which favoured representation by lawyers. Welfare-oriented courts saw themselves as taking the child's part and so viewed the lawyer's skills as redundant.

In many areas of child law children have no right to be legally represented. Reference is made to some of these and the problems in Chapter 6. But here they do and they, not their parents, can request legal aid. The parents are not entitled to legal aid because they are not regarded as a party to the proceedings. This is an unfortunate omission and it may be that lawyers will take their instructions from parents, who are not their clients, rather than children. This lacuna in the law has been repeatedly recognised, most recently by the Royal Commission on Legal Services,[167] and it is probable that it will be filled in due course.[168] Even so, in the context of criminal proceedings, the interests of parents and children conflict in only a minority of cases. There can only be any doubt as to the importance of representation so long as the juvenile court remains confused in its aims. Once it is accepted that it is a court not, for example, a family council and that it should respond to what children *do* rather than to what they *are*,[169] the functions of lawyers will be manifest. First, he is there to defend the child against the charges made against him. Secondly, if these are proved, his duty is to represent the child's interests at the disposition stage so as to ensure that he is only punished for what he has done.

(iii) Doubt has been cast on the independence of the decision-makers in the discussion of social enquiry reports. A number of other points must, however, be made. It is an elementary requirement of natural justice that extraneous matters such as social circumstances should only be considered once guilt has been established. But, given the confusion of purposes that reign in the juvenile court, it is not surprising that magistrates should discuss social enquiry reports with their authors, particularly where these are probation officers, prior to the court hearing. According to Carlen:

> of the thirty probation officers directly connected with the Metropolitan Court, only three claimed that they would *never* discuss a social inquiry report with a magistrate prior to the court hearing, nine said that they would discuss a report in certain circumstances but would ensure that all the main points of such discussion were repeated in court in front of the defendant, and eight said that they welcomed any chance to discuss reports with the magistrates.[170]

One probation officer justified his behaviour in this way:

> I may have put the information one way – for the client's benefit – and then I might want to go along with my report and see the magistrate and say, 'look, I said this – what I'm getting at is a bit more.' Uh – I'm not terribly happy about doing that because it does mean you're giving information that you haven't made public to the client – um – so it would be more a question of interpretation than of telling him anything that I hadn't put in the report. Like, you know, if I put 'This guy's inadequate' or 'of low intelligence', I might want to go to the magistrate and say, 'Look, he's as thick as two short planks.'

Carlen is writing of adult offenders, who, unlike juveniles, are given an opportunity to read reports on themselves. Although the practice is less necessary in the context of juvenile courts, it clearly takes place there too. This not only impugns the independence of the magistrates but renders the decision-making process less visible and accordingly less susceptible to control.

Indeed, the practice in the juvenile courts has been formalised into liaison committees. The eleventh report of the House of Commons Expenditure Committee in 1975 recommended the establishment in every local authority of 'liaison committees representing magistrates, teachers, social workers and probation officers . . . to discuss not only the progress of individual children in care or under supervision, but also more general matters such as the developments of intermediate treatment.'[171] Further, it was recommended that such committees should be able to compel the attendance of police officers 'where appropriate'. Liaison committees are now common. The innovation has provoked little comment, though it is difficult to see how magistrates who attend such meetings and discuss children in trouble can independently determine the guilt of those same children when they, as is often the case, appear before them at some subsequent time. It is important that all concerned in the juvenile court process should meet and discuss problems. But there is a world of difference between discussing a case in the abstract and focusing on a potential defendant. It can only be because the line between justice and welfare is so imperfectly drawn that to many participants this would appear to be no problem.

(iv) When adults are sentenced to a term of imprisonment the sentence is a fixed one, though the parole system has necessarily injected an element of indeterminacy. With juveniles it is otherwise. Since dispositions are supposed to be individualised, substantial discretion is given to magistrates, social workers and those in charge of institutions to decide how best to meet a child's 'needs' and also to decide when those 'needs' have been met so that he is rehabiliated. In theory the seriousness of the crime counts for little: 'the murderer was as eligible for the indeterminate commitment as the beggar.'[172] Such practices can easily result in arbitrary decision-making and have done so. There are wide disparities in sanctions imposed for the same offences: subjective attitudes and values, cultural and racial biases, sexual discrimination, all contribute towards these uneven practices.

The American Bar Association's Juvenile Justice Standards Project has called for determinate sentences with needs only a matter for consideration as regards the type of disposition within an already determined category of dispositions.[173] There are no such moves in this country though the American proposals have the qualified support of Morris.[174] But once we substitute justice and punishment for welfare and treatment, it becomes very difficult to support any notion of indeterminacy in the sentencing process or indeed in steps taken subsequently in the penal process.

(v) Closely related is the idea, also, in the American Juvenile Justice Standards, that sanctions for juvenile offenders should be proportionate to the seriousness of the crimes they have committed. The outcome of the case should be commensurate with the matter which brings the child before the court. This does not happen at the moment. There are discrepancies between the 'sentences' (they are not called this in the juvenile court but that is how the juvenile himself perceives them) a child may receive for the same offence (an injustice which was exposed in the United States by *Re Gault*)[175] and an absence of proportionality between 'sentences' given to children. Two ten-year-olds may be committed to care, one for a crime of violence, the other for a minor theft, and technically both could remain there for eight years. To say that such care orders are made in the best interests of those children does not deceive the children. As far as they and their families are concerned, they have been 'sentenced to eight years'.

Relating sanctions to the seriousness of the offence is fraught with difficulties as contemporary retributivists have found.[176] But these difficulties are not insurmountable. The American Bar Association's Juvenile Justice Standards suggest one scheme. It envisages five classes of juvenile offence, determined by the maximum sentences laid down for adult offenders. Maximum sentences are determined by the class of the offence.[177] The authors of *Justice for Children* propose six categories of offences and three of sanctions.[178] It is not necessary here to examine the pros and cons of each scheme, nor to suggest any other. These are details which can be worked out in due course. All I am concerned to establish here is the principle that the punishment should fit the crime.

Treatment Institutions

The question of children's rights is no less significant when we examine the institutions to which those who do wrong (as well as those who are wronged, as we shall see in Chapter 5) are sent by courts and administrative bodies. Space precludes more than a cursory examination of three main institutions.

The first residential institution that many children encounter is the observation and assessment centre. These centres can be looked at in two ways. They can be examined in terms of their official purposes and in terms of their real purposes. The supposed function of the centres is assessment. The assessment procedure 'is intended to provide a sophisticated analysis of a child's needs.' The House of Commons Expenditure Committee Report which states this goes on to note that 'to function adequately there must be sufficient skilled staff of all the necessary disciplines, an adequate number of assessment places and a suitable variety of possible placements for the children once assessed.'[179] But it is doubtful whether these centres can provide a sophisticated analysis, even if that is what they intend to do. For a start the child is in an alien environment. He does not fully understand why he is there or what he must do to get out. He is in a strange and uncertain world and his reactions and behaviour are not likely to be his normal ones. Observation and assessment centres are artificial. If the 'skilled staff of all the necessary disciplines' do not understand this, they may lack an 'appreciative perception'[180] of what they are involved in. But that begs the question. Sutton has tried to answer it. He asks:

> Where is the explicit knowledge base to which the organizers of observation and assessment might have recourse to help them in what they are doing? There is in fact none . . . . Nothing offers a concise guide as to what precisely is to be observed, why and how, and what are the structures of cause and effect that link these and other data together to arrive at an assessment of the needs and the fate of the individual child. Perhaps the fairest theoretical stance to be inferred from what has been published on observation and assessment is 'eclecticism'.[181]

Sutton is very much to the point when he says that 'observation' consists of little more than 'the personal impressions of residential staff who have little or no idea of the enormous technical problems of observing human behaviour'[182] and that data collected in this way plus information collated by a social worker and the opinions of the visiting psychologist and psychiatrist are then brought together and 'assessed'. The child must then wait until the recommended placement materialises.[183] And he may wait a considerable time, so long in fact that some children plead not to be moved because they have spent such a long time in a centre.[184] Some children spend long enough to need 'reassessing'. It is questionable whether assessment meets any of the criteria specified by the House of Commons Select Committee.

But is it intended to? There is a growing suspicion that assessment is merely a cloak for control. They are useful to the system in that they relieve staff in other establishments of difficult or disturbed children. They are warehouses,[185] transit camps. They are a threat to the potentially unruly and a way of containing the troublesome. Adult prisoners are first sent to a classifying centre but it is a prison and prisoners are classified in terms of the security risk they pose.[186] There is little pretence with adults that the purposes of assessment are anything other than containment. Should we not admit that this is the case with the young as well? A system which injects justice back into juvenile justice will have no place for the observation and assessment centre.

Many children who are committed to the care of the local authority are placed in community homes. When the residential care order[187] is implemented many more will be committed to community homes. What 'being in care' involves is considered fully in Chapter 5. A few comments directly related to care and the delinquent are in place here. Community homes were formerly approved schools and much of the pertinent research relates to the former institutions. It is, however, safe to assume the differences are few. But it is difficult to generalise about approved schools or community homes. There are significant differences between different homes, for example in their methods and style of administration.[188] In general, though, and despite the fact that most children in community homes are there not as a result of their misbehaviour, the ethos is 'reforming'.[189] Some are undoubtedly more liberal than others but in general the regime is penal, with an emphasis on discipline and with corporal punishment rife in many homes. Taylor *et al*. note that because the homes see their goal as reforming delinquents this 'legitimates not just day to day surveillance and control of most parts of children's private lives – their friendship patterns, relationship with home, sexual interests, correspondence, allocation of spending money – but also their incorporation into a variety of experimental programmes'.[190] They list various physical restraints (to which drugging may be added): it is difficult to be anything but appalled at measures taken in a supposedly civilised society to control children.

But, once again, the principal aim of the institution is treatment. As indicated earlier in this chapter, there is no doubt at all about the ineffectiveness of the treatment. Indeed, the Home Office Research Unit study, quoted earlier in this chapter, is of no doubt that 'much of what passes for "treatment" in institutions can . . . more properly be regarded as being concerned with reducing the ill-effects of residential living itself.'[191] Cornish and Clarke, the writers of this study, believe that organising programmes according to offender/programme typologies 'eases problems of control within the institution.' They comment: 'When innovations in an institution are made, for whatever reason, they come to be regarded as guarantors of increased therapeutic effectiveness.' In reality the effectiveness of the programmes is at best dubious.

Detention centres were introduced as an 'experiment'[192] in 1948. Their introduction was 'the price paid for the abolition of corporal punishment', their expansion is 'the "civilized alternative" to its reintroduction'.[193] On the one hand they are seen as a progressive idea designed to reduce, and ultimately end, the imprisonment of young offenders, yet on the other they are seen as a way of 'coming down hard' on delinquents and administering a 'short, sharp shock'.[194] In the period from 1960 to 1981 there was a tenfold increase in the number of juveniles sent to detention centres.[195] Detention centre disposals now constitute nearly 10 per cent of all 'sentences' on young offenders aged between fourteen and sixteen.[196] On 31 May 1982, 661 fourteen- to sixteen-year-olds were in junior detention centres (another 33 were in senior detention centres including one fourteen- and three fifteen-year-olds). Over half of the offences they had committed were of burglary, the next most represented offences being ones of theft and taking and driving away.[197] Perhaps 50 per cent of the offenders are already subject to a care order.

The success rate of detention centres is low. 73 per cent of boys released from junior detention centres in 1974 were reconvicted within two years.[198] Most re-offending occurs within the first six months while the memories of the punishment are freshest in the offender's mind. If these figures are depressing, they are rather worse than they look since at the time in question there was a period of compulsory after-care supervision of twelve months.[199] The figures would be worse if the follow-up period were extended.

Detention centres are a failure but we are now in the process of expanding the concept. They fit in well with the Conservative government's 'law and order' philosophy. A further experiment with shorter periods of incarceration introduced in 1979 is now confirmed by the Criminal Justice Act 1982 (s.4). In the past it was possible to send boys to detention centres for up to six months, although most 'sentences' were of three months. The new regime concentrates on a shorter 'sharp shock', of between three weeks and four months.

Detention centres are popular and are likely to expand rather than retract. 'Sentences' to a detention centre do have the merit of being short, determinate and directed towards punishment rather than treatment. In this latter point they differ from treatment measures only in intention, for the penal element is present in all treatment disposals as well. They are also relatively cheap to implement and this factor is not likely to pass unnoticed. What is worrying is the high level of institutionalisation of juvenile offenders in England. Commenting upon a United Nations survey which showed that Britain was one of the two top countries when it came to imprisoning young people, the Magistrates' Association said: 'if one country in the world is storing up trouble for itself by imprisoning large numbers (and a high proportion) of young people, it is Britain. The UN Survey shows that this, above all else, is Britain's major problem in the crime field.'[200] The problem is located within the community and that is where it should be solved.

Some Concluding Comments

Where do we go next? A number of proposals have been made. One that should be considered briefly is for decriminalisation, 'leaving the kids alone'.[201] If one accepts that all children are 'naughty' sometimes and that many break the law and, further, that nearly all mature into law-abiding citizens, the suggestion looks superficially attractive. If we add to this the evidence that control may lead to deviance[202] and stigmatises, the proposal begins to have considerable merit. But this has to be looked at another way as well. If we decriminalise, or not intervene in, the relatively trivial cases, we increase the stigma of those who are prosecuted. It is certainly the case that currently we intervene too often and too hastily. Many offences, particularly the so-called 'victimless crimes'[203] and 'status' offences, could be removed from the purview of control agencies. We could increase diversion, though how we do this remains a matter of some controversy: cautioning, in theory a useful approach, appears to be widening the net rather than screening out.[204] Even so, I would be prepared to risk an extension in the cautioning system and I would not allow police cautions of juveniles to be cited in the juvenile court, as they are now.

It is important, I believe, to have separate courts to deal with juvenile offenders and children who are in need of care. Whatever we call the latter ('family courts' seems the most favoured name),[205] it is important that the distinction between those who offend and those who are deprived or endangered is preserved. This argument applies with equal force to the institutions to which children are sent. Children who are removed from their parents because of home circumstances require care: those 'sent away' for an offence are, or should be, placed in an institution because they deserve punishment. It is quite wrong that the two categories of child should end up cheek by jowl in the same institution. As indicated in Chapter 5, it is the child in need of care who suffers. An important benefit emerging from this separation would be the recognition that the two were separate jurisdictions. It would mean, for example, that a local authority could appeal against the refusal of a care order in the case, for example, of a battered child. It cannot do this presently and so is forced to rely on a wardship jurisdiction.[206]

We have to accept that juvenile justice for offenders means inflicting punishment on them. We must not deceive ourselves (they are not deceived) into believing that we are treating them, that it is for their own good. We must recognise that we are imposing suffering. Once we accept that what we are doing is punishing, a number of implications follow. Because we are depriving of liberty, we must justify what we are doing. If offenders are to be punished they are to be punished because of what they have done, not to deter others and reform them. Of course, we must hope punishment will act as deterrence, individual and general, and help to rehabilitate. But we know it is likely to do none of these things.

In punishing a juvenile the most important criterion must be the offence he has committed, not his family background or his needs. One dimension of justice is fairness: injustice is created, and is perceived by the juvenile himself, when the punishment does not fit the crime.[207] It follows from this that the punishment of a child should never exceed that likely to be meted out to an adult offender. Hitherto, we appear to have accepted that children are less responsible for their crimes than adults but, in the name of treatment, we have often punished them more excessively. The *Gault* case in the United States is a striking illustration.[208] I am not advocating that children should receive the same punishments as adults, nor that they should be kept in the same institutions. Segregation of adult and young offenders is important: it is deplorable that juveniles are still held in adult prisons, even though they may not be sentenced to terms of imprisonment.[209] Nor am I suggesting that juveniles get the same sentences. Without developing the concept of responsibility.[210] which would be outside the scope of this book, it can, I think, be safely said that juveniles are not as responsible for their crimes as adults. This should be reflected in the sentences they receive. What is important is that they should never get a sentence which is longer than that which an adult could get under statute or would receive under the tariff system.[211] Finally, sentences should be determinate.[212]

Notes

1. An earlier experiment was juvenile prison hulks, first created in 1823. See W. Branch-Johnson, *The English Prison Hulks*, London, Phillimore, 1970.
2. It is discussed by P. Parsloe, *Juvenile Justice in Britain and the United States*, London, Routledge & Kegan Paul, 1978, pp. 116–17, and I. Pinchbeck and M. Hewitt, *Children In English Society* (vol. II), London, Routledge & Kegan Paul, 1973, pp. 460–5.
3. See J. Carlebach, *Caring For Children In Trouble*, London, Routledge & Kegan Paul, 1970. A Select Committee of the House of Lords in 1847 recommended the establishment of more institutions on Parkhurst lines. But Mary Carpenter's response to this (*Reformatory Schools For the Children of the Perishing and Classes For Juvenile Offenders*, published in 1851 and reissued by Woburn Press 1968) was more influential. See, further, Pinchbeck and Hewitt, *Children In English Society*, op. cit., pp. 469–74.
4. In 1854 and 1857 respectively.
5. Parsloe, *Juvenile Justice*, p. 119.
6. In Carpenter, *Reformatory Schools . . .*, p. 2.
7. Probation of Offenders Act 1907. On the practices of Matthew Davenport Hill, going back to 1841, see Parsloe, *Juvenile Justice*, p. 130.
8. Children Act 1908. The origins of the juvenile court are in the United States (see A. Platt, *The Child Savers*, Chicago, University of Chicago Press, 1977, 2nd ed.) but the earliest proposals in England were made by Benjamin Waugh in *The Gaol Cradle: Who Rocks It?*, London, Isbister, 1880 (4th ed.).

9. Introducing second reading of the Children Bill 1908 in the House of Commons, H.C. vol. 186, col. 1251.
10. Report of the Departmental Committee on *The Care and Treatment of Young Offenders*, London, HMSO, 1927, Cmd. 2831 (Molony Committee).
11. Hansard Parliamentary Debates, 5th series, H.C. vol. 261, col. 1179, 12 February 1932, per Oliver Stanley.
12. Report of the Committee on the *Care of Children*, London, HMSO, 1946, Cmd. 6922.
13. Children Act 1948 s.1 (now Child Care Act 1980 s.2).
14. In the Criminal Justice Act 1948.
15. See Criminal Justice Act 1948 s.17.
16. Report of the Committee on *Children and Young Persons*, London, HMSO, 1960, Cmnd. 1191.
17. Thus adopting the better social work practice of the 1950s. See J. Packman, *The Child's Generation*, Oxford, Blackwell, 1980 (2nd ed.), ch. 4.
18. London, Labour Party, 1964.
19. London, HMSO, 1965, Cmnd. 2742.
20. Longford Group, *Crime – A Challenge To Us All*, p. 16.
21. Ibid., p. 21.
22. White Paper, *The Child, The Family and The Young Offender*, p. 5.
23. Report of the Committee on Children and Young Persons (Scotland), Edinburgh, HMSO, 1964, Cmnd, 2306.
24. For contrasting pictures of juvenile panels see K. Murray, 'The Children's Panel' in F. M. Martin and K. Murray (eds), *Children's Hearings*, Edinburgh, Scottish Academic Press, 1976, p. 57; and P. Brown, 'The Hearing Process' in P. Brown and T. Bloomfield (eds), *Legality and Community*, Aberdeen, Aberdeen People's Press, 1979, p. 13.
25. See W. Cavenagh, 'What Kind of Court or Committee?', *British Journal of Criminology*, 6 (1966), p. 123; B. Downey, *Modern Law Review*, 29 (1966), p. 409; P. Fitzgerald, 'The Child, the White Paper and the Criminal Law', *Criminal Law Review* (1966), p. 607.
26. London, HMSO, 1968, Cmnd. 3601.
27. Ibid., para. 33.
28. Idem.
29. Ibid., para. 11.
30. See, further, A. E. Bottoms, 'On The Decriminalization of English Juvenile Courts' in R. Hood (ed.), *Crime, Criminology and Public Policy*, London, Heinemann, 1974, p. 319, for an analysis of the interests and ideologies involved from Ingleby to the passage of the 1969 Act.
31. The term was first used in *Children In Trouble*, London, HMSO, 1968, Cmnd. 3601, p. 9. A useful discussion of the origins, practice and implications is D. Thorpe, 'Intermediate Treatment' in N. Tutt (ed.), *Alternative Strategies For Coping With Crime*, Oxford, Blackwell, 1978, p. 64.
32. These are listed in s.1(2) of the 1969 Act.
33. As a result of the 1982 Criminal Justice Act. Before this, if criminal proceedings were brought under s.7(7) of the 1969 Act, it was not necessary to establish the need for care or control. See on this D. Thorpe *et al.*, 'The Making of a Delinquent', *Community Care*, 3 May 1979.
34. Minutes of Evidence to Expenditure Committee, 1975. It was a 'splendid means of assisting and treating the delinquent whose problems are mainly of an emotional or intra-familial nature' (para. 6.52).
35. See R. F. Sparks, 'The Depraved Are Not Just Deprived', *New Society*, 24 July 1969, pp. 12-15.
36. See D. Farrington and T. Bennett, 'Police Cautioning of Juveniles in London', *British Journal of Criminology*, 21 (1981), p. 123.
37. P. Cawson and M. Martell, *Children Referred To Secure Units*, DHSS Research Division, Research Report No. 5, 1979, p. 9.
38. S. Millham *et al.*, *Locking Up Children: Secure Provision Within The Child-Care System*, Farnborough, Saxon House, 1978, p. 40.

39.   See, further, A. Rutherford, *A Statute Backfires: The Escalation of Youth Incarceration In England During The 1970s*, London, Justice For Children, 1980.
40.   See *The Guardian*, 11 October 1979. For the Parliamentary announcement see H. C. vol. 973, cols. 1493–5, also reported in *The Times*, 16 November 1979.
41.   The regime is opposed by the Home Office (see *The Times*, 29 November 1979); for an insider's view see 'E529961', 'The Short, Sharp Shock', *The Times*, 13 August 1980.
42.   It is now also made legitimate by the latest legislation (Criminal Justice Act 1982 s.4).
43.   Section 22. See the White Paper, *Young Offenders*, London, HMSO Cmnd. 8045.
44.   See C. W. Hoffman, 'Organization of Family Courts, with Special References to the Juvenile Court' in J. Addams (ed.), *The Child, The Clinic and The Court*, New York, New Republic, 1927, p. 266.
45.   See Platt, *The Child Savers*; E. Schur, *Radical Non-Intervention: Rethinking The Delinquency Problem*, Englewood Cliffs, Prentice-Hall, 1973; and D. Matza, *Delinquency and Drift*, New York, Wiley, 1964, to name only the most significant statements.
46.   See E. M. Lemert, *Social Action and Legal Change*, Chicago, Aldine, 1970, and E. M. Lemert, 'Choice and Change In Juvenile Justice' *British Journal of Law and Society*, 3 (1976), p. 59. On the modest impact of the changes ushered in by *Gault*, see M. Sosin, 'Due Process Mandates and the Juvenile Court', *Journal of Social Services Research*, 1 (1978), pp. 321–43.
47.   One of the earliest indictments is F. Allen, 'Criminal Justice, Legal Values and the Rehabilitative Ideal', *Journal of Criminal Law, Criminology and Police Science*, 50 (1959), pp. 226–32.
48.   A. Morris *et al.*, *Justice For Children*, London, Macmillan, 1980.
49.   L. Taylor *et al.*, *In Whose Best Interests?*, London, Cobden Trust/Mind, 1980.
50.   See examples in S. Cohen (ed.), *Images of Deviance*, Harmondsworth, Penguin, 1971. For an appraisal see J. I. Kitsuse, 'The New Conception of Deviance and Its Critics', in W. Gove (ed.), *The Labeling of Deviance: Evaluating a Perspective*, New York, Wiley, 1980, pp. 273–84.
51.   See H. Becker, *Outsiders*, New York, Free Press, 1963.
52.   See Children and Young Persons Act 1969 s.1(2)(c), (d), (e).
53.   There are good examples in Taylor *et al.*, *In Whose Best Interests?*, p. 27. See also A. Sutton, 'Science In Court' in M. King (ed.), *Childhood, Welfare and Justice*, London, Batsford, 1981, p. 45.
54.   J. Lofland, *Deviance and Identity*, Englewood Cliffs, N.J., Prentice-Hall, 1969, p. 150.
55.   See B. E. F. Knell, 'Capital Punishment', *British Journal of Delinquency*, 5 (1965), p. 198, on death sentences. See also Platt, *The Child Savers*, Appendix, p. 193.
56.   Platt, ibid., p. 176.
57.   I. Rothman, *Conscience and Convenience*, Boston, Little, Brown, 1980.
58.   Ibid., p. 6.
59.   Platt, *The Child Savers*, p. xx (Introduction to 2nd ed.).
60.   But see the criticism in D. H. Thorpe *et al.*, *Out of Care: The Community Support of Juvenile Offenders*, London, Allen & Unwin, 1980, pp. 35–8.
61.   There are a number of other American studies, the conclusions of which are broadly similar to Platt's. See R. Mennel, *Thorns and Thistles: Juvenile Delinquency in the United States 1825-1940*, Hanover, New Hampshire, University Press of New England, 1973; S. L. Schlossman, *Love and the American Delinquent: The Theory and Practice of 'Progressive' Juvenile Justice*, Chicago, University of Chicago Press, 1977, the two best examples.
62.   See D. Katkin, 'Children and The Justice Process: Reality and Rhetoric', in D. Gottlieb (ed.), *Children's Liberation*, Englewood Cliffs, N.J., Prentice-Hall, 1973, pp. 53, 56–8.
63.   See W. S. Holdsworth, *A History of English Law*, London, Methuen, vol. III, (1923), (3rd ed.), p. 372 and vol IX, (1926), p. 140.
64.   See E. Ryerson, *The Best-Laid Plans: America's Juvenile Court Experiment*, New York, Hill & Wang, 1978, ch. 1.

65. See Schlossman, *Care and the American Delinquent. . .,* p. 13; J. M. Hawes, *Children In Urban Society: Juvenile Delinquency In Nineteenth Century America,* New York, Oxford University Press, 1971, pp. 46–7.
66. 'The Juvenile Court: its Legal Aspects', *Annals of the American Academy of Political and Social Science,* XXXVI, (1910), p. 49.
67. Ryerson, *The Best-Laid Plans. . .,* p. 65.
68. 213 pa. 48; 62A. 198 (1905).
69. See A. V. Dicey, *Introduction To The Study of The Constitution,* London, Macmillan, 1902 (6th ed.), and R. A. Cosgrove, *The Rule of Law,* Chapel Hill, University of North Carolina Press, 1980. See also D. Sugarman, *Modern Law Review,* **46** (1983).
70. G. Smith, 'Discretionary Decision-Making in Social Work', in M. Adler and S. Asquith (eds), *Discretion and Welfare,* London, Heinemann, 1981.
71. See M. Baxter, *The Meaning of Disability,* London, Heinemann, 1976. See also K. Curnock and P. Hardiker, *Towards Practice Theory,* London, Routledge & Kegan Paul, 1979.
72. H. Giller and A. Morris, *Care and Discretion: Social Workers' Decisions With Delinquents,* London, Burnett, 1981.
73. C. Lasch, *Haven In A Heartless World,* New York, Basic Books, 1977.
74. J. Donzelot, *The Policing of Families,* New York, Random House, 1979.
75. C. Lasch, 'Life In The Therapeutic State', *New York Review of Books,* XXVII, no. 16. 12 June 1980, p. 24, at p. 30.
76. London, HMSO, 1968, Cmnd. 3601, para. 33.
77. Lord Kilbrandon, 'Children In Trouble', *British Journal of Criminology,* 6 (1966), pp. 112, 115.
78. Cf. E. M. Schur, *The Politics of Deviance,* Englewood Cliffs, N.J., Prentice-Hall, 1980, p. 35. See also W. Gaylin *et al., Doing Good, The Limits of Benevolence,* New York, Pantheon, 1978.
79. London, HMSO, 1968, Cmnd. 3601, para. 13.
80. See. P. Priestley *et al., Justice For Juveniles,* London, Routledge & Kegan Paul, 1977; H. Parker *et al., Receiving Juvenile Justice,* Oxford, Blackwell, 1981.
81. See A. Cicourel, *The Social Organization of Juvenile Justice,* London, Heinemann, 1976.
82. See Giller and Morris, *Care and Discretion.* See also Giller and Morris, 'Supervision Orders: The Routinization of Treatment', *Howard Journal of Penal Reform,* **17** (1978), pp. 149–59.
83. See C. Stoll, 'Images of Man and Social Control', *Social Forces,* **47** (1968), p. 119.
84. See Giller and Morris, *Care And Discretion,* p. 112.
85. A. Morris, 'Juvenile Justice – Where Next?', *Howard Journal of Penal Reform,* 15 (1976), pp. 26, 32.
86. A. Morris and M. McIsaac, *Juvenile Justice?,* London, Heinemann, 1978, p. 129.
87. See F. M. Martin, S. J. Fox and K. Murray, *Children Out of Court,* Edinburgh, Scottish Academic Press, 1981.
88. Ibid.
89. See T. Bloomfield, 'Delinquency and Social Control: The Foundations of The Scottish System' in P. D. Brown and T. Bloomfield (eds), *Legality and Community: The Politics of Juvenile Justice in Scotland,* Aberdeen, Aberdeen People's Press, 1979, p. 44 at p. 68.
90. R. Emerson, *Judging Delinquents,* Chicago, Aldine, 1969.
91. See J. L. Schultz and F. Cohen, 'Isolationism in Juvenile Court Jurisprudence' in M. Rosenheim (ed.), *Pursuing Justice For The Child,* Chicago, University of Chicago Press, 1976, pp. 20, 35.
92. See M. Dean, 'Playing Hookey is Legal', *Guardian,* 31 July 1979.
93. Children and Young Persons Act 1969 s.1(2)(e).
94. R. White, *Absent With Cause,* London, Routledge & Kegan Paul, 1980.
95. See M. Rutter, *Fifteen Thousand Hours,* London, Open Books, 1979.
96. P. Schrag and D. Divoky, *The Myth of The Hyperactive Child,* New York, Dell, 1975, p. 221.

97. See P. Conrad, 'The Discovery of Hyperkinesis: Notes on the Medicalization of Deviant Behaviour', *Social Problems,* **23** (1975), p. 12.
98. See S. Box, 'Where Have All The Naughty Children Gone?' in National Deviancy Conference (ed.), *Permissiveness And Control,* London, Macmillan, 1980, p. 96.
99. C. Wright Mills, *The Sociological Imagination,* London, Oxford University Press, 1959.
100. '*Parens Patriae* and Vagueness in the Juvenile Court', *Yale Law Journal,* **82** (1973), p. 745.
101. For example, in *Gesicki* v *Oswald* 336 F. Supp 371 (1971), affirmed summarily 406 U.S. 913 (1972).
102. 416 U.S. 918 (1974).
103. See R. Greene and B. Esselstyn, 'The Beyond-Control Girl', *Juvenile Justice,* **23** (1972), p. 13.
104. A useful discussion is Anne Campbell, *Girl Delinquents,* Oxford, Blackwell, 1981, pp. 203 *et seq.* See also D. May, 'Delinquent Girls Before The Courts', *Medicine, Science and the Law,* **17** (1977), p. 203.
105. Institute of Judicial Administration and ABA, *Juvenile Justice Standards Project,* Cambridge, Mass., Ballinger, 1977, vol. 24, p. 37.
106. R. Page and G. Clark, *Who Cares?: Young People In Care Speak Out,* London, National Children's Bureau, 1977.
107. A recent example is the Black Report (Report of the Children and Young Persons Group), Belfast, HMSO, 1979, a justice model with pronounced welfare considerations, such as the indeterminate sentence.
108. See also A. Morris *et al., Justice For Children,* London, Macmillan, 1980, p. 34. See also D. May, 'Delinquency Control and The Treatment Model', *British Journal of Criminology,* **11** (1971), p. 359.
109. Cf. D. Matza, *Delinquency and Drift,* New York, Wiley, 1964. See also R. W. Balch, 'The Medical Model of Delinquency', *Crime and Delinquency,* (1975), p. 116.
110. See T. Hirschi, *Causes of Delinquency,* Berkeley, University of California Press, 1969, and H. Sandhu, *Juvenile Delinquency: Causes, Control and Prevention,* New York, McGraw Hill, 1977.
111. D. West and D. Farrington, *Who Becomes Delinquent?,* London, Heinemann, 1973, p. 190. Cf. M. Power *et al.,* 'Delinquency and The Family', *British Journal of Social Work,* 4 (1974), p. 13.
112. H. Wilson, 'Parental Supervision: A Neglected Aspect of Delinquency', *British Journal of Criminology,* **20** (1980), p. 203.
113. See S. Hall *et al., Policing The Crisis,* London, Macmillan, 1978, p. 38; L. Wilkins, *Social Deviance,* London, Tavistock, 1964; J. Young, *The Drugtakers,* London, MacGibbon & Kee, 1971.
114. See J. S. Wallerstein and C. L. Wyle, 'Our Law-abiding Lawbreakers', *National Probation* (March–April 1947), p. 107; L. T. Empey and M. L. Erickson, 'Hidden Delinquency and Social Status', *Social Forces,* **44** (1966), p. 546.
115. See The USA President's Commission on *Law Enforcement and Administration of Justice,* 1967, Field Surveys I, II and III.
116. R. Hood and R. Sparks, *Key Issues In Criminology,* London, Weidenfeld & Nicolson, 1970, p. 47.
117. Ibid., p. 51.
118. A. Morris *et al., Justice For Children,* p. 39.
119. N. Tutt, 'Treatment Under Attack' in B. Gillham (ed.), *Problem Behaviour In The Secondary School,* London, Croom Helm, 1981, p. 87.
120. Ibid., p. 90.
121. D. A. Romig, *Justice For Our Children,* Lexington, Mass., Lexington Books, 1978.
122. D. B. Cornish and R. V. G. Clarke, *Residential Treatment and its Effects on Delinquency,* London, HMSO (Home Office Research Study No. 32), 1975.
123. These statistics are taken from DHSS, *Offending By Young People: A Survey of Recent Trends,* London, DHSS, 1981, section 5.

124. Cornish and Clarke, *Residential Treatment*, p. 19.
125. See N. Walker, *Punishment, Danger and Stigma*, Oxford, Blackwell, 1980, p. 63.
126. See A. Stone, 'Overview: The Right To Treatment', *American Journal of Psychiatry*, 132 (1975), p. 1125.
127. P. Hardiker, 'Social Work Ideologies in The Probation Service', *British Journal of Social Work*, 7 (1977), pp. 131, 133.
128. H. Giller and A. Morris, *Care And Discretion: Social Workers' Decisions with Delinquents*, London, Burnett, 1981.
129. See A. Morris and H. Giller, 'The Juvenile Court — The Client's Perspective', *Criminal Law Review*, (1977), p. 198.
130. R. Page and G. A. Clark (eds), *Who Cares?: Young People In Care Speak Out*, London, National Children's Bureau, 1977, pp. 16–18.
131. See M. Dean, 'Juveniles "Gaoled" Without Legal Aid', *The Guardian*, 17 February 1982.
132. H. Parker, M. Casburn and D. Turnbull, *Receiving Juvenile Justice*, Oxford, Blackwell, 1981, p. 84 (24 per cent refusals in Huyton, 4 per cent in Liverpool: nationally the refusal rate is about 8 per cent).
133. Parker *et al.* call it 'Countryside'. The real identity was disclosed by R. Rohrer in the *New Statesman*, 3 July 1981.
134. H. L. A. Hart, *Punishment and Responsibility*, Oxford, Clarendon Press, 1968.
135. A doctrine which flourished in the Soviet Union in Stalin's time.
136. L. R. Anderson, *Human Toxicology*, 1982, notes 117 deaths in Britain in the period 1979–81 as attributable to glue-sniffing (for a comparison, 1,800 persons under nineteen were killed in road accidents in 1978).
137. See most recently Timothy Raison, H.C. vol. 6, cols 298–9 (Written Answers, 18 June 1981).
138. There is no record of the number of glue-sniffing-connected prosecutions. See Hansard H.C. vol. 14, col. 860 (9 December 1981) by Solicitor-General For Scotland.
139. In the Misuse of Drugs Act 1971.
140. N. Dorn, 'The Conservatism of the Cannabis Debate' in National Deviancy Conference (ed.), *Permissiveness and Control*, London, Macmillan, 1980, pp. 44, 46.
141. See P. Lerman, *Community Treatment and Social Control*, Chicago, University of Chicago Press, 1975.
142. See Farrington and Bennett, 'Police Cautioning of Juveniles in London'; DHSS *Offending By Young People*; and J. Ditchfield, *Police Cautioning In England and Wales*, London, HMSO (Home Office Research Unit Study No. 37), 1976.
143. *Young Offenders — A Strategy For The Future*, Chichester, Barry Rose, 1981.
144. Giller and Morris, *Care and Discretion . . .*, p. 27.
145. Recent evidence of biased decision-making are S. F. Landau, 'Juveniles and the Police', *British Journal of Criminology*, 21 (1981), p. 27 (police treat blacks more harshly), and T. Bennett, 'The Social Distribution of Criminal Labels', *British Journal of Criminology*, 19 (1979), p. 134 (police discrimination against working class).
146. See H. Parker *et al.*, 'The Production of Punitive Juvenile Justice', *British Journal of Criminology*, 20 (1980), p. 236.
147. 'Short, Sharp Shocks' and the measures in the Criminal Justice Act 1982 exemplify this.
148. The phrase is Leon Brittan's. See 'An Address' in *Getting On With Intermediate Treatment*, London, DHSS, 1979. See also N. Tutt, 'A Decade of Policy', *British Journal of Criminology*, 21 (1981), p. 246.
149. Cf. D. Fogel, *We Are The Living Proof: The Justice Model of Corrections*, Cincinatti, Anderson, 1976.
150. [1978] 1 All E.R. 180.
151. [1977] 3 All E.R. 961.
152. D. Matza, *Delinquency and Drift*, New York, Wiley, 1964, p. 115.
153. R. Anderson, *Representation In The Juvenile Court*, London, Routledge & Kegan Paul, 1978, p. 25.

154. Report of Inter-Departmental Committee on *The Business of Criminal Courts,* London, HMSO Cmnd, 1289 (1962).

155. P. Priestley *et al., Justice for Juveniles,* London, Routledge & Kegan Paul, 1977.

156. Anderson, op. cit., p. 16.

157. A. Morris, *Justice For Children,* London, Macmillan, 1980, p. 39.

158. Anderson, op. cit., pp. 28–9.

159. See M. Davies, 'Social Inquiry For The Courts', *British Journal of Criminology,* 14 (1974), p. 18.

160. J. Thorpe, *Social Enquiry Reports — A Survey,* London, HMSO (Home Office Research Study No. 48) (1979).

161. Anderson, op. cit., Table A II.4, p. 66.

162. See H. Parker *et al., Receiving Juvenile Justice,* Oxford, Blackwell, 1981.

163. A. Morris and H. Giller, 'The Juvenile Court — The Client's Perspective', *Criminal Law Review* (1977), p. 198.

164. See J. Carlin *et al.,* 'Legal Respresentation and Class Justice', *UCLA Law Review,* 12 (1965), p. 381.

165. Morris and Giller, 'The Juvenile Court. . .', p. 202.

166. Anderson, *Representation in the Juvenile Court,* ch. 4.

167. The Benson Report on Legal Services, London, HMSO Cmnd. 7648 (1979), vol. 1, 14.22–14.26.

168. It has now been promised. See 'Legal Aid for Parents At Last', *LAG Bulletin* (August 1982), pp. 1–2.

169. See F. Allen, *The Borderland of Criminal Justice,* Chicago, University of Chicago Press, 1964, p. 19.

170. P. Carlen, *Magistrates' Justice,* London, Martin Robertson, 1976, pp. 78–9.

171. Expenditure Committee Eleventh Report (1975), *The Children and Young Persons Act 1969,* London, HMSO.

172. See S. Fox, 'Philosophy and The Principle of Punishment In the Juvenile Court', *Family Law Quarterly,* 8 (1974), pp. 373, 377. See also T. D. Campbell, 'Punishment In Juvenile Justice', *British Journal of Law and Society,* 4 (1977), p. 74.

173. Institute of Judicial Administration and American Bar Association Juvenile Standards Project, *Standards for Juvenile Justice: A Summary and Analysis,* Cambridge, Mass., Ballinger, 1977.

174. A. Morris, 'Revolution in The Juvenile Court: The Juvenile Justice Standards Project', *Criminal Law Review,* (1978), p. 529.

175. 387 U.S.1.

176. See T. Sellin and M. Wolfgang, *The Measure of Delinquency,* New York, Wiley, 1964; C. Card, 'Retributive Penal Liability', *American Philosophical Quarterly,* Monograph no. 7 (1973); A. von Hirsch, *Doing Justice,* New York, Hill & Wang, 1976.

177. See Morris, 'Revolution in The Juvenile Court. . .', pp. 530–1.

178. Morris, *Justice For Children,* p. 72.

179. Expenditure Committee Eleventh Report (1975), *The Children and Young Persons Act 1969,* London, HMSO.

180. See D. Matza, *Becoming Deviant,* Englewood Cliffs, N.J., Prentice-Hall, 1969.

181. A. Sutton, 'Science in Court' in M. King (ed.), *Childhood, Welfare and Justice,* London, Batsford, 1981, pp. 64–5.

182. Ibid., p. 66.

183. This has been referred to as 'silting up'. See B. Davies *et al.,* 'The "Silting Up" of Unadjustable Resources and Planning of Personal Social Services', *Policy and Politics,* 1 (1973), p. 341.

184. See R. Parker, *Caring For Separated Children,* London, Macmillan, 1980, p. 107.

185. Cf. S. Cohen's description of prisons as 'human warehouses'.

186 See M. Fitzgerald and J. Sim, *British Prisons,* Oxford, Blackwell, 1981, (2nd ed.).

187. See Criminal Justice Act 1982 s.22.

188. See S. Millham *et al., After Grace–Teeth,* London, Human Context Books, Chaucer Press, 1975.

189. See L. Taylor *et al.*, *In Whose Best Interests?*, London, Cobden Trust/Mind, 1980, p. 50.
190. Ibid., p. 52.
191. Cornish and Clarke, *Residential Treatment. . .*, op. cit., p. 32.
192. See I. Crow, *The Detention Centre Experiment*, London, NACRO, 1979.
193. See H. Land, 'Detention Centres: The Experiment That Could Not Fail' in P. Hall *et al.*, *Change, Choice and Conflict In Social Policy*, London, Heinemann, 1975, p. 317 at p. 368. See also V. Choppen, 'The Origins of The Philosophy of Detention Centres', *British Journal of Criminology*, **10** (1970), p. 163. who refers to a 'strand of varied ideas'.
194. On 'short, sharp shocks' see M. D. A. Freeman, ' "Short, Sharp Shocks" — A Comment', *New Law Journal*, **130** (1980), p. 28, and N. Tutt, *Short, Sharp Shocks*, London, Justice For Children, 1980.
195. See Table 3.1.
196. Idem.
197. NACRO Briefing, *Juveniles In Custody*, London, NACRO, 1982.
198. *Prison Statistics 1977*, London, HMSO, 1978, p. 164.
199. D. H. Thorpe *et al.*, *Out of Care: The Community Support of Juvenile Offenders*, London, Allen & Unwin, 1980, p. 29.
200. *The Magistrate*, December 1975, p. 174.
201. See E. Schur, *Radical Non-Intervention: Rethinking The Delinquency Problem*, Englewood Cliffs, N.J., Prentice-Hall, 1973, p. 155.
202. See E. Lemert, *Human Deviance, Social Problems and Social Control*, Englewood Cliffs, N.J., Prentice-Hall, 1967.
203. See. E. Schur, *Crimes Without Victims*, Englewood Cliffs, N.J., Prentice-Hall, 1965.
204. Described by Parker *et al.* as a 'push-in' tendency: see their *Receiving Juvenile Justice*, pp. 36–8.
205. The name does not matter. I am troubled by the concept.
206. See *Re D* [1977] 3 All E.R. 481. The most recent judicial discussion of the overlap is Dunn L.J. in *Re E*, *The Times*, 25 January 1983.
207. See D. Matza, *Delinquency and Drift*, New York, Wiley, 1964, chs. 4 and 5.
208. 387 U.S. 1.
209. See Criminal Justice Act 1948 s.17.
210. See F. H. Bradley, *Ethical Studies*, Oxford, Clarendon Press, 1927. See also H. L. A. Hart, 'The Ascription of Responsibility and Rights' in A. Flew (ed.), *Logic and Language*, vol. 1, Oxford, Oxford University Press, 1951, p. 145.
211. On the tariff system see D. A. Thomas, *Principles of Sentencing*, London, Heinemann, 1979 (3rd ed.), part II.
212. The new youth custody sentence, introduced by the Criminal Justice Act 1982, is for that alone a step in the right direction.

4 CHILDREN WHO ARE WRONGED: THE PROBLEM OF ABUSE AND NEGLECT

In the eyes of the media and the general public child abuse and neglect are the examples *par excellence* of maltreatment of children. Hardly a day passes without a new item chronicling a case. Reports of enquiries follow thick and fast upon criminal trials and care proceedings. Parents are pilloried, government bodies and committed individuals search out ways of preventing tragedies and improving management techniques. But twenty years of concentrated effort, worldwide and inter-disciplinary, have left us no nearer a solution than we were when the problem was discovered. This, however, begs the question: for what is the problem? Much existing literature treats child abuse and neglect unproblematically. It has been convenient to construct a simple picture of a deviant act committed by an evil person, usually a parent, upon a helpless victim and to assume that the work of those who combat child abuse is value-free and absolutely altruistic.

This chapter takes a critical look at child abuse and neglect. It queries what we mean by abuse and by neglect. It raises questions about the decision-making process. How is behaviour classified? Are officials, medical personnel, police, social workers 'neutral observers of unambiguous events' or are they rather 'active agents'?[1] Is the child batterer the latest in a series of 'folk devils' to have generated a 'moral panic'?[2] Are the responses of control agencies justified or do they constitute an over-reaction? Does the complex system erected to manage child abuse and neglect protect children or does it batter them in a more insidious way than brutal parents? Does it work? Can anything work?[3] Is there a case for non-intervention and, if so, in what circumstances? This chapter attempts to answer these questions. It makes the assumption that an interpretation of a problem will govern or at least control the way it is approached. Neither of the two dominant understandings of child abuse and neglect makes any attempt to explain the phenomenon in terms of the status of the child in contemporary culture. Yet, it will be argued, it becomes easier to understand the wrongs perpetrated against children in terms of a denial of their full personality and integrity: in short, by denying them rights.

Children's rights or their absence, are very much a key to the understanding of abuse and neglect. Children without defined rights are by that very fact vulnerable.

It should, however, be added that when we talk of rights in the abuse and neglect setting we are talking about protection rather than autonomy. When we say of a child that he has the 'right' not to be beaten we are claiming on his behalf certain elementary protection. We are concerned about his welfare. If we accorded children greater recognition of their rights, there would be less abuse and neglect. It is then in the current context that rights in the sense of protection assume overwhelming importance.

The Problem of Child Abuse

Child abuse has always been with us but its recognition as a social problem dates from the 1960s.[4] In the past society does not appear to have been particularly troubled by its maltreatment of children. When Lloyd de Mause described the history of childhood as a 'nightmare from which we have only recently begun to awake',[5] he was particularly mindful of the universality of cruelty to children. The student of English society needs to look no further than classics of Victorian literature, *Oliver Twist, The Water Babies, Tom Brown's Schooldays, The Way Of All Flesh* or *Jane Eyre,* to observe the ways in which children were abused in an earlier century. The poems of William Blake themselves constitute a revealing insight, with the suffering of children being idealised.[6] Cruelty to domestic animals became a criminal offence in England more than sixty years before equivalent treatment of children.[7] In New York in 1873, where the situation was similar, an eight-year-old child, Mary Ellen Wilson, was removed from persons to whom she had been indentured by the Society for the Prevention of Cruelty to Animals on the ground that she was a member of the animal kingdom so that her case fell within the laws against animal cruelty.[8] In *The Classic Slum,* Roberts recalls Salford before the First World War:

> no-one who spent his childhood in the slums during those years will easily forget the regular and often brutal assaults on some children . . . . Among fathers administering such punishments were men who had received forty-eight strokes of the birch — at the local prison for small misdemeanours. . .[9]

Violence against children is firmly rooted in our history and culture.

But if physical abuse of children has always existed, why is its recognition as a social problem[10] such a relatively recent phenomenon? An investigation of this need go no further than the gatekeepers, the medical profession. In the past doctors were unaware of the possibility of abuse as a diagnosis.[11] In the twentieth century the mechanics of diagnosis have been improved by scientific progress, notably by the development of X-ray techniques.[12] The decision to X-ray, however, depends upon the doctor's definition of the situation. It requires him initially to doubt the parents' word. The medical profession was for long reluctant to believe that parents could inflict injuries on their children. A further impeding factor is enmeshed in the organisational ethics of the medical profession: the norm of confidentiality shielded the parents from exposure for a long time. Further, the medical profession was understandably reluctant to become involved in a criminal process over which they had no control and which they saw as of no value.

It was the radiologists who 'discovered' child abuse.[13] As a marginal medical group they had much to gain. As Freidson has written, it is 'one of the greatest ambitions of the physician . . . to discover or describe a "new" disease or syndrome.'[14] Of the barriers analysed only the disadvantages of getting involved with the criminal process affected them. But the potential for increased prestige, role expansion and coalition formation with psychodynamic psychiatry and paediatrics more than compensated for this. Further, as Pfohl puts it in an authoritative article

> the discovery of abuse as a new 'illness' reduced drastically the intra-organizational constraints on doctors' 'seeing' abuse . . . Problems associated with perceiving parents as patients whose confidentiality must be protected were reconstructed by typifying them as patients who needed help . . . . The maintenance of professional autonomy was assured by pairing deviance with sickness.[15]

The fact that child abuse was 'discovered' by the medical profession has left an important legacy. As Freidson has noted: 'medical definitions of deviance have come to be adopted even where there is no reliable evidence that biophysical variables "cause" the deviance or that medical treatment is any more efficacious than any other kind of management.'[16] People who work according to the medical ideology typically assume that it is better to impute disease than risk overlooking it, for they believe that the work they do is for the good of the person whom they treat.[17] The medical model assumes the problem is an individual one: treatment of the parent is thus seen to be the most reasonable intervention. This does not stop the system meting out 'punishment in the guise of help',[18] a practice which is a common feature of the 'therapeutic state'.[19] Undoubtedly legal responses to child abuse have been 'triggered'[20] by medicalisation of the problem. This is hardly surprising for lawyers themselves in the twentieth century have become accustomed to working within a model of rehabilitation (see Chapter 3).[21] But the medical model has been accepted by the community generally: indeed, this is the case also with the majority of known abusers.[22] Not surprisingly they prefer to be 'sick' deviants,[23] to criminal ones. To make people legitimately sick is implicit in the doctor's role.

The radiologists 'discovered' child abuse but it was other medical men who brought it to the attention of the general public. Paediatricians were the 'moral entrepreneurs'.[24] It was they who defined the problem and attempted an explanation. In doing so they put limits on the phenomenon which were clearer than perhaps was indicated by common-sense experience.[25] Paediatricians, unlike radiologists, had 'attained valued organizational status prior to the discovery' but they were again 'sliding toward the margins of the profession.'[26] The discovery of the battered baby provided them with a justification for attracting more resources and an enhanced status.

It was the eminent paediatrician, Dr Henry Kempe, whose work first attracted major attention to the phenomenon of child abuse. In 1962 he published an article on the clinical, radiological and psychiatric manifestations of serious injuries in children inflicted by parents and other caretakers. He coined the phrase 'battered baby syndrome' to refer to the phenomenon. This term remained in usage for a decade. Kempe attributed parental attacks on children primarily to psychiatric factors. The parents, he noted, were often of 'low intelligence'. They were 'immature, impulsive, self-centred, hyper-sensitive and quick to react with poorly controlled aggression.' He pointed also to alcoholism, sexual promiscuity, unstable marriages and minor criminal activities as common characteristics.[27] In Britain the problem was first 'discovered' by two orthopaedic surgeons, Griffiths and Moynihan, in 1963 in the form of the battered baby syndrome.[28] But it was paediatricians and forensic pathologists[29] who were largely responsible for propagating information about the problem.

Since violence against children was discovered by the medical profession it is not surprising that their interpretation of its causes and their prescription of remedies should have come to dominate thinking. The psychopathological model, with its emphasis on the individual and on sickness, has taken some shifting and has not been displaced totally even today. References to a 'syndrome'; common in the early years, are, however, no longer current. It is recognised that such an analysis, with an implication of a unitary causal process, is misleading. The term 'battered babies' was soon to give way to 'battered' and then 'abused' children. By the 1970s these notions in their turn had been replaced, in Britain at least, by the term 'non-accidental injury', usually abbreviated to NAI.[30] The expression is less emotive and also more accurate for abuse of children is more pervasive that what is generally understood by 'battering'.

An age-old problem thus required entrepreneurship by a professional interest group to legitimate and publicise it. Yet little more than twenty years after its 'discovery' child abuse is seen by the general public as the grossest of wrongs committed against children, though neglect is not seen in quite this light. Child abusers are seen as monsters.[31] We must not underestimate child abuse. Although we do not know with any certainty how widespread it is (much, of course, depends upon how it is defined), we know it is a problem of great seriousness. Children are maimed, some are even killed by parents. We must, however, not lose a sense of perspective. There are other evils perpetrated against children. More children are injured and killed as a result of accidents than acts of violence. The Court report noted that in 1972, 141,000 children were admitted to hospital as a result of accidents and 1,800 of these children died.[32] A very large percentage of these accidents are preventable. Children suffer (abuse and more generally) as a result of premature birth: we could successfully defeat the prematurity problem but we will not do so until we become more concerned and order our priorities accordingly.[33] The medical know-how exists: what is lacking is the resolve and the commitment of required resources. Then there is lead paint poisoning.[34] There is racial discrimination. There are inadequate schools. There is youth unemployment. There is child poverty and its correlates. But we do not get excited about these evils in quite the way that we do when confronted with a particularly brutal example of parental violence.

It is not difficult to understand why. The pinpointing of parental violence as the evil enables us to concentrate on 'them' rather than us. It results in an excessive concentration on one group of families.[35] It is comforting for us to view the child abusers as a race apart. The medical model reinforces the separation for it requires that abusing parents be studied in terms of what is 'wrong' with them.[36] And it requires exceptionalist solutions, for their 'problems are unusual, even unique, they are exceptions to the rule, they occur as a result of individual defect . . . and must be remedied by means that are particular and . . . tailored to the individual case.'[37] Zigler believes, and I find his arguments most persuasive, that there is something 'inherently erroneous in a classification system based on overt behaviour that would essentially divide parents into two groups, those who abuse their children and those who do not.' Instead, he prefers to conceptualise child abuse as a 'continuum on which everyone can be placed.'[38] But he admits that the 'continuum approach is threatening because within it the child abuser is viewed as very much like the majority of parents who have never been reported for child abuse.'[39] People usually try to distance themselves from those whom they consider to be deviant. The continuum approach to child abuse, Zigler notes elsewhere, 'offers a valuable perspective because it implies that, depending on the particular familial and environmental circumstances, all parents are capable of abusing their children.'[40] Were such a perspective accepted, we could expect greater empathy towards abusers. But it is not. The result is that abusers are seen as 'freaks'. They are identifiable targets upon which to vent anger. They are victims (though they may not be seen as such) to be blamed.[41] At the same time they enable us to divert our attention from lead paint poisoning or child poverty, matters about which we could do things if we were prepared to reconsider priorities and commit resources. Without in any way wishing to underestimate the gravity of child abuse, this is the context in which it must be seen.

What is Child Abuse?

Child abuse has been variously defined and there is no widely accepted definition. There is found in the literature narrow definitions which emphasise serious physical abuse (in Kempe's article — see n. 27 — for example, or in the American Bar Association's Standards relating to Abuse and Neglect)[42] ; broader definitions emphasising maltreatment (for example, in Fontana)[43] and broader definitions still, such as David Gil's which include any interference with the optimal development of children[44] and Eli Newberger's which sees child abuse as 'an illness with or without inflicted injury, stemming from situations in his home setting which threaten a child's survival.'[45] Arguments surrounding definitions of child abuse reflect ideological differences and may prove intractable.[46] Much depends on who is doing the defining and for what purpose. A definition for a reporting law, such as exists in each of the United States of America, or for management guidance (registers in this country) has very different functions from one developed for operational research. The definition selected may have important implications for civil liberties as it may for deciding how resources are to be distributed or who is entitled to services. Lawyers are likely to define abuse rather differently from doctors or social workers. Lawyers may wish to intervene only in serious cases[47] whereas doctors or welfare agencies may be prepared to intrude where there is any risk, to 'prevent an abusive case becoming a terminal' one.[48] Lawyers are likely to scrutinise the abuser's mental state to see what his intentions were: those who work within the psychological sciences may not think the abuser's mental state is quite so significant. It may matter less to them than to lawyers that the injury has resulted from an accident for they are likely to suppose that similar family dynamics are involved in both abuse and an accidental event.[49]

Accidents pose a problem for the would-be definer of child abuse. It is not always easy to distinguish intentional behaviour from that which is accidental. Some children suffer injury when placed in a situation in which 'accidental' injury occurs. Bourne and Newberger cite the following example:[50]

> a one-year-old child ingested a small quantity of bleach from a bottle that the parents had left on the kitchen floor. The youngster was treated at a Children's Hospital and released after the staff warned the family of the safety hazards in the home. Less than a month later, the child was again admitted to the hospital for ingestion of liquid furniture polish 'accidentally' left in the living room.

The doctor then filed a neglect report. As the authors note: 'the distinction between accidental and non-accidental injury has no significance with regard to the child's future safety when the accident is part of a pattern of neglect.'

Both the terms 'child abuse' and 'accident' are social constructions: they are not distinct categories. They are labels created by official agencies (doctors, hospital personnel, the police, social workers, coroners) who have the authority to decide whether a specific act or omission shall be designated as a case of deviance. The agent's moral beliefs and stereotypic definitions influence his definitions of, and reactions to, people's behaviour. Certain individuals are more likely to be defined abusers than others.

A number of situational factors,[51] within both the medical personnel and others concerned with abuse and the defined parents, assist this process. First, there is the possibility of a wide social distance between the agents and the parents. This facilitates the labelling and nullifies the potentiality of any organised resistance to the label by the deviant group.[52] The label is less likely to be applied if the doctor, for example, and the suspected abuser share similar socio-economic status and ethnic backgrounds. It is also true that the more serious the behavioural act in question, the less likely it is that social class or ethnic grouping will influence the process. But, otherwise, the injuries found in the children of higher status families are more likely to attract the classification of being 'accidents.'[53] Furthermore, once the label of 'abuser' has been affixed, social distance between the typer and the person typed in the transaction increases.

Secondly, once the label of 'child abuser' has been attached it is highly adhesive and accordingly difficult to remove. The result is that even 'innocent' behaviour of a parent, previously found to have abused a child, may attract attention and suspicion. Facts get interpreted selectively to confirm stereotype models.

Thirdly, there is, because of the publicity involved in scandals such as the Maria Colwell affair,[54] an increase in reported child abuse. But, because of the way the media report child abuse, stereotypes exist in the public's mind as to who the abusers are. Allegations that are made often conform to these stereotypes and thus tend to concern members of the lowest strata of society.

There is a fourth processive category. Hospital doctors are now cognisant with the symptoms of child abuse. Indeed, they may be more likely to be aware of the problem and to act upon their recognition than the general practitioner, particularly the one who services a predominantly middle-class clientele and who sees abuse more rarely anyway. But it is the poor who are more likely to take their child to a hospital casualty department and the more affluent who will see the family doctor as the man to attend to their child's 'accident'. The poor are accordingly more likely to reveal abuse.[55] Their abuse is not only more expected but also more visible. However, if the poor are more likely to reveal abuse and have abuse officially perceived, then characteristics become identified with the abuse 'syndrome' that are over-represented in the poor population. Abusers are found to be socially isolated, or one-parent families, or unemployed, or the children are found to have been born prematurely or the products of unwanted pregnancies. This has a spiralling effect, for families with these characteristics are automatically perceived to be 'at risk'. A family with these characteristics is far more likely to find an injured child perceived as having been deliberately traumatised than classified as 'accidentally' hurt.

Finally, the fact that child abuse is difficult to diagnose cannot be ignored. It means inevitably that much depends on the diagnostician's discretion. What the doctor knows about the family plays a not inconsiderable part in determining which side of the line the condition falls: 'abuse' or 'accident'. The decision as to whether a particular behavioural act is an accident or an abusive incident is thus far from value-free.[56]

Distinguishing abuse and accidents is one of the most basic of definitional problems. Differentiating physical chastisement from abusive behaviour has proved equally intractable. To some they cannot be distinguished: all forms of physical aggression against children constitute abuse. In the eyes of others, the difference is marked in terms of the perpetrator's motivation.

The Problem of Corporal Punishment

It was one of the paradoxes of current thought, policy and practice relating to children that battering children should cause horror and almost total condemnation whilst corporal punishment of children should remain socially sanctioned. The link between abuse and physical chastisement was not forged in the early literature on abuse but now few authorities writing on child abuse do not acknowledge a connection.[57] Certainly, it is a significant fact that in cultures where physical punishment of children is not sanctioned (these are admittedly few in number),[58] child abuse is not thought to take place and certainly does not take place on anything like the scale which we have experienced in Britain.

In Britain and much of the English-speaking world there is an institutional dimension to corporal punishment. The use in a school setting of a cane (in England), a tawse (in Scotland) or a paddle (in the United States) is not uncommon. Corporal punishment is also practised in children's homes.[60] It would be difficult not to be struck by the irony in this for some of the victims of such institutional discipline have been removed from their homes because of physical abuse upon them by their parents. Corporal punishment is often applied to the very young (Maurer quotes cases in the United States of children as young as two being badly beaten while attending day care centres),[61] the emotionally disturbed child as well as to those who are physically or mentally handicapped. Girls as well may be beaten, though in England at least this is relatively uncommon.[62]

English law permits reasonable and moderate physical chastisement by parents, teachers and others having 'lawful control or charge of a child'.[63] The Newsons' Nottingham studies show that 62 per cent of Nottingham babies had been smacked by the time they were one year old.[64] By the time they were four 97 per cent had been spanked, some with canes, straps, slippers or wooden spoons, but mostly with parental hands, on their legs and backsides. Seven per cent of mothers admitted to smacking more than once a day and 68 per cent between once a day and once a week.[65] By the time they were seven years old 22 per cent of these children had received corporal punishment with some implement and a further 53 per cent had been threatened in this way.[66] The higher socio-economic classes, the Newsons found, were less likely to threaten but just as likely as other groups to use an implement. Middle-class parents in Nottingham seemed to favour a cane, whilst working-class ones tended to use or threatened to hit the child with a strap or belt.

In the USA Stark and McEvoy found that 93 percent of all parents spanked their children[67] and Straus and Steinmetz[68] discovered that, as late as last year in high school, about half of the students experienced physical punishment or the threat of it. The most recent American research, reported by Gelles,[69] is even more revealing. A national probability sample of 2,143 families conducted in 1976 disclosed that 63 per cent of the respondents who had children between the ages of three and seventeen living at home mentioned at least one violent episode during the survey year (1975). The proportion of those reporting at least one violent occurrence in the course of raising a child was 73 per cent. Milder forms of violence were more common. But there was a large amount of serious violence which included threatening the child with a gun or knife. Three per cent admitted that at some time they had done this, that is an indication that between 900,000 and 1.8 million American children between three and seventeen have at some time been threatened with a deadly weapon by a parent. Astonishing though such figures are, they must underestimate the true incidence. The families interviewed were all intact families and the evidence suggests that there is more violence against children in one-parent families.[70] Furthermore, we would expect under-reporting rather than exaggeration. Perhaps, however, what is most disturbing is that parents admitted their violence against their children for this may indicate that they do not even consider such behaviour to be deviant; that, in other words, it is a perfectly legitimate way of rearing children. Elizabeth Elmer makes much the same point. She found that parents did not see physical punishment as 'even remotely related to abuse'. They were 'performing their duty', acting in accordance with 'the cultural heritage of America'.[71]

Are we to regard corporal punishment as child abuse for, if we are, it seems that abuse is not the exception but the rule. There is considerable difficulty in drawing a line between the two activities. Gil puts it like this: 'excessive use of physical force against children is considered abusive and is usually rejected in American tradition, practice and law. [However, there are] no clear cut criteria concerning the specific point beyond which the quantity and quality of physical force used against children is to be considered excessive.'[72] Is it then the case that so long as corporal punishment is a socially approved method of disciplining children we must invariably have child abuse? Zigler has written:

One of the single most important determinants of child abuse is the willingness of adults to inflict corporal punishment upon children in the name of discipline. Well over half of all instances of child abuse appear to have developed out of disciplinary action taken by the parent. All too often an adult begins disciplining a child with mild forms of punishment and ends up unintentionally harming the child. Parents often hurt children if they are unable to gauge their own strength and the physical vulnerability of young children and infants, or if they are unable to control their anger. Some parents are unaware that severe shaking can cause brain damage in young children. Parents are often shocked by the tragic outcomes of an incident in which their well-intentioned desires to impose needed discipline on a child results in severe physical injury.[73]

Much abuse of children is the result of corporal punishment which has gone wrong: either the consequence of deliberate action causing more harm than was intended or the product of loss of self-control. But it is the parental behaviour and not its consequences which should be regarded as abusive.

In contemporary societies, certainly in those of Western Europe and North America, it is children alone who may be subjected to physical chastisement. In Britain the only institution in which persons may be beaten are schools and community homes. Corporal punishment no longer remains a sanction in prisons or the armed services.[74] Ariès shows in *Centuries of Childhood*[75] how it was in part the institutionalisation of a systematised method of discipline on the part of adults against children which served to separate children from adults. Being subject to the application of force by others in authority has always been a badge of inferiority. That children can be hit is a reflection of their status.

In Britain we are most reluctant to abolish corporal punishment. As yet all attempts to do so have been limited to institutional corporal punishment. Three bills since 1973 have failed to progress through Parliament.[76] In Sweden by contrast legislation has removed from parents the right physically to chastise their children. When a clause to do this was added to the Parenthood and Guardianship Code it passed the Riksdag by 259 votes to 6.[77] When the House of Commons Select Committee issued its first report on *Violence In The Family*[78] in 1977, it made fifty-eight recommendations aimed at alleviating the problem of child abuse but it did not even question the use of corporal punishment. Its Canadian counterpart, the Robinson Committee in its report, *Child Abuse and Neglect*,[79] considered the problem but it too refused to recommend the abolition of physical punishment. In 1977 the American Supreme Court upheld[80] the constitutionality of corporal punishment in schools. In effect the court held that a severe beating by a school teacher was beyond review, and thus could not be 'cruel' within the terms of the American constitution.[81] But a doctor seeing the bruises inflicted would risk an action for negligence[82] if he failed to report his observations as symptoms of child abuse. Nor is this the only paradox, for a court might well uphold the removal of a child from his parents for the very same 'abuse' which schools have a licence to carry out.

Why should we be so unwilling to abolish corporal punishment, at least in schools and other institutional settings? I find Gil's view[83] that 'educational philosophies tend to reflect a social order and are not its primary shapers' persuasive. He continues:

> education tends to recreate a society in its existing image, or to maintain its relative status quo, but it rarely if ever creates new social structures. Violence against children in rearing may thus be a functional aspect of socialization into a highly competitive and violent society, one that puts a premium on the uninhibited pursuit of self-interest and that does not put into practice the philosophy of human co-operativeness which it preaches on ceremonial occasions and which is upheld in its ideological expressions and symbols.

Corporal punishment in schools and other institutions is highly significant for another reason as well. It conveys a clear message to parents that 'experts' see corporal punishment as an appropriate disciplinary measure.

Corporal punishment in schools has a weak deterrent effect.[84] It discriminates against the socially disadvantaged[85] (that is in state schools: of course, public school rituals have injected some equalisation). It teaches the use of physical aggression while militating against a positive environment for learning.[86] Furthermore, it is not 'the last resort' it is sometimes claimed to be.[87] For all these reasons it ought to be abolished. But above all else it should be rooted out because it is wrong. If a proposal were made to reintroduce flogging in prisons, or the navy, the case against would be made out on moral grounds. The case for the abolition of corporal punishment in schools and other institutions also rests on moral arguments.[88] It is demeaning and it undermines the child's integrity and legal personality. He has a moral right not to be beaten which the law should recognise. It is difficult to see how the evil of physical abuse of children can be eradicated so long as certain physical attacks on children are considered legitimate. The abolition of corporal punishment in schools, community homes and other institutions would symbolise society's rejection of violence against children.[89] A programme of public education could at the same time make parents aware of the dangers of hitting children and of the existence of the alternative educational and socialisation techniques.[90] It will take some time, perhaps several generations, before we reach the Swedish position. Meanwhile, children's names are entered on 'at risk' registers when attacked by their parents, but hardly an eyelid is raised when the children are beaten in schools or community homes.[91] The elimination of child abuse is a long and complex process. The removal of corporal punishment is merely one action that could be taken to reduce its incidence. Compared to the complexity and cost of other measures, it is relatively simple and would cost nothing. It is difficult to see how child abuse can ever be eliminated so long as we sanction the physical chastisement of children.

Towards a Definition and Taxonomy of Child Abuse

In the previous two sections of this chapter two problematic features of the concept of child abuse have been adumbrated, the difference between an accident and a deliberately inflicted injury and the blurred distinction between abuse and socially sanctioned corporal punishment. These reveal child abuse to be a political concept, a social construction, reflecting the interests and moral concerns of professional interest groups and the community more generally.

As already indicated, there is no consensus on a definition of child abuse. It may be that researchers and policy-makers do not need to define child abuse in the same way. But it may also be that the absence of an agreed definition has hindered both research and social action. It is clear to all that the original notions of a 'battered baby syndrome' are far too narrow because abuse is more pervasive than battering, affects children of all ages and has no unitary causal basis. On the other hand, the Gil approach (see note 44) is so all-inclusive that the concept itself is diluted. A definition must stress that abuse is not limited to battering and burning. Obviously, it includes gross neglect. However, drawn too widely, it would embrace just about everything that adults do to children. Physical chastisement once again causes problems. 'Normal' adults hit children. If we consider this to be abuse, as I have indicated it is tempting to do, then, short of abolishing corporal punishment, it is difficult to see what measures we could take. Do we enter the whole child population's names on 'at risk' registers? This would make a mockery of the registers and would achieve absolutely nothing. To limit abuse to abnormal parenting practices is also superficially attractive until one begins to consider what practices to include and by whose standards these practices are being judged.[92] Circumcising male babies has been considered by some to be sexual abuse.[93] The majority of the population would not consider it so, even though they do not do it. It would, I think, be otherwise, and rightly so, with female circumcision. The introduction of the notion of harm may be thought elucidating: abuse as the actions of parents and other caretakers which harm children. So long as one sticks to broken bones and bruises this causes few problems. But clearly 'harm' goes beyond this to embrace interference with a child's mental health and the suffering caused by neglect, malnutrition, failure to thrive and so on. But where then is the line to be drawn? Abuse could become as all-embracing a notion as Gil's concept of any force that compromises a child's capacity to achieve his physical and psychological potential. Neglect has its own problems and these are considered in a later section of this chapter.

We reach a conclusion — or rather no conclusion. It may be possible to achieve a satisfactory definition of child abuse for a specific and limited purpose: for a research project or a reporting law. Here we must be satisfied with a list of what abuse includes. The list does not purport to be exhaustive. Rather it is indicative of the contours of the concept. Abuse is a continuum. Different actions and omissions lie upon this continuum. At one end is the infliction of brutal force. Along the line lie other violent acts, acts where the intention is to do serious bodily or psychological harm to a child or acts where the wrongdoer is reckless as to whether such harm is caused or not. Next come less than serious assaults: those with and those without the use of an implement. The intention is to hurt and harm is caused, but unlike the previous category hospitalisation is not necessary. Further along the continuum lie injuries inflicted unintentionally. The parent's motive or its absence may be important in deciding what is to be done: measures taken to deal with harm unintentionally inflicted may be less intrusive or severe. But injuries inflicted unintentionally constitute abuse nevertheless.

A different type of physical abuse is sexual abuse. This too has many forms ranging from rape to incest to molestation to other types of sexual exploitation such as the use of a child for pornographic purposes. These too can be placed upon the continuum. Child victims of sexual abuse for long suffered in silence.[94] Only relatively recently did researchers begin to expose the magnitude of sexual exploitation.

Neglect also takes many forms. It can range from failure to feed or feed properly, resulting in malnutrition, to failure to clothe adequately or provide proper accommodation (the case of children recently living in a car is an extreme example)[95] to neglect of a child's health. It can include coldness or apathy towards the child, verbal abuse of the child, even leaving the child alone. Rejection of a child is another form of abuse and may result in failure to thrive or what has been called the 'deprivation dwarfism' syndrome.[96] The consequences of rejection may be every bit as traumatic as those of physical abuse. Further, emotional or nutritional neglect may lead to physical abuse. A child who is ignored may well become 'developmentally delayed': perceived as 'slow', he may then be subjected to physical ill-treatment. A child who receives inadequate nourishment may ruminate. This causes him to smell and this, in its turn, may lead to further neglect or abuse. But this said it should be stressed that many parents who physically ill-treat their children are far from neglectful of them: badly injured children are not uncommonly beautifully turned out.[97] They may well have been beaten because they fail to meet parental expectations of them.[98]

Our continuum thus includes three main types of abuse: physical and sexual abuse and neglect. Placing them in the order used here is not meant to suggest that sexual abuse is less serious than physical abuse nor of greater moment than neglect. It constitutes nothing more than an attempt at a typology, a classification which, it is hoped, will assist an understanding of the issues involved. To keep this chapter down to manageable proportions the emphasis, unless otherwise stated, is on physical abuse. Some of the problems surrounding neglect are considered in relation to the management of abuse and are raised also in the chapter on child-rearing and parental autonomy (Chapter 7).

Explanations of Child Abuse

There are today two competing interpretations of child abuse: one emphasises the problems within the parent himself (individualistic explanations); the other explains abuse in terms of the situation in which the parent finds himself (social explanations). One sees something wrong with the individual parent: the other with his environment. There is a third view, to which some reference has been made, and this, for want of a better word, indicts the culture: it provides an ideological explanation of the phenomenon.

The dominant explanation of child abuse stresses illness in the parent. As indicated already in this chapter, it was medical men who 'discovered' child abuse and this explanation of its aetiology bears their imprint. Throughout the 1960s and for much of the 1970s this explanation was pervasive and highly influential. It has taken something of a battering since but remains the primary interpretation. In the words of one of its critics, Richard Gelles, its theme is: 'anyone who would abuse or kill his child is sick.'[99] The psychopathological model of child abuse represents what the ordinary man in the street thinks about the parents of abused children. It has also been the mainspring for much of our social policy on the question. That we should want to think of abusing parents as 'sick' may tell us something about ourselves. As Gil puts it: 'parents . . . may derive gratification from the sickness-as-cause interpretation, since it may fill them with a sense of security. For if abusive behaviour were a function of sickness most parents could view themselves as free from the dangers of falling prey to it, since they do not consider themselves sick.'[100] As noted earlier in this chapter, the interpretation diverts attention from social conditions: if child abuse is the result of illness within the perpetrators, the social circumstances and cultural trends need not be questioned.

The psychopathological model conceptualises child abuse in terms of character traits or psychodynamics of individual abusing parents. It can be traced back to Freud's essay, 'A Child Is Being Beaten.'[101] The model is far from sophisticated. It is not clear, for example, whether child abuse is seen by its proponents as indicative of some abnormality or whether child abuse results from some underlying pathology which can be or has been judged by criteria other than the child abuse itself.[102]

One of the most authoritative and widely quoted of psychiatric studies of abusive parents is that by Steele and Pollock.[103] Their study was typically clinical and, although all sections of the white population were covered, their sample was hardly representative of the population as a whole. The authors note a wide spread of emotional disorders. They stress, however, unrealistic parental expectations of children, deprivation of basic mothering themselves, being themselves abused as children, intense, unresolved sibling rivalry, an obsessive, compulsive character structure, and unresolved Oedipal conflicts with excessive guilt. An NSPCC study, to give a second example, lists 'suggestive pointers': 'immaturity, impracticality and a tendency to flee into fantasy in the face of real problems.'[104] The fathers are said to be 'introverted schizoid personalities'. Most researchers agree that abusing parents are rarely neurotic or psychotic.[105] But some have diagnosed schizophrenia and psychopathy.[106] More commonly the parents are said to suffer a character or personality disorder, which allows for the uncontrolled expression of aggression.[107]

It is easy to criticise the psychopathological approach and I shall do so presently. Some aspects of it, however, do merit serious consideration. There can be no doubt that some, perhaps a small percentage, of abusing parents are disordered in some way. Certainly, some will be viewed by others in this way. Secondly, as Zigler expresses it, 'some individuals engage in abusive behavior even if they are not living in a stressful sociocultural situation, while other parents, no matter how much stress they are subjected to, never engage in abusive behavior.'[108] As he indicates this finding 'suggests' (perhaps it does more) that in some cases psychological problems account for abusive behaviour. But at best it only explains a limited number of cases.

There are a number of unsatisfactory features in the 'individual pathology' case.[109] The quality of the research leaves much to be desired. Most studies are distorted by sample bias. There are rarely control groups. Most studies do not test specific hypotheses. They 'start and end as broad studies with relatively untested commonsense assumptions.'[110] The model cannot account for the majority of incidents of abuse because the tendency is to posit a single causal variable and ignore other factors. It commonly argues, for example, that a parent, himself abused when a child, responds to this experience by physical abuse of his own children. It craves in support the Harlows's work on monkeys.[111] But first, empirical evidence gives only marginal support to the idea that an abusing parent experienced abuse when a child. Gil, for example, only found that 11 per cent of abusing parents were abused as children.[112] In one study, however, it has been traced through five generations of social work records.[113] Secondly, to extrapolate from monkeys in a laboratory setting to humans in their natural habitat is misleading. Thirdly, the 'experience of abuse' hypothesis may go some way towards explaining where the parent has learnt how to use violence, but it does not explain why it leads to child abuse as opposed to wife battering, football hooliganism or just plain thuggery.

Furthermore, the model does not explain why people possessed of the character traits which psychologists impute to child abusers do not necessarily act violently towards their children. It assumes that an act of abuse cannot occur unless the psychological 'illness' is present. It would thus seem to account both for too much and too little child abuse.

There is, further, little agreement as to the make-up of the alleged psychopathy. Gelles, having studied a representative selection of the research, noted that nineteen traits were referred to, but only 'four figure in the diagnoses of more than two authors.'[114] Not surprisingly, practically all the psychological research into child abuse is conducted *ex post facto*: as a result, it offers little analytical understanding of the genesis of the behaviour. To tell us that an abusive parent 'lacked control' or has 'impaired impulse control' does not tell us very much when we already know that he has perpetrated some gross act of violence against his child. Where the behaviour is not distinguished from its explanation, little predictive power is offered.

Given that the samples used are unrepresentative, we need to know much more about how abusive parents get referred, or refer themselves to psychiatrists or paediatricians. It is to be expected that when a parent comes to a psychiatrist having abused his child, the psychiatrist is apt to engage in what Kitsuse has called, 'retrospective interpretation of facts'.[115] Lofland in *Deviance and Identity* argues that 'the *present evil* of current character must be related to the *past* evil that can be discovered in biography.'[115] The pathological model requires that parents be studied in terms of what is 'wrong' with them. Goffman[117] writes of case records in mental illness cases that their purpose is 'to show the ways in which the patient is "sick" and the reasons why it was right to commit him and is right currently to keep him committed.' This is done, he says, 'by extracting from his whole life a list of those incidents that have or might have had "symptomatic" significance.' The process in the interview of the abusive parent is strikingly similar.

The psychological interpretation of child abuse has led almost inevitably to programmes which bear its imprints. Parents, since they are abnormal or 'sick', require extensive psychiatric treatment to enable them to overcome their 'illness'. They may be protected from penal measures (except in serious cases there has been a marked reluctance to invoke the criminal process)[118] but instead, they are subjected to what Ivan Illich called, 'interminable instruction, treatment and discrimination, which are inflicted . . . for professionally presumed benefit.'[119] The label is different but the stigma is equally permanent. It is well known that doctors 'seek safety by diagnosing illness rather than health'.[120] The rise of preventive medicine has led to attempts to identify potential high-risk cases: the predictive screening questionnaire[121] has accordingly been developed. This poses considerable methodological, ethical and social policy problems. Richard Light[122] has shown that false positive errors could potentially be as high as 85 per cent with the result that many parents would be mistakenly labelled. There would also be false negatives. Together this suggests low practical utility for an unacceptably high social cost.[123] Even in cases where the prediction may be thought accurate, the labelling process may be thought to interfere with a resocialising process.

Abusive or potentially abusive parents are also said to require social work intervention, and this despite the fact that the recidivism rate amongst parents known to a protective agency may be higher than it is in cases where there has been no social work intervention. Jordan explains why this may be so.[124] The danger as he perceives it is that 'the family can become a case, to be visited in a vague, supervisory way, to check up, for the social worker to cover herself.' He indicates that far from helping the 'client' the social worker can become part of the client's 'nightmare'. 'The situation is never defined; the reason for supervision is never spelt out; the problem is never really brought into the open.' This, he notes, quoting an NSPCC report,[125] is the basis for the research finding that, 'as applied to baby battering, anxious visiting by social workers of families actually increases battering.' He also makes the point that, in all the well-known tragedies about which full-scale inquiries have been held, the clients were not new referrals who had not been investigated speedily enough but cases known to a department, or more commonly several welfare agencies,[126] for a considerable period.

The emphasis on individual pathology has also led to the development of intervention programmes like Parents Anonymous[127] which rely on self-help. The support these groups can give may be invaluable in the short term to individual parents but they too reinforce the image of the inadequacy of the parents. They emphasise that they are incapable of rearing their children because of their own failings. The danger is that such programmes treat the symptoms rather than the causes of the problem.

This leads to the second interpretation. The medical world assumes the problem to be an individual one. The sociological interpretation of child abuse argues that its causes lie in the environment, in the socially polluted milieu in which typical (or stereotypical) child-abusers live. A leading advocate of this interpretation is David Gil. He argues that a major cause of child abuse is the stress and frustration which result from 'multi-faceted deprivations of poverty and its correlates, high density in overcrowded, dilapidated, inadequately served neighbourhoods, large numbers of children, especially in one-parent, mainly female-headed households, and the absence of child-care alternatives', as well as poor education and 'alienating circumstances in most work places'.[128] Gil does not suggest (though others do) that poverty is itself a direct cause of child abuse. Rather, he claims that it operates through an intervening variable, namely, 'concrete and psychological stress and frustration experienced by individuals in the context of culturally sanctioned use of physical force in child rearing.'[129]

This view of child abuse finds some support in Garbarino's research in New York State.[130] He found that socio-economic stress exacerbated by the unavailability of support systems for the family from the community is directly associated with the rate of child abuse. It accounted for 36 per cent of the variance in rates of child abuse across New York counties: economic conditions more generally affecting the family account for 16 per cent of the variance. Some caution must be exercised in examining these results for the data were derived from public agency sources where lower socio-economic classes were over-represented.[131]

There is considerable evidence of social deprivation amongst known child abusers. Parents tend to be poor, very young, socially isolated (a number of writers have noted an increase in child abuse at times of the year when people long for missing family support).[132] There is convincing evidence of an association between an unemployed or underemployed father or step-father in the household and a higher incidence of child abuse.[133] Many families in which abuse is known to take place have accommodation problems.[134] Gil found a positive correlation between mobility and the incidence of child abuse in a family. It is common to find that the fathers of abused children have criminal records. Mothers have often had to cope alone. Many of them were pregnant or recently confined at the time of the abuse. The abused children themselves are often the result of unplanned pregnancies.[135]

All this may be true but a link still has to be made between the poverty and the abusive action. The majority of those who live in a polluted socio-economic environment do not abuse their children. I have suggested elsewhere that part of the link may be found in social learning processes.[136] There is more violence in working-class communities and ghettos than in suburbs. Someone reared in an environment where violence is prevalent may learn that violence is a major resource in tackling life's problems. As Goode[137] has noted: 'most people do not willingly choose overt force when they command other resources because the costs of using force are high.' He, accordingly, hypothesises that the greater the other resources an individual can command, the less he will use force in an 'overt manner'. Working-class parents are deficient in social resources (prestige, communication skills, economic possessions), and may thus be constrained to use that very violence they have grown up with and see all about them. Could it be that violence is almost an inevitable feature of working-class existence[138] and that in some families, perhaps those where the psychological potential is also present, it is used against children? Children are obvious targets. They are weaker and more vulnerable; they may be 'responsible' for the poverty in which the parents find themselves; and crucially the use of force against children is socially sanctioned.

Of course, a theory of child abuse that relates it to the environment does not begin to explain it in the higher socio-economic classes. There are some, Leroy Pelton[139] for example, who are persuaded that child abuse is a working-class phenomenon, but their arguments are not convincing. He is, however, right to perceive that what he calls the 'myth of classlessness' diverts money from poverty programmes. But child abuse does exist in all sections of society. Straus, Gelles and Steinmetz,[140] indeed, have found that stress is more likely to lead to abuse in poor-to-middle-income families than it is in very poor or very wealthy families. According to Gelles, 'the reason why stress does not increase the risk of child abuse among the poor and well-to-do seems to be their ability and likelihood of reacting to stress. The poor . . . encounter stress as a normal part of their lives . . . . The well-to-do adapt to stress by using their financial resources to help alleviate problems.'[141] It is the middle-income bracket 'who struggle with every stressful event. Not poor enough to get welfare . . . , not well off enough to have financial security, they tend to resort to violence toward their children as a reaction to increased stress.'[142] They also found, however, that parents with the lowest income have the highest rate of violence.[143] Still not explained is why the upper-income groups abuse their children, even if they do so less frequently than the poor, and why middle-income families react to stress by turning to violence. The model, we may conclude, is only a partial one: it explains both too much violence (many people in deprived circumstances do not abuse their children) and too little (the better-off also abuse their children). Despite this the model remains a more convincing explanation of the phenomenon of child abuse.

Adoption of the sociological interpretation is less convenient than of the pathological one. It is more expensive to tackle the root sources of poverty than to provide treatment programmes after the event. But fixing the road on the cliff that causes the accidents is more sensible than providing for an ambulance service at the bottom of the cliff.[144] It would be outside the scope of this book, and certainly of this chapter, to list all the ways in which poverty and its correlates might be tackled. The present levels of unemployment (nearly four million in Britain) obstruct every kind of reform sought by those concerned about poverty. The reduction of this must be a prime target if we really want to decrease the incidence of child abuse. The need to raise living standards of low-paid workers, especially in our context those with children to support, is equally important. Half a million children in Britain live in families where the family income is below official poverty level, even though one or both parents go out to work full-time.[145] Almost one million children live in families that have to depend on supplementary benefits: supplementary benefit payments are low and clearly inadequate.[146] The parent of a ten-year-old receives £1.25 a day to cover all the child's needs — food, clothing, heating, travel, entertainment, and the costs incurred in school activities. Pensions and tax allowances (mostly for childless people) have kept up with inflation but we have not been able to maintain, let alone improve, the real value of child benefits. That we have favoured the childless as opposed to families with children has been a matter of deliberate policy.[147] It need not have been this way: it is what we have chosen to do. It reflects our priorities.

The point can be laboured. 'Inadequate housing produces a great deal of stress in parents and can turn difficult but normal circumstances of child upbringing into almost impossible ones.'[148] But a million and a half households live in homes officially considered to be unfit for human habitation;[149] over a million households are in council waiting lists whilst the stock of public housing is diminished by the sale of council houses;[150] over a quarter of a million children live in flats above the second floor in tower blocks, though it is accepted that families with young children should be transferred out of stressful conditions of tower block life.[151] We compel our poorest people to live in high-cost environments.[152]

We need to do more to help improve child care services, both facilities and alternatives. We know that many abused children were unwanted: we need, accordingly, to expand family planning services. The provision of homemakers or family aides might ease stress in families experiencing difficulties: it might also help to keep the families intact (thus saving the community money). But what exists at the moment is clearly inadequate. Child care alternatives, such as day-care facilities and nurseries, would free parents from the responsibilities of continuous care and reduce the incidence of child abuse. But they may also impede a bonding process.[153] Though this too may lead to child abuse, alternatives must be considered the least dangerous risk in stressful circumstances. The teaching of parenting skills must also be regarded as important.

We do not, in Britain, have a family impact statement[154] attached to new or proposed legislation or administrative changes. Elsewhere in this book I urge the adoption of such an idea. So many of the policies pursued, in relation to employment, income and housing, have taken so little regard of the effect that they have on families with children, that the need for such an assessment is now imperative. I do not argue that child abuse is caused by social considerations, such as those depicted here. But I believe at least part of the answer lies in improving the ecology of young families. I am confident that the removal of this social pollution would lead to a large decline in the incidence of child abuse.

A major fault in the environmental stress model lies in its inability to explain why circumstances of deprivation should lead to abuse of children. This is why we must look to another explanation of child abuse. It is difficult to put a name to it, other than to assert that it resides within the culture of a society. The cultural interpretation of child abuse looks at our basic attitudes, at our attitudes towards force and violence, at the way we regard children. The behaviour of child abusers on this level reflects societal forces. In a provocative article David Gil argues the cause of child abuse is to be sought in:

> a cluster of interacting elements, to wit, a society's basic social philosophy, its dominant value premises, its concept of humans, the nature of its social, economic and political institutions, which are shaped by its philosophy and value premises, and which in turn reinforce that philosophy and these values, and finally, the particular quality of human philosophy, values and institutions. For, in the final analysis, it is the philosophy and the value premises of a society, the nature of its major social institutions, and the quality of its human relations that determine whether or not individual members of that society will develop fully and in accordance with their inherent potentialities.[155]

Violence is common in asymmetric relationships, between master and slave, warder or policeman and prisoner or suspect as well as in male–female relationships. Physical force is used for disciplinary objectives in all these contexts. But nowhere is this clearer than in the relationship of adults to children. We should not limit ourselves to the rather obvious fact that physical punishment of children is culturally acceptable.

To understand violence against children or child abuse more generally, it is necessary to look at the definition of childhood prevalent in our society, at social policies which sustain different levels of rights for children, indeed, as Gil notes, different levels of rights for children from 'different social and economic backgrounds'.[156] But it is not just social policies to which we must look. The whole ethos of our society, though often described as 'child-centred',[157] is geared to seeing children as objects, rather than human beings in their own right. We no longer subscribe to notions of children as property but the legacies of such an ideology remain firmly implanted within our consciousness. It was never doubted that Maria Colwell[158] would be returned to her mother. Her mother wanted her back. The only decision, accordingly, was how to effect her return. No one bothered to consult the child herself. When a Sheffield mother decided that her daughter who suffered from Sotos Syndrome should be sterilised, that would have been the end of the matter had it not been for the chance intervention of an educational psychologist.[159] We are reluctant to interfere with parents. We have not got far from the point when a child was regarded as one of his parent's possessions, rather like the television set or refrigerator.[160] Many of us are inclined to kick them when they go wrong. Is it surprising that we should treat children differently?

If we understand child abuse in this way then its elimination as a social problem is a long way off. But we have already come a long way: we recognise child abuse as a social problem despite our social construction of childhood. Only twenty years ago we did not do so. At most, then, the problem of child abuse revolves about our definition of children, and the way we perceive them as property of their parents, almost as non-persons, as objects rather than participants in the social process. The move towards a recognition of children's rights is thus significant for it is only with a redefinition of the status and rights of children that the wrong of child abuse can be controlled and ultimately eliminated. This is the important link between child abuse and children's rights.[161] The end of child abuse awaits a social revolution. In the meantime, one initiative that we can take relates to corporal punishment. Governments, state and local, and local education authorities must take the lead in removing this from schools and institutions under their control.[162]

None of the three explanations depicted here is sufficient in itself. A multidimensional explanation must be sought. Child abuse cannot be understood in terms of one specific causal dimension. It is a complex problem and requires an understanding of the interaction between environmental stress and malfunctioning personalities and necessitates a location of this interplay in the wider structure and culture of society. However, strategies to contain and manage child abuse have hitherto emphasised psychopathology and, in doing so, have individualised the problem.

The Management of Child Abuse

Most comment on child abuse in the last ten years has centred on the problems arising out of its containment and administration. Although the amount of research on child abuse is extensive very little of it relates to the organisation and operation of services which are intended to deal with the problem. Most attention has focused on the system: bad news makes news. There have been over twenty formal inquiries into child abuse cases since the Graham Bagnall case in 1972.[163] A number of well-publicised criminal trials of parents and step-parents have also been conducted. There is a danger, but also an inevitability, in drawing conclusions from these inquiries and trials. As each new tragedy is splashed across the headlines, the critical reaction is to ask why it was allowed to happen. Social workers and others, but particularly social workers, are pilloried for their mismanagement of the case.

But we have not resolved and cannot resolve the basic dilemma. How are we to assess which children are at risk? We cannot do this with any precision. How are we to decide our priorities? Social workers are not just concerned with children. But even limiting themselves to children, if they concentrate on non-accidental injury they divert 'resources from the very much larger group of children who may be lying on the margin of child neglect, and indeed possibly suffering more than some victims of violence.'[164] Social workers must take calculated risks. As one told the Residential Care Association conference in 1974: 'if we attempt to create a system whereby all risk is eradicated we risk creating a system in which it is "death" to the kind of people we are trying to serve.'[165] Social workers could diminish risk by removing[166] from home all children thought to be 'at risk'. The Director of Social Services of Lambeth put this bluntly when he gave evidence to the House of Commons Select Committee. He said:

> I think that one of the causes of worry in the non-accidental injury field is the fact that a substantial number of the children are not in care. Of the 332 on our register at the moment, only 77 are in an establishment of some kind, or are fostered, or are in a hospital . . . . In other words, we have only really physically protected 77 of them. The other 240–250 are all at home with their parents and are on our register as subject to the risk of battery. Quite clearly, we have no way of ensuring that they will not be battered tonight, for example.[167]

It is all too easy to assume that removing a child is in his best interests. But 'the alternatives are not as happy as you might think', another social worker acknowledged in his evidence to the same committee.[168] He continued: 'If you think of the high turnover in children's homes and the shortage of long-term foster parents, to take a child away from home is not suddenly producing a panacea; it may be turning out an equally unhappy and disturbed child at eight-teen as if it had stayed with its parents.' He thought social workers were walking along knife edges.

It is furthermore difficult to see what social workers can do. Thus, Wayne Brewer, a four-year-old eventually killed by his step-father was said (by the director of social services) to be at risk from 'an impulsive kind of violence'. And, as the director added, 'unless you are there 24 hours a day it is difficult to protect a child in those circumstances, and difficult to know exactly what goes on in the home.'[169] In this case magistrates revoked the care order[170] contrary to the advice of social workers and substituted a supervision order with the recommendation that this should be 'on the basis of three or four times weekly.'[171] There was no way in which such a recommendation could be adopted — which is just as well, for one can well imagine the reaction of parents to such anxious, almost daily visiting.[172] It is common to assert that the magistrates were wrong to revoke the care order but when one reads the report it is clear that the social services department had no clear long-term plan for the child and that his mother and step-father could offer him some stability. Social workers are acquiring greater skills in handling the problem of NAI.[173] Child abuse specialists are now commonly appointed. The dilution of child care expertise, the result of reorganisation in the early 1970s,[174] is no longer as damaging as it was, because of this new injection of specialist workers. Social services departments remain starved of resources and this can cripple whatever skills individual specialists have. But that same public which vents righteous indignation when a tragedy occurs groans when money is levied from it to pay for social services.

Social workers are not the only personnel concerned with the management of child abuse cases. The police, the 'oldest social workers'[175] have long insisted that they '*must* be involved in all cases of violence'[176] against children. Their role in tackling child abuse remains controversial. The first DHSS circular on non-accidental injury made police attendance at case conferences a matter of marginal importance.[177] Castle, writing in 1976, noted that the question of police involvement had not been fully resolved, though he observed that police had attended half the conferences at which NSPCC officials were present during March, April and May 1976.[178] The difficulty is one of competing ideologies.[179] To the police (or at least a section of them) case conferences represent 'an inquisition, self-appointed at that level, to decide yea or nay to whether a prosecution should ensue.' They see this as 'against the natural spirit of justice.'[180] Social workers, on the other hand, find it 'very difficult to talk freely about their worries . . . if they feel the police are going to need to investigate further.'[181] Social workers and police divide on whether the best way of protecting children is to prosecute their parents. The House of Commons Select Committee recommended that a senior police officer should be invited[182] and by November 1976 a further DHSS circular was arguing that the police should be involved 'as closely as possible in the case conference structure'.[183] It recognised that the police should retain the capacity to take action independently of the case conference. Mutual confidence has increased in the last five years. Social workers have come to realise the value of the investigative skills of the police whilst the police themselves have become less heavy-handed and more prepared to evaluate action in terms of whether it is likely to protect the child or not.[184]

In all but the most serious cases the criminal law is something of a blunt instrument. In theory adults who assault their children should be treated in the same way as adults who assault strangers, be they other adults or children. But here a strict 'rights' approach does not bear fruit. There are a number of reasons for this. First, it is impossible to isolate the incident of battering from the total family situation: at least it is unwise to do so. The child may be, in most cases is, better off with his parents than in the alternative environments we as a society can offer him. Further, prosecutions may divide families. The punishment issue obtrudes once again: what is acceptable in different cultures varies and the total family situation must be assessed in terms of its cultural context.[185] Secondly, if a prosecution takes place it may be impossible to prove the case to the standard of 'beyond reasonable doubt' required by the criminal law. There are problems of evidence. Thirdly, there is the danger that if a parent fears prosecution he may neglect or delay to seek medical treatment for his injured child because of fear of the consequences. Fourthly, if the parent is acquitted, and given what has been said already this is quite likely, he may see the verdict as a vindication of the legitimacy of his behaviour and this may make social work with him extremely difficult to accomplish. On the other hand, if the parent is convicted, this may confirm his or her 'negative self-image'.[186]

The medical profession is also closely involved in child abuse. Its diagnosis requires its skills. If the matter is to get any further it is necessary that doctors report their suspicions. Beyond this there is not much that doctors can do. As indicated earlier in this chapter, the norms of confidentiality have obstructed doctors (parents are their patients too); so, at least until recently, has their education and training, which acquainted them inadequately with the symptoms of child abuse. The medical profession is a divided one (which profession is not?) and consensus is lacking on how best to tackle child abuse. The British Paediatric Association favours multi-disciplinary conferences 'rather than statutory notification by a single individual'[187] (an allusion to mandatory reporting on the American model). It is critical of the failure of family doctors to attend case conferences. Others within the medical profession are critical of the whole idea of case conferences and want a single decision-maker or small diagnostic conference. Many complain the conferences are too long, or unstructured or convened at inconvenient times of the day. Others are more critical still: an editorial in *The Lancet* in 1975[188] asked who were 'the battered':

is it the paediatrician, battered by too many case conferences and at risk of neglecting other needy families and ill children because this week he has cancelled his visit to the special care baby unit on Wednesday afternoon because of a case conference and has cancelled his Friday afternoon spina-bifida clinic in order to attend yet another case conference? The Friday conference, like the others, was attended by eight highly-paid, highly-trained professionals, who sat solemnly round a table discussing a robust, healthy child with a bruise on his bottom.

This is cynical but it cloaks an important truth. It is easy for administrative procedures, which are only a means, to become almost an end in themselves. They can take over, with the result that attention gets diverted from real issues of poverty and neglect.

There are thus a number of agencies[189] committed to protecting children against abuse. If one common theme runs through the reports of inquiries into child abuse cases it is that better co-ordination between agencies might have saved lives. Indeed, the DHSS argued before the House of Commons Select Committee that co-ordination was 'the key principle'.[190] The Committee itself noted that 'only by collective discussion can adequate decisions be reached.'[191] Rein[192] has characterised the problems that hinder co-ordination as duplication, discontinuity and incoherence. Duplication is an overlap of similar services and occurs when the functions of individual workers or policies of different agencies are designed without reference to those of other agencies. Discontinuity occurs when services which are related to each other but required at different points of time do not follow on consecutively: transfer is not negotiated smoothly. Incoherence is the failure of independent and specialised services to combine to solve a common problem.

The Maria Colwell case[193] is a paradigm of each of these faults. There was duplication between the East Sussex County Council Social Services Department and the NSPCC; discontinuity in the changeovers of supervision as first Maria came under one authority and then another; incoherence in the failure of the social services to work with education welfare among other agencies. The defects are found also in the Auckland case.[194] Duplication occurred between social services and the health visiting service, discontinuity between probation and after care and other agencies and incoherence in the failure of social services and health visiting service to combine effectively in the period when the father, a convicted child-killer, was left in sole charge of three small children, one of whom he subsequently killed.

One common feature of reports of inquiries is the constant assertion that it is 'a failure of a system compounded of several factors of which the greatest and most obvious must be that of the lack or ineffectiveness of communications and liaison.'[195] Often noted is the failure to call a case conference.[196] The case conference is the most obvious way in which 'systematic case co-ordination'[197] can take place. Together with the establishment of area review committees as policy-making bodies to co-ordinate programmes[198] and a central record of information, a system of registers, the holding of case conferences was part of the first DHSS guidance on the management of NAI.[199] But how useful a management technique are they?

A succession of official reports into the death of children have pointed to serious weaknesses and failures in case conferences. I limit myself to three of the most recent reports. Thus, in the Paul Brown Inquiry Report we read:

> the meeting then appears to have dissolved into unfocussed discussion and questions. The so-called minutes of this case conference were not so much minutes as haphazard verbatim notes. No coherent picture of the case conference emerges from these notes. They do however suggest that the case conference was not well chaired and that the discussion was allowed to ramble.[200]

The inquiry into the death of Malcolm Page discovered that there had been four case conferences over an eight-month period chaired by three different chairmen, with the fourth conference attended by only three people.[201] The report lists the tasks it sees a case conference performing:

— to share knowledge about the family as a whole including its history and information about individual members
— to try to diagnose the problem and assess the family, including the degree of risk of abuse to which *all* of the children of the family are exposed
— to allocate the case to a key worker responsible for its overall management
— to recommend to the key worker and others to whom responsibility falls or is assigned a treatment plan
— to decide whether or not to register any of the children
— to make recommendations about whether or not the parents and child should be informed of the fact and significance of registration
— to agree a review procedure, including who is going to undertake the monitoring of the case.[202]

This is the theory, but how much of it is carried out in practice? In the case of Maria Mehmedagi[203] very little of what happened conformed to anything like this model. First, no full review case conference was held within a reasonably short period of the first major incident. There was an initial conference but no further case conference was held for over three months, during which time vital decisions should have been taken. Secondly, there was no full written social history report prepared, giving all the background, the circumstances of the case and the various alternative courses open. The case conferences subsequently held were dictated more by the pressure of events than any conscious policy.[204] The crucial decision that the child should be returned home arose as a general assumption by those concerned (reminiscent of the Maria Colwell case) rather than a decision after all the factors and possible options had been considered.

But, as Hugh Geach intimates,[205] 'the fundamental weaknesses of case conferences go much further than the obvious failure of the system in the Malcolm Page tragedy', or, we may add, in any of the other cases. The ideal of systematic case co-ordination may be a worthy one but it is questionable whether professionals with entrenched ideological positions are capable of co-ordinating their efforts to achieve a common goal. Hallett and Stevenson[205] have defined the problems which make co-operation difficult, if not impossible. These include such issues as agency functions, role perspectives, status, professional attitudes, chairmanship and the position of case conferences within the decision-making processes of the various agencies. To what extent, for example, do the participants in a case conference understand the structure and functions of other agencies? The communication problems of police and social workers have been discussed earlier in this section. They are not the only problem. Geach quotes from a recent course on case conferences where neither social workers nor health visitors were properly able to define each other's role. A further obstacle to co-ordination is the value-laden subject-matter of many conferences. There is probably no agreement in the social work profession itself as to what being 'at risk' involves.[207] *A fortiori,* the differences between different professions on such an elusive notion are great. Meetings between professionals from different agencies need a clear base from which to operate. In too many case conferences this is missing. Add to this the fact that case conferences are expensive, loosely organised and structured and often badly chaired and one wonders what they achieve. It is doubtful whether it improves services to clients or strengthens the professional knowledge-base. It is a tempting thought to suggest that all the money spent organising them be used for the relief of child poverty. It is a fair bet that doing that would accomplish more than the current system achieves.

Registers: Whom do they Protect?

A second management technique is the keeping of registers of names of children who have been abused or are thought to be 'at risk'. Registers have proved more controversial than case conferences. Although kept by the NSPCC in the mid-1960s, the real origin of central registers is the recommendation in the DHSS Circular of 1974. The Circular stated that a 'central record of information in each area is essential to good communication between the many disciplines involved in the management of cases.'[208] It did not elaborate further: it did not state why it was thought to be essential, nor how it should be used. A further DHSS letter in 1976 offered some detailed advice but no guidance on these important questions. Noting that registers were immensely variable, it made a number of recommendations on confidentiality and security and the minimum requirements that should be satisfied by all register systems. It also gave a clue as to one of the possible motives for the establishment of a system of registers for it indicated that registers were useful guides to estimating the incidence of child abuse.[209] But this cannot be the primary purpose of registers. If it were, more attention would have been paid to the possibility of introducing mandatory reporting, though this, of course, in no way guarantees any accuracy.

The House of Commons Select Committee also noted that registers provided a 'record for statistical purposes'.[210] It stressed in addition that registers provide 'a safeguard for the child by aiding detection of a sequence of injuries and facilitating discovery of "mobile families".'[211] This begs the very question it should be answering. The Report also notes that 'registers are necessary in the interests of the child and . . . this should override all other considerations.'[212] That the child's interests should be paramount is not contested. What is debatable is whether the keeping of registers is the best way of achieving this and whether also it is concern for the child which is the primary motivating force in the setting-up and administration of registers. Solnit has argued that the child abuse mandatory reporting laws passed in the USA in record time in the 1960s 'were not intended and have probably contributed little to protecting children. They were intended mainly to safeguard the conscience and legal vulnerability of our adult society.'[213] I would argue that registers in Britain serve a similar function: they are used to protect the agencies involved rather than the children. Indeed, one Director of Social Services has been quoted as describing them as 'bureaucratic devices which act as an insurance policy for the local authority, instead of meeting the needs of clients.'[214]

There has been an epidemic of registering children. No one knows how many names are on registers, but one reliable estimate is 50,000.[215] But, as Solnit has noted, this spreads the net so widely that it 'does not distinguish sufficiently clearly between those who can be helped through identification and those who may be harmed by it . . . . The registers and reporting figures it has created satisfy the alarmists, but do not necessarily create or effectively encourage or support services.' His concern is that there has been 'too much reporting and too little services.' Services are spread so widely that those really in need are insufficiently helped. Clinical attention is imposed,

> a contradiction of threatening proportions [for] clinical care . . . depends on a voluntary engagement . . . and . . . rests crucially on feeling secure in the confidentiality of the engagement. If a child and parent know ahead of time that what they discuss with the helping persons will be communicated to the state . . ., then the capacity to reflect upon and cope with fears, anger, frustration, ghosts from the past, or any other feelings . . . is sharply limited and significantly distorted.[215]

There are also civil liberties issues here for information divulged may reach a case conference and through it the police.[217] Information may later be used to construe a minor injury on a child as an incident of child abuse.[218]

One of the main values of a system of registers is often said to be as an aid in diagnosis. It is envisaged that whenever a professional of any discipline confronts a child who exhibits symptoms of having suffered abuse he would check with the register to see if the child's name was on it, whether any agency was currently involved with the family, and whether another child in the same family had caused concern in any earlier period. A survey conducted by the British Association of Social Workers in 1976[219] found, however, that professionals were not making inquiries of the register. Thirty-nine had received fewer than fifty enquiries, some had received under ten, and three reported that they had had no inquiries in a year. Indeed, over half the registers had received less than 100 queries. These figures may underestimate the extent of usage, for not all queries may be recorded, but they do not suggest that the registers are being used as an aid to diagnosis. BASW commented: 'if they are not being used for diagnosis, one must ask what is the purpose of registers.'[220] In the five years since the BASW Report the indications are that the registers are being used no more frequently. In a letter to the DHSS, the Director of Social Services for Devon describes the use of registers as 'minimal' ('never more than five' a year). The situation in Newcastle mirrors that in Devon. In the London Borough of Wandsworth there were fifty-two inquiries in 1980.[221] Are registers becoming, as BASW anticipated they might, 'an overburdened and increasingly irrelevant list of children about whom professionals are concerned?'[222]

How do names get on to the register? 'A decision to place a child's name on the register should only be taken at a case conference.'[223] It is standard practice for the first case conference to decide whether or not a child's name should be placed on the register. There is wide variation in the criteria used by area review committees for placing children on the register. Some only place a name on the register if there is evidence of a non-accidentally inflicted injury. The difficulties of determining what is an accident have already been considered. In other areas the more nebulous concept of 'at risk' is used. This, as already indicated, is not an objective condition but rather a social construction. The most recent DHSS Circular has recommended the extension of the register system beyond non-accidental injury and the extremes of deprivation and neglect to 'children who suffer severe mental or emotional abuse.' This is explained to embrace 'severe non-organic failure to thrive' or adverse effects on 'behaviour and emotional development' where 'medical and social assessments found evidence of either persistent or severe neglect or rejection.'[224] Surprisingly, sexual abuse has not been added: the omission to do so has been criticised.[225] There is a case for emotional damage grounding social work intervention in some cases but what evidence is to be required to substantiate such damage? Perhaps 'evidence' is even an inappropriate word to use for there is no evidence that decisions will be taken on anything other than values and prejudices. The danger is that intervention will be grounded on vague concepts such as 'proper parental love' or 'inadequate parental affection'. This invites 'unwarranted or arbitrary intervention. It could be applied to parents who travel a great deal, leaving their children with housekeepers, who send them to boarding schools to get rid of them, or who are generally undemonstrative people.'[226] Of course, we know it won't.

The DHSS Circular does, it is true, concentrate on damage to the child. But is this the way that social workers and others concerned with the problem will see it? It is all too easy for agencies to concentrate on, even to seek out, parental behaviour. According to Gray, Cutler, Dean and Kempe's research,[227] some 25 per cent of parents provide parenting which could be criticised from some professional viewpoint or other, often as a result of a mixture of environmental and other social pressures and particular personality traits. We do not know enough about child development to be able to evaluate the long-term consequences of current neglect. Nor do we know whether a child will suffer less emotional trauma when he is removed from a home where he has been suffering emotional deprivation. The removal may be equally damaging: the new house or homes equally bad or worse or as bad in other ways. Intervention becomes easier to justify where there is evidence of actual harm, demonstrated by, for example, the child's anxiety, depression or extreme aggression, but the DHSS guidance makes no such proviso. Even to limit oneself to manifestations of the child's behaviour is not sufficient, for similar behaviour 'may for different reasons be a response to a wide range of different and even opposite psychic factors. And the same deep-seated emotional disturbance may lead to the most diverse manifestations of a child's behaviour.'[228] It is relatively easy to relate a child's physical injury to his parents' action, though as already indicated this is fraught with problems. It is a considerably more complex process to link emotional damage with actions or omissions to act that may be designated emotional abuse.

Once a child's name is on the register, what happens? Writing of mandatory reporting legislation in the USA, Paulsen noted that 'reporting is not enough. After the report is made, something has to happen.' He adds: 'no law can be better than its implementation, and implementation can be no better than resources permit.'[229] In similar vein, BASW, in its memorandum to the House of Commons Select Committee, argued that a register is not 'a panacea'. It is, the Association thought, 'a working tool, not an end in itself, and it can be counterproductive if workers are lulled into a false sense of security, when a child has been placed on a register.'[230] The question must, therefore, be asked: what is made available to families at risk? Is the fact that a child's name is on the register an admission ticket to the welfare pantry?[231] Does it assist with the provision of day care facilities or in securing better housing? There is little concrete information on this. Martel[232] found that nearly a third of the area review committees she questioned had made no decision on the crucial question as to whether families on the register should receive priority in the allocation of resources.

Registers raise a number of civil liberties issues as well.[233] There is no statutory obligation placed on social services departments to inform parents either that a case conference is to be called or of the placement of their child on a register. The House of Commons Select Committee thought parents should normally be informed and that responsibility for this should rest with the agency making the notification and not with the case conference.[234] Martel found that the majority of areas in the Family Service Unit survey had no policy at all on the question. Some informed families with all-agency agreement, some left it to the discretion of the key worker, and others informed families if they asked.[235] Geach, writing in 1980, thought that parents in most areas were not told (he estimated that up to 90 per cent of parents had no knowledge that their child's name had been placed on a register).[236] The DHSS gave no guidance until 1980. In its Circular of that year it recommended that

> unless in an individual case there are exceptional reasons for not doing so, parents should be informed that it has been decided to place their child's name on the register and should be given the opportunity to discuss and question the decision. When and by whom they are informed should be decided at the case conference.[237]

Questions have also arisen as to whether parents should have the right to be at, or represented at, case conferences. Allegations are made and judgments are passed which may influence decisions for years. At present parents have no rights to representation at case conferences. Further problems have centred on what information should be recorded and how much divulged and to whom. Martel found that in some areas anything was revealed.[238] With the dangers of stigmatisation, clear controls should be exercised to avoid this happening.

Registers have thus proved a troublesome feature of the management programme. There is no evidence that they have saved lives or helped families thought to be at risk. There is evidence of unwarranted stigmatisation. It is tempting to recommend that registers be dispensed with altogether. Short of this, an urgent and searching rethink of their aims is required. At the moment too many professionals are looking on them as panaceas rather than working tools. The result is more case-carrying: not necessarily better casework.[239]

A Moral Panic?

Twenty-five years ago the NSPCC noted in its annual report that 'cases of physical ill-treatment are less severe than they were' and that only a small minority of cases dealt with by them in the previous year stemmed from cruelty.[240] How different it is today with the same organisation pleading for more money to be available to tackle what is generally seen as an 'epidemic' of child abuse![241] What has changed?

I would argue that there is no more child cruelty today than in the mid-1950s. There may even be less. There is certainly greater awareness of child abuse. It is seen, in the words of *The Sunday Times* at the time of the Colwell affair, as a 'national scandal.'[242] There has also been an increase in social work activity centring around child care cases: fear of 'another Maria Colwell' seems to haunt social services departments.[243] The number of place of safety orders has rocketed; a new phenomenon of removing babies at birth has become common; the number of names on registers has increased rapidly. What does all this signify? How are we to account for a 350 per cent increase in place of safety orders in the three years following Maria Colwell's death;[244] the fact that fifty or more babies a year are being removed from their mothers at birth (that is by some thirty to forty social services departments who were surveyed);[245] and the fact that the vast majority of children appearing on registers come from families whose head is in a lower working-class manual occupation or is unemployed?[246]

Can what has happened be characterised in terms of a moral panic? According to Cohen, 'societies appear to be subject, every now and then, to periods of moral panic. A condition, episode, person or group of persons emerges to become defined as a threat to societal values and interests.'[247] He points out that sometimes the object of the panic is novel but at other times it has long existed though has not appeared in the limelight. Child abuse has caused a 'moral panic' in these terms, but why? To Hall and his colleagues moral panics are 'one of the principal forms of ideological consciousness by means of which a "silent majority" is won over to the support of increasingly coercive measures on the part of the state.' It lends legitimacy to 'a "more than normal" exercise of control.'[248] They also identify a number of 'significant spirals',[249] ways by which particular behaviour is made to seem increasingly more threatening. What they call 'thresholds' are one of the main escalatory mechanisms of the spiral. The higher something can be placed in a hierarchy of thresholds, the greater is its threat to the social order: concomitantly, the more severe the coercive response is likely to be. They identify three thresholds in the hierarchy: permissiveness, legality and violence. The child-abusing parent is violent and is thus to be seen as threatening to the social order.

The 1970s witnessed a number of similar moral panics directed at violent targets: muggers,[250] IRA terrorists[251] and pickets,[252] amongst others. Each in their own way struck at the fundamentals of the social order. But so did the child batterer, for nothing is more sacrosanct about English life than values associated with the family.[253] Panic about malaises within the social order led in the 1970s to a sustained 'law-and-order' campaign. Hall and his colleagues have charted this. They describe the way in which the 'state apparatuses' are progressively pushed into a 'more or less permanent "control" posture'.[254]

This has had a profound effect on the social work profession. Social workers have been forced into a more coercive relationship with families who depend on them. At an earlier period social workers concentrated on the poor because they 'needed' them: in the 1970s it was rather because they constituted a new source of deviance or potential deviance. Social workers are becoming more like policemen. There has been an emphasis on programmes to remove children from parents, to 'rescue' them. The Children Act 1975, though said to be a 'children's charter',[255] is to be seen in these terms. As Holman has written:

> it concentrates exclusively on facilitating the removal of children from their families and on reducing the rights of natural parents. It makes no provision whatsoever for income maintenance, it gives the deprived no greater access to housing, it places no duty on local authorities to install day care amenities, and it supplies no extra social work resources with which to promote greater contact with natural parents.[256]

Jordan too has detected a move away from the notion of supporting disadvantaged families. 'Social workers are increasingly being exhorted to act as rescuers, saving children from wicked or feckless parents.'[257] The Social Services are used 'as a means to accomplish the traditional tasks by reinforcing the work ethic, maintaining the sense of family responsibility, and keeping law and order.'[258]

The significance of this is not to be seen only in terms of increased intervention leading to more removals of children (what shows up in statistics on place of safety orders, care orders and so on) but also in terms of greater surveillance of poor families more generally. The category of child abuse has widened.[259] But, though the net has been cast wider, those whom it is likely to catch has not. The clients of social workers have not changed: the position which the social work profession occupies has shifted. The 'discovery' of child abuse may have done more for the social work profession than it has done for children.

Concluding Comment

A long chapter does not merit a prolonged conclusion. What I demonstrated in this chapter is that child abuse is an evil, though not a new one, and that current practices and policies are not tackling the problem. What they are doing is isolating and stigmatising a group of poor families and purporting to protect their children by rescuing them. Social workers, many of whom would ideally wish to be carrying out a preventive, welfare role, using section 1 money for example,[260] find themselves part of a social control mechanism embedded within 'law and order' politics. The Thatcher governments are the culmination of these policies. With unemployment up[261] and the stock of council houses depleted, with cutbacks in the social services and a stepping-up of the control culture, we cannot conquer child abuse. We lack the political will to do so. Indeed, if anything, we might expect child abuse to increase.[262] A government which believes in the 'short, sharp shock' is hardly likely to take an initiative on corporal punishment. Current politics may lead up to more abuse: current social work practices will undoubtedly find more. Only a radical rethink of the concept of childhood and an intensified poverty programme can do much to cut back on the number of children who suffer from parental cruelty and neglect.

Notes

1. See W. Clinton Terry III and D. F. Luckenbill, 'Investigating Criminal Homicides: Police Work in Reporting and Solving Murders' in W. B. Saunders and H. C. Daudistel (eds), *The Criminal Justice Process, A Reader*, New York, Praeger Publishers, 1976, pp. 79–95 at p. 92.
2. The terms are Stanley Cohen's. See his *Folk Devils and Moral Panics*, London, Paladin, 1973 (a second edition was published in 1980). See also Stuart Hall *et al.*, *Policing The Crisis*, London, Macmillan, 1978, and now see N. Parton, 'Child Abuse, Social Anxiety and Welfare', *British Journal of Social Work*, 11 (1981), pp. 391–414.
3. See the article by Joel Fischer, 'Does Anything Work?', *Journal of Social Service Research*, 1 (1978), pp. 215–43. See also (in relation to prisons) R. Martinson, 'What Works? —Questions and Answers About Prison Reform', *Public Interest*, 35 (1974), pp. 22–54.
4. On the history see Samuel X. Radbill, 'A History of Child Abuse and Infanticide' in Ray E. Helfer and C. Henry Kempe (eds), *The Battered Child*, Chicago, University of Chicago Press (2nd ed.), 1974. See also Ivy Pinchbeck and Margaret Hewitt, *Children In English Society*, vol. II, London, Routledge & Kegan Paul, 1973, esp. ch. 20.
5. de Mause, *The History of Childhood*, London, Souvenir Press, 1976, p. 1. See also his article, 'Our Forbears Made Childhood A Nightmare', *Psychology Today*, (April 1975), pp. 85–8.
6. See his *Songs of Innocence*.
7. Legislation to protect animals from cruelty dates from 1823: it was 1889 before child cruelty legislation was passed. The sponsor of the 1889 Act was 'anxious that we should give children *almost* the same protection that we give . . . domestic animals' (Hansard H.C. vol. 337, col. 229).
8. See V. Fontana, *Somewhere A Child Is Crying*, London, Macmillan, 1973; and Catherine J. Ross, 'The Lessons Of The Past: Defining and Controlling Child Abuse in the United States' in G. Gerbner *et al.*, *Child Abuse*, New York, Oxford University Press, 1980, pp. 63–81 at p. 75. The prosecution of the girl's mistress in 1874 led to the establishment of the New York SPCC.
9. R. Roberts, *The Classic Slum*, Manchester, Manchester University Press, 1971, p. 45.
10. See H. Becker (ed.), *Social Problems*, New York, Wiley, 1966, Introduction. See also M. Spector and J. Kitsuse, *Constructing Social Problems*, Menlo Park, Calif., Cummings, 1977. A useful explanation of the emergence of child abuse as a social problem is N. Parton, 'The Natural History of Child Abuse: A Study In Social Problem Definition', *British Journal of Social Work*, 9 (1970), pp. 431–52.
11. See, e.g. S. West, 'Acute Periosteal Swellings in Several Young Infants of the Same Family, Probably Rickets in Nature', *British Medical Journal*, 1 (1888), pp. 856–7.
12. Invented in 1895.
13. See S. Pfohl, 'The Discovery of Child Abuse', *Social Problems*, 24 (1977), pp. 310–23.
14. E. Freidson, *The Profession of Medicine*, New York, Dodd, Mead, 1970, p. 252.
15. Pfohl, op. cit., at p. 319.
16. Freidson, op. cit., at p. 328.

17   See T. Scheff, 'Decision Rules, Types of Error, and Their Consequences in Medical Diagnosis', *Behavioural Science,* **8** (1963), pp. 97–107. See also his *Being Mentally Ill,* Chicago, Aldine, 1966. A good example of this process at work is found in I. Illich, *Limits to Medicine,* Harmondsworth, Penguin, 1977, pp. 100–1.

18.   See A. A. Rosenfeld and E. H. Newberger, 'Compassion vs. Control: Conceptual and Practical Pitfalls in the Broadened Definition of Child Abuse', *Journal of the American Medical Association,* **237** (1977), pp. 2086–8

19.   See N. Kittrie, *The Right To Be Different,* Baltimore, Johns Hopkins Press, 1971.

20.   See E. Newberger and R. Bourne, 'The Medicalization and Legalization of Child Abuse' in J. Eekelaar and S. Katz (eds), *Family Violence,* Toronto, Butterworths, 1978, pp. 301–17, at p. 306.

21.   See F. Allen, *The Borderland of Criminal Justice,* Chicago, University of Chicago Press, 1964.

22.   Indeed, self-help groups like Parents Anonymous reinforce this image.

23.   See J. Gusfield, 'Moral Passage: The Symbolic Process in Public Designations of Deviance', *Social Problems,* **15** (1967), pp. 175–88.

24.   See H. Becker, *Outsiders,* New York, Free Press, 1963. See also E. Pfohl, *The Deviance Process,* New York, Van Nostrand, 1980, ch. 4.

25.   See E. Freidson, 'Disability As Social Deviance' in M. Sussman (ed.), *Sociology and Rehabilitation,* American Sociological Association, 1966. See also R. Gelles, *Family Violence,* Beverly Hills, Sage, 1979, ch. 3.

26.   See Pfohl, 'The Discovery of Child Abuse', p. 314.

27.   H. Kempe, 'The Battered Baby Syndrome', *Journal of the American Medical Association,* **181** (1962), pp. 17–24.

28.   D. L. Griffiths and F. J. Moynihan, 'Multiple Epiphyseal Injuries In Babies', *British Medical Journal,* no. 5372 (1963), pp. 1558–61.

29.   See K. Simpson, 'Battered Babies: Conviction for Murder', *British Medical Journal,* 1 (1965), p. 393; J. M. Cameron *et al.,* 'The Battered Baby Syndrome', *Medicine, Science and the Law,* **6** (1966), pp. 2–21. There are several other articles in issues of *Medicine, Science and the Law* of the period.

30.   See the DHSS circular LASSL(74)(13) of 22 April 1974 following the Tunbridge Wells Study Group on Non-Accidental Injury to Children of 1973. The proceedings were subsequently published in A. W. Franklin (ed.), *Concerning Child Abuse,* Edinburgh, Churchill, Livingstone, 1975.

31.   Cf. Jolly K. (an abusive parent) who told a US Senate Subcommittee in 1973: 'the deeds are monstrous, but we are not monsters.' Quoted in E. Hoffman, 'Policy and Politics: the Child Abuse Prevention and Treatment Act' in R. Bourne and E. H. Newberger (eds), *Critical Perspectives on Child Abuse,* Lexington, Mass., Lexington Books, 1979, pp. 157–70 at p. 162.

32.   *Fit For The Future,* Cmnd. 6684, HMSO, London, 1977 (see vol. 1, p. 42). In the USA it has been estimated that 28 million accidental injuries occurred annually among children under sixteen. See E. Zigler, 'Controlling Child Abuse: Do We Have the Knowledge And/Or The Will?', in G. Gerbner *et al.* (eds), *Child Abuse,* New York, Oxford University Press, 1980, pp. 3–32 at p. 4.

33.   See P. Townsend and N. Davidson, *Inequalities in Health,* Harmondsworth, Penguin, 1982.

34.   See D. Wilson, 'Petrol: Must our Children Still be Poisoned?', *The Times,* 8 February 1982; see also *The Times,* leading article, 'Poison In The Air', 9 February 1982.

35.   A point also made by O. Stevenson, 'Some Dilemmas In Social Work Education', *Oxford Review of Education,* **2** (1976), p. 2.

36.   See J. Mercer, 'Who Is Normal? Two Perspectives on Mild Mental Retardation' in E. Jaco (ed.), *Patients, Physicians and Illness,* New York, Free Press, 1972 (2nd ed.), See also W. Jordan, *Poor Parents: Social Policy and The Cycle of Deprivation,* London, Routledge & Kegan Paul, 1973.

37.   See W. Ryan, *Blaming The Victim,* New York, Vintage (revised 1976), p. 17.

38.   E. Zigler, 'Controlling Child Abuse in America: An Effort Doomed to Failure?' in Bourne and Newberger (eds), *Critical Perspectives on Child Abuse,* op. cit., pp. 171–

213 at p. 176.
39. Ibid., p. 177.
40. Zigler, 'Controlling Child Abuse . . .', in Gerbner *et al., Child Abuse,* p. 9.
41. Cf. Ryan, *Blaming The Victim.*
42. Part of the Juvenule Justice Standards Project, Cambridge, Mass., Ballinger, 1977. An introduction is E. Flannery, 'Synopsis: Standards Relating To Abuse and Neglect', *Boston University Law Review,* 57 (1977). They are criticised by R. Bourne and E. Newberger in ' "Family Autonomy" or "Coercive Intervention" ', ibid., pp. 663, 670.
43. V. J. Fontana, *The Maltreated Child: The Maltreatment Syndrome In Children,* Springfield, Illinois, Thomas 1970 (2nd ed.).
44. D. Gil, 'Societal Violence and Violence In Families' in Eekelaar and Katz (eds), *Family Violence,* op. cit., p. 14–33 at 14–15. See also Kerby T. Alvy, 'Preventing Child Abuse', *American Psychologist,* 30 (1975), pp. 921–8.
45. E. Newberger, 'The Myth of The Battered Child Syndrome' in *Current Medical Dialog,* 40 (1973), pp. 327–30. Also in Bourne and Newberger (eds), *Critical Perspectives. . .,* at p. 15.
46. See C. Stoll, 'Images of Man and Social Control', *Social Forces,* 47 (1968), p. 119.
47. For example, the American Bar Association's Standards (see Flannery, 'Synopsis: Standards Relating . . .', para. 2.1.)
48. See B. Fraser, 'Legislative Status of Child Abuse Legislation' in C. H. Kempe and R. Helfer (eds), *Child Abuse and Neglect: The Family and the Community,* Cambridge, Mass., Ballinger, 1977, p. 315. But cf. the English Children and Young Persons Act 1969 s.1.
49. See Bourne and Newberger, 'The Medicalization and Legalization of Child Abuse', op. cit., p. 308.
50. In Bourne and Newberger, op. cit., p. 701. See also G. S. Gregg and E. Elmer, 'Infant Injuries: Accident or Abuse?', *Paedriatics,* 44 (1969), p. 434.
51. See M. D. A. Freeman, 'Child Welfare: Law and Control' in M. Partington and J. Jowell (eds), *Welfare Law and Policy,* London, Frances Pinter, 1979, pp. 223–31, at pp. 225–7.
52. See E. Rubington and M. Weinberg, *Deviance: The Interactionist Perspective,* London, Macmillan, 1981 (4th ed.).
53. A consequence of which may be that middle-class children (in this instance) get less protection than their working-class counterparts.
54. The fullest description of which is the *Report of the Committee of Inquiry into the Care and Supervision Provided in Relation To Maria Colwell,* DHSS, HMSO, London, 1974.
55. On the greater visibility of the deviance of the poor more generally, see J. H. Skolnick and R. Woodworth, 'Bureaucracy, Information and Social Control: A Study of a Morals Detail', in D. Bordua (ed.), *The Police: Six Sociological Essays,* New York, Wiley, 1967, pp. 99–136. See also Pfohl, *The Deviance Process,* op. cit., pp. 110–14.
56. A good illustration in another context is Mary Cameron's study of shoplifting. See *The Booster and The Switch: Department Store Shoplifting,* New York, Free Press, 1964.
57. It is recognised by D. Gil, *Violence Against Children,* Cambridge, Mass., Harvard University Press, 1970; R. Gelles, *Family Violence,* Beverly Hills, Sage, 1979; N. Feshbach and S. Feshbach, 'Punishment: Parents' Rites versus Children's Rights' in G. Koocher (ed.), *Children's Rights and the Mental Health Profession,* New York, Wiley, 1976, pp. 149–70; as well as by Alvy, 'Preventing Child Abuse', op. cit.; Zigler's chapter in Gerbner *et al., Child Abuse,* and many others. But the NSPCC, for example, has not come out against corporal punishment.
58. But see, as regards China, R. Sidel, *Women and Child Care in China,* New York, Penguin, 1973. See also, as regards the Samia of Western Kenya, G. Fraser and P. L. Kilbride, 'Child Abuse and Neglect . . .', *Child Abuse and Neglect,* 4 (1980), p. 227.
59. See P. Wilby, 'The Cane: Who Uses It Abroad', *The Sunday Times,* 17 September 1978.
60. Though not in many areas and not in homes run by one of the largest of Britain's voluntary care organisations, the National Children's Home (abolished in 1972). See J. Dossett-Davies, 'Spare the Rod and Help the Child?', *Community Care,* 8 October 1981 pp. 16–17.

61. 'Corporal Punishment', *American Psychologist*, **29** (Aug. 1974), pp. 614–26. Also 'Violence Must End', *The Last Resort*, no. 7 (1978) p. 1.
62. The issue caused a riot (led to violence?) in Newcastle in January 1976. See *The Times*, 12 January 1976.
63. See Children and Young Persons Act 1933 s.1(7). See further, M. D. A. Freeman, 'Children's Education and the Law', *Legal Action Group Bulletin* (Sept. 1980), p. 212 at p. 213.
64. J. Newson and E. Newson, *Infant Care In An Urban Community*, London, Allen & Unwin, 1963.
65. Newson and Newson, *Four Years Old In An Urban Community*, London, Allen & Unwin, 1968.
66. Newson and Newson, *Seven Years Old In The Home Environment*, London, Allen & Unwin, 1976.
67. R. Stark and J. McEvoy, 'Middle Class Violence', *Psychology Today*, **4** (1970), pp. 52–65.
68. M. Straus and S. Steinmetz, *Violence In The Family*, New York, Dodd, Mead, 1974, pp. 159, 186.
69. R. Gelles, 'A Profile of Violence Toward Children In the United States' in Gerbner *et al.*, *Child Abuse*, pp. 82–105, reporting on M. Straus *et al.*, *Behind Closed Doors: Violence In The American Family*, New York, Anchor/Doubleday, 1980.
70. See E. Elmer, *Children In Jeopardy*, Pittsburgh, University of Pittsburg Press, 1967; Gil, *Violence Against Children*, op. cit.
71. See E. Elmer, *Children In Jeopardy*, Pittsburgh, University of Pittsburgh Press, 1967; p. 60 at p. 65.
72. Gil, *Violence Against Children*, op. cit., pp. 134–5.
73. Zigler in Gerbner *et al.*, *Child Abuse*, pp. 27–8.
74. It was abolished in prisons in 1967 (see Criminal Justice Act 1967 s.65) and in the armed services in 1881 (Army Act 1881, s.44).
75. P. Ariès, *Centuries of Childhood*, London, Jonathan Cape, 1962, pp. 258–62.
76. The lengthiest debate took place on the Protection of Minors Bill 1973. See Hansard, H.L. vol. 347, cols. 875–85, 893–965.
77. See E. Michael Salzer, 'To Combat Violence In The Child's World: Swedish Efforts To Strengthen The Child's Rights', *Current Sweden*, no. 229 (July 1979).
78. H.C. 329-i, London, HMSO.
79. *Child Abuse and Neglect*, House of Commons, Ottawa, 1976, p. 18.
80. 430 U.S. 651 (1977).
81. Which outlaws 'cruel and unusual punishment' (see Article 8).
82. See *Landeros* v. *Flood* 551 P. 2d. 389 (1975).
83. Gil, *Violence Against Children*, p. 142.
84. See P. Newell, *The Last Resort?*, Harmondsworth, Penguin, 1972.
85. See A. Clegg and B. Megson, *Children in Distress*, Harmondsworth, Penguin, and J. Kozol, *Death At An Early Age*, Boston, Houghton Mifflin, 1967.
86. See N. Feshbach, 'Corporal Punishment In The Schools: Some Paradoxes, Some Facts, Some Possible Directions' in Gerbner *et al.*, *Child Abuse*, op. cit., pp. 204–21.
87. See P. Wilby, *Corporal Punishment*, London, U.K. Association for the International Year of the Child, 1979.
88. It would be most difficult to justify corporal punishment in terms of retribution. I note this is never attempted: nearly all justifications are grounded in utilitarian-type arguments.
89. Official action, particularly legislation, is an important symbol of what is legitimate. See M. D. A. Freeman, *The Legal Structure*, Harlow, Longman, 1974, p. 55.
90. See S. Feshbach and N. Feshbach, 'Alternatives to Corporal Punishment: Implications For Training and Control', *Journal of Clinical Psychology*, **II**, no. 3 (1973), pp. 46–8.
91. It is arguable that a community home caning should be entered on the 'at risk' register. It is also arguable that it is unlawful. See Child Care Act 1980 s.18.
92. See M. Wald, 'State Intervention on Behalf of "Neglected" Children: A Search for Realistic Standards', *Stanford Law Review*, **27** (1975), pp. 985–1040.

93. See M. van Stolk, Paper to 2nd World Congress of International Society of Family Law, Montreal 1977 (unpublished). I have criticised this in 'Sexual Abuse of Children', *Family Law*, **8** (1978), pp. 221–5.

94. The subject of the first report of the British Association For The Study and Prevention of Child Abuse and Neglect (BASPCAN). See *Child Sexual Abuse*, Rochdale, BASPCAN, 1981.

95. See *The Times*, 8 August 1981.

96. See D. MacCarthy, 'Maternal Rejection and the Stunting of Growth' in DHSS, *The Family In Society*, London, HMSO, 1974, p. 86.

97. See J. Renvoize, *Children In Danger*, London, Routledge & Kegan Paul, 1974.

98. Zigler points out the significance of this in a middle-class setting. See 'Controlling Child Abuse. . . in America' in Bourne and Newberger, *Critical Perspectives on Child Abuse*, op. cit., pp. 187–9.

99. R. Gelles, 'Child Abuse as Psychopathology: A Sociological Critique and Reformulation', *American Journal of Orthopsychiatry*, **43** (1973), pp. 611–21. Also in his *Family Violence*, op. cit., ch. 1.

100. Gil, *Violence Against Children*, op. cit., p. 17.

101. See S. Freud, *Collected Papers*, vol. II, New York, Basic Books, 1959.

102. See Becker, *Outsiders*, op. cit.

103. B. Steele and C. Pollock, 'A Psychiatric Study of Parents Who Abuse Infants and Small Children' in R. Helfer and C. A. Kempe (eds), *The Battered Child*, Chicago, University of Chicago Press (2nd ed.), 1974, p. 89.

104. NSPCC Battered Child Research Department, *At Risk*, London, Routledge & Kegan Paul, 1976, p. 194.

105. An exception is S. M. Smith, *The Battered Baby Syndrome*, London, Butterworth, 1976. Cf. B. Melnick and J. Hurley, 'Distinctive Personality Attributes of Child Abusing Mothers', *Journal of Consulting Clinical Psychiatry*, **XXXIII** (1969), pp. 746–9.

106. See e.g. C. Ounsted, R. Oppenheimer and J. Lindsay, 'The Psychopathology and Psychotherapy of the Families: Aspects of Bonding Failure' in Franklin (ed.), *Concerning Child Abuse*, op. cit., p. 30.

107. See e.g., J. Holter and S. B. Friedman, 'Child Abuse: Early Case Findings in the Emergency Department', *Pediatrics*, **42** (1968), pp. 128–38, or E. H. Bennie and A. B. Sclare, 'The Battered Child Syndrome', *American Journal of Psychiatry*, **125** (1969), pp. 975–9.

108. Zigler in Gerbner *et al.*, *Child Abuse*, op. cit., p. 24.

109. A good review is J. Spinetta and D. Rigler, 'The Child-Abusing Parent: A Psychological Review', *Psychological Bulletin*, **77** (1972), pp. 296–304. See also Gelles, 'Child Abuse as Psychopathology. . .', op. cit.

110. In Spinetta and Rigler, ibid., p. 297.

111. H. F. Harlow and M. K. Harlow, 'Psychopathology in Monkeys', in H. D. Kimmel (ed.), *Experimental Psychopathology*, New York, Academic Press, 1971.

112. Gil, *Violence Against Children*, op. cit., p. 114 (14 per cent mothers; 7 per cent fathers). See also L. Allan, 'Child Abuse: A Critical Review of the Research and Theory' in J. P. Martin (ed.), *Violence and the Family*, Chichester, Wiley, 1978, p. 51.

113. See J. E. Oliver and J. A. Taylor, 'Five Generations of Ill-Treated Children in One Family Pedigree', *British Journal of Psychiatry*, **119** (1971), pp. 473–80.

114. Gelles, 'Child Abuse. . .', p. 614.

115. J. Kitsuse, 'Societal Reaction to Deviant Behavior', *Social Problems*, **9** (1962), p. 247. See also E. Schur, *Labeling Deviant Behavior*, New York, Harper & Row, 1971, p. 52, and E. Schur, *The Politics of Deviance*, Englewood Cliffs, Prentice Hall, 1980, pp. 13–14.

116. J. Lofland, *Deviance and Identity*, Englewood Cliffs, Prentice Hall, 1969, p. 150.

117. E. Goffman, *Asylums*, Harmondsworth, Penguin, 1968, p. 144. See also D. L. Rosenhan's 'On Being Sane In Insane Places', *Science*, no. 179 (19 January 1973), pp. 250–8.

118. See DHSS Circular, 'Non-Accidental Injury To Children: Area Review Committees', LASSL(76) 2 February 1976. Nineteen per cent of 5,700 known or suspected

cases in the last nine months of 1974 referred to juvenile court. Only 3.5 per cent led to prosecution of parents. Very few parents went to prison. See para. 33. I suspect the percentage of prosecutions has declined since 1974 rather than risen.

119.   Illich, *Limits to Medicine*, op. cit., p. 98.

120.   Ibid., p. 100.

121.   See C. Schneider *et al.*, 'The Predictive Questionnaire: A Preliminary Report' in C. H. Kempe and R. Helfen (eds), *Helping the Battered Child and His Family*, Philadelphia, Lippincott. See also M. D. A. Freeman, *Violence In The Home — A Socio-Legal Study*, Farnborough, Saxon House, 1979, pp. 108–11.

122.   R. Light, 'Abused and Neglected Children In America: A Study of Alternative Policies', *Harvard Educational Review*, 43, (1973) pp. 4556–98.

123.   See J. Daniel *et al.*, 'Child Abuse Screening: Implications of the Limited Predictive Power of Abuse Discriminants From a Controlled Family Study of Pediatric Social Illness', *Child Abuse and Neglect*, 2 (1978), pp. 247–59.

124.   B. Jordan, 'Is The Client A Fellow Citizen?', *Social Work Today*, 6, no. 15 (30 October 1975), pp. 471–5. Jordan develops this further in *Freedom And The Welfare State*, London, Routledge & Kegan Paul, 1976. See also Report of Review Panel of Somerset Area Review Committee for Non-Accidental Injury to Children, Wayne Brewer Inquiry, Taunton, Somerset C.C., 1977, para. 7.11.

125.   See A. Skinner and R. Castle, *78 Battered Children*, London, NSPCC, 1969, p. 20.

126.   Liaison failures are commonly pointed to in inquiries into child abuse cases.

127.   See B. Justice and R. Justice, *The Abusing Family*, New York, Human Sciences Press, 1976, pp. 204–9.

128.   D. Gil, 'Unraveling Child Abuse', *American Journal of Orthopsychiatry*, 45 (1975), pp. 346–58 at p. 352.

129.   Ibid.

130.   J. Garbarino, 'A Preliminary Study of Some Ecological Correlates of Child Abuse: The Impact of Socio-Economic Stress on Mothers', *Child Development*, 47 (1976), pp. 178–85.

131.   Light, 'Abused and Neglected Children In America', op. cit., has done similar analysis by re-analysing Gil's original findings (*Violence Against Children*). He found family stress due to the father's unemployment most closely related to abuse.

132.   See E. Newberger and J. Hyde, 'Child Abuse: Principles and Implications of Current Pediatric Practice', *Pediatrics Clinics of North America*, 22 (1975), pp. 695–715 at p. 706. See also NSPCC Battered Child Research Department, *At Risk*, op. cit.

133.   See Garbarino, 'A Preliminary Study. . .', op. cit.; Straus *et al.*, *Behind Closed Doors. . .*, op. cit. (rate was 62 per cent higher where husband was unemployed and nearly double where he was employed part-time); R. Parke and C. Collmer, 'Child Abuse: An Interdisciplinary Analysis' in M. Hetherington (ed.), *Child Development Research*, vol. 5, Chicago, University of Chicago Press, 1975, pp. 509–90; J. A. Baldwin and J. E. Oliver, 'Epidemiology and Family Characteristics of Severely Abused Children', *British Journal of Preventive Social Medicine*, 29 (1975), pp. 205–21; J. Cater and P. Easton, 'Separation and Other Stress in Child Abuse', *The Lancet*, 3 May 1980 (study showing 30 per cent child batterers in Dundee unemployed).

134.   Sometimes, no doubt, they move to avoid the limelight caused by the exposure of their behaviour towards their children.

135.   Skinner and Castle, *78 Battered Children*, op. cit. See also M. Lynch, 'Ill Health and Child Abuse', *The Lancet*, no. 7929, 16 August 1975, pp. 317–9. Allan, 'Child Abuse. . .', op. cit., pp. 53–5, contains a general review of the literature on this.

136.   M. D. A. Freeman, 'Family Violence: Interpretations and Solutions' in S. Lloyd-Bostock (ed.), *Psychology In Legal Contexts — Applications and Limitations*, London, Macmillan, 1981, pp. 165–81 at pp. 175–7.

137.   W. Goode, 'Force and Violence In The Family', *Journal of Marriage and the Family*, 33 (1971), pp. 624–36 at p. 628.

138.   See M. Straus, 'Normative and Behavioral Aspects of Violence Between Spouses', unpublished paper, 1977.

139.   L. Pelton, 'Child Abuse and Neglect: The Myth of Classlessness', *American Journal of*

Orthopsychology, **48** (1978), pp. 608–17.
140. Straus *et al., Behind Closed Doors. . .,* op. cit.
141. R. Gelles, 'A Profile of Violence Toward Children In The United States' in Gerbner *et al., Child Abuse,* op. cit., pp. 82–105 at pp. 98–9.
142. Ibid., p. 99.
143. See Straus, *et al.,* op. cit.
144. Cf. Gelles, 'Child Abuse as Psychopathology. . .', op. cit., p. 620.
145. See Hansard, H.C. vol. 955, cols. 597–603 (Written Answers) (3 August 1978).
146. See D. Piachaud, *The Cost of A Child,* London, Child Poverty Action Group, 1979, and D. Piachaud, *Children and Poverty,* London, Child Poverty Action Group, 1981.
147. See also to this effect D. Donnison, *The Politics of Poverty,* Oxford, Martin Robertson, 1982.
148. In House of Commons Select Committee on *Violence in the Family,* First Report, London, HMSO, 1977.
149. *Housing Policy,* Technical vol. III, Cmnd. 6851, London, HMSO, 1977.
150. See D. Webster, 'A "Social Market" Answer on Housing', *New Society,* **58** no. 991 (12 November 1981), pp. 269–72.
151. 'A Towering Problem For Children', *Community Care,* January 1979.
152. See D. Donnison, 'A Radical Strategy to Help The Poor?', *New Society,* **58** no. 989 (29 October 1981), pp. 183–5.
153. See M. Lynch, 'Ill Health and Child Abuse', op. cit. See also M. Ainsworth, 'Attachment and Child Abuse' in Gerbner *et al., Child Abuse,* op. cit., pp. 35–47.
154. See F. Field, *Fair Shares For Families,* London, Study Commission on the Family, 1980.
155. Gil, 'Unraveling Child Abuse', op. cit., p. 350.
156. Ibid., p. 351.
157. For example, by R. Fletcher, *The Family and Marriage In Britain,* Harmondsworth, Penguin, 1973 (3rd ed.), p. 138.
158. See DHSS Report of Committee of Inquiry Into Care and Supervision Provided In Relation to Maria Colwell, London, HMSO, 1974, para. 42.
159. See *Re D* [1976] 1 All E.R. 326.
160. Cf. M. Kellmer-Pringle, *The Needs of Children,* London, Hutchinson, 1975, pp. 69–70.
161. See M. D. A. Freeman, 'The Rights of Children in The International Year of The Child', *Current Legal Problems,* **33** (1980), pp. 1–31.
162. A number of local authorities and local educational authorities have abolished corporal punishment in institutions and schools. Unfortunately, the issue is something of a political football with Labour-controlled councils abolishing it and Conservatives re-introducing it or vice versa (see *Community Care,* 18 June 1981, p. 4). The Secretary of State for Social Services in the last Labour administration spoke out against corporal punishment in community homes (*Social Work Today,* **9**, no. 4 (1978), p. 2). His example has not been followed by the present Tory administration.
163. Shropshire County Council, Report of Working Party of Social Services Committee Inquiry into the Circumstances Surrounding the Death of Graham Bagnall and the Role of the County Council's Social Services, Shrewsbury, Shropshire C.C., 1973.
164. House of Commons Select Committee on *Violence in the Family, Minutes of Evidence:* Evidence of Association of Directors of Social Services by John Rea Price, H.C. 350-viii, London, HMSO, p. 253.
165. Geoffrey Banner, Assistant Director of Residential Care in Wiltshire, quoted in *The Times,* 12 September 1974.
166. By seeking care orders under Children and Young Persons Act 1969 s.1 or initially by place of safety orders under s.28 of that Act.
167. House of Commons Select Committee on *Violence in the Family. . .,* op. cit. (see note 164), by Mr. W. Johnson.
168. Ibid., p. 14, by Mr. J. Hillman, Assistant Area Officer of the London Borough of Hammersmith.
169. Quoted in *The Times,* 13 October 1976.
170. See Children and Young Persons Act 1969 s.21. There is no appeal against a revo-

cation, though local authorities sometimes get around this by resorting to wardship. See, e.g. *Re D* [1977] 3 All E.R. 481.

171. Report of Review Panel of Somerset Area Review Committee, op. cit., para. 4.19. There is a useful discussion of that case by R. Bacon, 'Child Abuse and Child Care', *Adoption and Fostering*, no. 90 (1977), pp. 36–43.

172. Cf. Jordan's remarks, p. 119. He added that parents often acted out their 'rebellious anger with us [i.e. social workers] on their children.'

173. See J. Roberts, 'Social Work and Child Abuse: The Reasons For Failure and The Way to Success' in Martin (ed.), op. cit., *Violence and the Family*, pp. 255–91. See also J. Pickett and A. Maton, 'Protective Casework and Child Abuse', *Social Work Today*, 9, no. 28 (14 March 1978), pp. 10–18.

174. Produced by the Seebohm Committee's report on Local Authority and Allied Personal Social Service, London, HMSO, Cmnd. 3703 (1968), leading to the Local Authority Social Services Act 1970.

175. House of Commons Select Committee on *Violence in the Family. . .*, op. cit. (see note 164), p. 56, by Chief Superintendent J. Keyte.

176. Ibid., p. 32 (Memorandum of Association of Chief Police Officers).

177. DHSS Circular LAASL(74)13: 'Others who may be invited when appropriate include police surgeons, police officers . . .' (para. 16(c)).

178. R. Castle, *Case Conferences: A Cause For Concern?*, London, NSPCC, 1976.

179. See Stoll, 'Images of Man and Social Control', op. cit.

180. HCSC, op. cit. (see note 164), p. 22 (Memorandum of Metropolitan Police CID).

181. Ibid., p. 248, by Miss Sally Beer (a Senior Social Worker and BASW representative).

182. HCSC, *Violence in the Family* (see note 148), para. 119.

183. DHSS Circular LAASL(76)26: also Home Office Circular 179/76.

184. As Mr. P. J. Outram of the NSPCC had hoped. See HCSC, op. cit. (see note 164), p. 135.

185. Cf. the point made by Dr. S. Hodgson (Specialist in Community Medicine and Chairman of the Area Review Committee of Ealing, Hammersmith and Hounslow AHA), ibid., p. 12.

186. See J. Court, 'Psycho-Social Factors In Child Battering', *Journal of Medical Women's Federation*, 52 (1970), pp. 99–106.

187. HCSC, op. cit. (see note 148), p. 141.

188. 31 May 1975.

189. Others include the NSPCC, Family Service Units, Health Visitors and the education service.

190. HCSC, op. cit. (see note 148), p. 62, by Mr. Roland Moyle.

191. HCSC, op. cit. (see note 164), para. 91.

192. M. Rein, *Social Policy*, New York, Random House, 1970.

193. DHSS, Colwell Inquiry, op. cit. A second inquiry was held by East Sussex C.C. itself: *Children At Risk*, Lewes, East Sussex C.C., 1975.

194. Report of Committee of Inquiry Into the Provisions and Co-ordination of Services to the Family of Auckland, DHSS, London, HMSO, 1975.

195. See DHSS Colwell Inquiry, op. cit., para. 240. On inquiries generally see A. Main, 'After The Horse Has Bolted — The Futility of Inquiries', *Social Work Today*, 11, no. 46 (5 August 1980), pp. 10–11.

196. For example, Essex A.H.A. and Essex C.A., *Inquiry into the Case of Max Piazzani*, Chelmsford, Essex C.C., 1974, para. 20(c); *Brewer Inquiry*, op. cit., para. 5.20; Essex C.C. and Essex A.H.A., *Report of Panel Appointed by Essex A.R.C. to Consider the Case of Malcolm Page*, Chelmsford, Essex C.C., 1981, para. 5.9; London Borough of Southwark, *Report of Independent Inquiry into Case of Maria Mehmedagi*, 1981, para. 135 (as to which see M. D. A. Freeman, 'A Second Maria: What Can We Learn From Inquiries into Child Abuse Cases?', *Justice of The Peace*, 145 (25 July 1981), pp. 440–1); Derbyshire C.C. and A.H.A. *Report by Prof. J. D. McClean concerning Karen Spencer*, Matlock, Derbyshire C.C., 1978, para. 3.35–3.37.

197. See J. Carter, 'Co-ordination and Child Abuse', *Social Work Service*, no. 9 (April 1976), p. 22.

198. I have considered these in Freeman, *Violence in the Home. . .*, op. cit., pp. 87–8.

199. LASSL(74)13.
200. *Report of Committee of Inquiry into Case of Paul Steven Brown,* London, HMSO, 1980, Cmnd. 8107.
201. See Malcolm Page Inquiry Report, op. cit., note 196, para. 5.8.
202. Ibid., para. 5.9.
203. *Report on Maria Mehmedagi,* op. cit.
204. Ibid., para. 135.
205. H. Geach, 'Case Conferences — Time For a Change?', *Community Care,* 27 August 1981, pp. 16–17.
206. C. Hallett and O. Stevenson, *Child Abuse: Aspects of Interprofessional Co-operation,* London, Allen.& Unwin, 1980.
207. The Malcolm Page Inquiry Report, op. cit., refers to the need to clarify thought about acceptable and unacceptable standards (para. 5.11).
208. LASSL(74)13, para. 17.
209. LASSL(76)2, para. 23.
210. HCSC, *Violence in the Family,* op. cit. (see note 148), para. 101.
211. Ibid.
212. Ibid.
213. A. Solnit, 'Child Abuse: The Problem' in Eekelaar and Katz (eds), *Family Violence,* op. cit. (note 20), pp. 243–52 at p. 246.
214. John Chant, quoted in *Social Work Today,* 9, no. 4 (20 September 1977), p. 2.
215. H. Geach, 'When Registers Lead To Abuse', *Community Care,* 12 June 1980, pp. 18–19 (also A. Morris *et al., Justice For Children,* London, Macmillan, 1980, p. 120).
216. A. Solnit, 'Too Much Reporting, Too Little Service: Roots and Prevention of Child Abuse', in Gerbner (ed.), *Child Abuse,* op. cit., pp. 135–46 at pp. 144–5.
217. P. Morris, 'Police: By Invitation Only?', *Community Care,* 22 March 1978. The police hold a most sophisticated computer.
218. An example is quoted by Geach, op. cit., at p. 19 (also A. Morris *et al.,* op. cit., p. 119).
219. BASW, *The Central Abuse Register,* Birmingham, BASW, 1978.
220. BASW in *Social Work Today,* 9, no. 3 (1977), p. 5.
221. This information is taken from 'Abuse Registers "Scarcely Used" ', *Community Care,* 19 March 1981.
222. BASW, *The Central Abuse Register,* op. cit.
223. See DHSS Circular, *Child Abuse: Central Register Systems,* LASSL(80)4, August 1980, para. 4.3.
224. Ibid., para. 2.2(c). On the original draft, which was wider, see the perceptive article by N. Parton, 'Recording Concern — The Case Against Child Abuse Registers', *Social Work Today,* 11 no. 25 (26 February 1980), pp. 12–14.
225. By BASPCAN, *Child Sexual Abuse,* op. cit., (note 94).
226. See M. Wald, 'State Intervention on Behalf of "Neglected" Children: A Search For Realistic Standards' in M. Rosenheim (ed.), *Pursuing Justice For The Child,* Chicago, University of Chicago Press, 1976, pp. 246–78 at p. 261.
227. See J. Gray, C. Cutler, J. Dean and C. H. Kempe, 'Perinatal Assessment of Mother-Baby Interaction' in R. Helfer and C. H. Kempe (eds), *Child Abuse and Neglect, The Family and the Community,* Cambridge, Mass., Ballinger, 1976, pp. 377–89.
228. See J. Goldstein *et al., Before The Best Interests of The Child,* New York, Free Press, 1979, pp. 75–7.
229. M. Paulsen, 'Legal Protections Against Child Abuse', *Children,* 13 (1966), p. 48.
230. House of Commons Select Committee, *Violence in the Family . . .,* op. cit. (note 164), p. 228.
231. Though it does (or did) note the power that this gives the social worker. See J. Handler, *The Coercive Social Worker,* Chicago, Rand McNally, 1973.
232. S. Martel, *Non-Accidental Injury,* London, Family Services Unit, 1977, p. 48.
233. See, generally, P. Hewitt, *Privacy: the Information Gatherers,* London, NCCL, 1977.
234. HCSC, op. cit. (note 148), para. 112.
235. Martel, op. cit., p. 52.

236. Geach, 'When Registers Lead to Abuse', op. cit., p. 18 (also A. Morris *et al., Justice For Children*, op. cit., p. 117).
237. DHSS, *Child Abuse,* op. cit., para. 4.6.
238. Martel, *Non-Accidental Injury,* op. cit., p. 50.
239. Cf. M. Paulsen, 'Child Abuse Reporting Laws: The Shape of the Legislation', *Columbia Law Review,* **67**, (1967), p. 1 at p. 3.
240. Annual Report, London, NSPCC, 1956.
241. See 1980 and 1981 Annual Reports (London, NSPCC). 615 cases in 1978; 1,383 cases in 1980.
242. 'Let Us End the Killings', 11 November 1973, p. 16.
243. See DHSS, *Social Service Teams: The Practitioner's View,* London, HMSO, 1978, p. 322.
244. See *Children in Care of Local Authorities — England,* DHSS Personal Social Services, Local Authority Statistics, A/F80/12. For the year ending 31 March 1980 there were 6,613 children under such orders, 2556 of them under five.
245. See A. Tredinnick and A. Fairburn, 'Left Holding The Baby', *Community Care,* **10** April 1980, pp. 22–5, and A. Tredinnick and A. Fairburn, 'The Baby Removed From Its Parents at Birth — Prophylaxis with Justice', *New Law Journal,* **130** (19 June 1980), pp. 498–50. I have criticised this in 'Removing Babies At Birth — A Questionable Practice', *Family Law,* **10** (1980), pp. 131–4.
246. See S. Creighton and P. Owtram, *Child Victims of Physical Abuse,* London, NSPCC, 1977.
247. Cohen, *Folk Devils . . .,* op. cit. (note 2), p. 1.
248. Hall *et al., Policing The Crisis,* op. cit. (note 2), p. 221.
249. Ibid. Cf. the 'amplification spiral' notion in L. Wilkins, *Social Deviance,* London, Tavistock, 1964, and J. Young, *The Drugtakers,* London, Paladin, 1971.
250. See as to which Hall *et al.,* op. cit.
251. See P. Taylor, *Beating The Terrorists,* Harmondsworth, Penguin, 1980.
252. See J. Rogaly, *Grunwick,* Harmondsworth, Penguin, 1977.
253. Hence in part the panic was inspired by 'permissiveness' which such measures of the 1960s as the legalisation of homosexual practices, the liberalised abortion law and easier divorce were thought to symbolise.
254. Hall *et al.,* op. cit., p. 222.
255. 'A nation's children represent a nation's future. How society treats its own children is a good reflection of the overall health and stability of that society', by David Owen, MP, Hansard, H.C. vol. 893, col. 1821. See also M. D. A. Freeman, *The Children Act 1975,* London, Sweet & Maxwell, 1976.
256. See R. Holman, *Inequality In Child Care,* London, Child Poverty Action Group/Family Rights Group, 1980 (2nd ed.), p. 29.
257. B. Jordan, *Family Rights: Two Paradoxes,* Birmingham, BASW, 1974.
258. B. Jordan, *Poor Parents: Social Policy and The Cycle of Deprivation,* London, Routledge & Kegan Paul, 1974, p. viii.
259. See the latest DHSS Circular, *Child Abuse: Central Register Systems,* op. cit., as an example.
260. See Child Care Act 1980 s.1 (formerly s.1 of Children and Young Persons Act (1963). See, generally, M. D. A. Freeman, 'Rules and Discretion In Local Authority Social Services Departments: The C.Y.P.A. 1963 In Operation', *Journal of Social Welfare Law,* **2** (1980), pp. 84–95.
261. See L. Burghes and R. Lister (eds), *Unemployment: Who Pays The Price?,* London, CPAG, 1981.
262. A point also made in an editorial in *British Medical Journal,* 'Recognising Child Abuse', No. 6218 (1980), pp. 881–2.

Most children live with their parents: a large number do not. The exact number of children separated from parents cannot be precisely given.[1] We know that about 100,000 children are in the care of local authorities and voluntary organisations,[2] but to this number must be added children in private foster homes[3] and mentally handicapped children in hospitals and units.[4] There are other categories as well.[5] An accurate estimate of children separated from parents, not including those at boarding schools and ordinary hospital cases, would be in the region of 120,000.[6] The legal and administrative framework is diverse rather than unitary. Children who have been privately fostered are afforded considerably less protection than children in the care of local authorities and voluntary organisations.[7] Mentally handicapped children generally have suffered neglect; often placed in large hospitals on a long-stay basis, their future has been and, despite some reforms, remains bleak.[8]

This chapter is mainly concerned with children who are in care. Some of these are not separated from their parents since they live with them, though they are technically in care. These children are home 'on trial',[9] mainly as a result of the determination of the parents.[10] In this chapter little attention is given to this group, aside from raising the question as to why more children are not returned in this way. I concentrate instead on children in care who live in residential care establishments such as community homes or who are boarded out with foster parents. Since I believe the former to be the main problem group the bulk of the chapter centres on them. Children in care are an 'at risk' population.[11] The majority come from deprived backgrounds and separation from their parents has rendered them yet more vulnerable. Overall, 7.8 per 1,000 of the child population are in care.[12] Over 29,000 of these children have been in care between one and three years and nearly 19,000 have been in care from three to five years. Over 27,000 have been in care for five years or more and two-thirds entered care under the 'voluntary' procedures for reception into care under the Children Act 1948 (now Child Care Act 1980).[13] Forty-six per cent of children in care live with foster parents.[14]

Mia Kellmer-Pringle[15] has identified a number of needs which children have

There are, she argues, four basic emotional needs which have to be met from the very beginning of life to enable a child to grow from helpless infancy to mature adulthood. These are the needs for love and security, for new experience, for praise and recognition, and for responsibility. Love and security is usually conveyed through a 'stable, continuous, dependable and loving relationship with parents (or permanent parent-substitutes).'[16] Children who are separated from parents may be offered not stability but rather the insecurity which multiple moves produce. Raissa Page, referring to children in the *Who Cares?* project, notes that the majority have had many moves from children's home to children's home (and foster home) 'almost as though they were required by statute to be peripatetic.'[17] Children in care may fail to develop relationships with parents or parent-substitutes. As a result they are liable to have, in the words of one leading authority, 'a personality characterised by a lack of guilt, an inability to keep rules and an inability to form relationships.'[18] Even where attachments develop there may be a lack of stimulation. Educability depends not only on inborn capacity but on environmental opportunity and encouragement. Absence of stimulation is associated with intellectual under-attainment and this adversely affects educational and vocational prospects.[19] Children also need to acquire independence and responsibility: children in care are often deprived of the opportunities to take responsibility and to participate in decisions which relate to their lives. There is thus every possibility that the development of children in care may become stunted or distorted. Everything possible, accordingly, should be done to keep children whenever possible out of care.

Inequalities in Child Care

Children in care come disproportionately from geographical areas of high social deprivation.[20] Local authorities with the highest percentages of children in care are inner London boroughs with extensive poverty, overcrowding and inadequate housing conditions. Thus, 24.6 per 1,000 of the child population of Tower Hamlets are in care, compared with 13.1 per 1,000 in Birmingham and 4.6 per 1,000 in Warwickshire.[21] Within authorities themselves children in care tend to come from the most socially depressed areas. Thus, research in Portsmouth[22] has revealed that two-thirds of the children in care were drawn from five of the city's sixteen wards. These wards were those with the highest proportions of unskilled manual workers, inadequate housing and lone parents. There is similar evidence from the Strathclyde region of Scotland.[23]

Socially deprived conditions create pressures which endanger family relationships and frustrate the attainment of child care objectives. Children brought up by families in the midst of poverty, with insecure employment and inadequate housing are vulnerable to separation from their parents. It is not surprising to find that children in care possess characteristics which are associated with social deprivation. It is common to find that they come from one-parent families.[24]

A study by the Birmingham City Council of children in its care revealed that 70 per cent came into this category.[25] Many children in care come from large families:[26] they are, of course, poor.[27] Thirdly, children in care are likely to come from financially deprived homes. The Birmingham study revealed that most of the households in its survey were on very low incomes at the time their children were admitted to care: more than half were dependent on state benefits; only a third had a man's wage coming into the home.[28] It does not need to be added that families with low incomes suffer other social deprivation. Fourthly, parents of children in care are drawn from the lower social classes.[29] A large percentage are unskilled manual workers. Children in care, in other words, tend to come from the social class most vulnerable to social deprivation. Fifthly, children in care are likely to come from homes which are overcrowded, structurally unsound or lack basic amenities: the extreme of housing deprivation is homelessness and many children are in care because their families are homeless. The Birmingham study found that only one in every twelve children in its care came from an owner-occupied house; 77 per cent had been living in rented accommodation and almost two-thirds in local authority housing. One-third of the children had lived in flats or bedsits or were abandoned or homeless.[30]

Poverty and its correlates do not inevitably lead to children coming into care. Many of the poor are able to keep their families intact. Nevertheless, the association between social deprivation and children in care remains a highly significant one. The fact that many cope, even against the odds, should not deflect our attention from those who do not and from a major reason why they do not. This is not to assert that all children, or indeed most, are in care because their families are socially deprived. Many children are in care because of cruel or neglectful behaviour by parents. It may be possible to understand this behaviour even if it cannot be exonerated. The parents' failings may be a reaction to outside pressures. This is supported by the research of Wilson and Herbert into low income families with five or more children.[31] All the families were below or just below the official poverty line while 79 per cent were in conditions of statutory overcrowding. They were all families in contact with social services. It was found that many parents did not pursue methods associated with developing the social, intellectual and future occupational skills of children. There was a lack of parental involvement but this did not stem from personal inadequacy in the sense of not caring about the children or of being unsure of good practices. The parents made valiant efforts to find time to spend with the children and did share the wider values of society in wanting them to succeed, be honest, reliable and the like. Wilson and Herbert explain child-rearing practices not in terms of inadequate parents but rather as a result of material shortages in the home and socially depriving environmental conditions in which children had to be raised. All the parents found their relationships with their children constrained by the effects of 'bad diet, lack of sleep, polluted air, untreated conditions of illhealth.'[32] Some had extra stresses of financial harassment, unemployment and invalid children.

This research is supported by other findings. Mintrum and Lambert's cross-cultural study found 'situational' constraints more influential than psychodynamic factors or beliefs.[33] They noted that overcrowded and materially stressful conditions were especially significant factors reducing the amount of affection and love mothers could show to their children.[34]

Children in care tend to come predominantly from families who have 'failed'. In many cases their parents are 'victims' of the economic system, of high unemployment,[35] of inner city decay, of racial discrimination,[36] of a social market theory of housing.[37] We tend to blame 'victims', as was made clear in Chapter 3. The children of these families can be seen as 'victims' of 'victims'. This has to be borne in mind when we consider the status of children in care. 'Being in care,' one child in the *Who Cares?* project is quoted as saying, 'you've got a cross on your back. You feel marked.'[38] Children in care see themselves as stigmatised, set apart from the ordinary life of the community in which they live. This affects every aspect of their daily lives; schooling, friendship, even applications for jobs. It is a common assumption that children in care must have done something wrong, otherwise they would not have been 'sent away'.[39] In fact only a small proportion of children in care have been committed to care because they have broken the criminal law. In the year ending 31 March 1980, about 2,000 children were committed to care because they were found guilty of an offence. Eighteen thousand children in care on that date were there for that reason.[40]

Children of the state are a vulnerable minority. Many of them are 'born to fail'.[41] For too long they have also been a forgotten minority. The Curtis report[42] in 1946 exposed the deficiencies in the system which provided for them at the end of the Second World War. The Children Act of 1948 was passed to remedy some of these inadequacies. It was not, of course, concerned with the rights of children. We would not have expected it to be. Instead there was expressed, officially at least, a caring philosophy. Stigma and sympathy, unhappy bedfellows that they are, have been the twin symbols of children in care ever since. But, as one child in *Who Cares?* said, 'The one thing I can't stand is people feeling sorry for us. That's worse than them thinking we're just a lot of yobbos.'[42] Rights are important because they transcend both these approaches. As indicated in the second chapter, they are important moral coinage. To have rights is to possess what children in care lack, namely dignity and respect. There can be few sections of the population who need to be able to claim rights more urgently than do children in care.

Preventing Children Coming into Care

There are too many children in care. Further, too many of these children are in residential care.[43] Children have the moral right not to be in care. Areas of similar social deprivation often have widely differing levels of reception into care. For example, in Hackney 19.7 children per 1,000 child population are in care, whereas in Newham the figure is 10.0; in Hammersmith it is 17.4 and in Brent 9.4. Birmingham's figure, already quoted, is more than double that of Dudley and nearly twice the proportion of Coventry, Sandwell and Walsall.[44] In part these discrepancies are to be accounted for in terms of differing social work practices. Children's 'need' for care is not an objective moral phenomenon. It depends very much on how agents of control, in each case social workers but also other professionals, define a situation. Examples of the process were given in the last chapter. The 'rescue' approach to child care is now firmly entrenched.

Many children, on any interpretation, are in care unnecessarily. There are, for example, children in care for no other reason that that their families are homeless or have inadequate accommodation. Receiving children into care for such reasons makes no sense. Not only does it break up families but it is also an enormous drain on the public purse. It costs £132 per week to keep a child in residential accommodation: this is 6½ times the cost of boarding out a child with foster parents.[45] Nevertheless, 1,400 children were in care on 31 March 1978 because their families were homeless and 8,900 because home conditions were unsatisfactory.[46] The London Borough of Barnet recently estimated that preventive work with families was saving it about £1.5 million a year that would otherwise have been spent on providing substitute care services. It is argued in the Barnet report that 'a social worker saves his or her salary three times over in preventive child care work alone.'[47] The biggest financial gains came, predictably, from keeping older children, who were more likely to get community home placements, out of care. The Director of Social Services stressed that it made sound financial sense, as well as being sound social work practice, to invest time, money and effort in intermediate treatment programmes, child-minding support programmes and mother and toddler group programmes to maximise these savings. Warwickshire has long carried out such policies.

Statute encourages preventive work. The Children and Young Persons Act 1963 encoded what was seen by the Ingleby committee[48] as good social work practice[49] by enabling a local authority to give 'assistance in kind or, in exceptional circumstances, in cash' to keep children out of care or eliminate the need to retain them in care. The provision is now s.1 of the Child Care Act 1980: psychologically, it is highly significant that the law on prevention is placed before that on receptions into care.[50] Certainly, many local authorities, including most of the areas of extreme social deprivation,[51] do use s.1 money to prevent children coming into care. But others do not. Returns for one year indicated that Hackney was making payments to 112.7 families per 10,000 population, whereas in County Durham only 1.2 families per 10,000 population were being assisted in this way.[52] About £200 million is spent each year by local authorities on children in care: local authorities also pay out £5 million a year as s.1 money. Current policies on public spending do not augur well for preventive work.

There is a wide variety of ways in which policies can be designed to keep children out of care. One recent study, *Caring For Separated Children*,[53] has identified three approaches. Primary prevention embraces those services which provide general support to families and reduce the levels of poverty, insecurity, ill-health or bad housing. This needs no elaboration in this context, save to indicate that current policies on employment, housing and state assistance with children (the levels of supplementary benefit and child benefit are egregious examples) fall far short of what is desirable if children are going to be kept within their families.

Secondary prevention is more specific. It emphasises help once problems have arisen; services to those who are thought to be at 'special risk'. Financial help under s.1 of the Child Care Act 1980 is an example. The allocation of day care is another. But day care, both full-time and part-time, is 'inadequate, uneven and unco-ordinated'.[54] Part of the problem springs from the division of responsibility between the DHSS, on the one hand, and the DES on the other. Back in 1975 the National Children's Bureau's journal, *Concern,* proposed integrated multi-purpose pre-school centres. It rightly saw little justification for 'perpetuating the artificial distinction between pre-school care and education.'[55] Since that time some forty community nursery centres have developed, set up by parents and local community groups and usually funded by Urban Aid. They are a hopeful sign for the future, if only governments and local authorities respond to an indubitable need. There is now a National Child Care Campaign.[56] This urges the minimisation of DHSS participation and the expansion of DES provision to embrace the concept of nursery centres. It is pressing for an appropriate training programme for child care workers. At present, the few community nursery centres excepted, there are only nursery schools which are usually part-time and utilised mainly by middle-class parents,[57] and day nurseries[58] which are, on the whole, reserved for the poor and deprived. Priority is given to 'children of working lone parents, children with a mental or physical handicap, those whose home environment is so socially impoverished or so strained that day care is considered necessary for their welfare, and those whose parents are, through illness or handicap, unable to look after them during the day.'[59] Places are scarce and long waiting lists are common: many of the children have been allocated places because they are thought to be 'at risk' at home. It is a scandal that funding for day nurseries is much lower than for nursery schools. There are now even hints that charges for nursery schooling are being considered to help reduce spending.[60]

Working-class families whose children are not allocated day nursery provision have only one other care alternative: private child-minding;[61] Only working mothers will resort to this. The exact number of children with child-minders is difficult to estimate. About 87,000 children are with registered child-minders. Many more will be looked after, with varying degrees of skill, unofficially. There are probably as many children with unofficial child-minders as with registered ones. Child-minding fees are much too high for most working parents though far from high enough to rescue child-minders out of the low-pay ghetto inhabited by most female 'homeworkers.'[62] In an unpublished report,[63] the DHSS has found that one-quarter of child-minders are so bad that they ought to be immediately de-registered; a third do not take babies; an overlapping third will not take black or Asian children. Existing child-minding provision is so poor that many children with child-minders would be no worse off, and some would be better cared for, were they living in residential care. There is a role for the child-minder, especially in the case of very small children. But its role should be residual and its uses should decline if and when the community nursery centre is centrally adopted. As a society we have looked too little at day care as an alternative to residential care. Day care is far from ideal, but children in day-care facilities do have regular daily contact with their parents, even if it is only early in the morning and for a short period in the evening. Local authorities spend only a small sum on day care, besides the many millions that goes on the residential care of separated children.[64]

Greater use of home helps might also prevent the need to receive some children into care.[65] Help in the home may make all the difference between managing and despairing. By giving mothers a break, by providing company, by acting as a safety valve, by providing a link with other services so that other help can be mobilised where necessary, they can prove a valuable resource in support of a family unit. Middle-class families may employ mother's helps or au pairs; working-class families have the same needs, even if they lack the resources to meet them. There has been a shift in the allocation of home helps away from families with children to provide support for the elderly.[66] This is not the place to consider social priorities. There can, however, be no doubt that greater provision of home helps and family aides would forestall receptions and committal to care.

Tertiary prevention aims 'at avoiding the worst consequences of a child actually having to spend long periods in substitute care. It would include preventing his remaining in care unnecessarily or in forms of care which were not appropriate to his needs.'[67] It stresses the importance of positive planning for children in care and of permanent placements where return to parents proves impossible. It is more appropriate to consider later in the chapter, when the right to a permanent placement is investigated.

Of all preventive measures the use of s.1 of the 1980 Act assumes overriding importance.[68] An analysis of the DHSS of purposes for which payments have been made indicates a wide variety of such purposes.[69] It is, however, thought a dominant consideration is often to prevent homelessness.[70] The London Borough of Wandsworth not long ago determined that accommodation would not be provided under s.1 for families with young children who were intentionally homeless. The Court of Appeal,[71] agreeing with Judge Mervyn Davies, has held this declaration to be invalid because it laid down a policy which fettered powers under s.1 in such a way that the facilities offered to a child under that section would not depend on the particular circumstances of the child or its family, but on a general policy not to provide accommodation when the parents were intentionally homeless within the meaning of the Housing (Homeless Persons) Act 1977. Judge Mervyn Davies said:

> since assistance under the 1963 Act [now the 1980 Act s.1] included the provision of accommodation it is plain that in every case where there is a family without a home for whatever reason, the local authority is obliged to consider whether the welfare of the child requires that some attempt be made to keep the family together. The local authority should on each occasion ask, should this child be taken from its homeless parents and received into care, or does his welfare require that, if some accommodation can be found for his family, that he remain with his parents.[72]

The importance of considering each case on its merits and not according to some 'blanket' policy is thus put beyond question. He saw that 'the mere existence of the resolution means that in operating s.1 of the 1963 Act there would be differentiation between children according to the conduct of their parents.'[73] 'Intentional homelessness' is an unfortunate concept for it embraces both fecklessness and victimisation. Why, as David Donnison asked recently,[74] do we consign the poorest people to the most expensive environments where they cannot cope, get into debt and default? The end result is eviction and often a label is attached of being intentionally homeless for they have, it is said, brought it upon themselves.

It may be that there are cases where it is better to receive the children of homeless parents into care: the case perhaps of 'a parent who continually changes homes and causes great stress and wrong to a child.'[75] But such cases are rare: homelessness is more often a misfortune than a sign of bad parenting. Yet we still read of cases where battles are fought between housing authorities and social services departments: the housing authorities evict or threaten to evict and expect the social services department to come to the rescue by receiving the children into care. Media attention was recently focused on one such battle fought over the Saunders family of Dover.[76] The Wandsworth decision is an important one. It is unlikely that any authority will now be brazen enough to make a declaration similar to that made by the Wandsworth social services committee. But what is more likely to happen is that informal policies to the same effect will emerge and these may be more difficult to quash.[77]

Prevention must remain a primary objective. That is why the implementation of the Houghton report on adoption[78] before the Finer Report[79] was to place the cart before the horse.[80] But in stressing prevention it must be recognised that it sometimes only defers the inevitable. Positive help may shore up a tottering family only to delay a decision thought to be unpalatable. Preventive help may also create greater dependence rather than fostering the ability to cope. We have to face the fact that we do not know if prevention works, and, if so, what forms of prevention work best.[81]

Whatever remains in doubt, of one thing we can be certain. There is no doubt that many children are 'taken' (I use this work deliberately though it is technically wrong)[82] into care unnecessarily. Many receptions and committals could be prevented. The 'rescue' policy now being pursued has led social workers to play safe. It has been estimated[83] that 8,000 children a year are being separated from their parents needlessly. In half of the cases dealt with by the National Council for One Parent Families, independent assessment has influenced the courts into deciding that children should remain with their parents. The NCOPF has put the blame for needless care on out-of-date information, poor and selective observation and assessment, and over-emphasis on psychodynamic factors. The emergence in the last few years of independent social workers[84] has provided a mechanism by which decisions of local authority social workers may be assessed and challenged. At present independent social workers are used in too few cases. Their establishment as a more common practice would lead to more intensive thinking on the part of those upon whom hinges the care-taking decision.[85] The value of an independent second opinion should not be underestimated.

Coming Into Care

Children come into care in a number of ways. The main reason for children being in care is that a court has committed them to care under the Children and Young Persons Act 1969. On 31 March 1980, 47,700 were in care for this reason. Another 44,300 had been received into care under s.1 of the 1948 Children Act (now Child Care Act 1980 s.2).[86] An increasing number of children (4,400 came into this category on 31 March 1980) are committed to care by a divorce court which has found 'exceptional circumstances making it impracticable or undesirable for the child to be entrusted to either of the parties to the marriage or to any other individual.'[87] This is a troublesome feature of our current high divorce figures: it is discussed further in the next chapter. Magistrates in domestic proceedings have similar powers to divorce court judges, but only a few children are committed to care by virtue of this jurisdiction.[88] They may also commit a child to care in guardianship proceedings,[89] but this action is rarer. Judges in wardship proceedings may also commit children to care.[90] This has become an increasingly common method of wardship disposal but there still were only approximately 500 children in care on 31 March 1980 who were committed in the course of a wardship hearing. Children may also be committed to care by a court which refuses an adoption application:[91] the number of care orders made amount to no more than a handful a year. Only receptions into care under s.2 of the Child Care Act 1980 (and assumptions of parental rights under s.3 of that Act), committals to care by a court in the course of wardship proceedings, and care orders under the Children and Young Persons Act 1969 need be considered any further in this context.

(i) Receptions into Voluntary Care

Reception of a child by a local authority into its care under s.2 of the 1980 Act is an entirely voluntary procedure. The section uses the word 'receive', not 'take', though judges and others often confuse the terms.[92] Section 2(3) underlines the voluntary nature of receptions: it provides that 'nothing . . . shall authorise a local authority to keep a child in their care . . . if any parent or guardian desires to take over the care of the child.' On the other hand, the local authority are under a 'duty to keep the child in their care so long as the welfare of the child appears to them to require it' (s.2(2)). The question posed accordingly is whether the local authority may refuse to hand over a child on a parental request and, if so, how.[93] The House of Lords has decided[94] that it may: a parental request for the child's return does not automatically terminate s.2 care. The House of Lords' speeches are ambiguous but it seems that as long as the child remains physically in the local authority's 'care', the authority may take further legal steps, the taking-out of a wardship summons or passing a resolution assuming parental rights if grounds exist, to keep the child. If the authority does not take these steps it ceases to have the legal authority to retain the child in the face of a parental request for the child's return. Where a child has been in care for six months parents must give 28 days' notice of their intention to remove the child.[95] The 28 days' period gives the local authority a 'breathing space',[96] time to consider whether to pass a section 3 resolution or begin wardship proceedings. In passing this provision, Parliament was accepting that 'a sudden move, without preparation, can be damaging to the child and may have long-term repercussions.'[97] The provision takes no account of a child's sense of time:[98] six months is a lifetime to a small child but is of lesser significance to an adolescent. Social services departments should take decisions rationally and not in response to pressure by parents. There seems no justification for allowing them to retain a child, or in the case of a child in care for six months to retain the child after 28 days have elapsed, when the parents want the child back. Lord Salmon's assertion in the *Lewisham* case that a local authority might 'well consider it to be their moral duty to keep the child long enough to have it made a ward of court,'[99] is, therefore, regrettable. That Lord Salmon couched the authority's powers in terms of 'moral duty' is significant: it is an express recognition that retaining a child is legally improper. Both the law and social work practice need clarification. Too much at present hinges on *ad hoc* decision-making by local authorities and this does nothing to enhance either the child's welfare or his parents' rights. Concern should also be expressed at the growing movement to terminate parental contact[100] and rights swiftly after a child's reception into care. It is becoming increasingly common for parental rights to be assumed within a few days of reception into care. It was recently urged by Ann Boswell, writing in *Adoption and Fostering*, that 'We should begin preparing parents for the possibility of permanent separation from their children the moment of reception into care.'[101] This is part of social work's 'new hard face – all or nothing, take responsibility or lose your rights.' It is, as Jordan has written, symptomatic of Thatcherite political economy and ideology.[102]

It is easy to criticise local authorities but little thought by policy-makers has gone into developing the structure within which social workers operate. What, for example, does 'care'[103] mean? Lord Scarman in the *Lewisham* case noted that s.2 was 'silent as to the powers exercisable by the local authority in the discharge of their duty'[104] to receive a child into care. Clearly, the authority has duties. They must provide accommodation and maintenance;[105] they must 'safeguard and promote the welfare of the child throughout his childhood.'[106] But what rights do they have? What is the legal relationship between the authority and the child in its care? Is it a relationship of guardian and ward? Certainly, the Curtis committee did not intend to suggest the creation of such a relationship.[107] It had in mind what is now called 'actual custody' of the child, that is, actual possession of the child. But 'actual custody' is now defined (in the Children Act 1975)[108] as having actual possession and not in terms of rights at all. It cannot be right that the local authority does not have any legal rights. It must, for example, have rights against foster parents, though these, I would suggest, emanate from the contract between the authority and the foster parents and not from status at all.[109] A local authority which has the authority to keep a child in its care must be in a different position from one which is detaining a child unlawfully in the face of parents who have come to remove their child. In the latter situation it may be apposite to describe the local authority's care as no more than actual custody. But what can we say of the former state of affairs? The distinction is an important one for a local authority may, if grounds exist, pass a parental rights resolution in respect of children in their 'care' under s.2. Is a child in 'care' whose parents have come to collect him if the local authority insists on holding him long enough to put through a s.3 resolution? It seems to me to be contrary both to the letter and spirit of the legislation to hold that such a child is in 'care'. On the other hand, a child in care for more than six months who is removed unlawfully from the care of the local authority remains in 'care' despite the fact that he is not in the possession of the authority. The authority in such circumstances might not be in a position to carry out its duties, but it surely would have the authority under the 1980 Act to pass a parental rights resolution.[110]

But what of the parent whose child is in care who does not want, or want at that moment, his child returned but who does want to be able to see his child or who disagrees with the arrangements the local authority has made regarding the child's accommodation? It would seem strange if the law were that a parent may remove his child at will (at least where the reception is under six months long) but that a local authority might be able to refuse the parent access to his child. However, it is common practice for local authorities to refuse access to parents.[111] This practice is supported by tenuous legal authorities. In *R* v. *Oxford City Justices ex parte H*,[112] where it was held that a putative father's application for custody under s.9 of the Guardianship of Minors Act 1971 ought to be heard even though the child was in care under s.3 of, what is now, the Child Care Act 1980, the court added that had the application been one for access it may have been that it should not have been heard since access was 'a quite different category', 'a matter which must necessarily be under the day to day and continuing control and discretion of the local authority.'[113] The remarks in this case, and in *Re Y*,[114] where similar comments were made, are strictly *obiter dicta* but have, nevertheless, persuasive force. As indicated they are consonant with social work practice and are widely supported by a body of opinion, perhaps best represented by the British Agencies for Adoption and Fostering.[115] The matter is one where clarification of the law is imperative. Legislation should provide for continuing contact between parent and child, save only where such contact is positively detrimental to the child.

(ii) Resolutions Assuming Parental Rights

Parents who request that their children be received into care may forfeit their parental rights should the local authority decide to assume those rights under the Child Care Act 1980 s.3. Voluntary care becomes involuntary care upon an assumption of parental rights resolution taken by a social services committee which in most cases merely rubber-stamps a decision of social workers.[116] Resolutions are becoming increasingly common. The number of children in care for whom the local authority assumed parental rights increased during the year ending 31 March 1979 by over 4 per cent to 18.4 per cent (a much lower percentage than in the previous two years). In 1973 the proportion of children in care under s.1 (now s.2) in respect of whom parental rights had been assumed was 25.3 per cent: by 1979 the percentage had risen to 40.1 per cent.[117] Part of the increase may be attributed to the extension in 1976 of the grounds for resolutions to include three years in care.[118] The increase also reflects a change in social work ideology away from prevention and rehabilitation and towards rescue.

The Curtis committee thought it 'objectionable . . . that the rights of a parent or other guardian should be extinguished by a mere resolution of a Council.'[119] It recommended that guardianship law be amended so that a local authority could apply to be made a legal guardian. Parliament did not heed this advice. Instead it left intact the resolution procedure of the 1930 Poor Law Act on to which was grafted a mechanism for objection and appeal by parents.[120] The

Children Act 1975 extended this so that parents or guardians (and the local authority) may appeal to the Family Division of the High Court against any confirmation or resolution of a resolution.[121] What Curtis thought objectionable a third of a century ago remains indefensible today despite the objection procedure and appeal system. The decision to divest a parent of parental rights and duties is, as Waterhouse J. said recently, 'a very serious one'.[122] It is, accordingly, one which should be taken by a court and not by, what the authors of *Justice For Children* called, a 'treatment bureaucracy'.[123] Waterhouse J. also thought that to sustain a resolution the conduct of the parent must be 'culpable, and culpable to a high degree'.[124] This is difficult to reconcile with the three years provision. That was introduced to help the so-called 'children who wait'.[125] It is desirable to move children through the child care system as rapidly as possible and positive planning for children in care is imperative. The three years provision may make adoption easier, it may even be a route to adoption but adoption is no panacea. There are children in care for three years who are there through no fault of their parents. The 'three years' provision may even discourage positive rehabilitative measures on the part of social workers who know that the mere efflux of time enables them to prevent parental reclaims. Thorpe found that 45 per cent of the parents in her samples had not been seen by a social worker for at least two years; 62 per cent did not know where their children had been placed.[126] Holman's research has produced similar results.[127] As the authors of *Justice For Children* say, commenting on these findings, 'parents can lose their children through default of the social worker rather than their own fault.'[128]

The three years provision is not the only unsatisfactory ground. Parents may also be deprived of parental rights if 'it appears to a local authority . . . that a parent . . . is of such habits or mode of life as to be unfit to have the care of the child.'[129] The vagueness of this standard is such that parents cannot know in advance whether their lifestyles will be seen to transgress it. The backgrounds of social workers are so very different from their clients that there is a danger that parents may be penalised when their behaviour deviates from the norm of middle-class morality. The ground is often used to deprive parents of rights where they are promiscuous or use proscribed drugs.[130] There is an increasing sense of disquiet at the way this ground operates. Were the test to be applied by a court then, as with 'neglect' provisions,[131] there would be considerable concern. But so long as the deprivation of parental rights rests on an administrative mechanism, on discretion largely beyond control, there is every reason to express extreme alarm.

The decision to divest a parent of rights should be taken only by a court. The existing grounds should be pruned with both the three years provision and the 'habits or mode of life' ground being abolished forthwith.[132] Defenders of the existing system point to the objection procedure which enables parents to challenge a resolution in the juvenile court. Few parents do in fact challenge resolutions. Only about 10 per cent of resolutions are objected to and adjudicated upon in the juvenile court, but failure to object must not be seen as admission by parents that the grounds exist and the local authority's actions are accordingly justifiable or that the criteria for passing a resolution have been satisfied. There is no obligation on local authorities to give parents advance warning of their intention to assume parental rights. Their obligation is to serve on the parents written notice of the fact that a resolution has been passed informing them of their rights to object and the effect of any objection. This is a highly formal procedure. It presumes a degree of competence and literacy. Many parents do not appreciate the consequences of the letter. There is no obligation on the social workers involved to visit the parents and explain the implications of a resolution. Parents upon whom notice is served may well be in stressful circumstances. The existing procedure does not extend sufficient protection to parents or to their children. A judicial hearing would afford greater safeguards.

It would not entirely overcome the problems. Courts would, as they do in other procedures relating to children, have to rely upon social enquiry reports.[133] At the moment reports prepared to support a resolution are short and littered with inexact psychological or pseudo-psychological concepts: terms such as 'manipulative', 'inadequate', 'infantile', 'schizoid'. There has, Sutton has cogently argued, been an 'unjustified reliance on premature professionalism'.[134] Science is misused to cloak assessments which are rather more subjective. Improvements will only be effected when judges, magistrates and lawyers learn to handle the data which currently blind them.

(iii) Wards of Court in Care

An increasing number of children are committed to care in the course of wardship proceedings. The court retains custody: the local authority is given care and control of the child.[135] The court has to be consulted about major decisions, such as whether an attempt should be made to rehabilitate the child with his parents, whether there should be long-term fostering with or without a view to adoption,[136] or whether the child can be transferred from one foster parent to another.[137] The court may also give directions as to access. In a recent case the Court of Appeal has said that it is 'unwise' for a court to try to direct the future of wards 'except in a broad way'.[138] It held that a judge was wrong to direct that the local authority should take all practical steps and means to return the child to its sixteen-year-old mother, who was also in care, and to see that the child was brought up by her.

Uncertainties and doubts remain. What, for example, is a 'major decision'?[139] Division of responsibilities between the court and local authority is in urgent need of clarification. The very status of care exercised by local authorities over wards is, to say the least, ambiguous. Children who come into care through a court committal order are not in section 2 care, though the powers and duties of the local authority under the Child Care Act 1980 operate as if the local authority had received the child into care under that Act, subject, that is, to the qualifications already made about major decisions. But if the children are not in s.2 care (and they are certainly not in s.3 care), they must be in care by virtue of the court order. But this tells us very little about the local authority's powers and duties. We know that parents cannot remove their children (this distinguishes the case from voluntary receptions); we know that directions may be given to the authority and that major decisions, whatever they are, may not be taken without the court being consulted. But more than that we do not know. It must be the case that a local authority cannot pass a parental rights resolution in respect of a child committed to its care in the course of wardship proceedings (or by a divorce or guardianship court). But it has to be said that the law is not stated with clarity anywhere. When powers were given to wardship, guardianship and divorce courts to commit children to care, it probably was envisaged that the powers would be exercised only in the rarest of cases. That was no excuse for creating the quagmire of concepts[140] that now exists. The problem is, however, now one affecting many thousands of children. Their status is uncertain: the question as to who is responsible for them remains unanswered. They must not be left in this land of limbo.

(iv) Care Orders

Care orders also raise a number of questions about children's rights. The biggest problem concerns the question as to who is to represent the child's interests in care proceedings.[141] Clearly, parents are not the right people to represent the child's case when it is their fitness to care that is being challenged. Despite this the Magistrates' Courts (Children and Young Persons) Rules 1970 provide that 'except where the relevant infant or his parent or guardian is legally represented . . . the court shall, unless the relevant infant otherwise requests, allow his parents or guardian to conduct the case on his behalf.'[142] Where parents conduct their child's case, it is difficult to avoid the conclusion that they are in fact protecting their own interests. Where the child is represented by a lawyer (about six in seven are), it may not be immediately obvious whether he is putting forward arguments based on his own inquiries, observations and assessments of the parents, or whether he has simply taken instructions from the parents. Legal aid is granted to the child, not his parents: the child is 'the person . . . brought before the juvenile court' within the meaning of the Legal Aid Act 1974 s.28(3). Lord Denning M.R. has tried to inject sense into this by saying that since a parent can be compelled to appear before the court he is also 'brought before' the court under the relevant statutory provision. His fellow judges were not convinced.[143] Since most children affected by care proceedings are too young to instruct a solicitor, it is only in the rarest of cases that instructions have not come directly from the parents.[144] It is almost as if the prosecution in a criminal matter were to take instructions from the defendant.

If the child's case is conducted in accordance with his parents' instructions, it must follow that, in cases where the interests of the child and his parents are in conflict, the child's welfare may be harmed rather than furthered by his own lawyer. A striking illustration of this process is the case of *Re S*.[145] Care proceedings were brought by a local education authority in respect of a boy whose parents objected to sending him to a comprehensive school so much that they refused to send him to any school at all. A care order was made and ultimately confirmed by the Court of Appeal. The problem highlighted in *Re S* was identified lucidly by Cumming-Bruce L.J. He said,

> I have a fear that the fact that the interests of the child may have been confused with the interests of the father may have made it difficult for the court at every stage from the Crown Court upwards to appreciate what the real interests of the child were. It may be that in cases raising such issues as the present the legal advisers of the child should consider very carefully how far it is consistent with their duty to the child to present a case which appears to be identical with that of a parent who holds somewhat obsessive views.[146]

The boy in fact appeared to share his father's views. But the general issue remains: the lawyer's duty is to represent the child but how is he to identify the child's views other than by consulting his parents? If, as is likely, they are opposed to care proceedings, can the lawyer disregard their instructions and, if he may, on what authority? If he does ignore the parents' instructions, from what source is he to get his information about the child? There may be others who will know about the child. The child himself may be able to express his wishes or, if very young, at least his feelings. Maria Colwell is said to have cried not to be removed from her foster parents.[147] It may be that what we need is a different sort of lawyer to take on cases of this sort, one with an elementary knowledge of the social and psychological sciences and some understanding of social work principles.

It may also be that the whole procedure of care proceedings is at fault. Care proceedings have been described by a former Lord Chief Justice as 'essentially non-adversary, non-party proceedings' entailing 'an objective examination of the position of the child.'[148] They are 'not set up in such a form as to provoke a contest between the local authority and the parents or, even more, the child and parents.' They are 'an objective enquiry'.[149] This conclusion enabled the court to admit hearsay evidence which was otherwise inadmissible. It is an interpretation which begs many questions. What other rules are to be relaxed in care proceedings? What form are care proceedings to take? What is the status of the parents in the proceedings?[150] How can 'parents and others concerned in the child's control . . . in some degree take part',[151] while at the same time ensuring that the child's interests are represented? It should be borne in mind that it was the child's solicitor in this case who used the hearsay rule to protect the mother and her cohabitant. In fact, had the hearsay rule not been relaxed the child concerned would have remained in a home where he was subjected to violence: at least until wardship proceedings had been commenced for in these 'the welfare of the child is . . . considered . . . first, last and all the time.'[152]

What emerges from a consideration of these two cases is the need for the child to have separate and independent representation in care proceedings. This is recognised in the Children Act of 1975. As a result, where there is an unopposed application for the discharge of a care or supervision order, the court must order that the parents shall not represent the child or otherwise act on his behalf, unless satisfied that it is not necessary to do so to safeguard the interests of the child.[153] Where it makes such an order it must appoint a guardian *ad litem* for the child unless satisfied that it is not necessary to do so. The court has the power under s.65 of the 1975 Act to grant legal aid for parents to be separately represented in these proceedings. The effectiveness of these provisions depends on magistrates and how they exercise their powers. For example, how easily are they satisfied that separate representation is not necessary to safeguard the child's interests? There is no real information on how the provisions are working.

There are other provisions in the 1975 Act relating to representation and these have not yet been implemented.[154] They enable the court in care proceedings, where there is or may be a conflict of interests between parent and child, to order that the parents may not represent the child or otherwise act for him in the proceedings. In such a case the court may appoint a guardian *ad litem* for the child. The powers are permissive, not mandatory. Failure to implement the provision is explained in terms of insufficiency of resources and the added burden of work on social workers and probation officers. Separate representation will not be necessary in every case, but in those in which it is it should be possible. It is inexcusable that seven years after the Act was passed, this part of it should not have been activated. The right of children to separate representation in proceedings where their interests may conflict with those of their parents is one of paramount importance. At the same time, the full rights of parents to participate in care proceedings must be recognised: the right to take part in the proceedings, the right to legal aid (recognised in another unimplemented provision of the 1975 Act)[155] and the right of appeal would give them some meaningful status in the court in which their conduct is often on trial.

The Welfare of the Child in Care

It is provided in s.18 of the Child Care Act 1980 that

in reaching any decision relating to a child in their care, a local authority shall give first consideration to the need to safeguard and promote the welfare of the child throughout his childhood; and shall so far as practicable ascertain the wishes and feelings of the child regarding the decision and give due consideration to them, having regard to his age and understanding.[156]

Local authorities are allowed to derogate from this duty where it appears to them to be necessary for the purpose of protecting members of the public.[157] Thus, they may restrict a child's liberty by placing him in secure accommodation, even though this is contrary to the child's interests. Nevertheless, the decision so to place a child is one to which the general duty to give first consideration to the child's welfare applies. There are many other decisions to which the general duty also applies: questions of reception, assumption of parental rights, assessment, reviews, discharge from care and other decisions, both from key decisions such as these and ordinary everyday matters. What does this statutory duty entail?

'First consideration' does not mean the same thing as 'first and paramount consideration', which is the test applicable in custody disputes and in wardship proceedings.[158] 'First and paramount' means, in the oft-quoted dictum of Lord MacDermott, 'the course to be followed will be that which is most in the interests of the child's welfare . . . . That is the first consideration because it is of the first importance and the paramount consideration because it rules upon or determines the course to be followed.'[159] 'First consideration' directs the local authority to 'consider specifically the welfare of the child and to give its welfare greater weight than other considerations.'[160] But it does not necessarily prevail over other considerations. The child's interest is to be 'weighted' but the question of weighted by how much is not answered.[161] The test *à propos* children in care is the same as that which courts and adoption agencies must apply in relation to adoption decisions.[162] It is clearly right in the adoption context to take account of matters other than the child's welfare. Otherwise it would be hard to resist most adoption applications. The argument is not as persuasive in the care context. If a local authority were obligated to view the child's welfare as 'first and paramount', many of the decisions discussed later in this chapter would have been decided in a way more favourable to children's rights.

There is only one reported case in which s.18 has been considered by a court. Dillon J. in *Attorney-General v. London Borough of Hammersmith and Fulham*[163] interpreted the phrase 'decision relating to a child in their care' narrowly. He stated that a preliminary decision to close a children's home was not one relating to any particular child, so that s.18 did not apply to it. Only when the home was closed would the local authority have to give first consideration to the welfare of each child when deciding how the child should be cared for. It was subsequently discovered that the local authority had acted unlawfully, since the closing of a home requires the approval of the Secretary of State.[164] This prevented the Court of Appeal deciding further on the meaning and scope of s.18. Dillon J.'s reading of the section is most unfortunate and not one that can have been intended by the legislature. The courts have elsewhere demonstrated an unwillingness to interfere with discretionary decision-making powers of local authorities.[165] A restrictive interpretation of s.18 is fully consonant with this approach.

Section 18 also refers to the wishes and feelings of children in care. It is the complaint of children in care, reflected in *Who Cares?*, that lip-service only is paid to the sentiments of s.18, particularly the part which requires 'due consideration' to be given to a child's wishes and feelings where these can be ascertained. The conflict between what professionals deem to be in the child's best interests and his wishes comes out well in one statement by a child quoted in *Who Cares?*: 'You can have the situation where the child's in care and doesn't want to see his parents. And yet your social worker can force you to go home, even if things are bad and you and the staff know it's not right.'[166] Individuals within a local authority may be very well aware of errors of judgement and harmful practices. But they are part of a large, unwieldy and diffuse bureaucracy within which change is easier to resist than implement.

Children in care now have national spokesmen with the creation of the National Association of Young Persons in Care (NAYPIC) and the Voice of the Child in Care, as well as supporters in such organisations as the Family Rights Group, Justice for Children and the Children's Legal Centre. But children in care remain a weak, unorganised group. They need someone to speak on their behalf. They need a buffer between themselves and those who make decisions about their lives. Of particular significance is the need to establish individual complaints procedures. Durham County Council has taken the initiative here[167] by issuing children in care with a rights guide which includes a contact card to be sent to the director of social services in the event of complaints. The guide sets out what constitutes ill-treatment (including corporal punishment and 'anything that takes away your dignity or self-respect')[168] and advises children who feel they are being ill-treated to tell the head of the establishment or social worker. The guide also contains an SOS card and tells the child that this may be sent to the director 'who will send someone to see you.' Other authorities are now following Durham's lead and Haringey has a Children's Spokesman scheme.[169] While not wishing to be critical of the Durham initiative, questions must be raised as to whether it is good enough: in particular it may be doubted whether a system which invites complaints to the very bureaucracy against whom the complaints exist is likely to exude confidence.

An unpublished report of the now defunct social services consumer body, the Personal Social Services Council,[170] found that most children in care they questioned 'seemed to feel that complaining about anything (for yourself or anyone else) to anyone within the system, e.g. social worker or residential worker, was unwise because it resulted in a much closer, and more critical, eye being kept on them.' The PSSC did not publish its report because it felt that complaints procedures were not the most urgent need of children in care. Cost was one consideration. Another was opposition from some groups of social workers to the establishment of such a system. It was particularly concerned with how genuine complaints could be distinguished from unwarranted ones. It is known that many social workers and residential social workers are opposed to what they call 'disturbed, manipulative' children having the power to lodge a formal complaint. The argument appears to be that these children would use the powers against social workers and that an already vulnerable profession would become more vulnerable. This is strange thinking. Children in care are the vulnerable group and they need protection against bureaucratic decision-making. Publicity has, however, been given to a case in Norfolk in which three children, having been unable to draw their complaint to the attention of social workers, consulted a solicitor and the predictable response was to label the children 'manipulative' and insist that the department was doing its best for them.[171]

Complaints systems, however, do exist. Cheshire has one. According to Maurice Speed, its Director of Social Services, 'the existence of the procedure stops any serious complaints arising.' Cheshire works on the assumption that all complaints are justified. All complaints (there are three or four a week) are referred, in the first instance, to the Deputy Director. He takes up the complaint with the principal officer concerned who investigates and presents a report. Any resulting action can be anything between referring the problem to the district officer; reviewing the procedure within the department; setting up a board of inquiry, headed by a principal officer of the DHSS; and calling on the DHSS to set up an independent inquiry. In Cheshire, the majority of complaints are simply dealt with and there has never been the need for a major inquiry. The model pursued by Cheshire is inadequate, but it is an important first step. As with complaints against the police[172] or lawyers,[173] it is important that there should be an independent lay element exercising surveillance over decisions taken by professionals. It is difficult to have confidence in any other system. Gill Wilton's comment that, 'those making the complaints will at least be secure in the knowledge that someone removed from the immediate situation will be looking at the problem with a dispassionate eye,'[174] is rather too complacent a position to adopt. There is a danger that the Cheshire system becomes merely an exercise in symbolic politics,[175] playing a pacification role. It is, nevertheless, a step in the right direction.

There is no reason why a child in care aggrieved by a decision should not refer the matter to a commissioner for local administration.[176] A fourteen-year-old girl in Cambridgeshire kept in solitary confinement in a secure unit for three months had her complaint upheld. She was even given a record player from her director of social services as a gesture![177] Where maladministration is proved this can lead to a social services department changing its policies. Ombudsmen do not have the power to change what local authorities are doing, only to comment critically upon them. This often has the same effect. One recent reference led to the first major independent assessment of the way social services departments arrive at decisions in case conferences. The case[178] was brought by the parent of a boy with Down's Syndrome when the local authority (Solihull) decided to remove him from a private school where he had been for six years. The Commissioner decided that the parents (not, be it noted, the boy) had suffered an 'injustice' at the hands of the social services department. Its decision, taken ostensibly in the interests of the child (he would be nearer home etc.) was in reality a cost-saving exercise. The Commissioner found four grounds of maladministration: (i) failure to provide the parents with the support they needed to come to terms with the decision to transfer their son; (ii) inviting the parents to a case conference, having already taken the decision to move him; (iii) failure to inform them when their son would be returned to the area; (iv) allowing an insufficent amount of time for the boy to adjust to the move. This ruling sets an important precedent. Many of the grounds of complaint, which the Commissioner substantiated as maladministration, could be invoked by children in care. Commissioners can, of course, only handle a few cases: they can only be approached by MPs or local councillors; and the processing of cases is a lengthy process. Too much faith must not be put in their ability to achieve very much for children in care.

Some indication of the problems confronting a child in care who wishes to take action against a social services department are the difficulties which confronted Graham Gaskin.[179] Gaskin spent his whole childhood in the care of Liverpool City Council. He had been in some fourteen foster homes in one of which he had been sexually assaulted and then in various institutions including a male psychiatric ward when only nine years old. He sought to bring an action against the local authority saying that it had been guilty of negligence or breach of duty and that his current psychological injuries and anxiety neurosis were due to that negligence or breach of duty. He applied under s.31 of the Administration of Justice Act 1970 for the disclosure of case notes and records relating to the time he had spent in care. He had in fact already seen them (a social worker incensed at his treatment had shown him them) but was now seeking official access to them. Without them he could not prove want of care but he believed these would provide the necessary evidence. Boreham J. dismissed his application and the Court of Appeal dismissed Gaskin's appeal. Boreham J. said it was 'necessary for the proper functioning of the child care service that the confidentiality of the relevant documents should be preserved.' Lord Denning M.R. used the floodgates argument.[180] if Gaskin's claim succeeded there would be many more such claims for damages. Neither of these arguments is convincing. If the child care service functioned properly there would be little need to challenge decisions. Successful claims for damages would only be common if the service was functioning totally inefficiently. Children need to be protected against negligent social workers, as they need to be protected from negligent parents.[181]

Children in this country are afforded quite inadequate protection against bad decisions and harmful practices. That much is clear. In looking to improve the complaints system one model which should be examined is that found in Quebec's Youth Protection Act.[182] This requires children to be informed of their rights, to be consulted on decisions or to be given the opportunity to accept or refuse them before they are finalised. There is also a Youth Protection Committee which has the responsibility of seeing that the rights laid down by the Act are respected and a local director of youth protection in each social services department. More promising still is the system operated by the Ville Marie social services department in Montreal.[183] They have community control and client participation at every level from policy questions to representation in individual cases. There are complaints task forces. Throughout the emphasis is on self-help. This is a far cry from our corporately managed bureaucracies. Were we to move in the direction of Ville Marie there would be rather less need for appeal systems. Until we do so better appeals and reviews systems are required. The Quebec Youth Protection Committee might well be a model to copy. The *Gaskin* decision is a barrier to such protection.

What Rights Do Children In Care Have?

In terms of our rights, before I came to 'Who Cares?' I hardly knew my rights — I thought it was all right for the staff to knock us about . . . It has happened at so many places I have been in.[184]

Are children in care cases or persons? Are they objects of decision-making processes? In an earlier chapter I posed some of the problems that giving children 'a say' in the family might cause. Children in care are not in the same position. There is no way in which one can equate flesh and blood parents with legal parents in a care setting. Policies are taken high up in bureaucracies by people who may never see the children. Day-to-day care is in the hands of poorly-paid, often untrained and inexperienced residential workers. There is rapid turnover in personnel: continuity in caring is absent. Secondly, there is not the close and meaningful interaction in a children's home that should exist with parents: homes are too big for this. Community homes need rules and regulations in a much more formal sense than does the organisation of a family.[185] Thirdly, important decisions are taken by social workers and residential social workers that no parent can take: for example, to put a child in a 'lock-up unit'. The case for children sharing in decisions that affect their lives is thus greater than in the context of a natural family.

There are some grievances vented by children in care about which the law can do little. Children in care often complain of the absence of privacy.[186] It is difficult to see what the law could do about this. They complain justifiably about the stigma which attaches to being in care. Whilst it is true that the abolition of the approved school[187] has done something to increase this, again it is difficult to see what state action could achieve. So much depends on educating the public and the media. There are other areas where the law may be able to intervene more meaningfully : questions of reviews, home closures, corporal punishment, drugging children in care are all matters on which the intervention of lawyers may be valuable. In the sections which follow I concentrate attention on areas where legal action may be effective.

(a) The Six-monthly Review

Under s.27(4) of the Children and Young Persons Act 1969, it is the duty of every local authority to carry out a review of a child's circumstances at least every six months with the intention of returning him to his family if this is in his best interests. According to *Who Cares?*, not all of those in care (we are talking here of teenagers) knew such a requirement existed. 'Where they had such knowledge it was not presented to them as a supportive step but in most cases as being mainly an administrative judgment.'[188]

Why should this be? Why should young people in care be excluded from involvement in decisions affecting them? One explanation of this may be sought in the dominant professional ideology that, to quote Stein,[189] 'many young people in care are disturbed and because of this their participation or involvement has little meaning'. Similar arguments, we have seen, have been used to argue against the introduction of complaints procedures. Children and young persons are often excluded because it is believed they need protection 'in their own interests'. They may, if present, hear something about themselves that may harm them: that, for example, they are the product of an incestuous relationship. Even if present, they are likely to be and feel isolated. One child in the *Who Cares?* group is quoted as saying: 'I was in a room with about 16 or seventeen people who were all sitting round a big table. They sat me half-way down and asked me questions . . there were so many questions that hurt me, a hell of a lot.'[190]

The six-monthly review tends to be a means of identifying the needs of a case, if even this, and is not so much concerned with the 'rights' of the young person. If, therefore, he is not allowed to be present or even not told that the review is taking place, this can be justified as being in 'his best interests'. He is a category of case anyway, and not an individual. Even if present, his presence may amount to little more than being like an exhibit in a criminal trial.

The British Association of Social Workers' Charter of Rights for Children in Care, formulated in 1977,[191] recognises this to a large extent. Principle 6 of the Charter states 'the child in care has a right to information concerning his circumstances and to participate in the planning of his future.' The comment on this explains:

Children should be aware of the reasons why actions are taken on their behalf, and, where appropriate, should be actively encouraged and enabled to share in the decision-making process. Even in situations in which the child's wishes cannot be acceded to, he has the right of participation, and disagreement if he so wishes. Individual respect of a child demands no less.

One young person in *Who Cares?* put this rather more stridently. He said:

> What we need to get over is we ought to be able to have a say in who is there discussing our lives. We ought to be able to speak for ourselves. And if we can't get our points across . . . we ought to have a spokesman for ourselves. Why don't the children have their own person they want to speak for them?[192]

At the very least, it may be thought, children should be able to request a second opinion if they disagree with the outcome of the review. At a recent meeting in London organised by the Children's Legal Centre and NAYPIC this was expressed in terms of a right of appeal.[193] I would go further than this to argue that children should have the right to be present at reviews and to participate in them. They should be entitled to have some independent person to speak for them, if necessary. It may be necessary to specify an age at which children are allowed to take part in reviews. Research indicates that twelve- to fourteen-year-olds reach adult levels of cognitive development.[194] There is thus little reason why they should not participate from (say) thirteen.[195]

The importance of presence and participation is not only that they will enable children to have a voice in their lives but that the review may assume the importance it ought anyway to have. Many reviews, the DHSS has itself admitted, are not carried out or are carried out perfunctorily.[196] There is not much evidence of the effect of reviews but what there is, for example, from a Newcastle study[197] suggests that they are 'administrative procedures rather than real dialogues' that 'radical rethinking of a child's treatment is militated against by a felt lack of alternatives and insufficient priority being given to preparation for the reviews, usually on the part of the fieldworker'. The Newcastle study found the system of reviews 'crisis oriented', not based on positive planning, 'where the placement is fully examined and the development of the child is monitored.' There is a statutory obligation to hold a six-monthly review (I suspect this duty is frequently broken). There is no obligation to indulge in positive thinking. 'No change' is a simple answer. If the child is involved, as he would be if he could participate, the incentive to plan a programme tailored to that child's needs would increase. Children would move through the system more quickly either to return home or to a permanent substitute placement.[198] The Secretary of State has had power since the Children Act of 1975[199] to lay down regulations as to the manner of reviews, the time-scale and frequency and the considerations to which the local authority is to have regard in reviewing cases. No regulations have been made. Better representation for children, in certain circumstances their presence and the presence of parents, should be made the subject of such regulations without further delay. It must be realised that reviews can actually gain from the presence of the children. As Skinner[200] found, they bring insight and maturity to the review: the review itself is often better focused as a result.

(b) Corporal Punishment

There are still local authorities and voluntary organisations which permit corporal punishment in community homes. It is arguable that the use of a cane in a community home is contrary to the welfare principle set out in s.18 of the Child Care Act 1980. It is certainly undesirable. Raissa Page explains why:[201] 'corporal punishment and physical ill-treatment are accepted by many children in care as natural and inevitable.' They accept it as a 'necessary trial of childhood'. She continues:

> we know that many children in longterm care first came into care because they had been ill-treated or seriously neglected by their parents. We also know that such children may rely on violent, aggressive behaviour to make their needs and feelings known . . . . Children in care have a real reluctance to confide in adults when they are being ill-treated. This reluctance may reflect the extent to which many children mutely accept physical and emotional cruelty as the norm, and the extent to which they feel adults in authority do not take them seriously.

If a child lives in a rigid atmosphere, which one dominated by fear of corporal punishment clearly is, 'the complete domination by external rules, prevents the development of internal control.'[202]

The Secretary of State for Social Services in the last government let all directors of social services know that he believed in the use of corporal punishment in community homes to be undesirable and improper in a professional caring relationship.[203] The Handicapped and Deprived Children (Abolition of Corporal Punishment) Bill in 1979 would have abolished the power to beat mentally handicapped, physically handicapped and deprived children but the Bill, like more general measures to do away with corporal punishment in schools, failed.[204] There is considerable irony in a state of affairs where a child can be removed from his home because he is thought to be at risk of non-accidental injury only to be placed in a situation where physical assaults upon him are institutionally sanctioned. It is arguable that a community home 'caning inflicts a non-accidental injury on a child which ought to be registered on the 'at risk' register. Many children are on registers for less serious matters. It is also somewhat ironic that Parliament has outlawed the taking of a photograph of a child being whipped when it obstinately refuses to outlaw the act itself.[205]

There is no justification for the retention of physical punishment in community homes. I would accordingly advocate the legal recognition of the immunity of a child in care from such ill-treatment. But we need to˙ go further for even where corporal punishment is formally abolished it continues to be practised. Attention, therefore, should also be given to the question of taking disciplinary action against staff who physically assault children.[206]

(c) Drugging Children in Care

Drugging children has become a common practice. In the United States the 'disease' of hyperactivity has been manufactured.[207] It is treated by administering drugs, stimulants such as methylphenidate (Ritalin), dexamphetamine (Dexedrine) and magnesium pemoline (Cylert); non-stimulants such as thioridazine (Mellaril) and antidepressant anticonvulsants, such as Dilantin, are also administered.[208] Ritalin is the most favoured treatment because it is supposed to be the most effective. Indeed, in the words of Sandoval *et al.,* 'depriving a hyperactive child of Ritalin is similar to depriving a diabetic of insulin.'[209] There are one million children labelled hyperactive in the United States today and the vast majority receive drug therapy. So-called hyperactive children can be, and are being, made more manageable through drug treatment. As Box writes, this provides

> comfort for the immediate clients of this drug treatment, the parents and the teachers. But as regards the real purpose of schooling, stimulant drugs have no proven efficacy, which throws doubt on the sincerity of those who administer them, or reveals the naivety with which medical solutions to non-medical problems are embraced.[210]

In Britain few children are labelled hyperactive, though British psychiatrists recognise hyperkinesis as a childhood disorder.[211] But 'it has been clear for some time that most of the children labelled hyperactive in the States would in Britain be described as children with a conduct disorder.'[212] They would be said to be 'maladjusted' or 'medium educationally subnormal'. Drugging these children may not be as common as it is in the USA, but drugging undoubtedly is practised. Box estimates that between 16,000 and 18,000 British schoolchildren receive medication for hyperactivity.[213] Furthermore, we know that it is common to tranquilise school phobics[214] and drugging children in hospital for subnormality for deviant social behaviour (screaming, swearing) has also been reported.[215] All this evidence reflects the triumph of the therapeutic state: the medicalisation of moral and political issues is all too common in the twentieth century.

Against this background, we should not be surprised to find that children in care are drugged. In 1977 doctors at a hospital near Dartford wrote to the British Medical Journal to inform the medical public that they were 'treating girls in a secure home for disturbed adolescents with the intramuscular depot preparations fluphenazine decanoate and flupenthixol decanoate.'[216] Doctors at an adolescent unit in St. Albans have also described how they use drugs to sedate children in care.[217] The National Association of Mental Health (MIND) expressed its concern over these practices to government ministers in 1980.[218] The association has argued that drugs, a tranquilliser, Depixol, and valium are being used to control children's behaviour. Medical responses are somewhat predictable. Thus the consultant psychiatrist who wrote to the *British Medical Journal* is quoted in *The Times* as saying that MIND's interpretation of the use of the drugs is 'absolute rubbish'. He insists that the drugs are used to 'help children who have serious behaviour disorders.'[219] But the Committee on the Review of Drugs has said that valium should not be used to treat behaviour disorders and the manufacturer of the drug Depixol has warned that it should not be given to children. Anti-psychotic drugs are known to produce unwanted neurological effects: long-term treatment is associated with abnormal movements described as tardive dyskinesia.[220] There are other side-effects too.

We know little about how prevalent the drugging of children in care is. We know rather more about the use of drugs in the education setting and the 'liquid cosh' in prisons. There is a danger that the practice of drugging children in care will spread. Medicalisation is a convenient way of not dealing with the roots of a problem. We are bound to be told that the drugs are in the child's best interests. We must not be convinced by this 'official' reasoning. Patterns repeat themselves and what we have here is the emergence of a new method of controlling children. It must be resisted. Children in care have the right not to be subjected to drugs unless the drugs are intended to cure a physical ailment.

(d) The Order Book

There are a number of areas where management considerations appear to prevail over the best interests of children in care. Drugging is, of course, one such question. Another is the order book system for purchasing clothes.[221] This makes children in care feel different from other children. It reinforces the stigma of being in care. 'You feel as if you are a beggar receiving from charity', said one child, quoted in *Social Work Today*.[222] The system serves to institutionalise children. It does not teach them how to use money. Above all it gives a restricted choice. There seems to be no valid reason why we should make shopping an humiliating experience for children in care.

A campaign has been mounted to abolish the order book system. The Residential Care Association has recommended that every child in care is allocated an allowance for personal clothing and items for personal use and that children, with a member of staff to guide them when necessary, be permitted to buy their own clothing to prepare them for a life outside care.[223]

The order book, like denying children the opportunity to do their own laundry, prepare their meals or do the shopping for the home, makes sense only if by 'sense' we mean 'administrative convenience'. It does little to assist the process of turning out capable, autonomous individuals. It remains a constant bone of contention amongst adolescents in care.[224] The order book should be abolished. Children in care should be given greater freedom in the choice of clothes. This freedom should also be extended to such matters as hair styles, spectacle frames and toiletries. Current practices conflict with both the letter and the spirit of s.18 of the Child Care Act 1980.

(e) Home Closures

The clash between management considerations and children's best interests comes out forcefully when decisions are taken to close homes, working teenagers' hostels and similar institutions. The Kingsthorpe children's home in Woodford Green run by Tower Hamlets was one such case: twice the local authority threatened to close it and twice intervention has kept it open.[225] The council proposed moving children whose ages ranged from fourteen to eighteen to another hostel ten miles away. In the end they moved them to council-owned accommodation in the area. There are important principles at stake in a case like this. Children in care need stability and shunting them around does not give them this. A social worker said of one fourteen-year-old in the Kingsthorpe case: 'he is a nice, well-adjusted kid, but a lot of his stability is Kingsthorpe.' The adolescent in question had had nine changes of home before he was seven.

Kingsthorpe is not an isolated instance. A similar decision was taken in Birmingham; another reported case concerned Earlsfield House in Wandsworth.[226] One in Hammersmith was challenged in the High Court (already discussed in this chapter). It was always doubtful whether a challenge would succeed. Children in care undoubtedly have a legal right to be consulted, so that in theory an injunction could be sought to stop a closure. The local authority has a statutory duty to ascertain the child's wishes and feelings; so in theory mandamus could be claimed on behalf of the children. It is, however, all too easy for a local authority to consult children or their representatives and then to ignore the views expressed. They need only be taken account of so far as is practicable. It may also be argued that a local authority's duty is too general or vague, with the result that a court might refuse to grant mandamus.[227] This is a weak argument in this instance. There is also the problem of who is to sue on the children's behalf.[228] Where the local authority has assumed parental rights, it would be expected in normal circumstances that it would act as the children's 'next friend'. But these are not normal circumstances. In the *Hammersmith* case, the initiative was taken by social workers, angered at the decision of their local authority, who sought and obtained the Attorney-General's fiat to a relator action being brought. Legal aid is generally unavailable for relator actions. It is situations like this which make it imperative that some organisation be set up to act as a children's advocate. Sweden and Norway have children's ombudsmen.[229] Some such institution is clearly needed in Britain as well.

(f) Contact with Family

Whatever the legal situation (whether, for example, the local authority has parental rights vested in it or not), good social work practice dictates that parents should be involved as much as possible in decisions relating to their children. Every effort should be made to preserve their relationship with their child unless this is harmful to him. The courts have been reluctant to grant applications for access,[230] except in those cases where they have specific power to give directions to the local authority.[231] In the past parents have made children wards of court in order to seek access, but it seems that this avenue is no longer open.[232] Where one parent has custody, access to the other parent has been said to be a child's right.[233]

Where the child is in care under s.2 of the 1980 Act, it should be the case that parents retain the right to access and do not require the local authority's permission.[234] The parent still has legal custody.[235] Furthermore, if access is a child's right, only a court can deprive him of his right of access in the interests of his own welfare.[236] But the courts have said that local authorities may control access.[237] In *Wards of Court,* Lowe and White have supported this control. They argue that: 'from the practical point of view it is essential for the authority to be able to limit access in so far as it is in the long term interests of the child, since the parent could otherwise thwart attempts to provide consistent and proper care for the child.'[238] Whether the courts are right (and I believe they are not), local authorities in practice do control access. Indeed, it is not uncommon for a local authority to refuse to tell the parents of the child's whereabouts. As Susan Maidment notes:

> The statutory scheme of the Child Care Act 1980 may be lacking somewhat in that there is no procedure whereby parents can formally challenge the exercise of a local authority's duty under section 18 . . . where the child is in section 2 care other than through the rather expensive and time-consuming wardship jurisdiction. The parent(s) may not in fact want the return of the child to their actual custody, yet they may wish to challenge for example, how often they are allowed to see the child. They may even wish to challenge the suitability of the care arrangements or the particular foster-home, despite having generally consented to the local authority determining a 'suitable form of care'.[239]

A place of safety order may create even greater injustice. Although it only lasts for 28 days and may not be renewed, it is often followed by interim care orders and it may be many months before the child is returned to the parents.

Delays can have extremely deleterious effects. The parents have no right of access to the child who anyway may be miles away, making visiting, if permitted, impracticable and infrequent.[249] There is no right of appeal against place of safety orders.

That parents can suffer an injustice in being denied access to their children is recognised in a report of the local commissioner for the administration of the North of England.[241] Parents of a child in a Manchester City council home had been denied visits for two months. Social workers had thought their visits were causing disruption. The local authority was purporting to apply what is now s.18 of the Child Care Act. But there is no evidence, certainly in the report, that the visits were detrimental to the child's welfare. It is unfortunate that parents should have had to appeal to the local 'ombudsman'. It would be even more unfortunate were children to have to do so. We now accept the right of an adopted child to search out his roots by requesting his original birth certificate.[242] Children in care too have a right to know about their identity.[243] Every effort should be made to keep up familial ties. There is a need for children in care to be given a sense of continuity in their lives: if nothing else, photographs, letters, diaries, etc. may provide this. Children should have the right to access to their parents and also to their siblings. As Allen Adams, MP said, in moving the Protection of Children in Care (Scotland) Bill, 'at the end of the day the children have no one to turn to except each other.'[244] He commented: 'It is a horrendous practice to split a family of children and put one in one home and one in another, or two with one foster and three with another. That is often done simply on grounds of administrative expediency.' His Bill to prohibit the placement of siblings under the age of twelve[245] in more than one residential establishment or with more than one set of foster parents made no progress in Parliament. Such measures should not be left to individual initiative: government action should be taken to outlaw the practice of splitting up siblings. Government action would also assist the preservation of familial ties. Parents should be helped to visit their children in care by paying them visiting expenses. Parents should be helped in their desire to have children home for weekends by paying them a proportion of child benefit.[246] These measures might be expensive but they would ultimately save money and, more importantly, promote the welfare of children.

(g) Locking up Children

An increasing number of children in care have their liberty restricted. There are currently 552 approved 'secure places'. The majority are provided by local authorities in community homes, though secure provision also exists in two Youth Treatment Centres which are under the control of the DHSS, and in privately run homes and National Health Service secure units. It is estimated that about 2,000 children a year are 'locked up' in care. In most cases locking up a child in an inappropriate system of control is a partial answer perhaps to the problems of often inadequate and inexperienced staff. But as far as the child is concerned it achieves nothing. The majority of the children are 'casualties of the care system'.[247] Their behaviour has offended the care authorities. In the words of Millham *et al*: 'the demand for security reflects the requirements of inadequate open institutions and community services rather than the needs of difficult children'.[248] Persistent absconders are often placed in secure units, though the evidence[249] is that children who abscond are commonly running away from unsatisfactory institutions. Further, many of the children have never been taken to court following an offence.[250]

Until 1983 the decision to place a child in secure accommodation was completely within the discretion of the local authority (or other authority) and there was no appeal structure. This gap has now been largely plugged by legislation.[251] No child under 10 may now be placed in secure accommodation without the prior consent of the Secretary of State. No child may be placed in secure accommodation unless he has a history of absconding and, if he absconds, it is likely that his welfare will be at risk or he is likely to injure himself or others if kept elsewhere than in secure accommodation. If the local authority wishes to continue the placement beyond 72 hours the child must be brought before a juvenile court within that time for authorisation of a continued placement. The court has to be satisfied that the criteria exist and may authorise a placement for a maximum period of 3 months (on subsequent applications 6 months). Interim orders are apparently possible where the court is not in a position to decide whether the criteria have been met — a strange provision. These reforms are to be welcomed though anomalies remain (for example, the extent to which the new law applies to Youth Treatment Centres). But the evil remains. In most cases locking up children in care is merely blaming the victims.

(b) Leaving Care and Afterwards

'Care' ends at eighteen or in some cases at nineteen. Insufficient attention has been paid to the problem of leaving care and postcare adjustment.[252] 'Is it eighteen when you're no longer in care?' said one youngster quoted in the Strathclyde study.[253] 'I was thinking of going to the Army or doing nursing. The only thing that worried me was that Matron said I could come here when I get my day off, but what would happen if this place was filled up? What would I do then?' As Parker *et al*. comment, 'final . . . discharge should not represent a major transition for the child.'[254] But, of course, it does. Part of the problem is connected with matters considered earlier in this chapter. Children in care are given too little independence, too little responsibility. Childhood should be an apprenticeship when the skills of living are acquired: for children in care this is all too rarely the case. Mia Kellmer-Pringle makes the point that 'prolonged institutionalisation during the early years of life leaves children very vulnerable to later stress.'[255] The education of children in care suffers; so, sometimes, does their health.[256] Children in care often miss essential assessments or treatment.[257]

Children are not prepared for leaving care. There is the problem of loneliness, of being cut off.[258] Mulvey found that the majority of young people had changed jobs at least twice in two years after leaving care; half of the youths had joined the Services; 7 per cent of the total were unemployed (the figure would, of course, be much higher today). A quarter of those leaving foster homes had lost contact with them. Those from children's homes had made the 'least satisfactory showing' after two years out of care. Mulvey concluded that nineteen- and twenty-year-olds deprived in this way of a normal home life are beset with uncertainties and experience greater difficulties than their peers with 'stable backgrounds', who can count on the support of a 'normal' home life.[259] There is an association between having been in care (along other factors) and subsequent delinquency,[260] illegitimate pregnancies and mental illness. We owe it to the children of the state to give them a better start in life. Many children in the *Who Cares?* group were understandably bitter about the ending of care. 'If you live with normal parents you're able to have a choice whether you leave home or not. But in care, you get kicked out on your heels.'[261] 'They plan your life for you and they don't let you come to your review and then all of a sudden they say "goodbye".'[262]

It is difficult to phrase the post-care treatment that children should receive in terms of rights. We could compel local authorities to supervise youngsters leaving care. We could require them to pay a certain sum of money. Many authorities already do both these things. What is required rather is a change in attitude towards children in care. By giving them greater responsibility, by ensuring that they acquire skills, education and training and by giving them the ability to acquire self-respect, we will be sending them out better equipped for life than we do at present.

Alternatives to Residential Care: The Right to Permanent Placement[263]

As a short-term measure, residential care has advantages. Children in residential care are known to have more contact with their parents than those in foster homes.[264] Thus the advantages of using it as a short-term measure to facilitate rehabilitation is clear. Indeed, as Jane Aldgate has suggested, there may even be a case for using residential care for older children who need a flexible but long-term placement in which they can maintain links with their natural family. But residential care cannot approximate to the conditions of a normal family existence. As one fifteen-year-old in residential care said,[266] 'it's not good to be in an institution all your life. You never find out what it's like to belong to a family — it makes you different . . . I'd like to be married and be a mother when

I grow up but I'll be a bit cold — I don't like all this love stuff. I can't stand being touched.'

Foster care is, of course, cheaper. In most cases it is also preferable. It should be used because it offers a better form of care for many, if not most, children deprived of their natural parents. Adoption mechanisms should also be put into operation. There are estimated to be 20,000 'children who wait' in institutions, and Adoption Resource Exchange and other agencies have demonstrated that homes could be found for many, if not most, of these. The evidence is overwhelming that older children, handicapped children, black children can all be adopted. The introduction of subsidised adoption[267] may help. One recent publication proclaims 'No Child Is Unadoptable'.[268] This overstates the case but its sentiment is worthy.

We must put our resources into finding new homes and families for children where rehabilitation with their natural parents is out of the question. But we must not put the cart before the horse. Every assistance, both financial and of a social work kind, must be given to parents to keep families together. We must not fall prey to the 'rescue' notions of social work to which reference has already been made. But we must consider the rights of children. Time limits are dangerous concepts and I do not, therefore, recommend that after a child has been in care for x number of years his parents should lose any chance of recovering him.

The construction of a right to a permanent placement is not easy. The goal of work with children in care should be 'normalisation'.[269] To develop into stable and secure adults children need parents. This was stressed at the very outset of this chapter. Despite the Rowe and Lambert study, *Children Who Wait,*[270] and the Children Act 1975, too many children are just allowed to drift. The Rowe and Lambert study coincided with the panic produced by the Maria Colwell case. The result is that too much social work goes into removing children, too little into deciding what becomes of them. Our system is plainly inadequate. We can learn from recent American experience.

American Review Procedure

Leading American students of child care, Fanshel and Shinn, have written that

> it is no longer considered that a child be afforded a placement situation in which his basic needs are being cared for . . . . A newly emphasised criterion is being used to assess the adequacy of an agency's performance, namely whether a child can be assured *permanency* in his living arrangements and *continuity* of relationship.[271]

The question remains: how best can this be done?

In the United States a system of third-party (i.e. non-agency) case reviews operates widely.[272] Some twenty-three states have a review procedure. In most it is the courts which do the monitoring. In New York since 1971, agencies charged with care, custody or guardianship of children have been required to petition the Family Court to review the foster care status of all children who have been in voluntary placement continuously for two years. A study of the New York review process indicates that children move more quickly through the system where there is a review structure. In Fanshel's study the proportion of children in foster care after two years was 'somewhere between 68% and 74%'.[273] In Festinger's study, conducted after the commencement of the review law, the comparable figure was 56.1 per cent.[274] Most of the states operating a review system use courts; others, such as South Carolina and Arizona, have appointed panels of citizens to determine if plans are being made for children in foster care.

No similar procedure operates in this country. In Humberside, however, an experimental project began in 1976 which introduced an outsider into the six-monthly review system.[275] Eight magistrates from the Juvenile Court Panel in Humberside attended review meetings for twelve months at sixteen community homes. The object of the exercise was different from that which is dominant in the American review system. It was to enable magistrates to familiarise themselves with the residential establishments and to strengthen the relationship between the Juvenile Court Panel and the social services department. In no way did any element of non-agency review intrude into this process. But the potentiality for such a review is present.

Positive planning for children in care is imperative. This is why I see independent reviews as a hopeful sign. In the United States, they have resulted in intensified programmes to return children home quickly or place them for adoption. Fewer children, accordingly, remain in the 'limbo'[276] of foster care. The review structure does, however, raise many problems. What is a review? Is it to be an adversarial hearing with arguments put by, or on behalf of, all interested parties? Or is it an administrative inquisition? Or is it, some might say despairingly, a mere formality?[277] Which institution is best suited to carry out the review? Is the judiciary, or the judiciary as at present constituted, a suitable review body? Is the review concerned with rights or ongoing needs? Certainly, the case for judicial review is stronger where rights are to be considered. How precisely can the goals of a review be set out? It is easy enough to state that its concern is with a child's welfare. But what exactly is that?[278]

Before we construct a right to permanent placement, before we introduce review procedures, there are, it is clear from this brief discussion, many issues which need further consideration. We must guard against 'parent bashing',[279] wholesale adoption policies which can lead, as one writer[280] has put it, to 'death by adoption'. On the other hand, as Shaw and Lebens argued in *What Shall We Do With The Children?*,[281] there is 'a need for quite radical organisational change'. Some of this change is already taking place. The Kent Special Family

Placement Project, Barnardo's New Families Project, Parents for Children[282] are all bodies committed to finding homes, roots and permanence for older, handicapped or difficult children. Children should not spend their childhood in residential care wherever this can be avoided.

Conclusion

Children in care have few rights at the moment. In this chapter I have argued that:

(i) Children should have the right not to be in care. Too many children are in care unnecessarily. Measures at state and local level could prevent children coming into care.

(ii) Children in care need adequate and independent complaint systems.

(iii) Children should have the right to participate in the six-monthly review process.

(iv) Corporal punishment in community homes and other residential establishments should be abolished.

(v) The drugging of children in care is an unacceptable practice.

(vi) The order book for purchasing clothes should be abolished. Management considerations should not be allowed to prevail over the best interests of the child.

(vii) Siblings in care should not be split up and everything should be done to keep up contact between a child in care and his family unless to do so would be positively harmful to the child.

(viii) The decision to put a child in secure accommodation should be taken only where no alternative exists. Save in the rarest of circumstances, it should not be taken against the best interests of the child.

(ix) Children who cannot return to their parents have the right to expect a permanent placement in a long-term foster home or to be adopted. There should be positive planning for children in care. It is believed that independent reviews would encourage this.

A number of other matters were considered. These included home closures and the problems of preparation for leaving care and after care. It is rather more difficult to formulate proposals as regards these matters. However, if section 18 of the Child Care Act 1980 were to be treated seriously, if the best interests of the children were placed before administrative convenience, many of the problems discussed in the sections on these subjects would disappear. Barbara Kahan, one of the prime movers behind the development of services for children in this country, has said that: 'What you do to children changes the world. Large numbers are being brought up away from home; they will affect the next generation.'[283] This is a lesson we ignore at our peril.[284]

Notes

1. See R. A. Parker, *Caring For Separated Children*, London, Macmillan, 1980, p. 23.
2. *Children In Care in England and Wales, March 1980*, DHSS, London.
3. 8,707 in 1976. The number is declining.
4. At the end of 1975 there were 5,140 children under sixteen in mental handicap hospitals and units in England and Wales.
5. Children in hospital, in homes for the disabled and in detention.
6. See Parker, op. cit., p. 24. Some of these will be living with relatives, guardians or friends.
7. See Foster Children Act 1980. See also R. Holman, *Trading In Children*, London, Routledge & Kegan Paul, 1973.
8. See M. Oswin, *Children Living In Long-stay Hospitals*, London, Lavenham Press, 1978.
9. The statutory legitimation of which is now Child Care Act 1980, s.21(2).
10. See J. Thoburn, *Captive Clients*, London, Routledge & Kegan Paul, 1980.
11. See SSRC, *Children In Need of Care*, London, SSRC, 1980, p. 29.
12. DHSS, *Children In Care . . .*, op. cit., p. 5 (Table 1).
13. Ibid., p. 7 (Table 3).
14. Ibid., p. 24 (Table A6).
15. M. Kellmer-Pringle, *The Needs of Children*, London, Hutchinson, 1980 (2nd ed.), p. 34 *et seq.*
16. Ibid., p. 34.
17. R. Page, 'Who Cares?', *Concern*, no. 26 (1977–8), pp. 17–21 at p. 18.
18. M. Rutter, *Maternal Deprivation Re-assessed*, Harmondsworth, Penguin, 1981 (2nd ed.), p. 113.
19. See M. Rutter and N. Madge, *Cycles of Disadvantage*, London, Heinemann, 1976, p. 114.
20. On the measurement of this see S. Holtermann, 'Areas of Urban Deprivation in Great Britain: An Analysis of 1971 Census Data', *Social Trends*, no. 6 (1975), p. 33.
21. DHSS, *Children In Care . . .*, op. cit. (Table A6).
22. *Children In Care*, Portsmouth, Social Services and Intelligence Unit, 1975.
23. Strathclyde Social Work Department, *Strathclyde's Children — A Sample Survey of Cases in Which The Regional Council Took Parental Rights Over Children in Its Care During 1978*, Glasgow, Strathclyde S.S.D., 1980.
24. See J. Packman, *Child Care: Needs and Numbers*, London, Allen & Unwin, 1969. See also Holman, *Trading in Children*, op. cit.
25. City of Birmingham Social Services Department, Child Care Review Group, Report 4: *A Study of a 10% Random Sample of All The Children in The Care of Birmingham City Council*, Birmingham, Birmingham C.C., 1979, para. 7.1.
26. See Packman, *Child Care*, op. cit.
27. See P. Townsend, *Poverty In The United Kingdom*, Harmondsworth, Penguin, 1979. (60 per cent of families with four or more children at or below poverty line compared with 21 per cent with one child, 30 per cent with two, and 31 per cent with three), p. 288.
28. Birmingham S.S.D., op. cit., para. 7.3.
29. See Packman, *Child Care*, op. cit.; Holman, *Trading in Children*, op. cit. (45 per cent lowest social classes). See also H. and E. Schaffer, *Child Care and The Family*, London, Bell, 1968 (31 per cent).
30. Birmingham S.S.D., op. cit., para. 7.4.
31. H. Wilson and G. Herbert, *Parents and Children In The Inner City*, London, Routledge & Kegan Paul, 1978.
32. See H. Wilson, 'Parenting In Poverty', *British Journal of Social Work*, 4 (1974), pp. 241–54 at p. 248.
33. Mintrum and Lambert, *Mothers In Six Cultures*, Chichester, Wiley, 1964.
34. See, further, R. Holman, *Poverty: Explanations of Social Deprivation*, London, Martin Robertson, 1978, pp. 228–31.

35. See L. Burghes and R. Lister, *Unemployment: Who Pays The Price?* London, C.P.A.G., 1981.
36. House of Commons, Fifth Report from the Home Affairs Committee, Session 1980–1, *Racial Disadvantage*, H.C. 424, HMSO, London, 1981.
37. See D. Webster, 'A "Social Market" Answer on Housing', *New Society*, **58**, no. 991 (12 November 1981), pp. 269–72.
38. Quoted in R. Page and G. Clark, *Who Cares?*, London, National Children's Bureau, 1977, p. 17.
39. Ibid., p. 16.
40. DHSS, *Children In Care . . .,* op. cit., Appendix A (Tables A1, A3).
41. See P. Wedge and H. Prosser, *Born to Fail?,* London, Arrow Books, 1973.
42. Page and Clark, *Who Cares?,* op. cit., p. 17.
43. DHSS, *Children In Care . . .,* op. cit., p. 24 (Table A6).
44. Ibid. The gap is, however, narrowing.
45. DHSS, *Children In Care . . .,* op. cit., p. 1 (Table 10) and p. 23 (Table A5). See also P. Sammons, 'The Costs of Child Care', *Adoption and Fostering*, no. 105 (1981), p. 7.
46. Nearly 9,300 children are in care because of unsatisfactory home conditions: another 8,500 for 'other reasons' including homelessness, op. cit., DHSS, *Children In Care*, Appendix A1, p. 16.
47. *Community Care*, 17 September 1981, p. 5.
48. *Children and Young Persons*, Cmnd. 1191 (1960).
49. See J. Packman, *The Child's Generation*, Oxford, Blackwell, 1981 (2nd ed.), ch. 4.
50. See M. D. A. Freeman, *The Child Care and Foster Children Acts 1980*, London, Sweet & Maxwell, 1980, s.1 (General Note).
51. See M. Hill and P. Laing, *Money Payments, Social Work and Supplementary Benefits*, Bristol, University of Bristol School for Advanced Urban Studies, 1978, pp. 8–17.
52. 1974–5, as quoted in Hill and Laing, ibid., at p. 9.
53. Parker, *Caring For Separated Children*, op. cit., p. 45. See also M. Kellmer-Pringle (ed.), *A Fairer Future For Children*, London, Macmillan, 1980, esp. ch. 4.
54. Ibid., p. 47.
55. Autumn 1975, p. 18.
56. See E. Ferri and D. Birchall, *Combined Nursery Centres — A New Approach to Education and Daycare*, London, Macmillan, 1981. See also *Who Needs Child Care? — The Results of A Survey in the West Green Area of Haringey*, 1981.
57. The percentage of three- to four-year-olds in nursery education is enormously variable. Twelve per cent of children under five are in a nursery or primary school (General Household Survey, 1979, as reported in *Social Trends*, no. 12, 1981, Table 13.3). It is 47 per cent in the London Borough of Merton and nil in Gloucestershire.
58. Also variable (three per cent under-fives in Camden to 0.8 per cent in Barnsley).
59. Ministry of Health Circular 37/38.
60. According to speeches of Sir Keith Joseph reported in *The Guardian*, 27 October 1981.
61. As to which see B. Jackson and S. Jackson, *Childminder*, Harmondsworth, Penguin, 1981. Fifty-seven per cent of children under five in full-day care and with child-minders. See *Social Trends*, no. 12, 1981, Table 13.4.
62. See S. Crine, *The Hidden Army*, London, Low Pay Unit, 1979; and A. Coote and B. Campbell, *Sweet Freedom*, London, Picador, 1982, ch. 2.
63. Discussed by H. Penn, 'Who Cares For The Kids?', *New Statesman*, 8 January 1982, pp. 6–8 at p. 7.
64. See Parker, *Caring For Separated Children*, op. cit., p. 135 (62 per cent of personal social budget spent on children and families goes on residential care and 16 per cent on day care, almost wholly on day nurseries).
65. See, further, M. Kellmer-Pringle, *A Fairer Future for Children*, London, Macmillan, 1980, p. 34.
66. See R. M. Moroney, *The Family and The State*, London, Longman, 1976, pp. 52–3.
67. Parker, op. cit., p. 45.
68. On which see J. Heywood and B. Allen, *Financial Help in Social Work*, Manchester, Manchester University Press, 1971; R. Lister and T. Emmett, *Under The Safety Net,*

Social Work, London, Routledge & Kegan Paul, 1979. See also M. D. A. Freeman, 'Rules and Discretion In Local Authority Social Services Departments: the C.Y.P.A. 1963 In Operation', *Journal of Social Welfare Law* (1980), pp. 84–96.

69.   Hill and Laing, *Money Payments . . .*, op. cit., pp. 8–25.
70.   Ibid., p. 17.
71.   [1981] 1 All E.R. 1162.
72.   Ibid., p. 1168.
73.   Ibid., p. 1169.
74.   D. Donnison, 'A Radical Strategy To Help The Poor?', *New Society*, **58**, no. 989 (29 October 1981), pp. 183–5 at p. 184.
75.   [1981] 1 All E.R. 1162, op. cit., p. 1171, by Templeman L.J.
76.   'Councils Fight Over Eviction', *Community Care*, 23 July 1981, p. 3.
77.   See S.A. de Smith, *Judicial Review of Administrative Action*, London, Stevens, 1980.
78.   Home Office/Scottish Education Department, Report of the Departmental Committee on the Adoption of Children, Cmnd. 5107 (1972), London, HMSO.
79.   DHSS, Report of the Committee on One Parent Families, Cmnd. 5629 (1974), London, HMSO.
80.   See M. D. A. Freeman, 'Children In Care: The Impact of the Children Act 1975', *Family Law*, **6** (1976), pp. 136–41.
81.   Parker, *Caring For Separated Children*, op. cit., p. 46.
82.   Children are either 'received' into care or committed to care by a care order or warrant.
83.   See Fletcher, 'These Children Must Not Be Taken Into Care', *Community Care*, 25 September 1980.
84.   See J. Levin, 'Independent Social Work Reports', *Legal Action Group Bulletin*, September 1981, pp. 203–5, and J. Tunnard (ed.), *Reports For The Court — Guidance For Independent Reporters*, London, Family Rights Group, 1981.
85.   But the concept has been criticised by leading social workers. See, e.g. Guy Mitchell, 'In The Private Interest', *Social Work Today*, **13**, no. 16 (22 December 1981), p.1.
86.   See *Children In Care In England and Wales, March 1980*, op. cit., p. 5 (Table 1).
87.   Under s.42(1) of Matrimonial Causes Act 1973. The figure is in *Children In Care In England and Wales*, op. cit., March 1980, p. 17.
88.   The powers are in s.10 of the Domestic Proceedings and Magistrates' Courts Act 1978. There are about 600 children in care under this provision. *Children In Care. . .*, op. cit., p. 17.
89.   See Guardianship of Minors Act 1971 s.9, as amended by s.2(2)(b) of the Guardianship Act 1973. There are about 400 children in care under this provision. See *Children In Care . . .*, op. cit., p. 17.
90.   See Family Law Reform Act 1969, s.7(2).
91.   Under Children Act 1975, s.17(1)(b).
92.   Examples are quoted in M. D. A. Freeman, 'Children In Care: The Impact of The Children Act 1975', *Family Law*, **6** (1976), p. 136.
93.   See M. D. A. Freeman, 'Retaining a Child in Care', *New Law Journal*, **129** (1979), p. 223, and 'Who Cares?', *New Law Journal*, **179** (1979), p. 648.
94.   In *London Borough of Lewisham* v. *Lewisham Juvenile Court Justices* [1979] 2 All E.R. 297.
95.   Child Care Act 1980, s.13(2) (first enacted by Children Act 1975, s.56).
96.   See Waterhouse J. in *Wheatley* v. *London Borough of Waltham Forest* [1979] 2 W.L.R. 543, 547.
97.   See Houghton Report on the Adoption of Children, op. cit., para. 152.
98.   As to which see J. Goldstein *et al.*, *Beyond The Best Interests of The Child*, London, Burnett, 1980 (revised ed.), pp. 40–9.
99.   *Lewisham* v. *Lewisham*, op. cit., p. 306.
100. Typified by BAAF publications such as M. Adcock and R. White, *Terminating Parental Contact*, London, BAAF, 1980.
101. A. Boswell, 'Relinquishing', *Adoption and Fostering*, no. 104 (1981), p. 22.
102. B. Jordan, 'Hard Faced and Unnatural', *Social Work Today*, **13**, no. 12 (24 November 1981), p. 1.

103. On this see S. Maidment, 'The Fragmentation of Parental Rights and Children In Care', *Journal of Social Welfare Law*, (1981), pp. 21–35, and M. D. A. Freeman, 'The Legal Battlefield of Care', *Current Legal Problems*, 35 (1982), p. 117.
104. *Lewisham* v. *Lewisham*, op. cit., p. 318.
105. See Child Care Act 1980, ss. 21, 22.
106. Ibid., s. 18.
107. *On The Care of Children*, Cmnd. 6922, para. 425(ii), London, HMSO, 1945–6.
108. Children Act 1975, 2. 87.
109. Foster parents sign a boarding-out agreement and are, clearly, agents of the local authority.
110. See to this effect Freeman, 'Children In Care . . .', op. cit., p. 138, and J. Eekelaar, 'Children in Care and the Children Act 1975', *Modern Law Review*, 40 (1977), p. 121.
111. Despite the guidance in the DHSS, *Foster Care: A Guide To Practice*, London, HMSO, 1976. See also the arguments of Juliet Berry, *Social Work With Children*, London, Routledge & Kegan Paul, 1972.
112. [1974] 2 All E.R. 356.
113. Ibid., p. 360, by Bagnall J.
114. [1976] Fam. 125.
115. See BAAF Publications, op. cit. It is admitted in the pamphlet that the group of parents 'who should be prevented from having personal contact with their children is probably quite small.' (Health Act 1983 ignores the problem.)
116. See, to the same effect, the opinion of the National Council for One Parent Families reported in *Community Care*, 22 October 1981, p. 2.
117. This is calculated from annual *Children in Care* publications. The statistics as such are not published.
118. See Children Act 1975, 2.56 (now Child Care Act 1980, s.3(1)(d).
119. *On The Care of Children*, Cmd., op. cit., para. 425.
120. Now in Child Care Act 1980, s.3(3)–(7).
121. Ibid., s.6 (added by s.58 of the Children Act 1975).
122. *Wheatley* v. *London Borough of Waltham Forest*, op. cit., p. 548.
123. A. Morris *et al.*, *Justice For Children*, London, Macmillan, 1980, p. 106.
124. *Wheatley* v. *London Borough of Waltham Forest*, op. cit., p. 548.
125. A phrase coined by J. Rowe and J. Lambert, *Children Who Wait*, London, ABAA, 1973.
126. R. Thorpe, 'Mum and Mrs. So and So', *Social Work Today*, 4, no. 22 (1974), pp. 691–5.
127. B. Holman, 'The Place of Fostering In Social Work', *British Journal of Social Work*, 5 (1975), pp. 3–27. See also his essay 'Exclusive and Inclusive Concepts of Fostering', in J. Triseliotis (ed.), *New Developments In Foster Care and Adoption*, London, Routledge & Kegan Paul, 1980, pp. 69–84.
128. Morris *et al.*, op. cit., p. 108.
129. Child Care Act 1980, s.3(1)(b)(iv).
130. A good recent illustration is P. Toynbee, 'To Tell a Mother She is Unfit . . .', *The Guardian*, 8 January 1982.
131. See M. Wald, 'State Intervention on Behalf of "Neglected" Children: A Search for Realistic Standards', in M. Rosenheim (ed.), *Pursuing Justice For The Child*, Chicago, University of Chicago Press, 1976, pp. 246–78.
132. In 1982 Parliament rejected the Child Care Bill 1982 which would have transferred jurisdiction to the court and removed the 'habits or mode of life' ground. See H.C. vol. 89, col. 866–70.
.33. As to which see L. Taylor *et al.*, *In Whose Best Interests?*, London, Cobden Trust and Mind, 1979, pp. 22–32.
134. See A. Sutton, 'Science In Court', in M. King (ed.), *Childhood, Welfare and Justice*, London, Batsford, 1981, pp. 45–104 at p. 95.
135. *Re W* [1964] Ch. 202, 210 by Ormerod L.J.
136. See *F* v. *S* [1973] Fam. 203.
137. *Re CB* [1981] 1 All E.R. 16.
138. *Surrey C.C.* v. *W.* (1982) 126 S.J. 155.

139. See R. Jones, 'Decisions on Important Steps', *Social Work Today*, **12**, no. 35 (10 February 1981), p. 15.
140. Discussed by Maidment, Freeman op. cit. (note 103).
141. See N. Warren, 'Representing Children In Care Proceedings', *Legal Action Group Bulletin*, July 1981, p. 155, and M. Hayes, 'Separate Representation In Care Proceedings', *Family Law*, 8 (1978), pp. 91–6.
142. Rule 17.
143. *R* v. *Welwyn Justices ex parte S, The Times*, 30 November 1978 (discussed in *LAG Bulletin*, January 1979, p. 1).
144. See B. Dickens, 'Representing The Child in the Courts' in I. Baxter and M. Eberts (eds), *The Child and the Courts,* Toronto, Carswell, 1978, pp. 273–98.
145. [1978] Q.B. 120.
146. Ibid., p. 144.
147. *The Guardian*, 16 October 1973.
148. In *Humberside C.C.* v. *D.P.R.* [1977] 3 All E.R. 964, 967.
149. Ibid.
150. See *R* v. *Milton Keynes Justices ex parte R* [1979] 1 W.L.R. 1062.
151. By Widgery L.C.J. in *Humberside C.C.* v. *D.P.R.*, op. cit., p. 966.
152. By Dunn J in *Re D* [1977] 3 All E.R. 481, 486.
153. Children Act 1975, s.64, inserting s.32A in Children and Young Persons Act 1969.
154. Ibid., inserting s.32B in CYPA 1969.
155. Children Act 1975, s.65.
156. Previously s.59 of the Childrens Act 1975, which expanded s.12 of the Children Act 1948; Health Act 1983, sch. 2, para. 55 (for voluntary organizations).
157. See s.18(3) of the 1980 Act.
158. See Guardianship of Minors Act 1971 s.1.
159. By Lord MacDermott in *J.* v. *C* [1970] A.C. 668, 724.
160. Lord Simon of Glaisdale in debate on Children Bill 1975; Hansard H.L. vol. 359, col. 544.
161. See Lord Chancellor's Memorandum on Children Bill 1975 (19 February 1975), referred to in M. D. A. Freeman, *The Children Act 1975,* London, Sweet & Maxwell, 1976 (note on s.3).
162. See Children Act 1975, s.3.
163. *The Times*, 18 December 1979.
164. Under the Children and Young Persons Act 1969, ss.37 and 38. See also *The Times,* 7 January 1980. A critical discussion of the case is M. D. A. Freeman, 'The Rights of Children and the Closure of Children's Homes', *Justice of The Peace,* **144** (1980), pp. 38–9.
165. The usual interpretation of *A* v. *Liverpool City Council* [1981] 2 All E.R. 385.
166. Page and Clark, *Who Cares?*, op. cit., p. 24.
167. Its booklet 'Guide For Children In Care' was discussed in *Community Care,* 4 October 1979.
168. Ibid., Section F.
169. See S. Cowling and R. Watson, *The Children's Spokesman's Scheme In Haringey*, London, A Voice For The Child In Care, 1982.
170. See G. Wilton, 'Processing Children's Complaints', *Social Work Today*, **11**, no. 1 (4 September 1979), p. 8.
171. *Community Care,* 6 September 1979, p. 2.
172. See Police Act 1976.
173. *Royal Commission on Legal Services*, London, HMSO, 1979, Cmnd. 7648, ch. 22.
174. Wilton, 'Processing Children's Complaints', op. cit.
175. See M. Edelman, *The Symbolic Uses Of Politics,* Urbana, University of Illinois Press, 1964.
176. Under the Local Government Act 1974. See, further, C. Cross, *Principles of Local Government Law,* London, Sweet & Maxwell, 1981 (6th ed.), pp. 82–6.
177. *Community Care,* 25 October 1979, p. 3.

178. *Community Care*, 20 August 1981, p. 3. See also L. Gostin, 'Case Confidence', *Social Work Today*, **13**, no. 3 (22 September 1981), p. 4.
179. [1980] 1 W.L.R. 1549. See also M. Fogarty, 'The Right to Know', *Social Work Today*, **13**, no. 18 (12 January 1982), pp. 10–11. The case has been raised in Parliament by David Alton, MP (H.C. vol. 12, cols. 282-8). See also now J. MacVeigh, *Gaskin*, London, Cape, 1982.
180. On the inadequacy of arguments used by judges, see W. Murphy and R. Rawlings, 'After the Ancien Régime: the Writing of Judgments in the House of Lords', *Modern Law Review*, **44** (1981), p. 617; *Modern Law Review*, **45** (1982), p. 34.
181. Cf. the remark of Katrin Fitzherbert, quoted in A. Morris *et al., Justice For Children*, op. cit., p. 121: 'A child can escape from negligent parents by being taken (*sic*) into care, but there is no escape from a negligent social worker.'
182. See Gouvernement du Québec, *La Protection des Jeunes en Danger*, Ministère de la Justice Service de l'Information, 1977.
183. See, further, O. Stone, *The Child's Voice in the Court of Law*, Toronto, Butterworths, 1982, p. 173.
184. Quoted in Page and Clark, *Who Cares?*, op. cit.
185. Cf. R. D. Schwart's study of different communal organisations in Israel, 'Social Factors in The Development of Legal Control', *Yale Law Journal*, **63** (1954), p. 471.
186. See *Who Cares?*, op. cit., ch. 5, and no. 4 of the Charter of Rights, p. 62.
187. By the Children and Young Persons Act 1969.
188. *Who Cares?*, op. cit., p. 40.
189. M. Stein, 'Children of the State', *Social Work Today*, **10**, no. 28 (1988), pp. 26-8 at p. 28.
190. *Who Cares?*, op. cit., pp. 41-2.
191. See *Social Work Today*, **8**, no. 25 (29 March 1977), pp. 7-9. See also 'Social Work in Child Care', ibid., pp. 19-20.
192. *Who Cares?*, op. cit., p. 43.
193. See C. Davey, 'A Share In Care', *Social Work Today*, **13**, no. 14 (8 December 1981), p. 4.
194. See J. Piaget, *The Moral Judgement of the Child*, London, Routledge & Kegan Paul, 1932, and W. Damon, *The Social World of the Child*, San Francisco, Jossey Bass, 1977.
195. It was suggested by children in care in a BBC television programme screened on 18 November 1979. See also L. Davis, 'A Voice In Their Lives', *Social Work Today*, **10**, no. 38, (5 June 1979), p. 20. See also G. Wilton, 'A Voice In Their Lives', *Social Work Today*, **10**, no. 34 (1 May 1979), p. 8.
196. DHSS, *The Cost of Operating The Unimplemented Provisions of The Children Act 1975*, London, HMSO, 1980.
197. It is unpublished but summarised in P. Sayer *et al.*, 'Positive Planning For Children In Care', *Social Work Today*, **8**, no. 2 (12 October 1976), pp. 9-11.
198. See Nottingham Social Services Department, *Report of Project Concerning Children In Care*, Nottingham, Nottingham SSD, 1975 (36 per cent inappropriately placed; 26 per cent could have returned home or been fostered but were not; some reviews 'superficial and cursory' and often no long-term plans).
199. Schedule 3, para. 71.
200. A. Skinner, 'Our Experience In Involving Children In Reviews', *Social Work Service*, no. 22 (February 1980), p. 42.
201. Page, 'Who Cares?', op. cit., p. 20.
202. See B. Bettleheim and E. Sylvester, 'The Therapeutic Milieu', *American Journal of Orthopsychiatry*, **18** (1948), p. 191.
203. See D. Ennals (then Secretary of State) in *Social Work Today*, **9**, no. 44 (1978).
204. See R. Kilroy-Silk, 'An Objectionable Objection', *Social Work Today*, **10**, no. 28 (13 March 1979), p. 1. The European Court of Human Rights has upheld corporal punishment as not in itself a breach of the Convention. But it decided that parents have the right to insist that their children are not corporally punished. See *The Times*, 26 February 1982.
205. Protection of Children Act 1978, s.1.
206. See also Davey, 'A Share In Care', op. cit.

207. See P. Conrad, 'The Discovery of Hyperkinesis: Notes in the Medicalisation of Deviant Behavior', *Social Problems,* **23** (1975), pp. 12–21. See also P. Conrad, *Identifying Hyperactive Children,* Lexington, Mass., Lexington Books, 1976.
208. See S. Box, 'Where Have All The Naughty Children Gone?' in National Deviancy Conference (ed.), *Permissiveness and Control,* London, Macmillan, 1980, pp. 96–122 at pp. 105–6.
209. J. Sandoval, N. Lambert and W. Yardell, 'Current Medical Practice and Hyperactive Children', *American Journal of Orthopsychiatry,* **46** (1976), pp. 323–4. See also D. Springmayer, 'Hyperactive Children and the Uses of Psychoactive Drugs: Treatment or Coercive Behavior Management?', *Journal of Contemporary Law,* **5** (1979), pp. 215–31.
210. See S. Box's introduction to Penguin edition of P. Schrag and D. Divoky, *The Myth Of The Hyperactive Child,* Harmondsworth, Penguin, 1981, p. 15.
211. See M. Rutter, *Helping Troubled Children,* Harmondsworth, Penguin, 1975.
212. See M. Bax, 'Editorial', *Developmental Medicine and Child Neurology,* **20** (1978), p. 277.
213. Rutter, *Helping Troubled Children,* op. cit., p. 21.
214. See H. Baker and U. Wills, 'School Phobia: Classification and Treatment', *British Journal of Psychiatry,* **132** (1978), pp. 492–9 (41 per cent of school phobics in this sample were given tranquillisers).
215. By P. S. Hughes, 'Survey of Medication In a Subnormality Hospital', *British Journal of Mental Subnormality,* **13** (1977), pp. 88–94.
216. Letter from M. S. Pepinpanayagan and R. A. Haig in *British Medical Journal,* **1** (26 March 1977), pp. 835–6.
217. See *Mind Out,* March 1981, p. 9 (letter of P. Bruggem *et al.*).
218. *The Times,* 28 May 1980.
219. Ibid.
220. 'Tardive Dyskinesia', *British Medical Journal,* **282** (18 April 1981), pp. 1257–8.
221. Page and Clark, *Who Cares?,* op. cit., 53.
222. The Who Cares Action Group, ' "As One Person Said . . ." ', *Social Work Today,* **11,** no. 6 (9 October 1979), p. 25.
223. See *Social Work Today,* **10,** no. 31 (1979), p. 2, and *Social Work Today,* **19,** no. 47 (1979), p. 6.
224. At a conference organised by the Children's Legal Centre and held in London in November 1981, it was a grievance frequently aired.
225. See J. Turner, 'Children not Cattle', *New Society,* 25 August 1978, p. 402. See also *The Times,* 8 July 1978, *The Guardian,* 8 November 1979, and *The Observer,* 4 November 1979.
226. *The Times,* 19 January 1981.
227. See H. W. Wade, *Administrative Law,* Oxford, Oxford University Press, 1978 (4th ed.), p. 603.
228. See on this J. Levin, 'Against The Cuts', *New Society,* 6 December 1979, p. 549.
229. Sweden's was established in 1972; Norway's in 1981. The Swedish one is discussed by E. Michael Salzer, *Current Sweden,* no. 229, July 1979.
230. See *Re K* [1972] 3 All E.R. 769; *Re W* [1979] 3 All E.R. 154.
231. See *Re Y* [1976] Fam. 125.
232. As a result of *A* v. *Liverpool City Council* [1982] 2 All E.R. 385.
233. *M* v. *M* [1973] 2 All E.R. 81.
234. Since, if access is denied, they may remove the child from care. See s.2(3) of the Child Care Act 1980.
235. The local authority has only actual custody.
236. See J. M. Thomson, 'Local Authorities and Parental Rights', *Law Quarterly Review,* **90** (1974), pp. 310, 314.
237. *Re K,* op. cit. (note 230); *R* v. *Oxford City Justices,* op. cit. (note 112).
238. N. Lowe and R. A. H. White, *Wards of Court,* London, Butterworths, 1979, p. 310. Cf. G. Kelly, 'The Lost Cord', *Social Work Today,* **13,** no. 12 (24 November 1981), pp. 7–9.

239. Maidment, 'The Fragmentation of Parental Rights . . .', op. cit., pp. 27–8.
240. See M. D. A. Freeman, *Violence In The Home — A Socio-Legal Study,* Farnborough, Saxon House, 1979, pp. 60–2.
241. See *The Guardian,* 28 September 1979.
242. See Children Act 1975, s.26, and T. Hall (ed.), *Access To Birth Records,* London, ABAFA, 1980.
243. A useful discussion of the issue is C. Wendelken, 'The Search For Identity', *Social Work Today,* 12, no. 19, (13 January 1981), pp. 8-10.
244. Hansard, H.C. vol. 3, col. 791, 29 April 1981.
245. Separation was to be permissible after the age of twelve only with the consent of the children concerned.
246. See as to this Family Rights Group, *In Care: A Money Guide For Families,* London, FRG, 1981. There is a clear association between a parent visiting his child in care and the chances of that child returning home. See J. Aldgate, 'Identification of Factors Influencing Length of Stay in Care' in Triseliotis (ed.), *New Developments in Foster Care . . .,* op. cit., pp. 22–40, and D. Fanshel and E. Shinn *Children In Foster Care — A Longitudinal Investigation,* New York, Columbia University Press, 1978.
247. See S. Millham *et al., Locking Up Children,* Farnborough, Saxon House, 1978, p. 186.
248. Ibid. See also Children's Legal Centre, *Locked Up in Care,* London, 1982.
249. See B. Audson, 'Unsuitable Cases For Treatment?', *Social Work Today,* 12, no. 36 (19 May 1981), pp. 10-14.
250. DHSS, *Children Referred To Closed Units,* London, DHSS, 1979.
251. See Criminal Justice Act 1982 s.25, Secure Accommodation Regulations 1983 and Health Act 1983, sch. 2, para. 50. See also M. Hughughi, *Troubled and Troublesome,* London, Burnett, 1978.
252. See T. Mulvey, 'After Care — Who Cares?', *Concern,* no. 26, 1977-8, pp. 26-30, and ' "As One Person Said . . ." ', *Social Work Today,* 11, no. 6 (1979), p. 25.
253. Strathclyde Regional Council Social Work Committee, *Room To Grow,* 1978.
254. Parker, *Caring For Separated Children,* op. cit. (note 1), p. 128.
255. M. Kellmer-Pringle, 'Whither Residential Child Care?', *Concern,* no. 26, 1977-8, pp. 5-10 at p. 6.
256. See IYG, *Whose Child?,* London, IYC, 1979, p. 9. A surprisingly high number of children in care die each year. This is commented upon critically by Parker *et al.,* op. cit., p. 129.
257. See C. Cooper, *Patterns of Family Placement,* London, National Children's Bureau, 1978.
258. See S. Godek, *Leaving Care,* London, Dr. Barnardo's, 1976.
259. Mulvey, 'After Care . . ., ' op. cit., p. 28.
260. See D. West and D. Farrington, *Who Becomes Delinquent?,* London, Heinemann, 1973, ch. IV.
261. Page and Clark, *Who Cares?,* op. cit. (note 38), p. 51.
262. Ibid., p. 52.
263. See M. Adcock, 'The Right of A Child To A Permanent Placement', in D. Rawstron (ed.), *Rights of Children,* London, BAAF, 1981, pp. 19-29.
264. 'Parents seem to find it easier to visit their children in a children's home than in a foster home', in *Who Cares?,* op. cit., p. 23.
265. See J. Aldgate, 'Advantages of Residential Care', *Adoption and Fostering,* no. 92 (1978), pp. 29-33.
266. IYC, *Whose Child?,* op. cit., p. 14.
267. Provided for in the Children Act 1975 s.32 and introduced in February 1982. See *Adoption and Fostering,* 6, no. 4 (1982), p. 4 on Devon's scheme (the first one).
268. By S. R. Churchill, published by Sage, London, 1979.
269. See G. James, 'Homes Fit For Children', *Social Work Today,* 11, no. 9 (1979).
270. J. Rowe and L. Lambert, *Children Who Wait,* London ABAA, 1973.
271. D. Fanshell and E. B. Shinn, *Children In Foster Care: A Longitudinal Investigation,* New York, Columbia University Press, 1978.

272.   See E. Cole, 'Conflicting Rights', *Adoption and Fostering*, no. 95 (1979), p. 35. See also K. Wiltse, 'Foster Care in the 1970s', *Children Today*, May/June 1979, p. 20.

273.   D. Fanshel, 'The Exit of Children From Foster Care', *Child Welfare*, **50** (1971), p. 65.

274.   T. B. Festinger, 'The Impact of the New York Court Review of Children in Foster Care', *Child Welfare*, **55** (1976), p. 211.

275.   See H. K. Bevan *et al.*, 'The Involvement of Magistrates In the Reviews of Certain Children In Care', unpublished paper, 1979.

276.   See R. Mnookin, *Child, Family and State*, Boston, Little, Brown, 1978, p. 577.

277.   See M. Wald, 'State Intervention on Behalf of "Neglected" Children: Standards for Removal of Children from their Homes', *Stanford Law Review*, **28** (1976), p. 623. He found that two-thirds of the review hearings took 2 minutes or less and the longest hearing only 20 minutes.

278.   See R. Mnookin, 'Child-Custody Adjudication: Judicial Functions In the Face of Indeterminacy', *Law and Contemporary Problems*, **39** (1975), p. 226 ff., particularly pp. 255-68.

279.   See J. Gibbs and R. Thorpe, 'The Natural Parent Group', *Social Work Today*, **6**, no. 13 (2 October 1975), pp. 386–9.

280.   J. Shawyer, *Death by Adoption*, Auckland, Cicada, 1979.

281.   M. Shaw and K. Lebens, *What Shall We Do With The Children?*, London, ABAFA, 1978, p. 22.

282.   See C. Lindsay Smith, 'Monitoring New Families Project', *Adoption and Fostering*, no. 95 (1970), p. 14, and 'Successful Planning in Essex', *Adoption and Fostering*, **6**, no. 1 (1982), p. 6.

283.   Quoted in D. Ball, 'What You Do To Children Changes The World', *Social Work Today*, **12**, no. 2 (9 September 1980), pp. 15–17.

284.   The Health and Social Services and Social Security Adjudications Act 1983 has effected a number of changes in the law. Most significantly restrictions are imposed on a local authority's power to terminate access to a child in care (though not one in voluntary care). Parents are to be allowed to apply to the juvenile court for an access order. The welfare of the child is the first and paramount consideration. A code of practice is promised (s.6 and Schedule 1, part I). The Act is progress but only limited progress. It will be possible to challenge a local authority's discretion only where it 'terminates' access, and not, for example, where it curtails it to irregular contact or makes visiting difficult or impracticable.

Divorce is an adult solution to an adult problem. The problem is age-old: the solution relatively new. In 1938 in England there were less than 7,000 divorces.[1] By 1970 the number of marriages dissolved had risen to 57,421,[2] and that was more than double what it had been a decade earlier.[3] The Divorce Reform Act of 1969, which liberalised the grounds for divorce and which took effect in 1971, has pushed the divorce statistics still higher. There are currently about 150,000 divorces a year.[4] The rapid increase in divorce is a widespread phenomenon. More significant than the number of divorces is the change in the incidence of divorce. It has been found that in Great Britain in 1976 there were approximately 10 divorces per 1,000 married persons: a 400 per cent increase in the divorce rate in twenty years.[5]

The proportion of divorces involving dependent children has also increased. In 1978, 60 per cent of divorces in England involved dependent children. This means that in that year nearly 86,000 couples who divorced had children under sixteen years of age — a total of nearly 163,000 children.[6] Seven years earlier, the number of children involved was barely half that number.[7]

One in three marriages today may expect to break up if the divorce rate continues at its present level. Between one in five and one in six children born today will witness their parents' divorce before they reach the age of sixteen.[9] The large increase in the number of one-parent families, and in the number of children in one-parent families, even since Finer reported in 1974, is mainly attributable to the upsurge of divorce.[10] The typical one-parent family today consists of a lone divorced or separated mother with one or two children.[11]

Divorce causes children trauma.[12] There is a clear association between marital disruption and deprivation.[13] When compared with children who have suffered bereavement, it seems that children from homes which have suffered marital disruption encounter hardships considerably more frequently. Delinquency also is 'associated with breaks which follow parental discord, or discord without a break'[14] rather than with the break-up of the home as such. Given the number involved and the multiple hardships and handicaps, surprisingly little attention has been focused on the children of divorce. Millions of pounds are spent researching rare diseases which afflict a handful of children. By contrast research into the causes and aftermath of divorce is very much a poor relation. Yet the children of divorce, 'the children of Armageddon', one American commentator[15] has dubbed them, are amongst the most vulnerable members of society.

Additionally, of course, the social cost of divorce is very large, particularly where there are dependent children. One estimate has put this at between half a billion and a billion pounds a year.[16] One effect of the paucity of research has meant that for too long truisms and myths have governed thinking about divorce and its impact on children: for example, that children prefer a divorce to an unhappy marriage; that the non-custodial parent should play a minimal role in parenting decisions.[17] Research has, however, now commenced, and, though many of these platitudes are firmly implanted in lay consciousness and legal practice, there is the hope that they may be displaced by a more rational social policy.

Divorce is an evil, though a necessary one. But unlike, for example, child abuse, the aim cannot be to eliminate it. The true evil anyway is marital discord and disorganisation. What can be improved is the decision-making process of divorce, particularly as this affects the principal victims of divorce, the children. There can be few areas of life where the treatment of children as property rather than as persons is better exemplified. And this has been accentuated by the growing trend towards private ordering of divorce which reduces further the already minimal reviewing capacity of courts.

With divorce it is easier to identify the wrong that children suffer than to spell out any code of rights. What rights should children have in relation to divorce? A right to choose which parent they prefer to remain with? Or should they have a right not to be asked to express a preference? A right to be separately represented in custody proceedings? But who is to represent the child and what is he to represent? A right to see the parent with whom they are not living? But how is such a right to be enforced? All of these rights and many others have been put forward. This chapter considers the merits and pitfalls of rights such as these. The gulf between rights as autonomy and rights as protection is at its sharpest in matters relating to custody of children. To what extent can children be allowed to choose, how free is their choice, or should they be protected from the consequences of expressing a view, with the decision being taken for them? These are matters on which there remain wide differences of opinion. These differences will remain so long as ideological cleavages and different images of man exist, But recent research, notably Wallerstein and Kelly's *Surviving The Break-Up*,[18] to which reference is made in this chapter, enables us to steer a path through some of the contradictory and often unsubstantiated assertions made in the literature and assists in the formulation of certain, hopefully informed, conclusions.

The Divorce Process and Children

Most divorces are undefended. Since 1977, when the 'special procedure' was extended to all undefended cases whether or not children were involved, this has meant that the divorce process is essentially an administrative mechanism.[19] The process of adjudication has effectively been transferred from the judge to the registrar. He examines the divorce petition and, if he is satisfied that the conditions for divorce are made out, issues a certificate. A decree is then pronounced by a judge in open court. This has aptly been described as an 'empty ritual'.[20]

Divorce is essentially a contest between a husband and wife. Historically, children were an 'ancilliary' matter and little attempt was made to safeguard their interests. This concerned the Morton Royal Commission which reported in 1956. The report noted that: 'passions are aroused in divorce and judgements distorted. One party may contest the other's claim to custody from spiteful or selfish motives. The children are then in the danger of becoming pawns in the struggle of wills.'[21] It concluded that a procedure was needed to ensure that parents themselves had given full consideration to the question of their children's future welfare and to make the control of the court over the welfare of the children more effective. Legislation was passed in 1958.[22] The law is now contained in section 41 of the Matrimonial Causes Act 1973. This provides that where there are relevant children of the family the Court is not to make a decree absolute of divorce (or nullity in the rare cases where this is asked for).

> unless the court, by order, has declared that it is satisfied − . . . (b) that the only children who are or may be children of the family to whom this section applies are the children named in the order and that −
> (i)   arrangements for the welfare of every child so named have been made and are satisfactory or are the best that can be devised in the circumstances; or
> (ii) it is impracticable for the party or parties appearing before the court to make any such arrangements; or
> (c)   that there are circumstances making it desirable that the decree should be made absolute or should be granted . . . without delay notwithstanding that there are or may be children of the family to whom this section applies and that the court is unable to make a declaration in accordance with paragraph (b) above.

This provision can offer children at best only minimal protection. And yet in most cases this fragile supervision of custody arrangements is all the legal system can offer children of divorcing parents.

The provision is designed for the uncontested custody matter, which most are. Indeed, the Courts have held that s.41 should not be used to hold up the grant of a decree absolute in cases where the interests of children will be considered in a contested custody application.[23] To enable the court to discharge its duties under s.41, the petitioner is required[24] to file with the petition 'a statement as to arrangements for children'.[25] Details are required of the child's proposed residence, child care arrangements, education or employment, financial provision and access. The official guide[26] for petitioners acting without a solicitor (the majority[27] since the removal of legal aid from the divorce itself) warns him that the proposed arrangements should be 'more than temporary'. He is encouraged to reach agreement with the respondent regarding the proposed arrangements. The respondent is given an opportunity to suggest alternative arrangements. If the case is being dealt with under the 'special procedure', as it will be if, as is likely, it is undefended, the registrar fixes an appointment for a judge to consider in chambers the proposed arrangements. The parties are given notices of the appointment but they are not obliged to attend. We do not know how many do but it is likely to be a very small proportion of divorcing parents. Whether anything might be achieved by compelling attendance is dubious.

It is easy to be critical of this procedure. It takes place in private. The judge has wide discretion to decide what to investigate, how to do so and what to do as a result of the investigation. There are no rules at all to circumscribe his inquisition. The conduct of this is entirely up to him. It is difficult to see, for example, how parents could object to the way an appointment was being conducted. As in all decision-making of low visibility, we cannot be certain that the values and prejudices of the individual judge do not intrude.[28] We have no way of knowing nor can we easily control judicial discretion. But look at what this has replaced. Formerly, there was a ritual enquiry made in open court during the hearing of an undefended divorce. Few parents were satisfied with this.[29] By contrast, Westcott has reported that parents are impressed that the judge takes the trouble to concern himself with the arrangements being made, the hearing apparently often reassuring the mother that she is 'doing the right thing'.[30] Murch notes that 'a preliminary investigation . . . suggests that most judges see their new task as to enquire further about the children and to test the parents' evidence, albeit in more informal ways than previously.'[31]

The judge does not have to approve the arrangements. But he nearly always does. There are, of course, a limited range of alternatives open to judges. As Eekelaar and Clive put it in their study *Custody After Divorce*:

> Even assuming the conditions in which the child is living are not very satisfactory, it would seldom be practicable or even sensible to transfer the child to the other parent (who may not want the child). If the proper solution lies in committing the child to the care of a local welfare authority, it is arguable that jurisdiction to do this already exists under the child welfare law and that it is by no means clear that it is appropriate to move a child from his home environment under the divorce jurisdiction in circumstances where

the requirements for such removal under child welfare law are not met.[32]

In Susan Maidment's survey[33] there was only one case out of ninety-five in which the judge declared himself not satisfied with the arrangements put to him. In that case a decree absolute was granted on the respondent's undertaking that she would bring this matter before the court within three months. She did not do so. In 67 per cent of the cases, the order was that the arrangements were 'satisfactory'; in 31 per cent that they were the best that could be made in the circumstances.

One thing the court can do is adjourn for further information, in practice for a welfare report. Eekelaar and Clive[34] found, surprisingly, that in uncontested cases nearly one in ten were adjourned. (In Scotland the percentage was considerably lower: 3 per cent.) The cases which courts tended to probe into further were those where it was proposed that a child's residence should change (these were rare), where there were many children involved, or where the children were living in different households or with a person other than the parent. Despite the investigation they found the courts intervened to change a child's place of residence in only 0.6 per cent of cases in England and Wales and only once in the Scottish sample of 203 cases. Whatever arrangements are approved there is anyway no real machinery, supervision orders apart, for ensuring that what is sanctioned is carried out and the evidence suggests far from total compliance with arrangements, particularly as regards access.[35] Supervision orders[36] are, however, sometimes made, particularly, it is thought, where this course of action is recommended in a welfare report. But the practice is variable. Eekelaar and Clive found it was ordered in 3.5 per cent of their English cases, though only once in their Scottish sample;[37] in Susan Maidment's smaller study, based in the North Midlands supervision orders were made in 8 per cent of cases.[38]

It will have been noted how all initiatives are taken by judges. They lack the expertise, training and often temperament to be the best persons to select cases which require further investigation. This has not escaped the notice of the Family Law Sub-Committee of the Chief Probation Officer's Conference and this in 1976 proposed that all divorce cases involving dependent children, should be referred by the registrar to the department of the Chief Welfare Officer. He 'should go through ever case involving children and all cases suggested by him should be put back for full investigation.'[39] As Jean Graham Hall has pointed out, this proposal 'amounts to a change of roles by welfare officers, from that of providing reports when called upon by the court, to becoming the initiating authority with prior right to decide whether reports should be made.'[40] She is critical of this. In principle I can see no objection to the proposal. Welfare officers are likely to be better judges of cases requiring investigation than are judges themselves. But in practice there are major problems. Each profession tends to designate a clientele which it believes needs its services and which, though it might not see it in this way, it can control.[41] Welfare officers, particularly probation officers, are likely to see the poor and the deviant particularly as requiring investigation and regulation in this way. Indeed, Murch[42] points out that the background to the welfare officers' proposal were investigations carried out in 1975 and 1976 into divorce petitions to see what proportion of families were already known to social services departments or the local probation service. Three studies revealed respectively 39 per cent, 43 per cent and 36 per cent of divorcing families were so known. These findings have been used to legitimate a practice which is spreading, but about which there is little information, under which names and addresses of all cases involving children are sent to the social services department and probation office covering the area where they live. If the family is known, then it is likely that a welfare report will be sought. As Murch notes, 'middle class families, not previously known to these organisations, will largely avoid being scrutinised'.[43] He quotes one chief probation officer as saying that the 'field of divorce is about the only element of preventative work left to our service. It is an area where we . . . can achieve some real benefit to a group of people at a critical and vulnerable point in their lives.'[44] This, of course, begs the question as to whether such intervention has beneficial or detrimental effects. This is considered in other chapters of this book in other contexts. Here the point need only be made that control of this nature may contribute to the very behaviour it aims to prevent.

The expectations of the Morton Commission have not been met. It had hoped that children's interests would be placed 'in the forefront'.[45] The Commission thought the 'main merit' of the scheme it put forward was that 'it would encourage . . . a sense of parental responsibility.' Indeed, it thought that 'if parents were thus made to realise at the outset their obligations to their children we would hope that they would sometimes decide to abandon the idea of divorce for the sake of their children.'[46] This hope is expressed periodically: indeed, there have been suggestions that divorce should not be permitted for couples with dependent children.[47] Mia Kellmer-Pringle, in her DHSS-commissioned study *The Needs of Children*,[48] has gone so far as to suggest two different forms of marriage: one designed to protect the interests of both partners which would be terminated readily at the request of either and another involving a more binding committment because the intention was to raise a family and put the needs of children above their own individual self-fulfilment. The latter contract would be much more difficult to terminate by divorce.[49] These are not practicable solutions in a society where divorce is as acceptable as is the case in Britain today. Morton's aspirations were built in another era since which there have been enormous social and cultural changes: we cannot expect them to succeed in the 1980s.

Private Ordering

It will be apparent that most custody dispositions result from arrangements put by parents to the court and that the courts themselves are able to exercise at best only tenuous control. It is one thing to accept this as inevitable, another to see it as positively desirable. But Goldstein, Freud and Solnit[50] unequivocally and Mnookin[51] more hesitantly think it is.

Goldstein *et al.* in *Before the Best Interests of The Child* (a book the general thesis of which is considered fully in the next chapter) argue that state intervention is justified only when one or both separating parents bring to the court their disagreement about the custody of the children. They claim that

> a child is thus (a) *protected from* intrusion if his separating parents can decide to continue to care for him jointly or separately or to entrust his care to a third party; and (b) *protected by* state intervention if either of his parents requests the court to choose which of them is to be responsible for his custody and care.[52]

From the point of view of the parents this proposal has much to commend it. For they, subject to what is said below, may well be in the best position to evaluate the comparative advantages of alternative arrangements. As John Stuart Mill put it: 'with respect to his own feelings and circumstances, the most ordinary man or woman has means of knowledge immeasurably surpassing those that can be possessed by anyone else.'[53] Parents can thus be expected in most cases to choose custody arrangements which are beneficial to themselves, just as entrepreneurs negotiating a deal can be assumed to conclude an agreement which conforms as closely as possible to the preferences of each. But should we equate children with ball-bearings or buttons?[54] This is what Goldstein and his colleagues would appear to do. Note their standard states that a *child* is protected from intrusion. It would be more accurate to phrase this as 'his parents are protected from intrusion'.

Mnookin recognises that the solution agreed to by the parents may be deleterious to the child of the marriage. In a recent paper of his he writes:

> It is . . . certainly possible that some parents may engage in divorce bargaining on the basis of preferences that narrowly reflect their selfish interests and ignore the chidlren's needs. A father may threaten a custody fight over the child, not because he wants custody, but because he wants to push his wife into accepting less support, even though this will have a detrimental effect on the children. A custodial parent, eager to escape an unhappy marriage, may offer to settle for a small amount in order to sever relations soon . . .[55]

In his 'Bargaining in The Shadow of the Law' he accepts that where there are dependent children 'the state obviously has broader interests than simply dispute settlement.' It also has 'a responsibility for *child protection.*'[56] He accordingly would limit parental freedom to decide on matters of custody to agreements which would not expose the child to neglect or abuse: in other words, the same minimum standard for child protection imposed on all families would apply also to divorcing parents.

The most substantial argument he raises in support of this is that 'since a child's social and psychological relationships with *both* parents ordinarily continue after the divorce, a process that leads to agreement between the parents is preferable to one that necessarily has a winner and a loser.'[57] A number of comments may be offered about this. First, it is of course true that in general adjudication tends to lead to an all-or-nothing solution.[58] But that is not necessarily so, as decisions on contributory negligence or awards of joint custody indicate. It is also clear that going to court has a polarising effect and that it tends to break or distort relationships rather than faciliating their future development. Bargaining, even with a third party added as mediator or conciliator, tends to avoid these dysfunctional consequences. What this shows is that out-of-court settlements are beneficial to the parents. But it does not follow from this that the child, the subject of the dispute, also comes out a winner.

Secondly, Mnookin makes the assumption that the process leads to a genuine agreement. But, as Eisenberg has written recently, 'an individual may be of average intelligence and yet may lack the aptitude, experience, or judgemental ability to make a deliberative and well-informed judgement concerning the desirability of entering into a given complex transaction.'[59] His concern is with situations where one party exploits the other's incapacity by inducing a bargain that a person with full capacity would not make. When this happens, Eisenberg argues, neither fairness nor efficiency support application of the principle that a bargain should be enforced to its full extent. Mnookin accepts that 'an analogous concept could be applied to divorce bargaining.'[60] He believes courts should reopen agreements where there is proof of exploitation. This, in Mnookin's terms, would require 'a showing that the terms of the agreement considered as a whole fall outside the range of what would have been acceptable to a competent person at the time of settlement.'[61]

The problem with Mnookin's reasoning is that a divorce settlement is not strictly analogous to a commercial bargain. Outside a slave society commerical contracts are not concerned with the disposal of human beings: bargains about custody and access are. Further, in no way can it be accepted that the children themselves are meaningful participants in the bargaining process. But there is a more basic distinction. Contracts about divorce are concerned with the dissolution of a status (marriage: the status of parenthood remains). The status is created by the contract of marriage. But the terms of this are not freely negotiated: rather they are imposed upon the contracting parties in the name of the public interest. Marriage is subjected to rules which have nothing to do with agreement.[62] Many of these rules may be out of date but that is another matter. If marriage is to be subjected to rules, then the case for imposing limits upon the private ordering of divorce, at least where there are dependent children, is a strong one. There is yet another argument against the preservation of contract as a private realm beyond state intrusion and that is that it presumes a dichotomy between public and private law, which soon disappears under investigation. Legal obligations are not the result of a meeting of wills but are imposed by the community and reflect its standards and goals, or those of the politically powerful. It is wrong to assume that the state neutrally endorses the will of contracting parties.[63] Private ordering may in fact be a mirage, an aspiration of liberals. It is one that must be reckoned with; indeed, given the performance of courts, one that can be readily understood. Nevertheless, I believe firmer, not looser, controls are required on private ordering of custody arrangements. This is considered further in the section on improving decision-making at the end of this chapter.

Custody Decisions: What Are The Child's Best Interests?

Where custody is uncontested, the judicial role is supervisory. In contested custody matters the court takes on an additional role, that of adjudication. In fact very few cases are contested. Eekelaar and Clive found only 6 per cent in their sample that were.[64]

How do the courts dispose of custody in contested cases? They get little assistance, in this country at least, from statute. The Guardianship of Minors Act of 1971 (re-enacting a 1925 provision) directs that where in any proceedings before any court the 'custody or upbringing' of a child is in question, 'the court . . . shall regard the welfare of the minor as the first and paramount consideration.'[65] These words, it has been held,[66]

> connote a process whereby when all the relevant facts, relationships, claims and wishes of parents, risks, choices and other circumstances are taken into account and weighed, the course to be followed will be that which is most in the interest of the child's welfare . . . . That is the first consideration because it is of first importance and the paramount consideration because it rules upon or determines the course to be followed.

Custody, in other words, is to be decided upon in accordance with the child's best interests. But what are these and how do judges determine them?

The most perceptive analysis has been undertaken by Robert Mnookin.[67] He points out that from the perspective of rational choice, the judge would wish to compare the expected utility for the child of living with his mother with that of living with his father (that is, of course, in the normal case where the dispute is not complicated by other factors). First, the judge needs information. Secondly, he needs predictive ability, to be able to assess the probability of various outcomes and evaluate the advantages and disadvantages of each. Thirdly, he needs some source for the values to inform his choice. All three of these requirements pose considerable problems.

Of the three the first is the easiest to surmount. The parties may themselves produce certain information. For example, they or one of them may have had the child psychiatrically examined. The courts are much more willing today to accept such evidence: it is not long since judges expressed the fear that the admission would lead to the medical profession deciding the case rather than themselves.[68] Wisely, the judges prefer parents to co-operate in jointly instructing a medical expert,[69] so that the court gets one opinion rather than two. The weight given to such evidence must inevitably depend on the judge himself (some are more sceptical than others)[70] and the circumstances of the case. Thus, Lord Upjohn in *J* v. *C*[71] distinguished cases where the child was suffering from illness, where the evidence 'must weigh heavily with the court', from those where the child was normal and happy where it might be 'valuable' but where it was only an element to support the 'general knowledge and experience of the judge', so that if he thought the child's welfare dictated a different course 'he should not hestiate to take risks . . . and go against such medical evidence.'

The courts may acquire information also from the reports of welfare officers. Eekelaar and Clive found regional variations but overall, in contested cases, fairly extensive use of the power to order such a report.[72] The courts prefer one welfare report wherever possible, though it is accepted that this may be impracticable in certain cases.[73] A good welfare report will compare the alternative environments. It will often incorporate a school report.[74] It may make recommendations.[75] The judge is not bound by these: they are to guide, not control his decision.[76] But it has been said that refusals to implement a welfare officer's report should be reasoned.[77] Parents (more correctly, parties to the proceedings)[78] are entitled to inspect the report[79] but it is apparently common to deny them access to it.[80] Unrepresented parents are always sent a copy by the court, which gives them at least one advantage over parents with a solicitor.[81] It is common for the welfare officer not to be in court when his report is considered. This makes it difficult to challenge the report.[82] Another problem is that a lengthy period of time can elapse between the making of the report and its consideration.[83] It is a cause for concern that courts must often act on out-of-date information. The whole process needs speeding up. Eekelaar and Clive found that in 45 per cent of contested cases where welfare reports are sought the case is adjourned for six months to await them.[84] A proper preliminary scrutiny of papers could obviate much of this delay.[85]

There are two other ways in which the court may increase its information. It can order the child to be separately represented and, if this is done, the Official Solicitor[86] will normally be appointed to act as guardian *ad litem* for the child. This course of action was becoming increasingly common but the tide has been stemmed by a Practice Direction in late 1981.[87] This states that in most cases the child's interest is sufficiently protected by a welfare report and that it is only in 'exceptional' cases that joinder of the child and his representation by the Official Solicitor is likely to assist the court. The Official Solicitor himself, David Venables, believes there are four categories of case where he may be useful: three are relevant here. First, where the child is of sufficient age (he suggests eight) to express an independent view; secondly, where the Court requires a specific task or independent enquiry to be carried out (for example, a psychiatric examination); and thirdly, where the case raises a difficult point of law or some unusual or difficult element.[88]

Finally, the judge[89] may interview the child in his chambers. This one English Lord Justice has described as a 'most desirable' practice.[90] The practice is common. Hall in 1966 found approximately half those questioned by him did consult children[91] Barrington Baker *et al.*, on the other hand, eleven years later, found that 40 per cent of registrars only rarely saw children and 31 per cent never did.[92] It has, however, been said by the Court of Appeal[93] that the judge should not give the child an undertaking that what he says will not be disclosed. This, Eekelaar remarks convincingly, 'puts the parties' representatives and an appeal court in an impossible position.'[94]

Judges rarely act possessed of full information. But even given that they had this and were thus in a position to specify possible outcomes, how are they to predict what the probable results of alternative outcomes are? The problem is that 'present-day knowledge about human behaviour provides no basis for the kind of individualized predictions required by the best-interests standard.'[95] There are competing theories of human behaviour related to different conceptions of the nature of man (for example, behaviourist models; psycho-analytic views and there are any number of these linked to different theorists, Freud, Jung, Klein, etc; theories based on child development associated with Piaget and so on). Furthermore, there is no consensus as to which, if any, of these views is the correct one. And even if there was a right answer, it is difficult to see how it could be a reliable guide to predict what is likely to happen to a particular child. 'No one', Goldstein, Freud and Solnit write, 'can forecast just what experiences, what events, what changes a child, or for that matter his adult custodian, will actually encounter.'[96] Anna Freud in a Lecture published in 1958 gave three reasons why prediction is 'difficult and hazardous'. Two presuppose the truth of her psycho-analytic perspective and can be ignored here. The third is that 'environmental happenings in a child's life will always remain unpredictable since they are not governed by any known laws.'[97]

The difficulty of making accurate predictions is attested to by the well-known Berkeley group study of 166 infants born in 1929. The aim of the study was to observe the emotional, mental and physical growth not of the disturbed, so often the subject matter of psychological study, but rather of 'normal' adults.[98] Arlene Skolnick summarising the research[99] notes that the most surprising, and for us the most interesting, research finding was 'the difficulty of predicting what thirty-year-old adults would be like even after the most sophisticated data had been gathered on them as children.'

Even if information was forthcoming to specify outcomes and their pro-bability could be estimated, the judge would still have to decide which set of values to use to determine what was in a child's best interest. How is utility to be determined? As Mnookin notes,[100] an obvious method would be to ask the person affected, namely the child, what he wants. We do not do so because we do not believe that the child has the capacity and maturity to determine his own utility. But is this necessarily right? It must be the case with very young children but is it necessarily consistent with the principles of liberal paternalism adumbrated in the second chapter to deny adolescents the capacity to specify the value-systems they uphold? This is not to ask them to choose their resi-dences, only to state the considerations the decision-maker should regard as dominant.

But whether or not we look to the child, other questions remain. Should best interests be looked at from a long-term or a short-term perspective? It is significant that the most recent English statutes refer to the need to 'safeguard and promote the welfare of the child throughout his childhood.'[101] Mnookin continues:

> The conditions that make a person happy at age seven to ten may have adverse consequences at age thirty. Should the judge ask himself what decision will make the child happiest in the next year? Or at thirty? Or at seventy? Should the judge decide by thinking about what decision the child as an adult looking back would have wanted made? In this case, the pre-ference problem is formidable, for how is the judge to compare 'happiness' at one age with 'happiness' at another age?[102]

What is 'happiness' anyway? When we refer to the child's best interests, are we stressing material welfare or spiritual? Is ultimate economic productivity an important consideration or are the more primary values, love, security and warmth in interpersonal relationships, of greater significance? The questions are endless but where is the judge to turn for answers? There is no clear consensus within society either as to the best child-rearing strategies or as to the approp-riate hierarchy of values.[103] Should, therefore, the judge rely on his own defi-nitions of happiness, the parents' (if they can agree) or the child's?

Nobody may know *the* answer, and there may not be one, but the judge has got to come to *an* answer. It is hardly surprising that a dispute over a child was chosen to demonstrate the wisdom of Solomon.[104] We ask the judge to do what no one can satisfactorily do: to predict, to make long-term extrapolations. What, of course, he is often forced to do is to weigh the relative merits of different kinds of environments and life-styles. He can only base his decisions on values and his own must inevitably intrude. This problem is graphically illustrated in the judgement of Justice Stuart, an Iowa judge, in the leading United States case of *Painter* v. *Bannister*.[105]

The case arose out of a dispute between a six-year-old's father and his maternal grandparents. The father had temporarily relinquished custody to them eighteen months earlier after the death in a car accident of his wife and daughter. He had now remarried. The case is thus not divorce-related but is highly pertinent nevertheless. The trial court ruled in the father's favour on the basis of parental preference. Two years later the Supreme Court of Iowa reversed the trial court's verdict, awarding custody to the boy's grandparents. The Court relied heavily on the testimony of a child psychologist. It maintained that its decision was in the psychological best interests of the child.[106]

The case is interesting for a number of reasons. First, it preferred psychological parents to a natural father. In doing this it demonstrated the diminishing importance of the 'blood tie'. As such it makes interesting comparisons with the contemporaneous English decision of *Re C(MA)*,[107] in which Ungoed-Thomas J. and the Court of Appeal, Willmer L.J. dissenting, turned down an adoption application in favour of allowing an illegitimate child of seventeen months to be brought up by his 'own people', a middle-aged father and his wife who was on the point of divorcing him. Secondly, *Painter* v. *Bannister* is informative of the ways expert evidence can come to dominate proceedings. The evidence of the child psychologist that the boy would 'go wrong' if he was returned to his father was a crucial factor in the court's thinking. He had not assessed the father. His testimony was based on adoption studies which found that the majority of 'children who are changed, from ages six to eight, will go bad, if they have had a prior history of instability.'[108] It is noticeable how 'social science data (e.g. adoption studies) and expert testimony could be used in custody disputes to highlight pathogenic consequences; the potential of risk became amplified and all the more ominous when bolstered by statistics and/or clinical diagnoses.'[109]

Thirdly, and most significantly in the context of trying to understand how values come to influence decision-making in disputed custody matters, the judge supplied evidence of his own thinking process more fully and frankly than is usual. He said:

The Bannister home provides Mark with a stable, dependable, conventional, middle-class, middlewest background and an opportunity for a college education and profession, if he desires it. It provides a solid foundation and secure atmosphere. In the Painter home, Mark would have more freedom of conduct and thought with an opportunity to develop his individual talents. It would be more exciting and challenging in many respects, but romantic, impractical, and unstable.

The judge pointed out that Mr. Painter's life was characterised by a 'Bohemian approach to finances and life in general', that the psychiatrist had classified him as 'a romantic and somewhat of a dreamer', that he had 'no concern for formal religious training', that he was a 'political liberal' and that at his wife's funeral he wore 'a sport shirt and sweater'. The judge, by way of defending himself, added that he was not intending to criticise the father but the father's values supported the conclusion to which the court had come. 'We believe', said the judge, that 'security and stability in the home are more important than intellectual stimulation in the proper development of a child.'[110] It is not difficult to believe when this is read that references to psychological parenthood and scientific data were but cloaks to cover opinions and value judgements far removed from any scientific process of evaluation. The case may be the exception rather than the rule, but there are other examples,[111] less graphic perhaps, certainly less frank in revealing values and biases, where similar processes are at work. It is easy to be critical and yet the point is that values must inevitably play a part. To an extent cases therefore depend upon which judge hears the case. The differences between judges are however minimised by the constraints of the institutional setting,[112] as well as by the rather homogeneous socio-economic and intellectual background of the judges.[113]

The Custody Decision-making Process

How do courts dispose of custody in contested cases? Eekelaar and Clive found that the fundamental principle underlying the court's decision-making was to preserve the residential status quo of the child.[114] They found that in only five cases (out of thirty nine) did this change, and in only two of these did the court order itself bring about a change.[115] In both the move was to the wife: one re-united separated siblings. It is of some interest that in the other the judge moved two children from the father to the mother against the recommendation in the welfare officer's report. In Maidment's sample there was no case in which a move took place as a result of a contested custody hearing.[116] The evidence thus suggests that a guideline similar to that depicted by Goldstein and his colleagues is applied by the courts. They have argued that placement decisions should safeguard the child's need for continuity of relationship.[117]

When one turns to the case law the impression is of the courts favouring the mother. There certainly once was a presumption that the mother should get custody at least of very young children.[118] Bowlby's views on maternal deprivation[119] cast a spell on judicial thinking. On occasions it still does.[120] Some believe that the fact the the mother usually comes out of a contested custody suit with custody reflects judicial preference.[121] It is, of course, also in the best interest of the state: in this sense divorce is a continuation of marriage.[122] Most dispositions in favour of the mother can be explained in terms of the fact that on separation that is with whom the children have stayed. Orders in the mother's favour, in other words, would appear to be merely supporting the residential status quo. But Susan Maidment[123] has produced some evidence that appeal courts in recent years have been giving mother custody where the status quo argument favoured the father. The evidence is flimsy and it cannot be said that a five-year sample of reported cases is statistically significant, but she does show that in several of the cases 'it was the judge's simple view that young children needed their mothers that was the dominant factor in the decision.' She also notes that reversals of custody were often in the face of welfare officers' recommendations. Certainly, however, some of the cases are not difficult to justify: thus, in one the mother regained custody because the father's Exclusive Brethren beliefs were deemed to provide the children with a handicapping milieu;[124] in another the father's attitude to access was 'destructive and damaging'.[125] I do not think that Maidment has proved that judges are biased towards mothers, though traces of Bowlbyism remain. What the cases do, I think, demonstrate is that proof of exceptional circumstances is required before a court will normally disturb the residential status quo of the child.

Another factor the courts have looked to in the past has been the parties' conduct.[126] Where it can be shown that an adulterous mother (or father — the cases are all concerned with mothers since it has long been thought a useful allegation for fathers to make to secure custody) is a bad mother, the reason may have some force.[127] But the courts have used conduct in the past as a bargaining counter to induce an errant wife to return and become reconciled to her husband.[128] But this factor is potent no longer. The question is not what the 'essential justice of the case' requires but 'what the best interests of the children' demand.[129]

The courts have stressed on a number of occasions[130] how important it is to keep siblings together whenever possible.[131] But they are prepared to split them where there is no better alternative.[132] The reluctance to separate siblings is less where there is a pronounced age gap and/or a sex difference.[133] Just occasionally a split which the courts justify as in the children's best interests will look a little suspect. One such case is *Re O*[134] where children of a mixed English–Sudanese marriage were split up, the son going to the father in the Sudan, the daughter staying with the mother in England. The court reasoned that the boy's prospects were good in the Sudan (he would eventually succeed to the father's business), but the girl was less adaptable and would be better off in England. In fact the court seemed equally concerned with justice and the father's rights as it did with the boy's welfare.

Other factors which influence the courts are continuity in religious education,[135] whether the parent can provide a parent-substitute[136] and whether an adequate home environment can be provided. A parent who can offer a child good accommodation must, other things being equal, have the edge over one who cannot.[137] The child's wishes are by no means ignored. They count for little when the child is very young and they may be discounted when they are thought to be the wishes of one of the parents 'assiduously instilled' into the child.[138] At least two American states have custody statutes which state that a judge must honour the child's preferences, in Ohio at the age of twelve and in

Georgia at fourteen. Other states have statutes which list the factors to which a judge should have regard in deciding custody, and these regularly include the child's wishes.

There are undoubtedly problems with relying on the wishes of children. There are questions of competence. The dangers of the child having been coached have been referred to. The child may be responding to promises made by one parent. Older children may think that a particular parent cannot survive their loss, with the result that their decision may be influenced by what they see as a parent's welfare rather than their own. Children may reject the parent whom they see as responsible for the separation. There is also the danger that a child may, by expressing his preference for one parent, do untold damage to his relationship with the other parent. The view, therefore, expressed in one recent English case,[139] that a child should have the right *not* to be asked to express any preference, has much to commend it. The older child faces an inevitable dilemma. If he fails to state a preference he invites the judge to make an un-desired decision. If he states a preference he risks hurting one of his parents and damaging his relationship with that parent. The dilemma is difficult, if not impossible, to resolve in the context of adversary proceedings at the end of which one parent is to be awarded custody.

It is difficult to state what the current English practice is. Judges regularly interview children and there are reported cases where the wishes of the child is said to be the dominant consideration.[140] It is, however, impossible to say how typical these cases are. It is probable that the child's wishes are the deciding factor in very few custody disputes.

Joint Custody

In England the court 'may make such order as it thinks fit for the custody and education of any child of the family who is under the age of 18.[141] The com-monest form of order gives custody to the wife with access to the husband.[142] The divorce court also has power to make 'split orders', giving custody to one parent and care and control to the other.[143] Such orders can cause problems[144] and in practice few are made.[145] The court may also give custody to both parents. This course of action has been commended in cases where each parent has something to offer the child and they can co-operate.[146] To call such an order joint custody, as English lawyers tend to do, is to run the risk of puzzling Americans for whom joint custody means what it says. By joint custody Americans envisage co-parenting. They would look aghast at Cretney's comment that 'care and control would, of course, have to be given to one parent.'[147]

Joint custody in its English law understanding makes little sense. Since 1973 both parents of a legitimate child have equal rights and these rights survive divorce.[148] Thus, an order giving one parent care and control and the other access would leave both parents with an equal say in matters such as the child's education and all other important issues.[149] Eekelaar and Clive observed, however, that the point was hardly appreciated by the courts, let alone by the parties.[150] In England joint custody orders are comparatively rare. This is hardly surprising in the circumstances.

The American practice of joint custody goes rather further than its English counterpart. Both involve, to quote the Wisconsin statute, 'equal rights and responsibilities to the minor child with neither party's rights being 'superior.'[152] The concepts, in other words, are not dissimilar: the practice is. Americans understand by joint custody shared custody or co-parenting.[153] Each parent has care and control so that custody is concurrent. Woolley defines it as follows:

> any method that permits the children to grow up knowing and interacting with each parent in an everyday situation, whether that comes about by splitting the time on a fifty-fifty basis each week or by having the children go live with the other parent for several years or more.[154]

Joint custody in the USA is commonly negotiated with alternating residences, with children living part of the time with one parent and part with the other. But this is not a necessary complication of joint custody: all that is necessary is that parents each continue to retain responsibility for the children's care and control. Grote and Weinstein state that it is 'more than an arrangement wherein one child resides with two parents – it is a flexible and open arrangement for living, sharing and loving.'[155]

At least twenty-seven states in the USA now have statutes requiring joint custody arrangements,[156] and one, New Jersey, has it as a result of a court decision.[157] The California statute is probably the most advanced. It begins

> The legislature finds and declares that it is the public policy of this State to assure minor children of frequent and continuing contact with both parents after the parents have separated or dissolved their marriage, and to encourage parents to share the rights and responsibilities of child rearing in order to effect this policy.

It emphasises that 'custody should be awarded in the following order of preference, according to the best interests of the child' (a) to both parents jointly . . . or to either parent'. Further, if both parents agree to joint custody or if either applies for joint custody, the court must state its reason for denial. Where the court makes an order for custody to either parent, it must consider 'which parent is more likely to allow the child . . . frequent and continuing contact with the non-custodial parent' (California Statutes 1980).

Joint custody orders are still relatively rare. They tend to be decreed when the parties agree an arrangement for joint parenting. But American courts have occasionally awarded joint custody when neither party, or only one party has requested it, and this despite the warning of the Chief Justice Breitel of the Court of Appeals of New York that 'it can only enhance familial chaos'.[158] There is evidence, albeit rather impressionistic, that joint custody can succeed. According to Roman and Haddad, it 'may, eventually, minimize parental conflict . . . because it appears more fully to satisfy the needs of both parents.'[159] Nor did they find the objection to joint custody, 'that it makes of the child a "yo-yo" whose loyalties are divided and whose stability is undermined by shifting living arrangements',[160] to be true. They argue:

> Under joint custody the feelings of both the parents and the children are more openly faced and expressed. Not only need the child never feel abandoned . . . , he also is enriched by experiencing the life styles and points of view of two adults who remain available and loving to him. The child is allowed to feel rooted in relation to both parents and to continue to value each relationship.[161]

To this the Nobles add the significant point that the arguments about child-rearing are found in most marriages but they do not have to become 'more shrill' on separation. 'In fact, removing the irritating factor of two unloving people living together can probably make them both more responsive to the needs of the children.'[162] Joint custody, it seems, can work where a couple is capable of reaching shared decisions in the child's best interests. It may only work for a minority. It involves commitment and it may also necessitate reasonable financial resources for, quite apart from the cost of implementing co-parenting arrangements, there may be need to resort to professional mediation should differences arise.

The importance of joint custody is that it disrupts the parent–child relationship less than other custody alternatives. It is, therefore, an ideal to be sought. In the United States it is in its early stages. In England it is barely known about. We could make joint custody orders under existing English legislation (we do, though they mean something different). The lead must come from divorcing couples. When their practices are affirmed by the judges acting in their supervisory role, the notion will emerge in public debate and in time there will be a demand for joint custody from people who at present would look sceptically at it. Not only is it better for children, but mothers and fathers[163] can also profit from it. If divorce is to continue to be as common as it currently is, we must find ways of taking the bitterness out of it. Joint custody arrangements as part of 'amicable' divorce[164] is one way of achieving this. Joint custody as co-parenting must be the goal but in the immediate future greater use of joint custody orders as they are currently understood would be psychologically valuable, whatever their theoretical legal superfluity.

Surviving the Breakup

For far too long discussion about the effects of divorce on children has been impressionistic. Only in the last few years have we begun to acquire knowledge regarding the impact of family breakdown on children. In the United States two major research studies have been published and these have begun the task of filling some of the gaps in our knowledge about what family rupture does to children and how they cope with it. One study (Wallerstein and Kelly)[165] arose out of a clinical investigation of 131 children and their parents from sixty predominantly white, middle-class families in Northern California who were followed for a five-year period from the decisive marital separation. The second by Hetherington and her fellow researchers[166] was Virginia-based and centred on thirty-six pre-school children and their divorcing parents, and a control group of thirty-six, who were studied for a two-year period following divorce. These are the only longitudinal studies of children in divorced families and to a large extent they corroborate each other. The studies are not without their defects and they can and will be criticised. But I emphasise here the positive side to the research, particularly of the Wallerstein and Kelly study. Their book is unquestionably the most illuminating documentary evidence of the divorce process and its effect on children yet published. Its findings force us to reject conventional wisdom on any number of issues, notably, access and step-parenting.

One of the values of Wallerstein and Kelly's study is that it constantly makes us re-examine our deep-rooted and often hitherto unquestioned assumptions. For example, it is commonly asserted that children are better off extricated from their parents' unhappy marriage.[167] Divorce is put forward as a positive benefit. Children, it is said, are relieved by divorce: they almost prefer it. But do they? Wallerstein and Kelly found that children actually prefer an unhappy marriage to their parents' divorce. For the children in their study, 'divorce was a bolt of lightning that struck them when they had not even been aware of the existence of a storm.'[168] It is parents who want a divorce: not their children. Wallerstein and Kelly found that for most parents who divorce there is ultimately an improvement in their psychological health, but this is not so for most of the children. They write: 'neither an unhappy marriage nor a divorce are especially congenial for children: each imposes its own set of stresses'.[169] For, 'whatever its shortcomings, the family is perceived by the child . . . as having provided the support and protection he needs. The divorce signifies the collapse of that structure, and he feels alone and very frightened.'[170] Of the children in the study, less than 10 per cent were relieved by their parents' divorce, despite the high incidence of exposure to physical violence during the marriage.

One of the central arguments in Wallerstein and Kelly's book is that there is an important link between a child's success in coping with divorce and his capacity to understand and make good sense of the sequence of disruptive events in his family. The basis of the divorce decision can, they show, have long-term consequences for the children.

> The child's efforts at mastery are strengthened when he understands the divorce as a serious and carefully considered remedy for an important problem, when the divorce appears purposeful and rationally undertaken, and indeed succeeds in bringing relief and a happier outcome for one or both parents.[171]

But perhaps only a third of divorces have such a rational foundation: others are stress-related, induced by an unexpected death, a tragedy, an accident, or linked to a severe psychological illness. The authors comment on these: 'since the decision to divorce did not address any particular problems within the marriage, there was no subsequent relief or sense of closure.'[172] There are also impulsive divorces 'undertaken without reflection or planning or any real consideration of consequences'[173] and divorces following a sudden unexpected revelation of infidelity. In the latter 'the children were often co-opted in the battle, and became the allies, confidants, and rescuers of the grieving parent.'[174] It is important that divorce be undertaken for rational reasons, for where it is not the child is burdened because the rupture makes no sense to him and brings no relief to any family conflict that he can identify.

Much depends on the age of the child.[175] The child's response to divorce is, Wallerstein and Kelly show, age-related. The youngest express fear; they regress; some have macabre fantasies shaped by their own limited capacity to understand the confusing events and their frightened perceptions of the parents' quarrels. Some of these children express painful bewilderment. The youngest children may see themselves as replaceable in just the same way as they perceive their fathers to be: they cannot conceptualise the other parent's departure as being directed at the other parent and not at them.

Children slightly older than this (six to eight years old) express grief and intense sorrow. They also expressed fear leading to severely disorganised behaviour and panic on occasion. Their thinking was often pervaded by fantasies of being deprived of food, toys and other important aspects of their life. Compulsive overeating was found to be not at all uncommon. The children were often angry at their mother 'for either causing the divorce or driving the father away.'[176] They tend to express their yearning for their father by copying him.

Children aged nine to twelve years have, Wallerstein and Kelly found, a layering of responses. That their responses differed from those of the slightly younger age group took Wallerstein and Kelly by surprise since psychological theory does not suggest a significant distinction. Others may be less surprised: developmental stages as depicted in psychological theory tend to be very rigid. Wallerstein and Kelly found courage, bravado, reaching out to others for help, denial and anguish. The unhappiness which these children experienced often galvanised them into vigorous activity which was 'a composite of coping and defensive strategies designed to help overcome those feelings of parentlessness which the children in this age group experienced as so humiliating and so threatening to their equilibrium.'[177] Some children attempted to effect a reconciliation of their parents. While younger children had expressed anger, for this age group the anger was 'a fully conscious, intense anger'.[178] It was 'well organised and clearly object-directed.'[179] Children were angry at the parent they blamed for the divorce. Some children in this age group experienced a shaken sense of identity. There were also somatic symptoms, headaches and stomach aches. Children tended to align with one parent, usually the mother: where the alignments were with the non-custodial parent they were short-lived, but alignments with the custodial parent remained strikingly stable eighteen months after separation.

For adolescents the problems take on a new dimension. 'Ordinary, expectable adolescent worries (are) intensified.'[180] They may be pressured into independence, worried about sex and marriage. One fourteen-year-old asked the project investigators whether it was true that the children of divorcees were also likely to experience marital problems. They also experienced a profound sense of loss and once again anger was a common response. There were loyalty conflicts too. Some expressed themselves aggressively. Others indulged in deviant behaviour like promiscuity. Some, however, increased in maturity and independence. Wallerstein and Kelly believe the adolescents who appeared to do well were those 'who from the outset had been able to maintain some distance from the parental crisis and whose parents had permitted them to do so without intruding on them.'[181]

Wallerstein and Kelly's study also involved looking at all the participants in the divorce process eighteen months and five years on from separation. They note that after eighteen months, 'the acute psychological disruptions precipitated by the dissolution of the family were ending . . . . The crisis-engendered responses . . . — the widespread fears, the grief, the shocked disbelief, and the new symptoms — faded or disappeared altogether.'[182] The majority of the children had been able consciously to put the divorce to one side. Wallerstein and Kelly find these improvements 'striking because they were not necessarily accompanied by comparable improvements in the parent–child relationships.'[183] They found that girls, though not adolescent girls, adjusted much better than boys, for whom the impact of divorce was more pervasive and enduring. Hetherington and her colleagues were also struck by this sex difference.[184] Wallerstein and Kelly observed 'considerable staying power' in the anger of the children and adolescents.

One visible consequence of the anger was the diminished relationship with the visiting parent. Nine- to twelve-year-old youngsters were visited less because they were angry, and they in turn became angrier because they were less visited. The relationship with their fathers thus deteriorated more than it had in any other age group.[185]

By the time five years had elapsed, some children were seen to have coped successfully, others not. Wallerstein and Kelly found that the factors that 'appeared to promote good adjustment in children of the divorced family are similar to those which make for good adjustments and satisfaction in the intact home.'[186] They note that

> families in which the children had a good outcome at five years were able to restabilise and restore the parenting after the initial, or sometimes extended, disorganization of the transition period. Custodial and uncustodial parents of the children who did well, separately or in cooperation with each other, retained their commitment to their children. In other families where children did well, one or both parents improved following the divorce and this was reflected in the parent–child relationship; or a third configuration was present where the divorce separated the child from a psychologically destructive parent. Finally . . . some children benefited from a remarriage.[187]

Irregular, erratic visiting by the non-custodial parent was found to have a negative effect on the child's adjustment to his new situation.

It has become common in the last decade to talk of the 'psychological' parent and to make the assumption that a child cannot relate positively to both parents unless both are responsible for everyday parenting. They key text for this school of thought is to be found in Goldstein *et al.*, *Beyond The Best Interests of The Child*. They write:

> Children have difficulty in relating positively to, profiting from, and maintaining contact with, two psychological parents who are not in positive contact with each other. Loyalty conflicts are common and normal under such conditions and may have devastating consequences by destroying the child's positive relationships to both parents. A 'visiting' or 'visited' parent has little chance to serve as a true object to love, trust, and identification, since this role is based on his being available on an uninterrupted day-to-day basis.[188]

The authors cite no evidence for this proposition, and when psychoanalytic sources are invoked no acknowledgement is made of the major criticisms[189] to which they have been subjected. The thesis is thus 'wide open to attack'.[190] Further, there is some evidence against what Goldstein *et al.* maintain. An American study by Keshet and Rosenthal[191] compared groups of children who spent varying amounts of time with each of their divorced or separated parents. It found that children (and parents for that matter) who spent at least 25 per cent of their time with each of their parents seemed to adjust best. While it could be that the explanation of the difference is that the children who adjusted best were those who were prepared best, 'the evidence is in the same direction as the hints that can be found in all the recent studies of children of divorced parents that continuing relations with both parents are desirable from the point of view of the children's adjustment.'[192] Martin Richards who makes this statement cites a number of sources,[195] of which Wallerstein and Kelly is the most compelling.

Wallerstein and Kelly stress the continuing psychological importance of both parents.

> Within the post divorce family, the relationship between the child and both original parents did not diminish in emotional importance to the child over the five years. Although the mother's caretaking and psychological role became increasingly central in these families, the father's psychological significance *did not* correspondingly decline. Even within remarriages, at least during the earlier years of these remarriages, though the stepfather often became very quickly a prominent figure to the children, the biological father's emotional significance did not greatly diminish, although his influence on the daily life of the child lessened.[194]

The in vogue phrase 'one-parent family' would, they note, have been considered 'a misnomer' by the children themselves. 'Children's self-images were firmly tied to their relationships with both parents and they thought of themselves as children with two parents who had elected to go their separate ways.'[195] Wallerstein and Kelly work within the same psychodynamic framework as Goldstein, Freud and Solnit, yet are able to provide substantial ammunition against their thesis. They stress, as against Goldstein and his colleagues, that children need a continuing relationship with both parents. They emphasise that both parents are central to the psychological health of children and adolescents alike. This leads them 'to hold that, where possible, divorcing parents should be encouraged and helped to share post divorce arrangements which permit and foster continuity in the children's relations with both parents.'[196]

My discussion of how children cope with divorce has been tied very closely to the Wallerstein and Kelly study which I regard as pertinent, perceptive and humane. But it is not beyond criticism. To get a more balanced view, I offer the following critical comments. First, the data are produced by a small, unrepresentative sample. I believe similar conclusions would be produced by replicating the study with different groups of children, but the point remains that the sample consisted of a middle-class Californian community. Secondly, the researchers were also acting as clinicians to help counsel families. The distancing role so important to further scientific accuracy was therefore absent. Further, since the researchers are psychoanalysts we may expect their questioning to have been oriented towards certain conclusions. But we do not know the questions or how they arrived at their interpretations. Thirdly, we do not know enough about the children, their relationships with their parents and others and their problems within the intact family. Without this knowledge, it is possible to argue that what Wallerstein and Kelly observed was but a continuation of a troubled childhood. These may be seen as serious criticisms but I do not believe they make serious inroads into the Wallerstein and Kelly thesis.

What they write has important implications on a number of matters. The matter of visiting arrangements and access is considered in the next section. Three comments on custody issues are pertinent before I pass on to access.

First, they stress how children can acquire new emotional meanings for parents within a divorced family. On marital breakdown parents may turn to their children as sources of support and love. Children are 'pressed into being advisors, practical helpers, buffers against loneliness and despair, replacements for other adults — in other words, parents for their own parents.'[197] Certain features of custody litigation are thus to be explained in terms of each parent's need for the 'child's presence to maintain self-esteem and to ward off self-criticism and depression. Litigation over custody thus may reflect the dependence of the adult on the child, and the adult's need to hold on to the child to maintain his or her psychic balance.'[198] This is an important insight which should be in the minds of everyone concerned with the divorce process. Custody arrangements and disputes should be seen in the light of this and not looked at, as they are at present, at face value. It is possible that if they were a few more arrangements would not be approved, and perhaps more fathers would be awarded custody. We cannot tell: there are too many imponderables.

Secondly, Wallerstein and Kelly have something to say about the child's own preferences in custody disputes. They believe their work suggests that 'children below the age of adolescence are not reliable judges of their own best interests and that their attitudes at the time of the divorce crisis may be very much at odds with their usual feelings and inclinations.'[199] They doubt the capacity of nine- to twelve-year-olds to make an informed judgement. They point to the long-lasting anger of these children, their eagerness to be co-opted into parental battling, their willingness to take sides, their compassion for a distressed parent. This evidence cannot be treated lightly. On the other hand, given the indeterminacy of the principles governing custody, it is unduly dismissive to use paternalistic arguments to undermine a child's own preferences.

A third point of interest is Wallerstein and Kelly's predictable support for the principle of joint custody. They put the arguments in its favour convincingly. In their eyes it does not mean 'a precise apportioning of the child's life, but a concept of two committed parents, in two separate homes, caring for their youngsters in a post divorce atmosphere of civilized, respectful exchange.'[200] Joint custody arrangements are one key to surviving the breakup. Where it is impracticable or undesirable then the encouragement and facilitating of access becomes another.

Questions of Access

Until very recently surprisingly little attention was paid to the question of access. Lawyers took no interest in it[201] and, though social scientists[202] took rather more notice of the tensions it generates and the way it atrophies with the passage of time 'unless there are unusual counter-factors at work',[203] to judge from the attention given to it, it must have seemed relatively unimportant. In the light of this, Maidment's study, which found that no order for access was made in about one-third of all divorces,[204] and Eekelaar and Clive's findings, that access was provided for in only 55 per cent of their sample,[205] should not have shocked, but they did. The findings followed hard on the Goldstein, Freud and Solnit bombshell that the custodial parent should decide whether the non-custodial parent was allowed to see his child or not.[206] From the perspective of the non-custodial parent divorce was to seem like adoption. It seems that anyway for many children the end of the parents' marriage is the end of all contact with their father. The longer separation goes on the less likely it is that children will be seen by the non-custodial parent. Visits gradually diminish or terminate.[207]

Goldstein *et al.* apart (their thesis will be considered critically in due course), everyone seems agreed that access is 'a good thing'. The courts, indeed, in England,[208] Canada[209] and the United States[210] have decided access is a child's right. For example, Wrangham J. in *M* v. *M* in 1973 said:

> The companionship of a parent is in ordinary circumstances of such immense value to the child that there is a basic right in him to such companionship. I for my part would prefer to call it a basic right in the child rather than a basic right in the parent.[211] That only means this, that no court should deprive a child of access to either parent unless it is wholly satisfied that it is in the interests of that child that access should cease, and that is a conclusion at which a court should be extremely slow to arrive.[212]

This is a very forceful statement which many would wish to applaud. But it is far from according with current practice; first, because the courts let so many access decisions go by default. The figures have already been quoted. Secondly, where orders for access are made, once the order is made the court takes no further interest. We know, for example, that approved arrangements are often not observed.[215] The machinery is lacking to superintend orders made and arrangements approved. Thirdly, access is sometimes ordered to promote a parent's right or the blood tie where it is not in the child's interests[214] or may even be positively harmful to the child.[215] Indeed, the courts claim to have the power to force a child to see a parent against the child's will, though it is difficult to see how such an order could be enforced against an older child.[216] Fourthly, where the child's interest in maintaining ties with non-custodial parent clash with the interests of the custodial parent, the courts tend to support the custodial parent. For example, if the custodial parent wishes to emigrate perhaps to take a new appointment, the courts are reluctant to stand in her way.[217] If she chooses to make access difficult or obstructs it entirely, the courts are reluctant to use the sanction of imprisonment[218] (as they should be, for penal sanctions should play no part in family disputes outside of domestic violence)[219] and almost as unwilling to change custody.[220] The custodial parent, in other words, has considerable freedom.

This is not lost on Goldstein, Freud and Solnit who in 1973 wrote: 'The non-custodial parent should have no legally enforceable right to visit the child, and the custodial parent should have the right to decide whether it is desirable for the child to have such visits.'[221] They would confer power on those who have the responsibility of child-rearing. This view, if implemented, would convert what is currently and unhappily common practice into a legal principle. But a continued relationship with the non-custodial parent appears to offer the child many psychological and social advantages. As Richards puts it,

> one of the most obvious is that it offers a wider variety of experience; the experience of a relationship with a second parent. A child is not denied a close and continuing relationship with a parent of each gender. This may be of special value in the development of his or her own gender identity.[222]

Further, it helps the child to overcome feelings of guilt, anger and depression. It should not make the acceptance of a step-parent more difficult: on the contrary, once a child sees that his relationships with both parents can survive his parents' divorce he can accept the introduction of a new adult into his life more easily. At a social level there are powerful arguments to support a continued relationship with both parents. It may act as a cushion to soften the economic, social and psychological blows of living in a 'one-parent family'. Most obviously, parents who have regular contact with their children and a close relationship are far more likely to pay maintenance willingly and promptly. Indeed, it may be that some fathers disappear from their children's lives to avoid paying maintenance, though absence of access does not affect their legal liability at all. The non-custodial parent may also be seen as 'a kind of insurance policy for children'[223] in the case of death, injury, illness or other disaster affecting the parent with custody.

Children certainly desire free access to the non-custodial parent. Indeed, Wallerstein and Kelly reported in a 1977 article that 'the only younger children reasonably content with the visiting situation were those seven- and eight-year-olds visiting two or three times a week, most often by pedaling to their father's apartment on a bicycle.'[224] There is no evidence that children are harmed or put at risk from frequent visits. Access visits may, of course, be difficult: it is often the only point of contact between ex-spouses. But the difficulties can be exaggerated. Murch found that the majority of those in his study were satisfied with their access arrangements.[225] But to suggest, as is commonly done, that visits should be diminished or stopped because they are unsettling is to misunderstand the relationship with the custodial parent. Without access the child may have no confidence in the non-custodial parent (he has left him): but why then should he have any more in the parent with whom he is living (that parent may go as well)? The best way to counter these legitimate fears is through continuity in both parental relationships. Furthermore, the frequency of a father's contact with the child is associated with a more positive adjustment of the child and with better functioning of the mother. Thus, Hetherington and her colleagues found no other support relationship as valuable for the mother raising children on her own as 'the continued, positive, mutually supportive relationship of the divorced couple and the continual involvement of the father with the child.'[226] Divorces which have the least detrimental effect on the normal development of children are those in which the parents are able to co-operate in their continuing parental roles. No research bears this out better than Wallerstein and Kelly's *Surviving The Breakup.*

They devote a large part of their study to a consideration of visiting arrangements. They are very critical of conditions imposed by courts which encumber difficult relationships which need encouragement if they are to prosper rather than wilt. As was to be expected, they found that it was friendliness between parents and the mother's interest in maintaining the father's visits which encouraged visiting by the father. They point to too many fleeting and infrequent visits, to ways in which the access visit can become an occasion for a 'crossfire of parental animosities'.[227]

Surviving The Breakup contains a thorough indictment of the legal processes which surround visiting arrangements. That 'reasonable visiting' should mean every second weekend, as it often does, reflects, they argue, the traditions of society which until recently went unchallenged. There was the cultural tradition which saw the father as sole wage-earner and the mother as parent. The father's ongoing role in parenting was relegated to secondary importance. 'Until the last decade', they observe, 'many fathers accepted this delimited role without thinking too much beyond its established boundaries. Thus, the majority of fathers quickly accepted twice a month visiting as representative of the lessened importance of their relationship with their children.'[228] Further, the nature of divorce proceedings themselves helps perpetuate customary visiting patterns. 'The adversary nature of the proceedings by definition implies that each . . . anticipates being a winner, not a loser. "Winning" has encompassed not just property settlement, but the issue of who shall own the children.'[229] Adversary justice does not allow for the interests of children to be adequately represented.

It is easy to argue that what is usual, what is in the precedents, is also 'developmentally correct, morally right'.[230] But to say that, for example, more frequent access is not in the child's interests is often a way of expressing the inconvenience that access causes the custodial parent. Wallerstein and Kelly found that despite the fact that two-thirds of the children in their study had contact with their fathers at a level defined 'by society, lawyers, and mental health professionals as "reasonable visitation" . . . only 20 per cent of them were at all content with the visiting situation.'[231]

From what has been written, it will be clear that decisions as to access are too important to be left to the custodial parent. The view presented in *Beyond The Best Interests of The Child* has little or nothing to commend it. It ignores the child's needs and desires as it does those of the non-custodial parent. It preaches continuity and autonomy but it encourages malice. Under the existing law access can be used as a weapon:[232] *a fortiori* if the standard suggested by Goldstein *et al.* were adopted. Invested with the power that Goldstein, Freud and Solnit would give the custodial parent 'one can visualize the blackmailing, extortion, and imposition which might be visited upon the non-custodial parent who wants to maintain contact with his or her child'.[233] Instead of promoting co-operation between parents, the view put forward in *Beyond The Best Interests of The Child* would encourage a situation where parents were forced to take each other on in a 'winner takes all' battle. It cannot be pretended that custodial parents, involved in what may have been a bitter divorce, can make objective decisions. The decisions they take may assist them (for example, by making them less helpless to deal with disruptive invasions of their lives by the absent parent); they may even sometimes be the best decision for the child; but we cannot be certain that the decision will be governed by the children's best interests. Nor must we forget possible reactions of the non-custodial (or potential non-custodial) parent. Will he be less willing to go in the first place? Will women be forced to lower their financial demands to induce his departure? Will there be more matrimonial violence and child abuse? Or, looked at another way, will non-custodial parents, and this means fathers in most cases, reduce their commitment to their children as a defence mechanism, so that they have less to lose?

The answer does not lie in the state renouncing responsibility and leaving access decisions to custodial parents. The present position is not satisfactory either. A rethinking of the issue of access is required, one that can be based on the concept that, as Wallerstein and Kelly put it, 'both parents remain centrally responsible for and involved in the care and psychological development of their children.'[234] Divorcing parents must be educated to accept this.[235] Currently, they are given negligible advice on access. How could this be improved? Both solicitors and welfare officers could play a part.[236] So, I think, could courts. In 1975 a committee of Justice, the British section of the International Commission of Jurists, of which I was a member, published a report entitled *Parental Rights and Duties and Custody Suits*. The most valuable, and indubitably the most lasting, feature of this is an excellent code of visiting practices drawn up by a leading paediatrician, Dr. Kenneth Soddy.[237] This explains in simple language the needs of children and their parents though it stresses that 'access visits are for the good of the child and are not a parental right.' There is a section which knocks down some common misconceptions about access. The code contains much practical information on how children's needs can be supplied. It distinguishes the needs of children of different ages. It contains a sensible list of things not to do, not to forget the children's private lives, not to force the visiting parent to rely on the park and the cinema, etc. The importance of a courteous and civil exchange is stressed. This code is not widely known about. It would make a lot of sense for divorcing parents to be given copies of this code. The state through legal aid currently spends approximately £72 million on divorce:[238] the circulation of this code, or one like it, would cost very little.

The courts have a part to play as well. If the norm is to be 'continued involvement',[239] this is what the courts should stress. At present access often goes by default. Courts rarely refuse access where it is asked for[240] but, as indicated earlier, it is often not sought. Judges should use their powers under s.41 of the Matrimonial Causes Act 1973 to find out why an access order is not being requested: what arrangements have the parties finalised; what relationship between each parent and the child; are there practical difficulties; is the parent who is not to get custody genuinely disinterested in continuing a relationship with his child[241] and, if so, why? The courts need to probe in this way. Answers to these questions may well indicate the need for a welfare report. There may also be a need for a report when a dispute arises over access. It is all too easy for the courts to respond by reducing or terminating access, but what should be explored are ways of resolving conflict so as to enable contact with the non-custodial parent to continue. An effective conciliation service, such as the one which operates in Bristol,[242] could do much to smooth relations between parents and assist parents to preserve relationships with their children in the aftermath of divorce.

Step-parenting: Adoptions and Name Changes

About one-third of divorcees remarry with the result that children acquire step-parents.[243] The National Children's Bureau's longitudinal study of children born in 1958 shows that by 1974 4 per cent of them were living with a step-parent, usually a step-father.[244] Unpublished data from the 1976 OPCS Family Formation Survey indicate that in 1976 about 7 per cent of all children under seventeen were step-children.[245] The majority will be children whose parents have divorced but some will be illegitimate children and others will have lost a parent as a result of death. The problems for each type of reconstituted family are different, though they overlap. For our purpose only the step-family formed out of divorce is of concern.

In English law step-parents do not have parental rights.[246] Nor *qua* step-parent do they have any duties. As an adult in charge or control of a child certain duties, for example protection, arise but these accrue to any adult in a caretaking role. The duty to maintain is dependent upon the step-parent having 'treated' the child as a child of the family.[247] When custodianship is brought into operation, step-parents will be given a right to apply for custody of their step-children after three months' actual custody where the person with legal custody consents or after three years without consent.[248] The application will be decided according to the overriding principle of the child's welfare.[249] The effect of a custodianship order will be to give legal custody[250] to the applicant. This is a lesser concept than parental rights so that the parent would retain greater powers than the custodian. But even this small solace is denied the step-parents who are our concern because the 1975 Act precludes applications for custodianship in respect of a child already the subject of a divorce court order.[251] Instead, he may apply to the divorce court for a custody order. The effect of this so far as the step-parent is concerned is not clear.[252]

In a book on children's rights it is not the step-parents' absence of parental rights which is of primary concern, but the effect that their absence may have on the welfare of the child of the reconstituted family. English social and legal policy is not consistent. It does little to maintain contact between a non-custodial parent and his child but it puts barriers in the way of establishing new relationships between the child and his step-parent. If access to a non-custodial parent were real the case for vesting parental rights in a step-parent would be difficult to sustain. But given the fact that so many fathers disappear from the lives of their children upon marital breakdown, the case for recognising a new factual situation and improving the status of the step-father is cogent. Many step-fathers see themselves as the father[253] and many of the children regard their step-father as their father. With the peak year for divorce now the fifth of marriage[254] many children will be very young, and some will not even be born, when their fathers cease to play a parenting role.

The increase in the number of divorces has thus led to a demand by mothers and their new husbands to adopt the mother's children of a dissolved marriage. In 1964 there were 2,291 adoptions of legitimate children where one of the adopters was a parent. By 1968 there were 4,038 such orders and by 1975 the annual number had peaked at 9,262.[255] By 1980 the number was down to 3,668.[256] The decline is largely the result of legislative intervention in 1975. Section 10(3) of the Children Act provides that where an adoption application is made by a parent and step-parent of the child 'the court shall dismiss the application if it considers the matter would be better dealt with under section 42 of the Matrimonial Causes Act 1973.' The matter can only be dealt with under s.42 where there has been a divorce (or nullity),[257] so that s.10(3) does not affect step-parents who achieve this status by marrying unmarried mothers or widows.[258] The legislation followed in the wake of judicial opposition to such adoptions and a recommendation in the Houghton Committee on adoption published in 1972. A county court judge had voiced his opposition as early as 1968[259] and the President of the Family Division twice expressed his disapproval

of the step-parent adoption.[260] In the first of these cases the President was prepared to explain away the father's seeming lack of concern for his children (for
example, his failure to turn up at arranged times for access) as 'a temporary
drifting apart and a withdrawal by the husband/father, when a marriage is
breaking up.'[261] In the second he postulated the child's right not to be deprived
of his actual father. 'The courts should not encourage the idea that after the
divorce the children of the family can be reshuffled and dealt out like a pack of
cards in a second rubber of bridge.'[262]

The Houghton Committe thought that 'the legal extinguishment by adoption
of a legitimate child's links with one half of his own family was inappropriate
and could be damaging.'[263] It had little information available to it about step-
families or step-parent adoptions. Its case was barely reasoned at all. The research
of Masson and Norbury, however, shows that 'in all but a small number of cases,
by the time of an adoption application the link had already been broken or had
never existed.'[264] Legal and social policy was thus, it seems, changed on the
basis of an unresearched and unsubstantiated assertion. We are told that step-
parent adoptions distort real relationships. It may, however, be that in many
cases it is their absence that does this. ' "Dad" is the man in the house who
loves and disciplines (children), not the shadowy figure of the past now barely
remembered.'[265] The Children Act itself is unable to uphold its own logic for
it contains a provision restricting the removal of a child from foster parents
with whom he has had his home for five years if the foster parents apply for
adoption.[266] This may only 'freeze'[267] the position and it does not guarantee
an adoption but it favours foster parents in a way in which a step-parent is not
so favoured. Ironically, it may sever ties with parents who are in contact with
their children, whereas the step-parent provision prevents the severance of legal
ties which factually may not exist because the natural father has disappeared
from the child's life.

The statutory provision presumes that courts will be capable of distinguishing
cases in which a child's welfare would be better promoted by joint custody than
by adoption. It is clear that they cannot do so. Hence inconsistency of interpretation of s.10(3) both at county court[268] level and in the Court of Appeal is
not unexpected. What is remarkable, though, is that one Lord Justice, Ormrod,
has been instrumental, first in restricting step-parent adoptions even beyond
legislative intention, and then in engineering almost a complete change of
policy, and all in less than five years.[269] In *Re S* in 1977[270] an adoption order
was refused. The children had 'acquired, as children of the family of the natural
parent and step-parent, all the material advantages which adoption can provide
. . . . The advantages of adoption in these cases will, therefore, have to be found,
if at all, in the intangible results which may flow from it.'[271] The distinction
between material advantages and intangible results is not easy to state. What, for
example, is the assumption of the step-father's surname? Are stability and
security intangible, as Ormrod L.J. insinuates they must be? He thought that

custody recognised the reality of the situation, whereas adoption imposed an artificial status. In this case all the parties wanted an adoption and the natural father had actually agreed to one. He took little interest in his sons, rarely saw them though he lived locally and paid maintenance irregularly and in diminishing amounts. The fact that the children wanted to be adopted was apparently of no significance. Ormrod L.J. reversed the statutory onus: the question he said was whether adoption would safeguard and promote the welfare of the child better than the existing arrangements. In this case it would not. In a case not long after *Re S*, an adoption was refused at the request of paternal grandparents. The court thought it was for the boy's welfare not to be severed from his grandparents now or in the future, when he might join the family business. Further, 'the child was already integrated within his new family and making an adoption order added nothing to his welfare.'[272]

Already before *Re S* in 1977, a case, also called *Re S*,[273] had shown that step-parent adoptions would sometimes be allowed. The step-father in this case had been the 'father figure in the child's life' from an early age. The natural father had disappeared from the child's life. The adoption order was said to be 'formal recognition of the factual situation'. Two more recent cases are of much greater significance. In the first, another *Re S*,[274] the father's contact with a four-year-old boy was limited to a few moments when he visited him in the nursing home some three weeks after he was born. The step-father had been 'very much on the scene' from the time the boy was six months old. The judge refused an adoption, relying it seems on the 1977 Court of Appeal ruling in *Re S*. Presumably he thought that an adoption order would not safeguard or promote the welfare of the child better than the existing arrangements. The Court of Appeal allowed the appeal and made an adoption order. 'It was really a case of integrating this child into the (new) family legally and bringing the legal situation into direct relationship with the human situation, which should be the objective in most of these cases.' Ormrod L.J. thought that if the instant case 'did not pass the test of s.10(3) successfully' (itself an ambiguous statement) 'it would be very hard indeed to imagine any such case in which a parent with custody, married to a step-parent, could ever succeed in convincing the court that an adoption order should be made.'

It is possible to distinguish this case from the 1977 *Re S* on its facts. Indeed, there are some remarks in Ormrod L.J.'s judgment which appear to do this. The child in the later case had had virtually no contact with his father: in the 1977 case the children had grown up familiar with him. But the fact cannot be disguised that in the later case the judge, applying a principle laid down by the Court of Appeal, could find no benefit in adoption. In *Re D*[275] once again an adoption was refused. The children were thirteen and ten and a half and wished to be adopted. Contact with their father had ceased and he agreed to an adoption. But the judge said no because the girls had a proper recollection of their father as a father. In refusing the application he followed the recommendation of the guardian *ad litem*. The Court of Appeal overturned this decision. Ormrod L.J. rejected his earlier interpretation of s.10(3). He said:

> The section requires the court to dismiss an application for adoption if it considers that the matter would be *better* dealt with by means of a joint custody order. It is not a question of showing that an adoption order is itself better. The court has to consider whether or not the matter can be *better* dealt with by means of a joint custody order.[276]

He thought the adoption order would be beneficial. He could have done this by invoking the security argument which he used in *Re S* in 1979. But he did not. Instead, he argued that since the children desired adoption not to grant an order might have harmful effects on them.

> I would be very hestitant, in a case where the natural father is consenting and the children wish to be adopted, to stand in the way of an adoption order being made. The children might well see this as 'an intrusion by authority' and an unnecessary one which they will not understand and will resent.[277]

Further, Ormrod L.J. was critical of the arguments of the guardian *ad litem* that adoption was inappropriate since the children fully recollected their father. 'This is not', he said, 'a crucial distinction.' It was not a reason for refusing an adoption order. The guardian *ad litem* had also submitted that an adoption would sever the child's ties with the father's family but Ormrod L.J. would have none of this. That might be the effect in law but 'there is no reason why if everyone is agreeable, children . . . should not see their (paternal) grandparents should it be desirable.' This does, of course, make such continuing contact dependent on the mother and step-father and as such is reminiscent of Goldstein *et al.*'s proposal on access. The court could have made an adoption order subject to conditions as to access by the grandparents[278] but it did not do so.

The policy on step-parent adoptions appears to have changed. But is there any wonder that local practice on step-parent adoptions should be so variable? How are county court judges to keep up with these shifts in opinion and reasoning? Masson and Norbury compared three local authority areas.[279] In one, post-divorce step-parents continued to get adoption orders just as they had before the 1975 Children Act. Full orders were made in 96 per cent of the cases in 1975 and in 1978. In a second area 'judges held strong views on step-parent adoptions'[280] and adoption was virtually unobtainable by step-parents. In 1975, 91 per cent of applications were granted. In 1978, the percentage of successful applications by step-parents was 9 (in real terms, one case out of eleven). In the third area the picture, they note, was less clear-cut but the percentage of successful applications dropped by just over a quarter from 87 per cent to 64 per cent. Masson and Norbury are right to be concerned about these discrepancies. Equally significant is the fact that in absolute numbers applications dropped in all three areas, by 49 per cent in the first area, by 92 per cent in the second and by 60 per cent in the third. Would-be applicants in areas 2 and 3 were strongly discouraged from making applications. Masson and Norbury found that few applications for joint custody were being made, so it seems that step-parents did not find the alternative provided in s.10(3) acceptable. Now that the Court of Appeal appears to be adopting a more flexible attitude towards step-parent adoptions, can we expect all local courts to come into line and, if so, how long will it take for the news to percolate from The Strand?

The reversal in policy by the Court of Appeal, if that is what it is, is difficult to interpret. Legal changes cannot always be understood in terms of judicial reasoning. To locate it in ideology[281] is too grandiose, particularly since the time-span is so short and the decisions and leading judgments all belong to one judge. But whatever the explanation, which may be nothing more than a realisation on Ormrod L.J.'s part that he was wrong or that the implications of his 1977 ruling were counter-productive, the present policy articulated in the 1981 and 1982 cases is, I believe, closer to grass-roots opinion. More importantly, it is more in tune with children's best interests. The refusal to allow adoption by step-parents was an ill-thought-out measure and the initial judicial response was intemperate. Both demonstrated the way in which the concept of adoption is still closely tied to the needs of adults,[282] whatever the rhetoric[283] about the child's welfare being the 'first consideration'. If the end of marriage did not spell the end of a child's relationship with his father in so many cases, the demand for step-parent adoptions would diminish and would be relatively easy to stifle. In England in the 1970s we took the easy way out: we placed an embargo on step-parent adoptions rather than doing anything to buttress the very relationships which such adoptions would largely destroy. Now that we appear to have reversed the ban on step-parent adoptions we are less likely than ever to institute processes to make the goal of preserving family ties meaningful. In the short term the reversal may be welcomed but its long-term effects are likely to be detrimental to the welfare of children.

Although surnames have no legal significance in England, it is customary to call a wife and children by the husband's surname. When a marriage ends and a former wife remarries it is common for her to change her own name to that of her new husband. If she has custody, which is most likely, she may wish to change the children's names as well. Her new husband may want this and so may her children who may feel awkward if they bear a surname different from their mother. If an adoption takes place this solves the problem.[284] But whatever the reversal of policy most children will not be adopted by their step-fathers. The attitude of English law to the sensitive question of whether name changes are allowed has wavered.

It is clear from the early cases[285] that neither parent has the right unilaterally to change the child's name but that if it is changed it might be against the child's best interests to order it to be changed back.[286] The Matrimonial Causes Rules state:

> Unless otherwise directed, any order giving a parent custody or care and control of a child shall provide that no step (other than the institution of proceedings in any court) be taken by that parent which would result in the child being known by a new name before he or she attains the age of 18 years, or being a female, marries below that age, except with the leave of a judge or the consent in writing of the other parent.[287]

The judge would, of course, be guided by what is in the child's best interest. The law seems clear but the cases show a marked difference of approach. The earlier view, already referred to, was that a change of name was an important matter which should be permitted only when the child's welfare demanded that this should be done. In *Re WG*,[288] The Court of Appeal took the view that the mother's change of her daughter's name, following her remarriage, at the request of the school headmistress, was not in the long-term interests of the child. Cairns L.J. stressed the importance of maintaining a link with the father, unless he had ceased to have an interest in the child or there were grounds which made it undesirable for him to have access to the child at all. But then in *R(BM)* v. *R(DN)*[289] and *D* v. *B*,[290] courts suggested that it was all really a storm in a teacup, that a change of name was relatively unimportant and that fathers were laying too much emphasis on it. Thus, in *R(BM)* v. *R(DN)*, Ormrod L.J. said: 'We are in danger of losing sense of proportion.'[291] In *D* v. *B* he was insistent that parents should behave sensibly and not fight over 'formalistic things that do not matter much.' He argued:

> What is real is that the father and the child should know one another, that the child should, in course of time, come to recognise the fact that D is his natural father, and, so long as that is understood, names are really of little importance, and they only become important when they become a *casus belli* between the parents.[292]

Judges in these cases recognised that name changes were designed to avoid embarrassment, not to destroy links between a child and his father.

The conflict between the two views has now been resolved in favour of the earlier view. The Court of Appeal in *W* v. *A*,[293] following Latey J. in *L* v. *F*,[294] refused to allow a change of name even though the child was emigrating to Australia with his mother and stepfather. In *L* v. *F*, Latey J. took the view that names were a matter of importance. He said that the fact that the children's surname was different from that of the mother and their half-sister would not cause them embarrassment. They would have 'a better sense of security if there was co-operation between the parents and the step-father.' That may be so but what if, as is common, there is no such co-operation? The conflict, as Susan Maidment puts it, is 'between the principle of honesty in family relationships as against the needs of the new family.'[295] English law appears to be coming down in favour of openness. That is right where the children have a continuing relationship with the parent who does not have custody of them, but not, I would suggest, where such a relationship has ceased to be meaningful. If we are weighing up embarrassment against preservation of family ties then the latter must win out every time if for no other reason than that it is in a child's best interests to retain such ties. But in many cases the desire to maintain the original surname will reflect nothing more than sentimentality.

Improving Decision-making

The idea that divorce should provide a 'clean break' has now become so popular[296] that judges have had to be constrained from imposing one in cases where there are children.[297] It is thus accepted that financial obligations towards dependent children outlast the end of a marriage. But for many children marital rupture is the end of their relationship with the non-custodial parent, who is in most cases the father. As far as custody arrangements are concerned, courts play an insignificant role. Few cases are contested and in those which are the residential status quo is confirmed in all but a few. Private ordering has become the norm. But parents bargain in 'the shadow of the law'[298] so the contribution the courts can make is not negligible. There are better agreements to which parents can come and better decisions that courts can make than those that currently dominate the divorce scene in England, decisions that would recognise that parenthood continues when marriage fails. Joint custody which symbolises the continuing parenting role of both parents is thus an ideal at which to aim. Greater, not lesser, control of access arrangements is desirable. It makes sense for the courts to concentrate their efforts on contested cases. There are too many divorces for the courts to make any real impression on more than a few, and if the parties have sewn up the arrangements relating to the children it can be rare that the courts can achieve anything. It is, however, not surprising that more children than ever are being committed to the care of a local authority because it appears to the court that 'there are exceptional circumstances making it impracticable or undesirable for (them) to be entrusted to either of the parties to the marriage.'[299] How then can decision-making be improved? Three possible strategies are here considered: two (representation of the child's views and conciliation) are welcomed; of the third, the Family Court ideal, I am more sceptical.

(a) Representation of the Child's Views

The first is to appoint someone who is independent of the parents to present a case on behalf of the child. Numerous commentators had advocated this.

Three models of legal representation of children have been identified:[300] the adversary, *amicus curiae*, and social work models. The adversary role is traditionally combative: it envisages a lawyer using his skills within the framework of a trial governed by strict rules of law and procedure to convince a court that the cause for which he argues has merit and should prevail. The *amicus curiae* model is 'comparably legalistic but neutral as to outcome':[301] it assists the court to resolve a conflict by presenting another perspective from the strictly partisan cases represented by the opposing parties. The social work model is intended to help the child 'by proposals, concession and collaboration to put (him) into the most satisfactory condition that can be achieved.'[302] Models may also be distinguished into those which regard the representative as an officer of the court and those which see him as independent of it; and into those which believe the representative should have legal training and experience, those which envisage social work skills to be more valuable to the task and those which would construct a hybrid role for the representative.

It is clear that if lawyers are to represent children, they require skills which the run-of-the-mill lawyer is apt to lack. Genden notes that 'a child may have less need for a litigation specialist than for a lawyer who has competence and familiarity with non-legal resources.'[303] It is important, for example, that someone representing a child should know how to interview him[304] and how to communicate with him.[305] It is easy to 'deny or minimize the reality of the child's feelings.'[306] In thinking about representing a child in divorce proceedings we have to recognise that it is likely that each parent will think he or she knows what is best for the child. It will not be possible to turn to the parents, as it might be, for example, in care proceedings, and get one view. Where the child is of an age to express a view the representative may be able to take instructions from him. But where he is too young to do so, his representative would have to take his instructions from elsewhere. To take them from the parents would be self-defeating. The likelihood is that he would commission specialists' reports predicting the child's future in alternative environments and act upon these. But if this is all he does there is an argument for saying that a judge can equally well call for a welfare report and does not require the information to be mediated by someone representing the child. The role of the lawyer may differ depending on the age of the child.

There is also a danger that a lawyer may, as Dickens put it, fall

under the spell of fashionable theories and dogmas that cause him to apply preconceptions and stereotypes to the individual child . . . . Inept and doctrinaire advocacy may too easily become the norm when the court is satisfied that simply by appointing a representative for the child the court has safeguarded his interests.[307]

There is a danger also that the appointment of a lawyer to represent the child may become a formalistic step which in no way guarantees that the child's best interests are furthered. On the other hand, a lawyer may be valuable as an antidote to a welfare report, if he has the ability to challenge unsound evidence, where, as is not uncommon, unsubstantiated opinion masquerades as fact. It is also suggested recently that the child's lawyer may perform an important function as a mediator by helping the parents and their lawyers to reach some kind of agreement concerning custody as expeditiously and painlessly as possible.[308] This does, of course, presume that the child is represented at an early stage in the dispute. He is much more likely to be appointed only with the commencement of litigation.

There is, I believe, a case for children in divorce proceedings being independently represented. From what has been said, it is by no means an open and shut case. On balance I think such appointments would be valuable but in no way would they constitute a panacea. Indeed, unless carefully monitored they could, as indicated, create problems of their own. Of the three models the *amicus curiae* approximates closest to the ideal form of representation. The social work form of representation would amount to another variant of welfarism and would duplicate the function of the divorce court welfare officer's report. A strictly adversary approach is likely to embitter proceedings yet further and this can be of no benefit to the child.

Justice favoured the representation of children in custody suits by an officer of the court, what it called a 'Children's Ombudsman'.[309] He, or members of his office, would have training in both law and applied social sciences and among other things his duty would be 'to act as overseer of children's interests in custody suits.'[310] He would be a 'clearing agency', with power to request a welfare report.

> He would act as the child's spokesman and would have the duty of instructing solicitors and counsel to represent the child's interests so that the interests of the child might be separately represented to the court independently of the adults . . . concerned . . . . As the child's spokesman, it would be his particular duty to ensure that the views of any child able to express them, verbally or otherwise, were ascertained in the absence of the parents . . . and then made known to the tribunal.[311]

I was a signatory to this proposal in 1975 and still subscribe to it. I would envisage that the intervention of the 'Children's Ombudsman' would be required in all contested custody disputes and in uncontested cases where the court has any doubts as to the nature of the arrangements put to the court by the parties. There are precedents for such an institution. British Columbia has 'family advocates',[312] Ontario the Official Guardian[313] and New York a system of Law Guardians.[314] The New York legislation states:

This act declares that minors who are the subjects of family court proceedings should be represented by counsel of their own choosing or by law guardians. This declaration is based on a finding that counsel is often indispensable to a practical realization of due process of law and may be helpful in making reasoned determinations of fact and proper orders of disposition. This part establishes a system of law guardians for minors who often require the assistance of counsel to help protect their interests and to help them express their wishes to the court.

The Law Guardian is an advocate, defending legal and constitutional rights; a guardian, taking into consideration the general welfare of the child as well as his legal rights; and an officer of the court, with the duty of interpreting the court and its objectives to both the child and his parents, and of bringing to the court all material facts.

In England we have the Official Solicitor but in comparison with North American models his powers are limited. He cannot initiate proceedings on behalf of the child nor can he intercede to represent the child unless ordered to do so by a court.[315] The English Matrimonial Causes Rules actually provide for a higher standard of protection for the child's property than his person.[316] One critic[317] thought this 'curious' but it is perfectly consistent with attitudes and policies towards children. The Official Solicitor's office is involved with a wide range of issues and is not merely concerned with children, though its expertise in the area cannot be questioned. Yet, as the Official Solicitor himself recently recognised, his staff are career civil servants and 'while I try to choose "horses for courses" in assigning them to their duties I cannot claim that they are, nor would I want them to be, hand picked for dealing with children's cases.'[318] His predecessor saw his primary responsibility 'as being to give the child a voice in the proceedings.'[319] He stressed the importance of exploring 'every avenue which might lead to an agreed order.'[320] Agreed orders are desirable but whether an institution can set itself this goal and at the same time be a representative of the child is dubious. If the child is to be more adequately represented, an institution such as that envisaged by *Justice* or closer to the North American models is imperative.

This is not to underestimate conciliation to which I turn.

(b) Conciliation

Divorce terminates marriage but not its problems. Divorce adjudication looks backward and measures the parties and their conduct against legal norms and societal expectations: it rarely looks to the future relationship of the parties which is so important where there are children. Courts impose solutions and stifle constructive dialogues; hence the importance of conciliation. Separating couples may find it difficult to engage in rational discussion about matters such as custody and access. The importance of such discussion from the point of view of the children cannot be over-emphasised.

The Conciliation Service attached to the Provincial Court (Family Division) of Toronto defines conciliation as 'a process by which parties are helped to identify and clarify the issues between them and are assisted in making agreement on some or all of those issues — especially, but not limited to, dispute over custody and access to children.' English divorce legislation stresses the importance of reconciliation[321] though it does very little to assist it, but the concept of conciliation had not caught the imagination in 1969. Even today lawyers would tend to think in terms of reconciliation rather than conciliation.[322] But reconciliation is unattainable save in a small minority of cases. Effective conciliation is a real possibility as evidence from North America, Australia and this country[323] now demonstrates. Conciliation services in England depend on local initiative (a well-known and successful experiment has operated in Bristol since 1979); the opportunity to give them support, ideological[324] and financial, has arisen but has not been taken. There is, indeed, some doubt as to whether existing schemes can survive.

It is difficult to estimate how successful conciliation schemes are: much depends upon the critera of success adopted. Research by Davis at Bristol into the Bristol scheme found evidence of agreement, or some possibility of agreement, between the parties in 81 per cent of the conciliation cases studied.[325] These were cases in which both parties accepted appointments and therefore were motivated, however intransigent their problems, to find a solution. On the other hand, solicitors, from whom the references came, presumably sent their most difficult cases. Of the ninety-eight cases monitored by the research, 40 per cent resulted in total agreement on all contested issues. But where do the children stand in all this? There are two ways of looking at it. It is possible that in an effort to reach an agreement the children's interests are squeezed out. This may well happen sometimes but I prefer to think that the help given in the conciliation process may ultimately redound to the children's benefit. We are, Goldstein, Freud and Solnit remind us,[326] looking for the least detrimental alternative for the children. We are looking for solutions beyond divorce, to custody and access arrangements which cause least heartache and despair. Short-term help can enable parents to focus their attention on the future needs of the marriage and of the family, rather than harping on the past, on the failure of the marriage and on recriminations. The earlier arrangements can be worked out the better. If there are difficulties, for example, over access, conciliation 'should be the first resort, not a last-ditch attempt. Long-standing access disputes are much harder to resolve if a pattern of rejection and counter-rejection has become established.'[327]

It may be argued that the establishment of an independent conciliation service is unnecessary since the work can be done within the traditional framework of welfare services. There is a growing appreciation in the probation service of the importance of the counselling role.[328] It has, however, to be recognised that the divorce court welfare officer's role is investigative. The results of his inquiries are reported to the court. His report contains recommendations and may not be seen by the parties. He is likely to be identified by the parties as part of the welfare machinery and to be feared. He is a social control agency. Furthermore, his approach to his task is likely to be the very antithesis of what is required of a conciliator. For example, it is usual to see the two parents separately. I am dubious of the ability of a welfare officer satisfactorily to combine two different roles and would expect the social control task to overshadow that of assisting in a conciliation process. But half a loaf is better than no bread at all and attempts by some probation services to embrace the conciliation task is, therefore, to be applauded. The goal must, however, be an independent conciliation service.

It has to be accepted that disputes between parents at the time of separation have profound and long-term consequences for the parents themselves and more particularly for the children. That is why, as Eekelaar and Clive stressed, 'there is room for adapting our procedures to the urgency of these situations in recognition of the importance of their resolution in the interests of the children concerned.'[329] In these terms the significance of conciliation cannot be underestimated.[330]

(c) The Family Court

Would the establishment of a Family Court be equally valuable? Most of those who advocate conciliation of family disputes certainly think so: indeed, the two are often thought to go hand-in-glove. There can be few commentators on family matters who have not propounded the cause of the Family Court.[331] They are not necessarily agreed on the details, but there is general consensus, as Manchester has written, that the Family Court should be 'a "caring court" with social and welfare services integrated within it as part of a total team operation.'[332] I am rather less enthusiastic. I have presented my arguments elsewhere.[333]

In brief, I do not believe that the ideals which the Family Court is said to embody would be implemented by its establishment. The annals of legal history are strewn with examples of institutions and practices which have had unintended (or unproclaimed) consequences.[334] The juvenile court, considered in Chapter 3, is a paradigm example.

Critics of the existing system are concerned with its impersonality, insensitivity and remoteness. They want to make it more efficient and more effective by making it more responsive to the needs of the family, as they perceive these. Proponents of the Family Court are not alone in their desire for more informal justice.[335] It is a widespread concern. But can it succeed? It was Max Weber[336] who first noted that movements towards informalism contained the seeds of their own self-contradiction and so were ultimately doomed. Programmes which seem to weaken the hierarchies of power may actually establish new channels through which they can be expressed or even strengthened. We've seen it with the growth of the regulatory sanction[337] spawned by the 'new property'[338] state. The medicalisation of deviance[339] by the therapeutic state is yet another example. What we get is a 'dispersal of social control.'[340]

The Family Court ideal is part of what has been aptly called the 'triumph of the therapeutic'.[341] This century has witnessed a continual expansion of sur-veillance by professionals over family life. We have become dependent on the providers of expert services, sometimes not only for the satisfaction of needs but their 'very definition'.[342] The therapeutic state, Lasch reminds us, leaves the family 'always "justifed" in theory and always suspect in practice.'[343] It is not difficult to envisage developments that would enable us to substitute for 'thera-peutic state', 'family court'. But that should not surprise anyone, for the Family Court is merely one of the latest of a line of the progeny of the therapeutic state.

Family Court design proposals do not come to grips with these fundamental issues at all. Take, for example, the fullest, most authoritative discussion of the Family Court in Britain. This is found in the Finer Report on one-parent families published in 1974.[344] Although disdainful of American family courts which, it says, are 'committed to a social work philosophy which regards family break-down as a phenomenon to be dealt with primarily by diagnosis and treatment' and which are as much a 'therapeutic agency as a judicial institution',[345] it advocates the employment of court social workers. The welfare part of the court would be expected to 'demonstrate a commensurate degree of professional integrity and expertise',[346] that is on a par with the integrity and formal expertise of the court. The problem is that we are talking of different types of expertise. Lawyers have formal expertise: they work with legal authorities and there are accepted interpretational techniques. Social workers aspire to expertise based on empirical knowledge: the knowledge base, however, is more questionable.[347] The Finer Report envisages court welfare services providing 'assistance for people with marital problems.'[348] But the Report does not expand on the work tasks it expects welfare services to undertake. It does not see social workers as decision-makers, rather as handmaidens. They are to make social and welfare enquiries and reports. Others have been prepared to see a non-legal component to the decision-making process.[349] But in the context of a Family Court, the line between informed (sometimes not so informed) opinion and decision-making is easy to transverse and experience of juvenile courts demonstrates how difficult it is to separate them into watertight compartments. Finer's proposals are relatively conservative. The report is cautious about making the court more informed.[350] It is careful to separate fact-gathering and decision-making.[351] Other blueprints are more prepared to adapt existing procedures, to humanize the administration of family law and in so doing to sacrifice the benefits we associate with courts.

There is a lot wrong with the existing structure and Finer and others have identified some of the problems. But there is a danger in throwing out the baby with the bathwater. Not the least value of a 'regime of rules',[352] of the forms and rhetoric of law is that it may on occasion 'inhibit power and afford some protection to the powerless.'[353] In our context these are the children of divorce. That the existing legal structures have not afforded them much protection is a reason for improving upon them, not throwing them out totally and embarking on an uncharted voyage of discovery, particularly when the voyage may turn out to resemble a previous journey which has been far from successful, namely the juvenile court. We must not let our concern with the insensitivity of traditional legal mechanisms turn us away from the unqualified good in the rule of law. We may find adversary processes inappropriate, even dehumanizing or alienating. Yet the formalism and rule of law which accompanies them affords a measure of protection to the weak. It also inhibits the power of welfare professionals.

Notes

1. There were 6,092 decrees absolute (but 9,970 petitions for divorce).
2. Civil Judicial Statistics, 1970, Cmnd. 4271, London, HMSO, 1971, p. 64 (Table 10).
3. In 1960, 27,870 petitions for divorce were filed. There were 23,369 decrees absolute of divorce.
4. In 1980 there were 153,874 decrees nisi granted, 8 per cent up on the previous year. 177,415 petitions were filed in 1980, 6 per cent up on 1979. See Judicial Statistics, Annual Report 1980, Cmnd. 8436, London, HMSO, 1981, p. 63, and Tables D.8 (b) and (c).
5. Office of Population Censuses and Surveys, *Demographic Review*, London, HMSO, 1977, p. 59.
6. L. Rimmer, *Families In Focus*, London, Study Commission On The Family, 1981, p. 35. In 1976, 13 out of every 1,000 children under sixteen were involved in divorce. See R. Leete, *Changing Patterns of Family Formation and Dissolution in England and Wales 1964–76*, OPCS, London, HMSO, 1979, p. 95.
7. 26 per cent in 1971.
8. See J. Haskey, 'The Proportion of Marriages Ending In Divorce', *Population Trends*, 27 (1982), p. 4.
9. See Rimmer, *Families in Focus*, p. 36.
10. Finer estimated 620,000 families in Great Britain were one-parent families in 1971 (this is thought to have exaggerated the figure by 50,000 since it failed to account properly for cohabitation). By 1976 the figure had grown to 750,000. In 1980 the National Council for One Parent Families estimated 920,000 with about a million and a half children, that is one family in eight. In some areas of London nearly one in three families is a one-parent family.
11. One in three single parents are divorced mothers and another one in five are separated mothers. See OPCS, Monitor GHS 80/1 (1980), London, OPCS, Table 3.
12. See, generally, J. S. Wallerstein and J. B. Kelly, *Surviving The Breakup*, New York, Basic Books, 1980.
13. See the Finer Report on *One-Parent Families*, Cmnd. 5629, London, HMSO, 1974, part 5, and D. Marsden, *Mothers Alone*, London, Allen Lane, 1969.
14. See M. Rutter, *Maternal Deprivation Reassessed*, Harmondsworth, Penguin Books, 1981 (2nd ed.), p. 100.
15. See A. Watson, 'The Children of Armageddon: Problems of Custody Following Divorce', *Syracuse Law Review*, 21 (1980), p. 55.

16. See J. Dominian, *Marriage in Britain 1945–80*, London, Study Commission on the Family, 1980, p. 17.
17. See W. Goode, *Women In Divorce*, New York, Free Press (reissued in 1965, originally published as *After Divorce*, 1956), pp. 329–30, quoting the opinion of divorced mothers.
18. Wallerstein and Kelly, op. cit.
19. On this see G. Davis and M. Murch, 'The Implications of The Special Procedure In Divorce', *Family Law*, 7 (1977), p. 71.
20. By J. Eekelaar, *Family Law and Social Policy*, London, Weidenfeld & Nicolson, 1978, p. 143.
21. Morton Royal Commission on *Marriage and Divorce*, London, HMSO, 1956, Cmnd. 9678, para. 366.
22. Matrimonial Proceedings (Children) Act 1958 s.2.
23. *A* v. *A* [1979] 2 All E.R. 493.
24. Matrimonial Causes Rules 1977, r. 8(2), Form 4.
25. The form is to be found in S. Cretney, *Principles of Family Law*, London, Sweet & Maxwell, 1980 (3rd ed.), p. 471.
26. *Undefended Divorce*, London, Lord Chancellor's Office, 1977, p. 13.
27. Though most still consult solicitors even if they do not represent them. See G. Davis *et al.*, 'Special Procedure in Divorce and the Solicitor's Role', *Family Law*, 12 (1982), p. 39. In 1980 98 per cent of divorces were by special procedure.
28. Cf. A. K. Bottomley, *Decisions In The Penal Process*, London, Martin Robertson, 1973.
29. See E. Elston *et al.*, 'Judicial Hearings of Undefended Divorce Petitions', *Modern Law Review*, 38 (1975), p. 609.
30. J. Westcott, 'The Special Procedure — One Year Later — A Practitioner's View', *Family Law*, 8 (1978), p. 209 at p. 210.
31. M. Murch, *Justice and Welfare In Divorce*, London, Sweet & Maxwell, 1980, p. 212.
32. J. Eekelaar and E. Clive, *Custody After Divorce*, Oxford, SSRC, Centre for Socio-Legal Studies, 1977, para. 13.25.
33. S. Maidment, 'A Study in Child Custody', *Family Law*, 6 (1976), pp. 195, 236.
34. Eekelaar and Clive, op. cit., para. 4.4 and Table 20.
35. See J. Hall, *Arrangements for the Care and Upbringing of Children*, Law Commission Working Paper No. 15 (1968).
36. Under s.44 of the Matrimonial Causes Act 1973.
37. Eekelaar and Clive, *Custody After Divorce*, paras. 5.5, 12.7.
38. Maidment, 'A Study in Child Custody', p. 237.
39. Chief Probation Officers Conference, Report of Family Law Sub-Committee, *Divorce Court Welfare*, September 1976.
40. J. Graham Hall, 'The Future of the Divorce Court Welfare Service', *Family Law*, 7 (1977), pp. 101, 102. Cf. S. Maidment, 'The Future of the Divorce Court Welfare Service — An Alternative View', *Family Law*, 7 (1977), p. 246.
41. See R. Scott, 'The Construction of Conceptions of Stigma by Professional Experts' in J. Douglas (ed.), *Deviance and Respectability*, New York, Basic Books, 1970, p. 255.
42. Murch, *Justice and Welfare*, op. cit., p. 197.
43. Ibid., p. 198.
44. Ibid., pp. 197–8.
45. Morton Royal Commission, para. 376.
46. Ibid., para. 377.
47. See, e.g. Sir Jocelyn Simon's 'The Seven Pillars of Divorce Reform', *Law Society Gazette*, 62 (1965), p. 344.
48. M. Kellmer-Pringle, *The Needs of Children*, London, Hutchinson, 1980 (2nd ed.), pp. 127–9.
49. See also *The Times*, 15 February 1980 (report of Press Conference to launch book).
50. J. Goldstein, A. Freud and A. Solnit, *Before The Best Interests of The Child*, New York, Free Press, 1979.
51. R. Mnookin and L. Kornhauser, 'Bargaining In The Shadow of The Law: The Case of

Divorce', *Yale Law Journal*, **88** (1979), p. 950 (also as Mnookin alone in *Current Legal Problems*, **32** (1979), p. 65, to which article subsequent references are made), and 'Divorce Bargaining: The Limits on Private Ordering', unpublished paper, 4th World Congress of International Society on Family Law, Harvard, June 1982.
52. Goldstein *et al., Before The Best Interests of The Child*, p. 31.
53. J. Stuart Mill, *On Liberty,* London, Dent (Everyman Edition), 1910, p. 133.
54. Cf. S. Macaulay, 'Non-Contractual Relations in Business', *American Sociological Review,* **28** (1963), p. 55.
55. Mnookin, 'Divorce Bargaining', op. cit., pp. 22–3.
56. Mnookin and Kornhauser, 'Bargaining In The Shadow. . .', p. 69.
57. Ibid., p. 70.
58. See V. Aubert, 'Competition and Dissensus', *Journal of Conflict Resolution,* **7** (1963), p. 26, and 'Courts and Conflict Resolution', *Journal of Conflict Resolution,* **11** (1967), p. 40.
59. M. A. Eisenberg, 'The Bargain Principle and Its Limits', *Harvard Law Review,* **95,** (1982), pp. 741, 763.
60. Mnookin, 'Divorce Bargaining . . .', op. cit., p. 10.
61. Ibid., pp. 10–11.
62. See L. Weitzman, *The Marriage Contract,* New York, Free Press, 1981.
63. See, further, M. Horwitz, *The Transformation of American Law,* Cambridge, Harvard University Press, 1977, ch. 6; G. Gilmore, *The Death of Contract,* Columbus, Ohio, Ohio State University Press, 1974; D. Kennedy, 'Form and Substance In Private Law Adjudication', *Harvard Law Review,* **89** (1976), p. 1685; A. Kronman, 'Contract Law and Distributive Justice', *Yale Law Journal,* **89** (1980), p. 472. Cf. C. Fried, *Contract As Promise,* Cambridge, Harvard University Press, 1981.
64. Eekelaar and Clive, *Custody After Divorce,* op. cit., para. 6.1.
65. Guardianship of Minors Act, 1981, s.1.
66. By Lord MacDermott in *J* v. *C* [1970] A.C. 668, 710. This dictum has been approved on a number of occasions.
67. R. Mnookin, 'Child-Custody Adjudication: Judicial Functions In the Face of Indeterminacy', *Law and Contemporary Problems,* **39,** no. 3, (1975), p. 226 at pp. 255–68.
68. See, e.g. Pearson, L.J. in *Re C(L)* [1965] 2 Q.B. 449, 469-70.
69. *B(M)* v. *B(R)* [1968] 3 All E.R. 170.
70. See (1966) 116 N.L.J. 1389; *Re E(P)* [1969] 1 All E.R. 323. For similar Australian examples see *Lynch* v. *Lynch* (1965–6) 6 F.I.R. 433; *Neill* v. *Neill,* ibid., p. 461.
71. Lord Upjohn, *J* v. *C,* op. cit., p. 726.
72. Fifty three per cent of contested cases (Eekelaar and Clive, *Custody After Divorce,* op. cit., para. 6.3 and Table 25). Maidment, 'A Study In Child Custody', op. cit., produced a figure of 18 per cent for all cases (including uncontested ones).
73. *C* v. *C, The Times,* 7 November 1972; *Re B* (1973) 3 Fam. Law 43.
74. *Leech* v. *Leech* (1972) 116 S.J. 274.
75. Seventy per cent of the Eekelaar and Clive sample did (*Custody After Divorce,* op. cit., para. 13.26). The recommendations were usually followed.
76. *J* v. *J* (1979) 9 Fam. Law 91.
77. *Re C* (1973) 9 Fam. Law 50.
78. One, for example, might be a step-parent.
79. Matrimonial Causes Rules 1973, r. 95(3)(b).
80. See Murch, *Justice and Welfare,* op. cit., pp. 118ff.
81. Ibid., p. 127.
82. Ibid., p. 132.
83. Ibid., p. 135, where the figure of 36 per cent who last saw the welfare officer more than three months before the hearing is produced.
84. Eekelaar and Clive, *Custody After Divorce,* op. cit., para. 4.8 and Table 3.2.
85. See Graham Hall, 'The Future of the Divorce Court', op. cit.
86. See N. Turner, 'Wardship — The Official Solicitor's Role', *Adoption and Fostering,* no 88 (1977), p. 30, and N. Lowe and R. A. H. White, *Wards of Court,* London, Butterworth, 1979, ch. 8.

87. [1982] 1 All E.R. 319, see also *Re F* [1982] 1 All E.R. 321.
88. 'The Official Solicitor: Recent Developments', *Adoption and Fostering*, **6**, no. 3 (1982), p. 45 at p. 46.
89. But not, *semble*, a magistrate who may hear a contested custody suit. See *Re T, The Times*, 16 January 1974 (also in (1974) 4 Fam. Law 48).
90. Megaw, L. J. in *Hayes* v. *Hayes* [1974] 1 All E.R. 1145, 1147.
91. Hall, *Arrangements for the Care . . .*, p. 15.
92. B. Baker *et al.*, *The Matrimonial Jurisdiction of Registrars*, Oxford, SSRC, Centre for Socio-Legal Studies, 1977, para. 5.10, Table 18.
93. In *Hayes* v. *Hayes*, op. cit., p. 1148.
94. Eekelaar, *Family Law and Social Policy*, op. cit., p. 220.
95. See Mnookin, 'Child-Custody Adjudication . . .', p. 258.
96. J. Goldstein, A. Freud and A. Solnit, *Beyond The Best Interests of The Child*, New York, Free Press, 1979, p. 51.
97. A. Freud, 'Child Observation and Prediction of Development: A Memorial Lecture In Honour of Ernst Kris', *The Psychoanalytic Study of The Child*, **13**, (1958), pp. 97–8.
98. See J. MacFarlane, 'Perspectives on Personality Consistency and Change from the Guidance Study', *Vita Humana*, **7**, (1964), p. 115.
99. A. Skolnick, *The Intimate Environment: Exploring Marriage and The Family*, Boston, Little Brown, 1973, p. 378.
100. Mnookin, 'Child-Custody Adjudication. . .', p. 260.
101. See s.3 of Children Act 1975 and s.18 of Child Care Act 1980.
102. Mnookin, 'Child-Custody Adjudication', p. 260.
103. A good example of this is the way the views of Benjamin Spock have changed.
104. See 1 Kings 16–28.
105. 140 N.W. 2d 152 (1966).
106. See 'Alternatives to "Parental Rights" in Child Custody Disputes Involving Third Parties', *Yale Law Journal*, **73** (1963), p. 151; J. Goldstein, A. Freud and A. Solnit, *Beyond The Best Interests. . .*,
107. [1966] 1 All E.R. 838.
108. In L. C. Halem, *Divorce Reform: Changing Legal and Social Perspectives*, New York, Free Press, 1980, p. 206.
109. In W. Mischel, *Personality and Assessment*, New York, Wiley, 1968, p. 116.
110. The boy was later returned to his father at his request.
111. *J* v. *C* [1970] A.C. 668; *Re B* [1971] 1 Q.B. 437; *Re C(MA)* [1966] 1 All E.R. 838.
112. See K. Llewellyn, *The Common Law Tradition: Deciding Appeals*, Boston, Little, Brown, 1960; R. Dworkin, *Taking Rights Seriously*, London, Duckworth, 1977.
113. See J. A. G. Griffith, *The Politics of The Judiciary*, London, Fontana, 1981 (2nd ed.).
114. Eekelaar and Clive, *Custody After Divorce*, para 13.4. See also *Rostron* v. *Rostron* [1982] 3 F.L.R. 270.
115. Ibid., para. 6.5.
116. Maidment, 'A Study In Child Custody', p. 236.
117. Goldstein *et al.*, *Beyond The Best Interests. . .*, pp. 31–2.
118. See *Re S* [1958] 1 W.L.R. 391; *Re F* [1960] 2 Ch. 238.
119. Popularised as J. Bowlby, *Child Care And The Growth of Love*, Harmondsworth, Penguin, 1953. The original is a WHO publication (1951). See also J. Bowlby, *Attachment*, London, Hogarth Press, 1969.
120. See, e.g. *Southgate* v. *Southgate* [1978] 8 Fam. Law 246, and see M. D. A. Freeman, 'Bowlby Rides Again', *Justice of the Peace*, **143** (1979), p. 574. See also *L* v. *L* [1981] 2 F.L.R. 48; *M* v. *M* [1980] 1 F.L.R. 380.
121. For example, A. J. Bradbrook, 'The Role of Judicial Discretion in Child Custody Adjudication in Ontario', *University of Toronto Law Journal*, **21** (1971), p. 402. Cf. F. Bates, 'The Changing Position of the Mother in Custody Cases', *Family Law*, **6** (1976), p. 125.
122. See C. Delphy, 'Continuities and Discontinuities in Marriage and Divorce', in D. L. Barker and S. Allen (eds), *Sexual Divisions and Society: Process and Change*, London, Tavistock, 1976, p. 76.

123. S. Maidment, 'Child Custody: Unfair to Fathers?', *The Times*, 9 April 1980. See also her pamphlet published by the NCOPF (*Child Custody: Do Fathers Get A Raw Deal?*).
124. *Hewison* v. *Hewison* [1977] 6 Fam. Law 207.
125. *Cutts* v. *Cutts* [1977] 7 Fam. Law 209.
126. *Re L* [1962] 1 WLR 886.
127. See the New Zealand case of *D* v. *R* [1971] N.Z.I.R. 952 and the Ontario case of *Nielsen* v. *Nielsen* [1971] 16 D.L.R. (3d) 33.
128. See Lord Denning M.R.'s remarks in *Re L*, op. cit., p. 890.
129. By Ormrod L.J. in *S (BD)* v. *S (DJ)* [1977] 1 All E.R. 656, 660. See also *Re K* [1977] 1 All E.R. 647.
130. See, e.g. *Bowden* v. *Bowden* [1974] 4 Fam. Law 92; *Re P* [1967] 1 W.L.R. 818.
131. Cf. the discussion about children in care, Chapter 5.
132. See *Re P* [1967] 2 All E.R. 229, where separation was described on the facts as the least bad course to adopt.
133. See *Angrish* v. *Angrish* [1973] 3 Fam. Law 108.
134. [1962] 2 All E.R. 10.
135. *Re M* [1967] 3 All E.R. 1071 (see particularly Willmer L.J. at 1074).
136. *Re F* [1969] 2 Ch. 238.
137. Ibid.
138. *Re S* [1967] 1 All E.R. 202, 210 by Cross J. See also *Doncheff* v. *Doncheff* [1978] 8 Fam. Law 205, and *Cossey* v. *Cossey* [1981] 11 Fam. Law 56.
139. *M* v. *M* [1977] 7 Fam. Law 17.
140. An example is *Marsh* v. *Marsh* [1978] 8 Fam. Law 103.
141. Matrimonial Causes Act 1973, s. 42(1).
142. Custody was given to the wife in 76 per cent of the cases in Eekelaar and Clive's sample, *Custody After Divorce*, Table 34.
143. *Wakeham* v. *Wakeham* [1954] 1 W.L.R. 366.
144. *S* v. *S and T* [1963] 107 Sol. Jo. 475; *S* v. *S (orse D)* [1968] 112 Sol. Jo. 294.
145. See Eekelaar and Clive, *Custody After Divorce*, op. cit., Tables 33 and 34, and Maidment, 'A Study in Child Custody', Table 3.
146. See *Jussa* v. *Jussa* [1972] 2 All E.R. 600.
147. S. M. Cretney, *Principles of Family Law*, London, Sweet & Maxwell, 1980 (3rd ed.), p. 477.
148. Guardianship Act 1973, s.1.
149. But either may take decisions if the other has signified disapproval of its exercise or performance in that manner. See Children Act 1975, s.85(3).
150. Eekelaar and Clive, *Custody After Divorce*, paras. 13.16–13.17 and Table 34 (3–4 per cent of cases). According to a recent statement of the Lord Chancellor, joint custody orders occur in only about 2 per cent of divorce cases (see (1981) N.L.J. 543). Usually they are only made by consent.
152. Wis. Stat. Ann. of 247.24 (West Cum. Supp. 1978–79), effective 1 February 1978.
153. Other terms used are joint parenting and co-custody. M. Galper, *Co-parenting: A Source Book For The Separated or Divorced Family*, Philadelphia, Running Press, 1978, p. 16, lists the various terms in use to describe this type of custody arrangement.
154. P. Woolley, 'Shared Custody', *Family Advocate*, 1 (1978), p. 6.
155. D. Grote and J. Weinstein, 'Joint Custody: A Viable and Ideal Alternative', 1 J. Divorce 43, 45 (1977).
156. Listed in D. Freed and H. Foster, 'Family Law in the 50 States: An Overview', *Family Law Quarterly*, 16 (1983), pp. 289, 352. See, further, H. J. Folberg and M. Graham, 'Joint Custody of Children Following Divorce', *University of California Davis Law Review*, 12 (1979), pp. 523, 542–44.
157. *Beck* v. *Beck* (1981) 86 N.J. 480.
158. In *Braiman* v. *Braiman*, 378 N.E. 2d, 1019, 1021 (1978).
159. M. Roman and W. Haddad, *The Disposable Parent: The Case For Joint Custody*, New York, Penguin, 1979, p. 117.
160. Ibid., p. 118.
161. Ibid., p. 120.

162. J. Noble and W. Noble, *The Custody Trap*, New York, Hawthorn Books, 1975, p. 160.
163. See Folberg and Graham, 'Joint Custody . . .', pp. 553–6.
164. See R. Blood and M. Blood, 'Amicable Divorce: A New Lifestyle', *Alternative Lifestyles*, 2 (1979), p. 483.
165. Wallerstein and Kelly, *Surviving The Breakup*.
166. See the following papers by E. M. Hetherington *et al.*, 'Divorced Fathers', *Family Co-ordinator*, 25 (1976), p. 417; 'The Aftermath of Divorce' in J. H. Stevens and M. Mathews (eds), *Mother–Child, Father–Child Relations*, Washington DC, NAEYC, 1978; 'Play and Social Interaction in Children Following Divorce', *Journal of Social Issues*, 35 (1979), p. 26; 'Divorce: 'A Child's Perspective', *American Psychologist*, 34 (1979), p. 851.
167. For examples of this see Halem, *Divorce Reform . . .*, op. cit., chs. 4, 6 and 7.
168. Wallerstein and Kelly, op. cit., p. 11.
169. Ibid., p. 307.
170. Ibid., p. 35.
171. Ibid., p. 17.
172. Ibid., p. 21.
173. Ibid.
174 Ibid.
175. Like Goldstein *et al.*, *Beyond The Best Interests of The Child*, p. 40, Wallerstein and Kelly stress the child's sense of time.
176. Wallerstein and Kelly, op. cit., p. 70.
177. Ibid., p. 73.
178. Ibid., p. 74.
179. Ibid., p. 75.
180. Ibid., p. 85.
181. Ibid., p. 95.
182. Ibid., p. 162.
183. Ibid., p. 164.
184. See, e.g., E. L. Hetherington *et al.*, 'Divorce: A Child's Perspective', *American Psychologist*, 34 (1979), pp. 851, 853.
185. Wallerstein and Kelly, op. cit., pp. 173–4.
186. Ibid., p. 215.
187. Ibid.
188. Goldstein *et al.*, *Beyond The Best Interests . . .*, op. cit., p. 38.
189. See, especially, D. Katkin *et al.*, 'Above and Beyond The Best Interests of the Child: An Inquiry Into the Relationship between Social Science and Social Action', *Law and Society Review*, 8 (1974), p. 669.
190. See Roman and Haddad, *The Disposable Parent . . .*, op. cit., p. 110.
191. H. F. Keshet and K. M. Rosenthal, *Fathers Without Partners: a Study of Fathers and the Family After Marital Separation*, Totowa, N.J., Rowan and Littlefield, 1980.
192. See M. P. M. Richards, 'Post-Divorce Arrangements For Children: A Psychological Perspective', *Journal of Social Welfare Law*, (1982), pp. 133, 143.
193. Also R. Weiss, *Marital Separation*, New York, Basic Books, 1975, and *Going It Alone*, New York, Basic Books 1979, and Murch, *Justice and Welfare In Divorce*.
194. Wallerstein and Kelly, *Surviving The Breakup*, p. 307.
195. Ibid.
196. Ibid., p. 311.
197. Ibid., p. 103.
198. Ibid.
199. Ibid., p. 314.
200. Ibid., p. 310.
201. The first serious legal academic article dates from 1975. See S. Maidment, 'Access Conditions In Custody Orders', *British Journal of Law and Society*, 2 (1975), p. 182. See also J. Payne and K. Kallish, 'A Behavioral Scientific and Legal Analysis

of Access', *Ottawa Law Review,* 13 (1981), p. 215.

202. For example, see W. Goode, *After Divorce,* New York, Free Press, 1956; D. Marsden, *Mothers Alone,* London, Allen Lane, 1969; and V. George and P. Wilding, *Motherless Families,* London, Routledge & Kegan Paul, 1972.

203. From W. Goode, *After Divorce,* p. 316.

204. Access granted in 68 per cent of cases (S. Maidment, 'A Study of Child Custody', *Family Law,* 6 (1976), pp. 199–200).

205. Eekelaar and Clive, *Custody After Divorce,* para. 5.7.

206. Goldstein *et al., Beyond The Best Interests of The Child.,* p. 38.

207. See W. Goode, *After Divorce,* p. 313, and J. A. Fulton, 'Parental Reports of Children's Post-Divorce Adjustment', *Journal of Social Issues,* 35, no. 4, (1979), p. 126.

208. *M* v. *M* [1973] 2 All E.R. 81. See also R. S. Benedek and E. P. Benedek, 'Post-divorce Visitation: A Child's Rights', *Journal of American Academy of Child Psychology,* 16 (1977), pp. 256, 257.

209. *Knudslein* v. *Rivard* 5 RFL (2d) 264 (Alberta Family Court 1978).

210. *Bernick* v. *Bernick* 505 P.2d (14 Colorado C.A.) (1972).

211. As was said in *S* v. *S and P* [1962] 2 All E.R.1, 3 by Willmer L.J.

212. Wrangham J. in *M* v. *M*, p. 85.

213. See Hall's research in *Arrangements for the Care and Upbringing of Children.*

214. See *Re T* [1973] 3 Fam. Law 138; *D* v. *D* [1974] 4 Fam. Law 195. See also *Csicsiri* v. *Csicsiri* 17 R.F.L. 31 (Alberta S.C. 1974) and *Tassou* v. *Tassou* 23 R.F.L. 351 (Alberta S.C. 1975).

215. *Re N* [1975] 119 Sol. Jo. 423.

216. *B* v. *B* [1971] 3 All E.R. 682. Cf. *Sheppard* v. *Miller* [1982] 3 F.L.R. 124.

217. *Nash* v. *Nash* [1973] 2 All E.R. 704. Cf *P(LM)* v. *P(GE)* [1970] 3 All E.R. 659 (where conclusion was same though greater attention was given to child's welfare). See also now *Barnes* v. *Tyrrell* [1982] 3 F.L.R. 240 and *Bates* v. *Morley* [1982] 3 F.L.R. 244

218. *Re K* [1977] 2 All E.R. 737; *R* v. *R* [1980] 10 Fam. Law 56.

219. See M. D. A. Freeman and C. M. Lyon, 'The Imprisonment of Maintenance Defaulters', *The Howard Journal,* XX (1981), p. 15.

220. *V — P* v. *V — P* (1978) 10 Fam. Law 20.

221. Goldstein *et al., Beyond The Best Interests . . .,* pp. 38, 116–21.

222. See M. Richards, 'Post-Divorce Arrangements for Children: A Psychological Perspective', *Journal of Social Welfare Law* (1982), pp. 133, 143.

223. Ibid., p. 145.

224. J. S. Wallerstein and J. B. Kelly, 'Part-Time Parent, Part-Time Child: Visiting After Divorce', *Journal of Clinical Child Psychology,* 6 (1977), pp. 51, 52.

225. Murch, *Justice and Welfare in Divorce,* p. 71 (Table 16) (74.4 per cent in one sample, 67 per cent in the other).

226. Hetherington *et al.,* 'Divorced Fathers', p. 246.

227. Wallerstein and Kelly, *Surviving The Breakup,* p. 142.

228. Ibid., p. 133. See also J. and E. Newson, *Infant Care in the Urban Community,* Harmondsworth, Penguin, 1972, and A. Oakley, *Becoming A Mother,* Oxford, Martin Robertson, 1979.

229. Wallerstein and Kelly, *Surviving The Breakup,* p. 133.

230. Ibid., p. 134.

231. In J. B. Kelly, 'Children of Divorce: At Separation and Five Years Later', paper at SSRC and Psychology Conference 1981, Oxford, p. 23, to be published in 1983 by the Centre for Socio-Legal Studies, Oxford.

232. See Fulton, 'Parental Reports of Children's Post-Divorce Adjustment', op. cit.

233. In H. Foster, 'A Review of Beyond The Best Interests of the Child', *Williamette Law Journal,* 12 (1976), pp. 545, 551.

234. Wallerstein and Kelly, *Surviving The Breakup,* p. 134.

235. It is clear from sociological research (see N. Hart, *When Marriage Ends: A Study In*

Status Passage, London, Tavistock, 1976) that people do not know what is expected of them or where to seek advice.

236. See Murch, *Justice and Welfare in Divorce.*
237. *Parental Rights and Duties and Custody Suits,* published by *Justice,* London, 1975, at p. 51.
238. Some two-thirds of civil legal aid expenditure can be attributed to matrimonial cases. See Legal Aid 31st Annual Reports of Law Society 1980–1, London, HMSO, para. 27. The total expenditure on legal aid is £108,431,856; Ibid., Appendix 21, p. 27.
239. In Richards, 'Post-Divorce Arrangements', p. 146.
240. See Eekelaar and Clive, *Custody After Divorce.*
241. See J. Eekelaar, 'Children in Divorce: Some Further Data', *Oxford Journal of Legal Studies,* 2 (1982), pp. 63, 71 (Table 2).
242. On which see L. Parkinson, 'Bristol Courts Family Conciliation Service', *Family Law,* 12 (1982), p. 13.
243. See R. Leete, *Changing Patterns of Family Formation and Dissolution In England and Wales 1964–76,* London, OPCS, HMSO, 1979, p. 6. In the USA it has been calulated that in 1977 13 per cent of all children under eighteen were living in families in which one of the two parents was not the biological parent.
244. See K. Fogelman, *Britain's Sixteen-Year-Olds,* London, NCB, 1976, p. 30.
245. Quoted in J. Burgoyne and D. Clark, 'Reconstituted Families', in R. N. Rapoport *et al.* (eds), *Families In Britain,* London, Routledge & Kegan Paul, 1982, p. 290.
246. *Re N* [1974] 1 All E.R. 126. See also S. Maidment, 'The Step Relationship and Its Legal Status', *Anglo-American Law Review,* 5 (1976), p. 259.
247. See Matrimonial Causes Act 1973, s.52. See also s. 25(3).
248. See Children Act 1975, s.33(3)(a), (c).
249. Ibid., s.33(9).
250. Defined in s.86 of Children Act 1975.
251. Ibid., s.33(5), (8), unless the other parent is dead or cannot be found.
252. For agreement (and a fuller discussion of this point) see S. Maidment, 'Step-Parents and Step-Children: Legal Relationships in Serial Unions', in J. Eekelaar and S. Katz (ed), *Marriage and Cohabitation in Contemporary Societies,* Toronto, Butterworth, 1980, pp. 428–9.
253. J. Burgoyne and J. Masson, 'The English Step-Family', (unpublished paper) note that on adoption forms a number of step-fathers describe their relationship to the child as 'father by marriage' (p. 7).
254. Haskey, 'The Proportion of Marriages Ending In Divorce', p. 5.
255. On adoption patterns see P. Selman, 'Patterns of Adoption In England and Wales since 1969', *Social Work Today,* 7 (1976), p. 194.
256. See OPCS Monitor FM3 81/1.
257. Or judicial separation but this could not entitle the parties to remarry.
258. But they still have to surmount s.3 of the 1975 Children Act.
259. Judge Grant at Edmonton County Court. See *Child Care News,* no. 179 (October 1968), p. 7, and M. Freeman, 'Adoption and The Burden of Proof', *New Law Journal,* 119 (1969), p. 345.
260. *Re D* [1973] Fam. 209; *Re B* [1975] Fam. 127.
261. *Re D* [1973] Fam. 209, 216.
262. *Re B* [1975] Fam. 127, 132.
263. Houghton Committee, *Adoption of Children,* Cmnd. 5107, London, HMSO, para. 105. The First Report to Parliament on the Children Act 1975 (H.C. 268 (1979–80) said: 'The whole field of adoption by parents and step-parents is largely unexplored' (para. 32).
264. In J. Masson, 'Step-Parent Adoption', *Adoption and Fostering,* 6, no. 1 (1982), pp. 7, 10.
265. In M. Freeman, 'Adoption — Existing Policies and Future Alternatives', *Family Law,* 9 (1979), pp. 142, 144.
266. Section 29, following Houghton Committee, op. cit., para. 161.
267. By David Owen MP, Children Bill Standing Committee 1975, col. 403. He continued:

'We are not giving rights to foster parents . . . we are giving rights to the children.'

268. Both the DHSS, through a circular, and the High Court, have indicated that magistrates' courts should not hear step-parent adoption cases.

269. For an account of this volte-face which uses unreported cases as well, see the excellent article by R. Rawlings, 'Law Reform With Tears', *Modern Law Review*, 45 (1982), p. 637.

270. [1977] 2 All E.R. 671.

271. Ibid., p. 675.

272. *Re L.A., The Times*, 27 April 1978 (also (1978) 122 S.J. 417).

273. *Re S* (1974) 5 Fam. Law 88 (decided before the passing of the Children Act 1975).

274. *Re S* (1979) 9 Fam Law 88. See also *Re P*, unreported but discussed in Rawlings, 'Law Reform With Tears', op. cit., pp. 643–4.

275. *Re D* (1981) 2 F.L.R. 102.

276. Ibid., p. 104.

277. Ibid., p. 107. See also *Re D* (1982 unreported) in Rawlings, op. cit., p. 647.

278. See *Re J* [1973] 2 All E.R. 410; *Re S* [1975] 1 All E.R. 109, in both of which continuing access by a putative father was approved.

279. Masson, 'Step-Parent Adoption', op. cit.

280. Ibid., p. 9.

281. As Albie Sachs and Joan Hoff Wilson do: see *Sexism and the Law: A Study of Beliefs and Judicial Bias*, London, Martin Robertson, 1978, pp. 51–2.

282. See Freeman, 'Adoption — Existing Policies . . .', op. cit., p. 142.

283. In s.3 of Children Act 1975.

284. Some names are changed prior to the adoption application. See Burgoyne and Masson, 'The English Step-Family', op. cit. (11.5 per cent in this study).

285. *Re T* [1963] Ch. 238; *Y* v. *Y* [1973] Fam. 147.

286. As in *Y* v. *Y*, where four years had elapsed.

287. Matrimonial Causes Rules 1977, p. 92(8).

288. *Re WG* [1976] 6 Fam. Law 210.

289. *R(BM)* v. *R(DN)* [1978] 2 All E.R. 33.

290. *D* v. *B* [1979] Fam. 38.

291. *R(BM)* v. *R(DN)*, op. cit., p. 39.

292. *D* v. *B*, op. cit., pp. 50–1.

293. *W* v. *A*, [1981] Fam. 14.

294. *L* v. *F, The Times*, 1 August 1978.

295. Maidment, 'Step-Parents and Step-Children . . .', p. 425.

296. See *Minton* v. *Minton* [1979] A.C. 593, and Law Commission, *The Financial Consequences of Divorce* (Law Com. No. 103, Cmnd. 8041, London, HMSO, 1980, and Law Comm. No. 112, London, HMSO, 1981).

297. *Moore* v. *Moore* (1981) 11 Fam. Law 109; *Dipper* v. *Dipper* [1980] 2 All E.R. 722.

298. See Mnookin and Kornhauser, 'Bargaining In The Shadow of The Law . . .'

299. Matrimonial Causes Act 1973 s.43(1). There were 4,400 in care on 31 March 1980 under this section. See DHSS, *Children In Care In England and Wales March 1980*, London, DHSS, 1982, p. 17. Eekelaar and Clive, on the other hand, in *Custody After Divorce*, op. cit., found this happened in only 0.3 per cent of the cases in their sample.

300. See I. Dootjes, P. Erickson and R. Fox, 'Defence Counsel in Juvenile Court: A Variety of Roles', *Canadian Journal of Criminal Corrections*, 14 (1972), p. 132; also W. V. Stapleton and L. Teitlebaum, *In Defense of Youth: A Study of the Role of Counsel in American Juvenile Courts*, New York, Russell Sage Foundation, 1972, ch. 1.

301. See B. Dickens, 'Representing The Child In The Courts' in I. Baxter and M. Eberts (eds), *The Child and the Courts*, Toronto, Carswell, 1978, p. 273, 280.

302. Ibid.

303. J. K. Genden, 'Separate Legal Representation For Children: Protecting The Rights and Interests of Minors In Judicial Proceedings', *Harvard Civil Rights — Civil Liberties Law Review*, 11 (1976), pp. 565, 589.

304. On interviewing children, see H. Dent and G. Stephenson, 'An Experimental Study

of the Effectiveness of Different Techniques of Questioning Child Witnesses', *British Journal of Social and Clinical Psychology*, **18** (1979), p. 34.

305.   As to which see M. Crompton, *Respecting Children*, London, Edward Arnold, 1980.

306.   See Clare Winnicott, *Social Work in Child Care*, Bristol, Bookstall Publications, 1964, p. 43.

307.   Dickens, 'Representing The Child . . .', p. 294.

308.   Note 'Lawyering For The Child: Principles of Representation In Custody and Visitation Dispute Arising From Divorce', *Yale Law Journal*, **87** (1978), p. 1126.

309.   *Justice, Parental Rights . . .*, op. cit., p. 39ff.

310.   Ibid., para. 89(l).

311.   Ibid., para. 91.

312.   Unified Family Court Act 1974, s.8.

313.   See *Re Reid* (1967) 67 D.L.R. (3d)46.

314.   Family Court Act 1962 s.241.

315.   On the limits of his jurisdiction see *Re D* [1976] Fam. 185, 197 by Heilbron, J.

316.   Cf. Rules 72 and 115.

317.   Jennifer Levin, 'The Legal Representation of Children', *Family Law*, **5** (1975), pp. 129, 131.

318.   David Venables, 'The Official Solicitor . . .', op. cit., p. 46. Only 10 per cent are engaged in children's cases.

319.   See Turner, 'Wardship — The Official Solicitor's Role', op. cit., p. 32.

320.   Ibid., p. 34.

321.   Matrimonial Causes Act 1973, s.6.

322.   See A. H. Manchester and J. M. Whetton, 'Marital Conciliation in England and Wales', *International and Comparative Law Quarterly*, **23** (1974), p. 339. See also Eekelaar, *Family Law and Social Policy*, op. cit., pp. 144–51.

323.   See L. Parkinson, 'Bristol Courts Family Conciliation Service', *Family Law*, **12** (1982), p. 13.

324.   The Law Commission missed the opportunity to stress conciliation in its report on magistrates' jurisdiction in 1976 (Law Com. No. 77).

325.   Quoted in Parkinson, 'Bristol Courts . . .', op. cit., p. 14.

326.   Goldstein *et al.*, *Beyond The Best Interests . . .*, p. 53.

327.   Parkinson, op. cit., p. 14.

328.   See D. Millard, 'The Divorce Court Welfare Inquiry', *Justice of the Peace*, **141** (1977), p. 765; M. Wilkinson, *Children And Divorce*, Oxford, Blackwell, 1981; and P. Francis *et al.*, 'Mightier Than The Sword', *Social Work Today*, **14**, no. 17 (4 January 1983), p. 8.

329.   Eekelaar and Clive, *Custody After Divorce*, para. 13.30.

330.   The importance of arbitration in family disputes has been stressed by the American Chief Justice Warren Burger. See *New York Times*, 25 January 1982, p. A19, cols. 1, 2, 3. See also now new Practice Direction (1982) 3 FLR 448 (as from 1 January 1983 Principal Registry of Family Division to operate pilot scheme of conciliation in contested custody and access cases: where child eleven or over, he is to be brought to the conciliation appointment since 'it will sometimes be appropriate for the child to be seen by the registrar or the welfare officer.')

331.   For Family Court proposals see the Finer Report on *One-Parent Families*, Cmnd. 5629, 1974, London, HMSO; *Justice, Parental Rights*, op. cit., paras. 85ff; J. Graham Hall, *Proposal For a Family Court*, London, National Council for the Unmarried Mother and Her Child, 1973; Murch, *Justice and Welfare in Divorce*, op. cit. (which I discuss in (1981) 145 J.P. 173) and many others.

332.   A. H. Manchester, 'Reform and The Family Court', *New Law Journal*, **125** (1975), p. 984.

333.   M. D. A. Freeman, 'Questioning The De-Legalisation Movement in Family Law: Do We Really Want a Family Court?', paper at 4th World Congress on Family Law, Harvard, 1982.

334.   Cf. R. Merton (ed.), *Unanticipated Consequences of Social Action: Variations on a Sociological Theme*, New York, Academic Press, 1981.

335. For a good survey of the delegalisation movement see Richard L. Abel (ed.), *The Politics of Informal Justice* (2 vols.), New York, Academic Press, 1982.

336. See G. Roth and C. Wittich (eds), *Economy and Society*, Berkeley, University of California Press, 1968, vol. II, pp. 641–90.

337. See R. Kagan, *Regulatory Justice*, New York, Russell Sage Foundation, 1978.

338. See C. Reich, 'The New Property', *Yale Law Journal,* 73 (1964), p. 733; M. A. Glendon, *The New Family and The New Property*, Toronto, Butterworths, 1981.

339. See P. Conrad and J. Schneider, *Deviance and Medicalization: From Badness to Sickness,* St. Louis, Mosby, 1980.

340. In S. Cohen, 'The Punitive City: Notes on the Dispersal of Social Control', *Contemporary Crises,* 3 (1979), p. 339.

341. By Philip Rieff, *The Triumph of The Therapeutic: Uses of Faith After Freud*, Harmondsworth, Penguin, 1966.

342. In C. Lasch, 'Life In The Therapeutic State', *New York Review of Books,* **XXVII**, no. 16 (12 June 1980), p. 27.

343. Ibid., p. 30.

344. Finer Report, op. cit., sections 13 and 14.

345. Ibid., para. 4.281.

346. Ibid., para. 4.325.

347. See A. Sutton, 'Science In Court' in M. King (ed.), *Childhood, Welfare and Justice,* London, Batsford, 1981, p. 45, and G. Pearson, *The Deviant Imagination*, London, Macmillan, 1975.

348. Finer Report, op. cit., para. 4.328.

349. Which Finer advocates (see paras. 4.288 *et seq*.).

350. Finer Report, op. cit., paras. 4.402–4.404.

351. Ibid., para. 4.405.

352. See D. Kennedy, 'Form and Substance In Private Law', *Harvard Law Review,* 89 (1976), p. 1685.

353. See E. P. Thompson, *Whigs and Hunters,* London, Allen Lane, 1975, p. 266.

7 WHO KNOWS BEST? CHILD-REARING DECISIONS, PARENTS AND THE STATE

The relationship between the family and the state is one of the perennial questions of history.[1] Today, striking the right balance between autonomy and social intervention remains a pre-eminent policy decision for all concerned with family matters.[2] A focal point of the debate is child-rearing. There are a number of policy models. One, commonly espoused in the past but in seeming decline until its recent activation by neo-conservatives[3] such as Goldstein, Freud and Solnit,[4] is basically non-interventionist. It argues that standards for intervention should be pitched at a minimum and that intervention should be countenanced only in cases of clear abuse. An alternative model advocated by some is directed towards the destruction of family influence and transmitted advantages. At one level this involves policies such as the taxation of inheritance or comprehensive schooling, both matters of some controversy in Britain today: at another level this requires, as it does in the Platonic ideal as practised in the Communist bloc of Eastern Europe, complete conformity to community norms and little or no recognition of family autonomy. Thus, Bronfenbrenner can quote an official Soviet handbook thus:[5] 'Our parents are not without authority either, but this authority is only a reflection of social authority. In our country the duty of the father toward his children is a particular form of his duty towards society.' There is perhaps an intermediate model which employs the notion of affirmative action in an attempt to compensate those disadvantaged by their family background. This is increasingly acceptable to policy-makers in Western democracies, though intensely controversial.[6] It is furthermore dubious whether such policies achieve much: cycles of disadvantage are so firmly entrenched.[7] This chapter is an examination of family autonomy and state intervention which focuses on issues of child-rearing. The debate is central to that concerned with children's rights for it revolves around restraints on the power of parents to make decisions on their children's behalf and, in so doing, control their lifestyles. It also makes us confront the question of a child's autonomy. Furthermore, though it is rarely seen in this light, state intervention may result in burdens being assumed by families, for example, to care for a mentally handicapped child or the elderly, and this raises the moral question as to whether those who assume such burdens should be entitled to compensation from the state:[8] indeed, whether in certain circumstances the child himself should also have such a claim.[9]

Is Parental Autonomy Important?

Children need parents: that much is not in dispute. All children have certain needs,[10] physical and psychological, and these can best be satisfied by parents. Parents generally act in the child's best interests.[11] Indeed, children's rights are normally best secured in the context of a functioning family. Children have an interest in receiviing guidance, support and assistance and it is usually to parents that they turn for these things. Indeed, it may be that without such parental succour a child may be unable to acquire the necessary insight and strength to mature to adulthood.

The state is no real substitute for flesh and blood parents. As Goldstein, Freud and Solnit argue in *Before The Best Interests of the Child*:

> the law does not have the capacity to supervise the fragile, complex inter-personal bonds between child and parent. As *parens patriae* the state is too crude an instrument to become an adequate substitute for flesh and blood parents. The legal system has neither the resources nor the sensitivity to respond to a growing child's ever-changing needs and demands. It does not have the capacity to deal on an individual basis with the consequences of its decisions, or to act with the deliberate speed that is required by a child's sense of time.[12]

It may be doubted also whether legal intervention is capable of improving parenting. 'It must be recognised', Andrew Watson has written, 'that most of the parenting process is automated and unconscious, and therefore not susceptible to change through simple moral or legal admonition.'[13] He argues, most convincingly, that changes in parenting approaches require an understanding of that behaviour and a re-examination of its premises. Legal systems cannot create appropriate parental impulses.

The costs of intervention may also be great. It may polarise the family. It may undermine family stability and harmony. In putting the case for a child's privacy, as I shall do later in this chapter, I do not leave out of account the fact that children may have an interest in family privacy. Parents need to feel 'comfortable and confident about their child-rearing. Anything that undermines this sense of competence will have extremely serious effects on the children.'[14] By intrusion the state may achieve nothing but it may thwart much. Child-rearing is a risk-taking enterprise. Decisions have to be taken and sometimes taken immediately. One of the strongest arguments in favour of parental autonomy is that parents should not be inhibited by the fear that their judgement will be countermanded. It has to be recognised that in many cases there is 'a band of possible reasonable decisions'.[15] Whether recognised as such or not, state intervention sometimes conveys the impression of there being a single right answer.

The Philosophy of Minimum State Intervention

Because parental autonomy is considered important, the case for leaving state intrusion into the family to cases of clear abuse is commonly put both by legal commentators[16] and judges.[17] The United States Chief Justice Burger in the recent case of *H.L.* v. *Matheson*[18] (the case involved a child's privacy challenge to a Utah statute requiring parental notification in advance of the performance of an abortion on a minor) stressed the state interest in reinforcing the parental role in child-rearing. It was this interest, together with the necessity to protect an immature minor against an improvident decision (as he saw it), which enabled him to uphold the Utah legislation. The philosophy of minimum state intervention in the family was expressed most forcibly in another United States Supreme Court case in 1944 (*Prince* v. *Massachusetts*).[19] The case arose out of a conflict between Jehovah's Witnesses and the Commonwealth of Massachusetts. The latter was trying, somewhat dubiously, to extend its child labour legislation to prevent a child selling religious literature on the streets. The Supreme Court had already invalidated a Nebraska statute limiting the teaching of foreign languages, partially because it interfered with the right of parents to control the education of their children[20] and struck down an Oregon law requiring that parents educate their children in the public schools.[21] In the latter case a unanimous Court relied on the Nebraska decision to conclude that the Constitution protected the parents' right to 'direct the upbringing and education of children under their control.'[22] In *Prince* v. *Massachusetts* Justice Rutledge said: 'it is cardinal with us that the custody, care and nurture of the child reside first in the parents, whose primary function and freedom include preparation for obligations the state can neither supply nor hinder.'[23] There was, he argued (and he cited the Nebraska and Oregon cases in support) a 'private realm of family life which the state cannot enter.'[24] The Commonwealth of Massachussetts' legislation was accordingly held unconstitutional. The Court, however, recognised that the 'family (was) not beyond regulation in the public interest.'[25]

Justice Rutledge's remarks have been regularly cited with approval in recent American jurisprudence. They are given a similar accolade by the authors of *Before The Best Interests of The Child*.[26] It is here that the fullest statement of minimum state intervention in family matters is articulated. Goldstein, Freud and Solnit come close to treating the family as a private area outside the law. They write:

The child's need for safety within the confines of the family must be met by law through its recognition of family privacy as the barrier to state intrusion upon parental autonomy in child-rearing. These rights — parental autonomy, a child's entitlement to autonomous parents, and privacy — are essential ingredients of 'family integrity'.[27]

It will be noted how they conflate psychological needs into legal rights without so much as a hint of justification. Their purported justification for minimum state intrusion is both psychologically and philosophically grounded. The basis is in part their notion of psychological parenthood which they developed in their earlier monograph, *Beyond The Best Interests of The Child*.[28] This requires, as described there, day-to-day interaction, companionship and shared experiences. And it requires

> the privacy of family life under guardianship by parents who are autonomous. The younger the child, the greater is his need for them. When family integrity is broken or weakened by state intrusion, his needs are thwarted and his belief that his parents are omniscient and all-powerful is shaken prematurely.[29]

They conclude, in the face of very considerable and convincing empirical evidence to the contrary,[30] which they dismiss as 'simplistic',[31] that the effect on the child's developmental progress is 'invariably detrimental'.[32] If this prognosis is taken at face value, which it cannot be, no state intervention in the family could ever be justified. Furthermore, we could never expect adoption to be successful.[33]

Goldstein, Freud and Solnit also adduce a philosophical rationale for their position. A policy of minimum coercive intervention by the state is said to accord also with their 'firm belief as citizens in individual freedom and human dignity'.[34] These notions may be superficially attractive to some, but in a world of basic structural inequalities individual freedom can be so exercised as to undermine not only the liberty of others but also their human dignity. In a world where the pursuit of inequality[35] has become fashionable[36] it is not surprising that the dangers of these remarks of Goldstein *et al.* can be so readily glossed over. More attention has been given to inequalities of class, race and sex than within age structures[37] but the adult-child complex and especially parent-child relationship is a microcosm of the asymmetry found in these other dimensions. Bill Jordan puts the point well when he writes that: 'the case against intervention in family life often rests on the freedom of more powerful members (usually husbands in relation to wives and parents in relation to children) to exercise their power without restriction.'[38] Failure to intervene can, therefore, ensure the prevailing of a parent's will over a child's legitimate interest and though some of these interests may be trivial (choice of clothes or television programmes), others may be fundamental (abortion,[39] sterilisation,[40] life-saving surgery[41]).

There is, nevertheless, more than a core of truth in Goldstein, Freud and

Solnit's arguments. What is questionable, however, is their simplistic view of autonomy.[42] To them it is 'there', taken for granted and unproblematic. They ignore the ways in which the autonomy they value is constructed and regulated by legal processes. The law is the cultural and institutional underpinning of autonomy. It gives and it takes away. Families, that is parents for our purposes, have as much autonomy as the law allows them. Long ago it imposed restrictions on parental views regarding child-rearing. Thus we have today compulsory restrictions on child labour and we insist upon certain vaccinations. In their day each of these policies was resisted[43] and each is by no means uncontroversial today. It is not surprising that Goldstein and his colleagues do not consider such state intrusions: the status quo, particularly when long established, is beyond recall, at least in their view.

The Dangers of State Interference

'By its intrusion' into the family, 'the state may make a bad situation worse; indeed, it may turn a tolerable or even a good situation into a bad one.' So argue Goldstein and his colleagues.[44] Michael Wald makes much the same point.[45] It is difficult to contradict this. At its crudest the case for non-intervention is that intrusion does not work. Thus, for example, there is evidence that police and social work intervention does not have its intended effects. Faced with deviance, it aims to rehabilitate and yet it is just as likely to exacerbate delinquency amongst publicly-labelled youth as those against whom there had been no intervention.[46] There is similar American evidence.[47] Scott has shown how agencies established to rehabilitate the blind frequently encouraged their subjects to 'play the kind of deviant role traditionally reserved for the blind'.[48] Intervention legitimates itself, for to the extent that the client meets agency expectations, stereotypic beliefs are actualised. Scheff's work on mental illness comes to similar conclusions: he demonstrates how mental patients are rewarded for playing the deviant role, that is concurring in the diagnosis and behaving accordingly.[49]

Earlier in the book reference has been made to the effects of intervention on child abuse. There is no evidence that the increased control mechanisms of the last ten or fifteen years have conquered, or seem ever likely to conquer, violence against children. The NSPCC study,[50] which found that anxious visiting by social workers might actually increase the incidence of hostile acts against children, provides would-be interventionists with a sobering jolt. The NSPCC research finding, it will be recalled, was of a 60 per cent rebattering incidence in a sample of cases known to the NSPCC contrasted with a figure less than half that where there had been no intervention. Of course, there is no guarantee that children removed from home will not suffer similar or even worse hardship in substitute homes. There is evidence that some do.[51]

A second argument which may be used to support policies of non-intrusion relates to the standards conventionally used to measure parental conduct. Vague language invites unwarranted and arbitrary interventions.[52] Where vague standards are used it is difficult to give parents advance warning of what is required of them. A firmly entrenched maxim of the criminal law is *nulla poena sine lege*. Since the consequences of falling foul of the standards in child protection legislation is, or can be, little short of penal, similar considerations should apply. That is why Goldstein, Freud and Solnit insist, and rightly so, that parents should be given a fair warning, so that clear, precise standards govern the decision to intervene. The obvious parallel is, what H. L. A. Hart has called, 'the doctrine of fair opportunity' in the criminal law.[53]

There is no doubt that vague neglect laws, for example, which are all too common, do increase the likelihood that intervention will take place where it is harmful to the child. Where the standards are insufficiently precise 'decision making is left to the ad hoc analysis of social workers and judges.'[54] There is evidence that their decisions are often reflections of their own personal values and that interventions and removals are unnecessary. Social enquiry reports are replete with judgments for which there is no evidence.[55] Parental rights resolutions, particularly on the habits and mode of life ground, often express cultural biases.[56] Vague standards can all too easily be employed to impose the standards of one section of the population on another. There are different types of parenting, as a cursory reading of the Newson and Newson studies of their Nottingham cohort[57] or of Elizabeth Bott's *Family and Social Network*[58] demonstrates. Middle-class parents place a high value on the internalisation of values, reasoning, initiative and self-direction; working-class parents are more likely to emphasise obedience. Disciplining practices are also divergent: though both use corporal punishment,[59] working-class discipline is more physical, middle-class tending to use reasoning and the withholding of love and reward rather more. There are regional and racial differences as well as class differences. Nor do the ethnic minorities constitute a homogeneous population: Asian families are organised very differently from those whose origins are in the Caribbean. Statutory agencies often lack the expertise and knowledge to cope with the problems of West Indian youth.[60] Critics of the practices of intervention employed by such agencies allege, sometimes with considerable justification, that these operate so as to impose middle-class and white standards of appropriate parenting on working-class parents and on the parents of black children.

These problems are aggravated because a 'rescue' ideology demands greater intrusion into family privacy and more interference with parenting decisions. As indicated in an earlier chapter, the Maria Colwell case caused a moral panic amongst social workers in this country and the adoption of 'safety first' measures. Thus, there has been an increase in place of safety orders, in the removal of babies at birth, in resolutions assuming parental rights. The placing of children's names on 'at risk' register has reached epidemic proportions. Being 'at risk' is not like suffering from measles. It is not an objective condition but is rather a label or social construction.[61] Whether a child is deemed to be at risk or not depends upon a subjective interpretation. In part this depends on the values of the individual social worker but it is not entirely an individual decision-making process. Each agency develops a particular clientele which it designates as a control problem. As Freidson has noted,[62] in defining and classifying a universe which they claim needs their services, all control agencies in effect become responsible for drawing clearer lines than in fact exist in everyday life or in the processes by which the people concerned were originally led into their services. Agencies also develop processing stereotypes, simplified images as to the moral character of the person being processed, their motives, etc. Unique background characteristics are submerged in standardised background expectancies. These stereotypes are learned during socialisation (including social work training), from the media, as well as 'on the job'. Blumberg,[63] writing of lawyers, though his remarks may be readily generalised, sees stereotypes as generated and used as a response to the demands of bureaucratic organisations on its personnel to appear efficient, process a large volume of cases, reduce uncertainty and ambiguity in disposition and promote a smooth flow through the system. Placing children's names on a register may help some children, though the evidence of its having done so is difficult to find: it undoubtedly provides a solution[64] to one of social work's problems.[65]

Justifying State Intervention

The case for non-intervention has been shown to be considerable. The dangers of intervention cannot be denied. State-supervised child-rearing would anyway be inconsistent with our political and cultural traditions.[66] But some parents do abuse their children and some children do need protection. Children in some cases do have a privacy interest which the state must recognise. But, as Chief Justice Burger stated recently in the United States Supreme Court in *Parham* v. *J.R.*:[67] 'the statist notion that governmental power should supersede parental authority in *all* cases because *some* parents abuse and neglect children is repugnant' (he said to 'the American tradition' but this may be generalised to include this country and much of the Western World). Considerations have to be balanced and lines have to be drawn. Not even Goldstein, Freud and Solnit, who adopt the most extreme position of all thinkers on the subject, espouse a totally *laisser-faire* policy. It is, I believe, useful to examine their criteria for intervention. These are, I shall argue, too narrowly drawn but they give us some critical insight into the problems of line-drawing. Most significantly for our purposes their grounds enable us to focus on children's rights. Goldstein *et al.* pay no attention to these at all: indeed, they are totally eclipsed in their monograph.

Their first ground is that a parent has requested that the court determine the custody of a child.[68] This ground would exist if separated parents failed to arrive at a custody decision themselves or either or both requested a voluntary termination of their parental rights. A consequence of this is that court intervention would not be permitted where parents were in agreement as to a child's disposal, even where the court sensed or was convinced that the placement chosen by the parents was unsuitable. They would not, in other words, allow a court to review a custody arrangement, satisfactory to both parents, to ascertain whether it was in the child's best interests. There is some sense in this proposal since coercing parents into accepting an arrangement that neither wants may well do more harm than good. Moreover, our courts have more than enough to do without undertaking the burden of uncontested cases. Using resources, judicial and social work, for contested cases makes more sense.[69] And yet the nagging feeling remains that this once more relegates the child to the status of chattel. Are his wishes and feelings to count for nothing? Should we allow courts to abrogate responsibility in this way? Are we sacrificing rights on the altar of expediency? The problems are greater than Goldstein *et al.* indicate. The solution, as I indicated in the previous chapter, is not clear-cut and if I reach the same conclusion as Goldstein and his colleagues, I do so only because I believe the legal system is impotent to do more for children in this crucial area.

Secondly, Goldstein, Freud and Solnit envisage that where familial bonds or psychological parentage exist between non-parental caretakers and children, such a caretaker, a foster parent or relative, might seek to become the legal parent, or at any rate might refuse to relinquish the child to his parents or to a state welfare agency.[70] It is not difficult to envisage this: it is happening all the time. In such a situation, Goldstein *et al.* argue, state intervention can be justified. The time for intervention, they say, 'is when both the child and caretaker have turned to and accepted one another.'[71] Although, we are told, 'the complex process of forming psychological parent-child relationships is not beyond description,[72] its timetable cannot be set precisely.'[73] Despite this admission, they argue that 'parental rights must rest on objective data which are readily obtainable with the minimum of intrusion.'[74] To this end they put forward statutory periods (twelve months for a child under three years at the time of placement and twenty-four months for a child of three years and older at the time of placement, periods which they stress are 'time *with* (caretakers) and not time *away* from (parents).'[75] They see these time spans coupled with the caretaker's wish to continue custody as reliable indicators for granting legal recognition to the new relationship and terminating the legal relationship between the children, absent parents and state agencies. To this they make one exception: older children, more than three years old at the time of placement and in continuous parental care for three years at the time of placement, who had not been separated from parents because they had inflicted or attempted to inflict serious bodily injury on them, or because they had been convicted of a serious sexual offence against the child concerned *and* whose parents were still their psychological parents, would first be the subject of a 'special hearing' designed to determine psychological parenthood and whether the child's return to his parents would be the 'least detrimental alternative'.[76] They add: 'in the event that such evidence is inconclusive, the child's relationship to his long time caretakers should be given legal recognition.'[77] Where termination of parental rights is effected, Goldstein *et al.* view adoption as the preferred solution, but, failing this, they advocate what they call *'care with tenure'*.[78]

They do not spell out care with tenure. In conception it appears not far removed from the notion of custodianship introduced[79] into English law by the Children Act 1975.[80] It is suspect in rather similar ways. First, it is imprecise: with 'care with tenure' we do not know at all to what rights and duties it gives rise. Secondly, the process of divesting of parental rights appears as an administrative procedure, rather like English resolutions to assume parental rights[81] and accords little due process to parents or protection to children. Thirdly, the whole policy of imposing time-scales militates against working with natural families to reintroduce their children. Presumptions are a poor substitute for proper fact-finding. Furthermore, it is difficult to defend a concept which does not distinguish the reason why a child is in care. There is a strong ground for distinguishing between a child voluntarily placed with foster parents, perhaps because of bad housing conditions or illness, and one removed from parents because of abuse or neglect. It is also significant that, even in the case of older children, their wishes and feelings are imputed rather than sought out.

A third ground for intervention is 'the death or disappearance of both parents, the only parent or the custodial parent — when coupled with their failure to make provision for their child's custody and care.'[82] This, they say, is 'designed to provide the state with the authority to discover and to safeguard children for whom no day-to-day care arrangements have been made by parents who die, disappear, are imprisoned or hospitalized.'[83] Much of this is uncontentious. Clearly, the law has to provide for abandonment, a parent's sickness and other emergencies, and English law in common with other systems does.[84] Where the standard developed here is novel is in authorising intervention only if the absent parent failed to make provision for the care of the child. Further intervention would only be allowed if the substitute parent's actions brought him within another of the grounds for intervention. But we know how unsuitable are many private fostering arrangements.[85] Should we, therefore, as Goldstein *et al.* seem prepared to do, leave placements to parents? This runs counter to the trend in English legislation which is to extend local authority control over private fostering arrangements.[86] Control is elusive but this should not encourage us to give up trying. The Goldstein, Freud and Solnit standard is unwise. This should not blind us to the fact that arrangements by local authorities can also go tragically wrong.[87] But proper superintendence of substitute care should eliminate most of the errors.

The fourth ground posited in *Before The Best Interests of The Child* is even more controversial and dubious. It is 'conviction, or acquittal by reason of insanity, of a sexual offense against one's child.'[88] The ground is concerned with children whose parents 'use them as sexual partners'. The ground is unduly restrictive because protective intervention is authorised only after a conviction of the adult in criminal proceedings. There are a number of objections to this. The trend in the treatment of sexual abuse within the family is to see it as a social problem concerned with family dysfunction. There is a move, which few would attack, away from penal responses.[89] It is recognised that here, if nowhere else, the criminal law is a clumsy instrument. Yet implicit in this standard is an inevitable swing back to punitive responses. Again, if we look at this from the perspective of the child, what does the standard achieve?

First, it will allow most sexual abuse to continue. As Appleton asks: 'What of the teenager who does not want to put his parents behind bars?'[90] Secondly, if intervention must await a conviction, there must be inevitable delays in taking measures to protect children. It is difficult to see what advantages there can be in this. Thirdly, the narrowness of the test means that protective measures will be ruled out where a conviction is not obtained because of a technicality. The standard would also prevent any intrusion where the sexual offence was committed by, for example, the mother's boyfriend. Fourthly, although Goldstein, Freud and Solnit are alert to the fact that 'harm done by the inquiry may be more than that caused by not intruding',[91] they are prepared to subject children to an involvement in the criminal process which is not attuned to their needs and which is likely to perpetrate greater harm to them than any juvenile court placement process. It is difficult to understand how authors who express concern for family integrity and protection of the family from invasion of its privacy can possibly want to encourage the continued use of the criminal law and its processes to tackle incest and other sexual offences against children.[92] It should be added that Goldstein *et al.* do not wish to protect the family, that is parents, from intrusion into their private lives because they wish to further children's autonomy in sexual matters. There are some who do.[93] This is, however, one of the least acceptable concessions to a child's (an adolescent's) privacy.

The fifth of Goldstein, Freud and Solnit's grounds for intervention is 'serious bodily injury inflicted by parents upon their child, an attempt to inflict such injury or the repeated failure of parents to prevent their child from suffering such injury.'[94] In limiting the ground for intervention in this way they are excluding neglect, emotional harm, inadequate supervision and similar standards. So far so good. But they go on to define serious bodily injury narrowly. The ground is intended

> to provide protection to children who are brutally kicked, beaten or attacked by their parents. It is meant to safeguard children whose parents may have attempted to injure them, for example, by starvation, poisoning or strangling . . . . It is designed to safeguard children from parents who prove to be

incapable of preventing their child from repeatedly suffering serious injury or being exposed to such harm.[95]

But extreme cases, it seems, deserve extreme measures. Intervention is limited to 'serious injuries', thus ruling out of court a whole range of conduct which is deleterious to children, but when serious bodily harm has been inflicted, they are firm in their conclusion that parental rights should always be permanently terminated. 'Parental maltreatment', they claim,

> leaves psychological scars which endure long beyond any physical healing and preclude a child from regaining the feeling of being safe, wanted and cared for in his parents' presence — the very emotions on which his further developmental advances need to be based.[96]

They believe that battered children should always be adopted. Their position is totally inflexible and not easy to comprehend, for parents who batter their children can be helped to become adequate caretakers.[97] Children returned to parents who have abused them do not develop very differently from those placed in foster homes or, for that matter, from working-class children brought up by their own parents, or a parent, in comparable environments.[98]

We have here a rigid one-dimensional rule.[99] It must be asked why, if the consequences of serious bodily injury are to be so drastic, so many other forms of abuse fall short on Goldstein, Freud and Solnit's criteria of warranting intervention at all. It seems odd, to say the least, that a parent who beats his child should risk losing him but one who chains his child to a bed or locks him in a cupboard or insists on cross-dressing him or her should be immune from state intervention. On Goldstein, Freud and Solnit's standard, they are.

One of the reasons why they limit themselves to 'serious bodily injury' is that so many other standards of abuse are so inherently vague. They make a legitimate point. But *mutatis mutandis*, the same criticism may be levelled by their invocation of *serious* bodily injury; for what is a 'serious injury'? The answer to this surely depends on values upon which no consensus can be guaranteed. What is a 'brutal' assault? Is the parent's motive relevant? Can his cultural or subcultural background be considered relevant? In societies where corporal punishment of children is sanctioned these are by no means inconsiderable questions. English law permits moderate and reasonable physical chastisement of children,[100] but can parents know in advance what this standard entails? And how are we to deal with cases of serious injury which result from accidents which occur in the course of punishing a child? Is this an area where it is difficult to give parents the 'fair warning' that is regarded as essential? If so, it may be as difficult to defend this ground for intervention as those based on emotional harm. More clearly needs be spelt out if a ground for intervention based on the infliction of bodily damage is to be supported, as, of course, it must be. Furthermore, it must be recognised that failure to intervene in cases of less than serious injury may result in danger signs not being picked up. As is well known, minor injuries often forewarn of more dangerous traumas.[101] Unfortunately, there is another side to the coin for we know that intervention can have the effect of a self-fulfilling prophecy.

The sixth ground for intervention hinges on failure to take medical care. It is, I believe, the most controversial of all the bases for interference put forward by Goldstein, Freud and Solnit. They argue that intervention can be justified only where there is a

> refusal by parents to authorize medical care when (i) medical experts agree that treatment is non-experimental and appropriate for the child, (ii) denial of that treatment would result in death; and (iii) the anticipated result of treatment is what society would want for every child — a chance for normal healthy growth or a life worth living.[102]

Adequate medical care is defined in as narrow a way as possible: the child must be faced with death and not, for example, the prospect of blindness or lameness; there must be medical consensus on the type of intervention and on the fact that it is therapeutic; and, dealing specifically but not exclusively with 'defective newborns', the child must have a chance to live 'a normal life or a life worth living'.[103] On this too they assume a consensual standard.

The ground, as set out, raises profound social, medical, ethical and legal issues. The authors' reasons for limiting intervention are similar to those they adduce throughout their book. They do not want the views of professionals, be they doctors, social workers or judges substituted for those of parents. They are not convinced that outside professionals are any more capable of taking decisions than parents. Indeed, they believe that decisions other than life or death are only 'preferences for one style of life over another.'[102] Further, they argue that neither law nor medicine provides 'the ethical, political or social values for evaluating health care choices.'[103] They are not prepared to see parental motives evaluated by judges or doctors or social workers.

The posited ground is sufficient to allow for court intervention in cases in which parents, for religious or other reasons, oppose medical care for a child facing imminent death. There is no difficulty thus countering the objections of Jehovah's Witnesses to blood transfusions where these are necessary to save a child's life.[104] Their willingness to martyr themselves for their religious beliefs cannot be rationally extended to their children. But outside this relatively non-controversial area, cases may arise to expose the limits of the Goldstein *et al.* standards. For example, what is 'non-experimental' treatment? Is a procedure experimental because it is not orthodox?[105] Are we not to allow an adolescent to take the risk of being cured by treatment which is still at the experimental stage? What is a 'life worth living'? Who should take the decision as to which lives are worth living? There is surely a distinction, which Goldstein and his colleagues do not acknowledge, between giving parents some autonomy and allowing someone else to review the decisions they take. They are thus critical of the decision in the Connecticut case of *Hart* v. *Brown*.[106] The case arose out of a decision by parents to save an eight-year-old daughter's life by a kidney transplant from her healthy twin sister. Acting on medical advice, the parents consented to surgery but the hospital would not operate without a court review. The court upheld the parents' decision, though not their 'autonomy to decide'[107] and Goldstein *et al*. are critical of this. They are concerned that neither doctors nor judges are trained or in any other way qualified to impose their values about what is right for children or families in such situations. But this is not the point at issue. In such cases as an isograft kidney transplant there is a strong case for an objective review of the decision. Nor is it necessary for a judge, or a doctor or social worker merely to impose his or her own prejudices and views. There clearly ought to be guiding standards and these ought to be broadly acceptable to most of the community. It may be difficult to decide upon these, as it is, for example, with abortion decisions,[108] but this should not discourage us from trying to formulate principles.

The Goldstein, Freud and Solnit standards are even more vulnerable in cases where failure to treat leads to irreparable harm but not death. A case which arose in the Pennsylvania Supreme Court in 1972 is a striking illustration of the problem.[109] The child was sixteen and suffered from a curvature of the spine as the result of polio. A spinal fusion was required to straighten his spine and prevent him becoming totally bedridden. The mother, a Jehovah's Witness, refused her consent to blood transfusions essential to the operation. The Court remanded the case for determination of the boy's wishes: after talking with him the lower court concluded that he did not want the operation and his wishes were honoured by the Supreme Court. The majority opinion is close in sentiment to the Goldstein *et al*. approach (though they would not have consulted the child). Thus, Chief Justice Jones states: 'We are of the opinion that as between a parent and the state, the state does not have an interest of sufficient magnitude outweighing a parent's religious beliefs when the child's life is *not immediately imperiled* by his physical condition.'[110] If spinal surgery can be ordered, what, he asked, about a hernia or gall bladder operation or a hysterectomy? What indeed? Are these decisions which are to be left to parents? Surely not. More persuasive is the dissent in the Pennsylvania case. Justice Eagen wrote: 'By the decision of this Court today, this boy may never enjoy any semblance of a normal life which the vast majority of our society has come to enjoy and cherish.'[111] Furthermore, he recognised that a crippled child 'under the direct control and guidance of his parents' could not make an independent judgement. The decision of the majority can be criticised because it did not recognise that the child was not fully autonomous and did not ensure that he received the care that we must assume he would have wanted had he been able to exercise an independent judgement. In making this criticism I am accepting the liberal paternalistic argument that Ricky Green, in the case just considered, lacked rational capacities and had chosen a decision which would prevent him subsequently becoming rationally autonomous. Just as a child may be protected from actions that would result in his death (as Goldstein *et al.* concede), so, I would argue, he may legitimately be protected against disabling or irreparable injuries. The rational good of being able to get about was permanently denied Ricky Green by the Pennsylvania courts partly because they saw a parent's religious beliefs as paramount and partly also because they accepted an adolescent's non-independent judgement of what was best for him.

It is worth comparing the *Green* case with a couple of other American decisions. In *Re Seiferth*[112] a New York court refused to find a fourteen-year-old boy a neglected child, even though his father would not compel him to undergo the surgery recommended for the repair of a cleft palate and harelip. In Goldstein, Freud and Solnit's words, the court was unwilling 'to substitute its or a state agency's value preferences for those of the responsible parents.'[113] The court reasoned that

> less would be lost by permitting the lapse of several more years, when the boy may make his own decision to submit to plastic surgery, than might be sacrificed if he was compelled to undergo it now against his sincere and frightened antagonism.[114]

This decision is readily justifiable: there was no evidence of any psychological harm to the boy and the possibility that coerced treatment might do more harm than good. Furthermore, the condition was not likely to deprive the boy of a rational good and it was reversible at a later time. This contrasts with *Re Sampson.*[115] A fifteen-year-old boy suffered from a severely deformed face ('grotesque and repulsive', according to Judge Elwyn in the case). Corrective surgery was dangerous and could have been performed more safely when the boy reached maturity. The parent refused consent to necessary blood transfusions. A New York court, however, mandated treatment on the ground of alleged psychological harm to the boy from delaying the surgery. It is difficult to defend this decision. The alleged psychological harm was speculative. Evidence that the boy had developed a healthy personality was ignored. Goldstein *et al.* are scathing in their criticism of the decision. The judge, they say, adopted the 'role of prophet, psychological expert, risk-taker, and all-knowing parent.'[116] They continue:

> Genuine humility would not have allowed a judge to believe that he, rather than Kevin's mother was best qualified to determine the meaning of a 'normal and happy existence' for her son. In Kevin's eyes, either might be proven 'wrong' retrospectively. But nothing can qualify a judge to make that

prediction with equal or greater accuracy than a parent. Nor is any judge prepared or obligated, as are parents, to assume day-to-day responsibility for giving their Kevins the personal care they may require. Judges cannot be substitute parents and courts cannot be substitute families.[117]

These are weighty arguments but the decision can be justified without appealing to them. Here was a disability which did not appear to be causing harm. It was reversible at some subsequent time. Furthermore, it was possible to envisage a relatively normal life even in the absence of treatment at some time.

None of these considerations applies to *Re D*, [118] the well-known English sterilisation case decided in 1976, where the court stopped a proposed sterilisation taking place. In *Re D* an application was made via wardship proceedings by an educational psychologist employed by a local authority to prevent an eleven-year-old suffering from Sotos Syndrome from being sterilised. It should be stressed that it was a chance intervention: we know that other similar sterilisations had taken place. The proposed operation had the consent of the girl's widowed mother. The girl was precocious in development and presented behaviour problems which suggested that she might become pregnant in the near future. There was medical evidence that any child she might have could be abnormal. Reliance on the view that parents (and in this case medical experts too) know best would have deprived the girl 'of a basic human right, namely the right of a woman to reproduce.'[119] Heilbron J. held that 'if performed on a woman for non-therapeutic reasons and without her consent, [it would be] a violation of such right.'[120] The proposed sterilisation was stopped. The decision is a correct one on the criteria just formulated. A sterilisation would have robbed the girl of a rational good. It would have produced irreversible harm and we cannot say that at some putative time in the future she would have regarded it as the right step to have taken.

The case also exposes the limitations of the approach of Goldstein and his colleagues. Their grounds for intervention are based on parental failures to meet particular standards. But the mother in *Re D* was not neglecting or inflicting injury on her daughter (or at least this is not how she saw it). If anything, she was trying to protect her daughter from dangers she thought she would lack the maturity to fend off. Bernard Dickens expresses this particularly well.[121] He comments that the

tests [in *Before The Best Interests*] seem to lack the fine tuning required to deal with the situation presented by *Re D*, since they are directed primarily at decisions to remove children entirely from parental custody and control. Further, they are concerned with parents whose treatment of their children falls short of legislated or judicially set minimum standards of care. They seem not to address parents whose well-meaning and conscientious initiatives are misguided or insensitive in ways denying children future rights. The tests set by *Before The Best Interests* are illustrated by failure to come up to the standards and do not consider deviations from norms of child-rearing by, for instance, over-protectiveness. They do not deal with causing harm to children by violating or pre-empting their human rights, such as their rights of reproduction.

In a sense the problem can be generalised by noting that the *Before* guidelines are too clear-cut, too rigid, too polarised. Just as there are adults on the one hand and children on the other, so there are 'black' decisions and 'white' decisions. There is no understanding of grey areas, any more than there appears to be of the rights of wishes of adolescents.

Some Problem Areas

The last section concluded with a general discussion of the interests involved in the medical treatment of children. In this section the theme is continued by focusing on three problem areas all of which stand at the interface between law and medicine and all of which accordingly raise not only legal, social and ethical questions but medical issues too. The problem areas selected are the life or death issues concerned with defective newborn children; questions relating to an adolescent's rights to birth control, to use contraception and seek abortion; and, thirdly, the problem of the institutionalisation of mentally ill children. As with medical treatment, and medical experimentation[122] (which for reasons of space is omitted from the book), the questions have been more thoroughly explored in the United States than in Britain. But the issues (the absence of a written constitution embodying a bill of rights apart) are the same as responses to early English initiatives in the areas demonstrate. American literature and case law are thus freely drawn upon.

(i)   Defective Newborns

In 1981 English courts were confronted with the problem of the defective newborn child for the first time:[123] the 'baby Alexandra' case[124] was a successful wardship application by a local authority to authorise surgery against parental wishes; a few months later Dr. Leonard Arthur was charged with murder and eventually acquitted of attempted murder after an emotionally charged trial.[125] Both children suffered from Down's Syndrome: one lived as a result of court action; the other died but the fact that the doctor had acted from purely humane motives seems to have been the prevailing factor. What the Alexandra case made explicit, the Arthur verdict to an extent clouds. I concentrate on the Alexandra decision because it centred on the decision-making process. The trial of Dr. Arthur was *ex post facto* and few can have doubted the verdict to which the jury would come.

The facts of *Re B* (the 'Alexandra' case) are relatively straightforward. She was born in July 1981 and suffered from Down's Syndrome. She was also born with an intestinal blockage (duodenal artresia) which would be fatal unless it were operated upon. She would in fact have starved to death. Her parents took the view that it would be kinder to let her die. They therefore refused to consent to surgery. The doctors made contact with the local authority (the London Borough of Hammersmith and Fulham) which made the child a ward of court and asked the court to give them care and control and to authorise them to allow the operation to be carried out. The judge made the necessary orders. When the child was transferred from the hospital at which she was born to another hospital for the operation, the surgeon declined to operate when informed that the parents objected. The local authority accordingly returned to the judge and he, after hearing the parents, refused his consent to the operation taking place. The local authority appealed. Inquiries showed that other surgeons were prepared to perform the operation. It was estimated that if the operation were successful (the prognosis for such surgery being good), the child would have a life expectancy of twenty to thirty years.

The Court of Appeal saw the question as: 'whether it is in the interests of this child to be allowed to die within the next week or to have the operation?'[126] It devolved upon the court to decide whether 'the life of this child is demonstrably going to be so awful that in effect the child must be condemned to die, or whether the life of this child is still so imponderable that it would be wrong for her to be condemned to die?'[127] The court held that it was wrong that the child's life should be terminated because, in addition to being a mongol, she had another disability. Accordingly, it saw its duty to decide that the child should be allowed to live. Dunn L. J. thought that Alexandra should be 'put into the same position as any other mongol child.'[128] The Court of Appeal thought the first instance judge was at fault in being influenced by parental views rather than deciding what was in the best interests of the child.

Goldstein, Freud and Solnit have not, so far as is known, commented upon this decision. But their view on the case is clear from remarks in *Before The Best Interests of The Child*. They quote Duff[129] to the effect that: 'families know their values, priorities and resources better than anyone else. Presumably they, with the doctor, can make the better choices as a private affair. Certainly, they, more than anyone else, must live with the consequences . . . .'[130] An argument commonly used to support passive euthanasia of defective newborns is the cost to the family and community of keeping them alive.[131] Thus, Duff and Campbell acknowledge that there are 'limits of support that society can or will give to handicapped persons and their families.'[132] Such families bear psychological as well as economic burdens. Goldstein *et al.* insist accordingly that where children are 'saved' against parental wishes 'the state must take upon itself the burden of providing the special financial, physical and psychological resources essential to making real the value it prefers for the child.'[133] This may involve finding foster or adoptive parents: at the least it involves fully financing special care requirements. Philippa Foot is right to characterise such arguments pro passive euthanasia as 'not for their sake but to *avoid trouble to others*'.[134] This she finds unacceptable as do I. Nor am I impressed by Brandt's defence of the relevance of cost. 'Is it obvious', he argues, 'that the continuation of a marginal kind of life for a child takes moral precedence over providing a college education for one or more of his siblings? Some comparisons will be hard to make, but continuing even a marginally *pleasant* life hardly has *absolute* priority. . . .'[135] It is not obvious: it clearly requires reasoned argument and this can be presented. Nor is it fair to suggest that all interventionists see life as an absolute priority, though some pressure groups clearly do.

The argument that if the state is going to step in and override parental wishes then it must be prepared to shoulder the cost has been much in evidence in Britain in the aftermath of *Re B*.[136] Thus estimates of how much the care of Alexandra is going to cost the local authority in question have been given considerable attention by the media. But ultimately, and despite Brandt's arguments, decisions such as those in the *Re B* case must be taken on moral grounds, not economic considerations.

The case sparked off considerable controversy. The British Paediatric Association[137] immediately took the line that parents must ultimately decide whether a severely handicapped baby is to be treated. This view is consonant with the principles set out in the British Medical Association's *Handbook of Medical Ethics*. It is there stated that 'adult patients can make their own decisions but for an infant the parents must ultimately decide.' The principles do, however, go on to urge that doctors 'attend primarily to the needs and rights of the individual infant.'[138] The BMA view is thus far from clear-cut: indeed, it shares with much of the community an ambivalence. Others are more certain. Thus an organisation was formed shortly after the Alexandra decision to promote the rights of parents to make the decision as to whether their severely handicapped newborn babies should live or die.[139] The opposite position is taken by Life. The great advantage of their position is that every human being is entitled to the same care, foetus or baby, handicapped or not. One commentator in *The Times* described the Court of Appeal's decision as 'the cruel folly'.[140] 'Those who call for legal intervention in preference to the quickly reached decisions made between parents and trusted doctors seem to me', wrote Claire Tomalin in that article, 'to lack understanding of the moral capacities of ordinary people.'[141] She has called for parents to be able to make their decisions 'privately and peacefully and with people whose goodwill [they] can trust.' It certainly seems that parental acceptance or rejection of a handicapped child influences doctors more than their own assessment of the child's quality of life. A recent survey of 280 paediatricians showed that in cases where parents rejected the child, only 36 per cent would recommend surgery for a Down's Syndrome baby needing an intestinal operation to live, but where the parents accepted the baby the percentage favouring surgery rose to 64 per cent.[142]

The non-interventionist view thus has considerable support. The fault with the thesis, it seems to me, is that the alternative is not between withholding medical assistance so that the child dies and being burdened with the care of the child, though critics of interventionism often insist it is. There is a third option, namely, the termination of the parental relationship and with it parental rights, powers and duties. Robertson puts his finger on it when he writes:

> while parental discretion to terminate the parental relationship may be justified, it does not follow that parents should also have the right to decide whether the child lives or dies. Clearly, discretion to terminate a relationship of dependency does not mandate that one has the power to impose death on the terminated party.[143]

Furthermore, to make a distinction between killing and letting die is little short of casuistry: the child dies without dignity and in distress. As Harris put it: 'we should be absolutely sure that we face squarely the full impact of what we are doing . . . if we disguise the facts from ourselves and others by various distancing strategies we may permanently shield ourselves from the full awareness of what we are about.'[144]

There are both procedural and substantive problems at issue. Most of the discussion has centred on the procedural questions. Thus, Goldstein and his colleagues within outer and narrow limits leave the decision to the parents and expect them to get some assistance from doctors. But neither parents nor doctors are disinterested parties and they cannot accordingly act dispassionately. Each has a committed personal interest in the decision. If we are looking for a rational decision, we should not turn to them. Outside superintendence of decision-making is crucial. The courts are far from an ideal forum for decision-making in such matters, yet it is difficult to find a more suitable alternative. Nor should we expect *ad hoc* decisions to emanate from courts any more than we would wish judicial pronouncements to be reflections of individual values and preferences.[145] What is required is a code of principles to govern such cases.[146] Doctors, social workers and not least moral philosophers have a part to play in developing these principles. They can be tested and evaluated in real human cases in courts. The clearer they become the less need there will be to refer cases to courts.

What are these principles? First, the presumption must always favour life, unless it is proved otherwise. The child himself cannot, of course, be consulted. On the theory of liberal paternalism adumbrated above, the child must be protected against death unless we can say rationally on his behalf that he, given his disability, would not choose to live. There are children with no real life possibilities who can only lead a vegetable existence.[147] There are others who with standard medical treatment have life possibilities.[148] I like the distinction made by Angela Holder between treatment which can cure the condition for which it is performed and that which cannot. She argues:

> if a Down's baby has an intestinal obstruction or . . . an infant has a fistula, either one of which can be cured by relatively simple surgical procedures *and* if those procedures would clearly be performed by court order if necessary on an otherwise normal newborn, then it is arguable that treatment is legally required. On the other hand, neurosurgery for a paralyzed newborn is by no means 'ordinary care', since normal babies do not require it. Second, the condition for which surgery might be performed is not curable, and thus the operation may be regarded as both futile and one that would subject the baby to more pain than he would have felt if left alone. Third, if the child survives he may well have sufficient self-awareness to suffer the agonies of knowing his limitations and to be tormented by them. Thus, it may be possible to justify as good medical practice a determination that a child whose condition is incurable should not be subjected to surgery for that condition solely to keep him alive.[149]

Bernard Dickens simplifies this in the following useful way: 'The mongoloid child with bowel obstruction may be in the same position as a normal child refused a necessary blood transfusion by parents who are Jehovah's Witnesses; the medical care in issue will restore normal function to the part of the child's body for which it is indicated . . . .'[150] He argues that it cannot lawfully be withheld and I concur in this.

(ii) The Adolescent's Rights to Birth Control

Can a teenage girl use contraceptive devices or undergo an abortion without her parents' consent? English courts have not had to consider these matters, though in one recent case the court skirted the abortion issue. In *Re P*,[151] a girl in local authority care wanted an abortion. Her parents objected and the authority hesitated 'to override the natural feelings of parents who oppose[d] the termination.'[152] It accordingly made the child a ward of court[153] and an abortion was mandated despite the parental objections. Since the girl was in care under a care order, the local authority had the same powers as the parents would have had apart from the order.[154] It did not in fact have to consult the parents at all. It was, however, good social work practice to do so. But more significantly the question must arise as to whether the girl, who was fifteen, could have given consent to the abortion herself. It seems to have been assumed both by the local authority and the judge that she could not do so. The Family Law Reform Act 1969 s.8(1) allows a minor to consent to a surgical operation including an abortion at the age of sixteen, but since the 1969 Act does not affect the validity of any other consent (s.8(3)), a younger child capable of understanding what is involved may also give effective consent. All the evidence in this case suggested that the girl in question, who was mature for her age, fully understood what termination of her pregnancy involved and was aware of all the 'pros' and 'cons' of taking such a decision. It is a pity that this point was not taken, for a clarification of the law is long overdue.[155]

In the United States by contrast the nettle has been firmly grasped by the Supreme Court. In *Planned Parenthood of Missouri* v. *Danforth*,[156] *Bellotti* v. *Baird*[157] and *Carey* v. *Population Services International*[158] the Court limited parents' control over their children by extending to minors the constitutional right to privacy. In *Danforth* the Court struck down a Missouri statute that required parental consent as a necessary condition of a child's having a legal abortion. Justice Blackmun, writing for the majority, argued that the statutory parental veto power would be unlikely to strengthen the family unit 'where the minor and nonconsenting parent are so fundamentally in conflict and the very existence of the pregnancy already has fractured the family structure.'[159] In *Bellotti* v. *Baird* the Court invalidated a requirement of notice to parents that stopped short of granting parents a veto power. Justice Powell noted that 'many parents hold strong views on the subject of abortion, and young pregnant minors, especially those living at home, are particularly vulnerable to their parents' efforts to obstruct both an abortion and their access to court.'[160] He held that the Constitution guarantees minors the opportunity to seek judicial authorisation for an abortion without parental notice or consent. However, the opinion allows for statutes to require parental notice to be given under some circumstances. It countenances the denial of a minor's request if it concludes that 'her best interests would be served thereby' and 'the court may in such a case defer decision until there is parental consultation in which the court may participate.'[161] In *Carey* v. *Population Services International* the Court held unconstitutional New York's legislation which prohibited the sale of contraceptives to minors under sixteen. The prohibition was struck down because there was no evidence that it rationally furthered the goals of discouraging teenage sexual activity or safeguarding their physical health. The judges were, however, careful not to be seen as approving of teenage sexual activity. Justice Stevens said he would describe as 'frivolous' the argument that a 'minor has the constitutional right to put contraceptives to their intended use, notwithstanding the combined objection of both parents and the State.'[162]

Is the United States Supreme Court right to have limited parental control as they have done in this group of cases? Is sexual activity an area in which we should recognise an adolescent's right to personal autonomy? It is worth pondering the arguments put by those who favour constraints on adolescents. Inevitably, there are moralistic arguments. But if contraception enables adults to regulate the consequences of their sexual activities rationally, as it does, it also assists adolescents to achieve the same ends. The moralistic condemnation of abortions performed upon girls who are minors finds its support in reasons which apply with as much ethical force to adults as they do to minors. If abortion is morally permissible then what is sauce for the adult must be sauce for the adolescent as well. There are paternalistic arguments too but, if anything, these are weaker and certainly so in the case of adolescents. Given the experimental and extra-marital nature of the sexual activities of adolescents it must be in their interests, not contrary to them, to use contraceptives. Indeed, if the principles of paternalism are followed through, adolescents will be taught about the uses and availability of contraceptives. As far as abortion is concerned, this must be in the interests of most pregnant adolescent girls, since, as Justice Powell acknowledged in *Bellotti* v. *Baird*, 'considering her probable education, employment skills, financial resources, and emotional maturity, unwanted motherhood may be exceptionally burdensome for a minor.'[163] It is difficult to see what arguments could be put in favour of parental veto or notice in the name of paternalism to stop a girl having an abortion which is in the interests of many pregnant adolescents.

The arguments against crediting adolescents with autonomy in relation to contraception and abortion are thus suspect. This does not mean that in the exercise of such autonomy they will not make mistakes. But having rights entails developing the capacity to take personal responsibility. In the development of that capacity, mistakes will be made. Rights are not always exercised wisely, sometimes they are abused or misused, but this is not an argument for denying them. It is an argument for proffering advice, so in relation to contraception and abortion sex education becomes a matter of pre-eminent importance, but the sovereignty of persons require that they be final authority when it comes to exercising rights.

(iii) Institutionalisation of Mentally Ill Children

The recent United States Supreme Court of *Parham* v. *J.R.*[164] has brought into focus yet another issue revolving about parental decision-making and children's rights. The case concerned children committed to mental hospitals without adequate procedural protections. The Court concluded that a parent or guardian might effect an admission to a mental hospital. It stated that 'precedents permitted the parents to retain a substantial, if not the dominant, role in the decision, absent a finding of neglect or abuse.'[165] It favoured the 'traditional presumption that the parents act in the best interests of the child.'[166] Nevertheless, it recognised that the risk of error involved was sufficiently high to require a pre-commitment inquiry by a neutral factfinder. It thought, however, that the admitting psychiatrist constituted an adequately neutral and independent decision-maker. It was argued that more formal due process proceedings would unduly discourage parents from making needed commitments, with little gain in accuracy. It was thought that a post-commitment hearing could satisfy due process requirements with less cost to family harmony, since, as Justice Brennan noted, 'the family autonomy already will have been fractured by the institutionalization of the child.'[167]

The *Parham* opinion was given shortly before the publication of *Before The Best Interests of The Child* but an earlier article[168] of Joseph Goldstein's was available to the Court, and was influential in the decision. The opinion of the Supreme Court does, however, depart to a considerable degree from the position upheld by Goldstein and his colleagues. It recognises, as after *Danforth* it had to do, that children had interests in liberty from detention and treatment. Indeed, Justice Brennan in a partial dissent recognised that children committed to mental hospitals by the state (that is, in this instance, social workers) were entitled to a pre-admission commitment hearing. The Court also accepted that adolescents, capable of admitting themselves, had additionally the legal power to leave a mental hospital.

The decision is something of a compromise. It recognises the state's interest in avoiding unnecessary and destructive interventions.

> The State in performing its voluntarily assumed mission also has a significant interest in not imposing unnecessary procedural obstacles that may discourage the mentally ill or their families from seeking needed psychiatric assistance. The *parens patriae* interest in helping parents care for the mental health of their children cannot be fulfilled if the parents are unwilling to take advantage of the opportunities because the admission process is too onerous, too embarrassing or too contentious.[169]

Watson would have preferred the court to have defined the admission process 'solely as a therapeutic contract between family and doctor.'[170] He argues that 'to conceptualize automatically hospital admission as a danger to the child's welfare . . . runs counter to the Court's preferences for parental privacy.' He is concerned that protection of parental decision-making, rather than children's liberty interests, should have been the opening questions in *Parham*.'[171]

The dangers inherent in this approach are profound. Szasz[172] has depicted some of them. Analogies with tonsillectomies, appendectomies and other similar medical procedures, to which the Court in *Parham* drew attention, are not apposite, for, as Watson himself concedes,

> the child's medical symptoms [of mental illness] may stem from parental problems . . . and the child may serve as the scapegoat and a symbolic focus for intrafamily conflicts. This sort of admission differs from hospitalization for other medical purposes because it presents the question under what circumstances the state should intervene into family psychological or social difficulties that hinder the development of the child.[173]

The question posed in *Parham* v. *J.R.* may have been different from *Danforth*, for example, but the principles involved are the same. Here we are faced with children lacking developed capacities and never likely to achieve full autonomy. Their welfare had to be protected but it had to be protected both against the excesses of parental authority and what are acknowledged to be the negative effects[174] of institutionalisation. What the children in *Parham* had the right to expect was the sort of individualised care through which they would be enabled to achieve whatever rational independence they could. But the Court paid no attention to the children at all. Richards[175] has commented with considerable justification that the Supreme Court, often so 'conscientiously committed to indicating and elaborating the rights of children', here fell short of 'even recognising the ethical issue.' He notes that where the conflict is parent versus adolescent, as in *Danforth*, or parent and child versus school, as in *Tinker*[176] or *Goss* v. *Lopez*[177] (but not, of course, *Ingraham* v. *Wright*[178]) the Court 'can grapple with the issue'. Where, on the other hand, 'the issue is parent-and-state versus child, the Court loses its footing.'[179] Richards describes *Parham* as 'Plato's moral refuse bin'.[180] Institutions which house the mentally ill are little removed from Plato's conception.[181]

The United States Supreme Court decision in *Parham* v. *J.R.* is a low water-mark for children's rights. In order to support parental autonomy or the *parens patriae* power of the state the Court quite simply ignored the moral status of the children involved. And yet the consequence of so doing was in all probability to place children in institutions which did not further their welfare. Even on the narrow child-saving conception of children's rights *Parham* is thus a flawed decision.

I have concentrated on one United States decision because for all its defects it is at least a discussion of important moral issues. In England we have not even reached the stage of litigating the competing interests of parents, children and the state in matters relating to institutionalisation of the mentally ill, and this despite recent re-appraisals of the law[182] and new legislation.[183]

What Voice for the Child?

In most of the cases considered in this chapter the views of the children, in so far as they had views, were congruent with, or at least assumed to be congruent with, those of their parents. The problem has, however, been raised as to what weight to give to the child's views where he disagrees with the decision taken by his parents. This will not happen often: given a child's socialisation it will be a rare and courageous child who is both capable and willing to express an independent view. Even where the child does express an opinion, we cannot be sure whether it is he who is truly speaking. These problems are acute in custody battles on divorce and many of the implications of a child's preference for one parent rather than another were considered in the previous chapter. Judges may be more aware of the problem in custody suits than in the context of decisions relating to child-rearing. Their fears are, however, expressed in these cases too. Thus, in a case where care proceedings were brought in respect of a child whose father refused to send him to school because he had an implacable objection to comprehensive schooling, Cumming-Bruce L.J., after noting that the boy's views were similar to his father's, commented:

> I have a haunting fear that the fact that the interests of the child may have been confused with the interests of the father may have made it difficult for the court . . . to appreciate what the child's interests were. It may be that in cases raising issues such as the present, the legal advisers of the child should consider very carefully how far it is consistent with their duty to the child to present a case which appears to be identical with that of a parent who holds somewhat obsessive views.[184]

It is quite clear that this was an instance where the court could overrule the father's decision without any qualms. Indeed, this would seem a paradigm example of an area where a child's views have little relevance, in so far as his views were to prefer no schooling to comprehensive schooling. We should choose for children, being guided by the goal of wishing to maximise those interests which will enable them to develop life plans of their own. As Gerald Dworkin put it in a recent paper: 'We ought to preserve their share of what Rawls calls "primary goods";[185] that is, such goods as liberty, health, and opportunity, which any rational person would want to pursue whatever particular life plan he chooses.'[186]

But what if the child had disagreed with his father? To what extent should notice have been taken of his view? The interest in the American Supreme Court case of *Wisconsin* v. *Yoder*[187] lies principally in the attitude taken to this matter in Justice Douglas's dissenting opinion. The question the Supreme Court had to answer was whether Amish parents could withdraw their children from public schools at the eighth grade. The education the children would receive would, their parents argued, be detrimental to those about to live an Amish life. The Supreme Court upheld the parents' claim. The 'primary role of the parents in the upbringing of their children is now established beyond debate as an enduring American tradition',[188] wrote the Chief Justice (Burger). There was no conflict, or discernible conflict, between the Amish parents and their children, only one between the Amish community and the state authorities of Wisconsin. But, what if there had been? Justice Douglas took up this issue.

> On this important and vital matter of education, I think the children should be entitled to be heard. While the parents, absent dissent, normally speak for the entire family, the education of the child is a matter on which the child will often have decided views. He may want to be a pianist or an astronaut or an oceanographer. To do so he will have to break from the Amish tradition.

It is the future of the student, not the future of the parents, that is imperiled by today's decision. If a parent keeps his child out of school . . ., then the child will be for ever barred from entry into the new and amazing world of diversity that we have today. The child may decide that that is the preferred course, or he may rebel. It is the student's judgment, not his parents', that is essential . . . if he is harnessed to the Amish way of life his entire life may be stunted and deformed. The child, therefore, should be given an opportunity to be heard before the State gives the exemption which we honour today.[189]

Justice Douglas saw the possibility of the parents' religious views being imposed upon adolescents and he opined that where a child was mature enough to express conflicting desires, it would be an invasion of the child's rights to permit 'such an imposition without canvassing his views'.[190]

The issue can arise in areas other than education. One of the most acute is where the child wishes to leave home. There is no categorical answer in English law to the question: when can I (or my child) leave home? The school-leaving age is sixteen and this is often thought to be the age at which a child may leave home. But care proceedings may be brought until the age of seventeen and wardship until the age of majority. The question as to whether a child has the right to leave home arose in the state of Washington case of *Re Snyder*.[191] The court's view was basically protectionist. 'Our paramount consideration', it said, 'must be the welfare of the child.' The issue, as it saw it, was whether there was substantial evidence to support a finding that 'the parent-child relationship has dissipated to the point where parental control is lost.'[192] The court in *Re Snyder* had no doubt that it had.

Re Snyder concerned an adolescent girl aged sixteen. The *Polovchak cause célèbre* revolved about a twelve-year old.[193] He had emigrated with his parents from the USSR to the USA, but his father had not liked America and decided that he and his family should return to the Soviet Union. But Walter, aged twelve, decided he liked America and wanted to stay. He accordingly ran away from home and refused to accompany his parents back to the Soviet Union. An extraordinary legal battle then commenced with political overtones of considerable magnitude. The American Civil Liberties Union, which has campaigned for children's rights, supports the father's case. An ACLU lawyer is quoted as saying: 'We believe kids have rights, but not that a 12 year old has the right to choose where his family should live.'[194] It does not seem to me that that is what Walter Polovchak is claiming. He is claiming the right to decide where he lives.

He won the first round of the battle. A Chicago juvenile court declared Walter 'a minor in need of supervision' and put him into foster care. The same day the United States government granted him political asylum and assigned FBI officers to guard him against being snatched by Soviet agents. But the Illinois Court of Appeal voided the order which had removed Walter from his parents' custody. The court declared:

We have serious doubts as to whether the state would have intervened in this realm of family life and privacy, had the parents' decision to relocate involved a move to another city or state. The fact that the parents have decided to move to a country which is ruled under principles of government which are alien to those of the USA should not compel a different result.[195]

Walter remains in Chicago. The US Department of Justice, in a move unprecedented in the case of a child, has issued a 'departure control order', under which all US border guards and custom officials are instructed to prevent Walter's departure from the USA. The battle continues: if it drags on much longer Walter, now fifteen, will be of age from the point of view of Russia and the state of Illinois[196] and will be able to decide where he wants to live.

There can be very little doubt that the publicity of this case and the decision taken are a reflection of its political overtones. Had Walter been French he would have been compelled to return to France, if that is what his parents wanted. But the political issue is very relevant and cannot be ignored. What Walter was saying was that life was better for him in Chicago than the alternative in Lvov. I am sure he is right and I believe he could be proved right on objective criteria. But rather than pursuing the *Polovchak* case, let me try to generalise. Who is to make the decision and upon what criteria?

There are three models. There is the Goldstein, Freud and Solnit approach which would give unqualified endorsement to parental authority to decide in a case such as this. In their view the child does not begin to have an independent interest. His interests and those of the parents are identical. The core of truth in this is children, certainly while young, internalise parental values, so that in most cases their interests are likely to coincide with their parents. The problems with this view have been spelt out in this chapter. We do not allow parents who are Jehovah's Witnesses to deny their children a lifesaving blood transfusion because of their religious beliefs. We do not even ask whether the children share those beliefs. Goldstein and his colleagues agree with our taking this course. The identity of interests idea would condemn some children to death (Alexandra,[197] for example) and rob others (the girl in the Sheffield sterilisation case,[198] for example) of basic human rights.

A second approach is that which emphasises that the decision-maker, whoever it is, should consider first and foremost the best interests of the child. So much has been written about this doctrine that it is hardly necessary to explore it further. Courts and administrative agencies acting in the best interests of children, as they have perceived them, have often made decisions which aggravate rather than ameliorate the child's situation. Decisions taken are often no better than those parents would have made. This is not to rule out the 'best interests' doctrine but it is difficult to give it by itself unqualified approval. If the doctrine is endorsed it still becomes in every case a question of deciding what the individual child's best interests are or of finding a criterion against which to judge a child's welfare. This is to be found within the third model.

A third possible approach is to see parents as representing[199] their children's interests. With older children this may mean nothing more than putting their child's wishes forward. This doctrine offers very little guidance in the case of young children. With adolescents the problems are likely to arise where parents do not agree with the views of their children. How should they act? Dworkin argues that 'we ought to choose for [them], not as they might want, but in terms of maximizing those interests that will make it possible for them to develop life plans of their own.'[200] This may not assist the Walter Polovchaks of this world much, particularly if what they want and what is in their long-term interests coincides and their parents are not prepared to represent those views. But it is a useful idea to conjure with where, for example, an adolescent is not prepared to undergo surgery required to prevent him becoming totally bed-ridden. It will be remembered that in the *Green* case[201] the boy's wishes were sought and honoured by the court. His wishes prevented an operation which was necessary if he were to have the opportunity of acquiring primary social goods, such as liberty, health and opportunity. But what if he had wanted the operation and his parents had been unwilling, as, indeed, his mother was? One can, I think, still adopt the view that parents prima facie are supposed to represent their child's views, but hold that representation should cease where it can be shown to a court that parental decision-making is not geared towards a maximisation of primary social goods. It is to be assumed that the matter would only be litigated where there was a difference of opinion between a parent and a child. It would presumably only come to attention in matters of gravity or urgency and where the medical profession or a social welfare agency was appraised of the case.

My tentative solution is for a combination of the second and third decision-making models. This would, I believe, provide (i) for children's views to be recognised; (ii) for it to be acknowledged that parents do usually represent those views; and (iii) for parents to be overridden by a court where it can be shown that they are (a) not representing a child's views or (b) representing a child's views which on criteria of maximisation of primary social goods are not in the child's best interests. Further work is needed to delineate these goods. This is far from an ideal programme but it acknowledges the existence of children's rights which the Goldstein, Freud and Solnit position does not. Further, although it acknowledges the differences between young children and adolescents, it accepts the necessity for the interests of all non-adults to be taken account of in decision-making processes which affect them.

Notes

1. See S. Kamerman and A. Kahn, *Family Policy*, New York, Columbia University Press,

1978, and R. M. Moroney, *The Family and the State: Considerations For Social Policy*, London, Longman, 1976.

2. See J. Coussins and A. Coote, *The Family In The Firing Line*, London, CPAG/ NCCL, 1981.

3. The clearest philosophical statements of this are to be found in R. Nozick, *Anarchy, State and Utopia*, New York, Basic Books, 1974, and F. Hayek, *Law, Legislation and Liberty*, London, Routledge & Kegan Paul, 1982 (revised ed.). A brilliant, informed critique is P. Green, *The Pursuit of Inequality*, New York, Pantheon Books, 1981.

4. See J. Goldstein, A. Freud and A. Solnit, *Beyond The Best Interests of The Child*, New York, Free Press, 1979 (revised ed., originally published in 1973), and *Before The Best Interests of The Child*, New York, Free Press, 1979.

5. U. Bronfenbrenner, *Two Worlds of Childhood: U.S. and U.S.S.R.*, New York, Russell Sage Foundation, 1970 (re-issued with new preface by Simon & Schuster 1972), p. 5. The handbook quoted is by Makarenko and dates from 1954.

6. See M. Cohen, T. Nagel and T. Scanlon (eds), *Equality and Preferential Treatment*, Princeton, N. J., Princeton University Press, 1976.

7. See M. Rutter and N. Madge, *Cycles of Disadvantage*, London, Heinemann, 1976.

8. Cf. R. Plant, H. Lesser and P. Taylor-Gooby, *Political Philosophy and Social Welfare*, London, Routledge & Kegan Paul, 1980.

9. The issue was raised acutely in the case of the 'thalidomide children' and more recently with those brain-damaged by whooping cough vaccine but the claim can and should be generalised.

10. See M. Kellmer-Pringle, *The Needs of Children*, London, Hutchinson, 1980 (2nd ed.).

11. For a judicial observation to this effect see Justice Stevens in *H.L.* v. *Matheson* 450 US. 398, 423-24 n.1 (1981). See also *Parham* v. *J.R.* 442 U.S. 584, 603 (1979).

12. Goldstein *et al.*, *Before The Best Interests of The Child*, pp. 11-12.

13. A. Watson, 'Children, Families and Courts: Before The Best Interests of The Child and Parham v. J.R.', *Virginia Law Review*, **68** (1980), pp. 653, 665.

14. Ibid. p. 664. See also *Poe* v. *Gerstein* (1975), 517 F. 2d 787, 794 15th Cir.

15. By Lord Hailsham in *Re W* [1971]. A.C. 682, 700.

16. For example, Watson, 'Children, Families and Courts. . .', op. cit.; R. Keiter, 'Privacy, Children and Their Parents', *Minnesota Law Review*, 66 (1982), p. 459; D. Richards, 'The Individual, The Family and The Constitution', *New York University Law Review*, **55** (1980), p. 1; M. Wald, 'Thinking About Public Policy Toward Abuse and Neglect of Children', *Michigan Law Review*, **78**, (1980), p. 645; R. Mnookin, 'Foster Care— In Whose Best Interest?', *Harvard Educational Review*, **43** (1973), p. 599; M. Wald, 'State Intervention on Behalf of "Neglected" Children', *Stanford Law Review*, **27** (1975), p. 985, and *Stanford Law Review*, **28** (1976), p. 623.

17. Many examples are to be found in this chapter.

18. *H.L.* v. *Matheson*, pp. 409-10.

19. *Prince* v. *Massachusetts* 321 U.S. 158 (1944).

20. *Meyer* v. *Nebraska* 262 U.S. 390 (1923).

21. *Pierce* v. *Society of Sisters* 268 U.S. 510 (1925).

22. Ibid., at pp. 534-5.

23. *Prince* v. *Massachusetts*, op cit., p. 166. See also *Ginsberg* v. *New York* (1968) 390 U.S. 629, 639.

24. *Prince* v. *Massachusetts*, idem. The commitment to family privacy is found also in cases on local zoning ordinances, e.g. *Moore* v. *City of East Cleveland* 431 U.S. 494 (1977).

25. *Prince* v. *Massachusetts*, op cit., p. 166.

26. Goldstein *et al.*, *Before The Best Interests of The Child*, p. 217.

27. Ibid., p. 9.

28. In Goldstein *et al.*, *Beyond The Best Interests of The Child*, at pp. 17-20: see also *Before The Best Interests of The Child*, at pp. 40–57.

29. *Beyond The Best Interests of The Child*, op cit., p. 9.

30. For example, M. Rutter, *Maternal Deprivation Re-Assessed*, Harmondsworth, Penguin.

1981 (2nd ed.); A. M. Clarke and A. C. B. Clarke, *Early Experience: Myth and Evidence*, London, Open Books, 1976; B. Tizard, *Adoption: A Second Chance*, London, Open Books, 1977; J. Kagan, R. Kearsley and P. Zelazo, *Infancy: Its Place in Human Development*, Cambridge, Mass., Harvard University Press, 1978.
31. *Beyond The Best Interests...*, p. 200.
32. Ibid., p. 9.
33. For evidence of its success see J. Seglow, M. Kellmer-Pringle and P. Wedge, *Growing Up Adopted*, London, National Foundation for Educational Research, 1972, and B. Tizard, *Adoption...*, op cit.'
34. Goldstein *et al.*, *Before The Best Interests...*, p. 12.
35. Cf. P. Green, *The Pursuit of Inequality*.
36. Witness the intelligence/IQ debate, the development of socio-biology and the backlash against feminism. See also K. Joseph and J. Sumption, *Equality*, London, John Murray, 1979.
37. For example, J. Cobb and R. Sennett, *The Hidden Injuries of Class*, New York, Random House, 1972; C. Jencks, *Inequality*, New York, Basic Books, 1972; M. Barrett, *Women's Oppression Today*, London, Verso, 1980; R. Miles, *Racism and Migrant Labour*, London, Routledge & Kegan Paul, 1982.
38. B. Jordan, *Freedom and the Welfare State*, London, Routledge & Kegan Paul, 1976, p. 60.
39. See *Re P* [1982] 80 L.G.R. 30.
40. See *Re D* [1976] Fam. 185.
41. See *Re B* [1981] 1 W.L.R. 1421.
42. See, similarly, J. Hodges, 'Children and Parents: Who Chooses?' in *Politics and Power vol. 2: Sexual Politics, Feminism and Socialism*, London, Routledge & Kegan Paul, 1981, pp. 49-65.
43. And not only by a lunatic fringe: Lord Shaftesbury opposed compulsory education and Herbert Spencer compulsory immunisation.
44. Goldstein *et al.*, *Before The Best Interests...*, p. 13.
45. See M. Wald, 'Thinking About Public Policy...', *Stanford Law Review*,27 (1975), pp. 985, 992.
46. See D. P. Farrington, 'The Effects of Public Labelling', *British Journal of Criminology*, 17 (1977), p. 112; D. P. Farrington *et al.*, 'The Persistence of Labelling Effects', *British Journal of Criminology*, 18 (1978), p. 277.
47. M. Gold and J. R. Williams, 'The Effect of Getting Caught', *Prospectus*, 3 (1969), p. 1; S. Ageton and D. S. Elliott, 'The Effects of Legal Processing on Self-Concept', *Social Problems*, 22 (1974), p. 87. The *locus classicus* is, of course, D. Matza, *Becoming Deviant*, Englewood Cliffs, N.J., Prentice Hall, 1969.
48. R. Scott, *The Making of Blind Men*, New York, Russell Sage Foundation, 1969.
49. T. Scheff, *Being Mentally Ill: A Sociological Theory*, Chicago, Aldine, 1966.
50. A. Skinner and R. Castle, *78 Battered Children: A Retrospective Study*, London, NSPCC, 1969.
51. The most recent publicised case is that of Shirley Woodcock in Hammersmith. On the report see *Social Work Today*, 14, no. 20 (1983), p. 3.
52. But cf Sanford Katz, *When Parents Fail: The Law's Response to Family Breakdown*, Boston, Beacon Press, 1971.
53. H. L. A. Hart, *Punishment and Responsibility*, Oxford, Clarendon Press, 1968.
54. In M. Wald, 'State Intervention on Behalf of "Neglected" Children' in M. Rosenheim (ed.), *Pursuing Justice For The Child*, Chicago, University of Chicago Press, 1976, pp. 246, 251.
55. See A. Morris *et al, Justice for Children*, London, Macmillan, 1980; L. Taylor *et al.*, *In Whose Best Interests?* London, Cobden Trust/Mind, 1980; A. Sutton, 'Science in Court' in M. King (ed.), *Childhood, Welfare and Justice*, London, Batsford, 1981, p. 45.
56. NCOPF, *Against Natural Justice*, London, NCOPF, 1982.
57. J. Newson and E. Newson, *Patterns of Infant Care; Four Years Old In An Urban Community; Seven Years Old In The Home Environment*, all London, Allen &

Unwin, 1963, 1968 and 1976 respectively.

58.   E. Bott, *Family and Social Network*, London, Tavistock, 1971 (2nd ed.).

59.   Newson and Newson, *Patterns of Infant Care*.

60.   K. Fitzherbert, *West Indian Children In London*, London, C. Bell, 1967.

61.   See, further, M. D. A. Freeman, 'Child Welfare: Law and Control' in M. Partington and J. Jowell (eds.), *Welfare Law and Policy*, London, Frances Pinter, 1979, p. 223.

62.   E. Freidson, 'Disability As Social Deviance' in M. Sussman (ed.), *Sociology and Rehabilitation*, Washington D. C., American Sociological Association, 1966.

63.   A. Blumberg, 'The Practice of Law as a Confidence Game: Organizational Co-optation of a Profession', *Law and Society Review*, 1 (1967), p. 15.

64.   If it does not create the additional problems described in Chapter 4.

65.   Cf. G. Pearson, 'Social Work as the Privatized Solution of Public Ills', *British Journal of Social Work*, 3 (1973), p. 209.

66.   See Justice McReynolds's rejection of Plato's 'ideal Commonwealth' in *Meyer* v. *Nebraska* 262 U.S. 390, 401-02 (1923). See also *Pierce* v. *Society of Sisters* 268 U.S. 510, 535 (1925), *Bellotti* v. *Baird* 443 U.S. 622, 637-38 (1979); *Wisconsin* v. *Yoder* 406 U.S. 205, 218 (1972); and 'Developments In The Law — the Constitution and the Family', *Harvard Law Review*, 93 (1980), pp. 1156, 1214-16.

67.   *Parham* v. *J.R.* 442 U.S. 584, 603 (1979).

68.   Goldstein *et al.*, *Before The Best Interests*. . ., p. 31.

69.   See J. Eekelaar and E. Clive, *Custody After Divorce*, Oxford, SSRC, Centre for Socio-Legal Studies, 1977.

70.   Goldstein *et al.*, *Before The Best Interests*. . ., p. 39.

71.   Ibid, p. 41. See, further, C. Curtis, 'The Psychological Parent Doctrine in Custody Disputes Between Foster Parents and Biological Parents', *Columbia Journal of Law and Social Problems*, 16 (1981), p. 149.

72.   See J. Bowlby, *The Making and Breaking of Affectional Bonds*, London, Tavistock, 1979.

73.   Goldstein *et al.*, *Before The Best Interests*. . ., p. 42.

74.   Ibid, p. 45.

75.   Ibid., p. 48.

76.   As to the meaning of which see *Beyond The Best Interests*. . ., ch. 4.

77.   Goldstein *et al.*, *Before The Best Interests*. . ., p. 48.

78.   Ibid., p. 49.

79.   But not yet implemented.

80.   Children Act 1975, s.33. I have written on it in two places: 'Custodianship — New Concept, New Problems' (1976) 6 Fam. Law 57, and 'Custodianship and Wardship' (1977) 7 Fam. Law 116.

81.   Under s.3 of Child Care Act 1980 (the origins of this administrative procedure go back to the Poor Law Amendment Act 1889).

82.   Goldstein *et al.*, *Before The Best Interests*. . ., p. 59.

83.   Idem.

84.   By providing for reception into care (Child Care Act 1980 s.2) and for care proceedings and place of safety orders under the Children and Young Persons Act 1969. Also for prosecutions under the Children and Young Persons Act 1933 s.1.

85.   See R. Holman, *Trading In Children: A Study of Private Fostering*, London, Routledge & Kegan Paul, 1973.

86.   See Children Act 1975 ss. 95-97 (now in Foster Children Act 1980).

87.   See the case of Shirley Woodcock, op. cit. Other cases are the Richard Clark, the subject of an inquiry in 1975, and Frankland cases.

88.   Goldstein *et al.*, *Before The Best Interests*. . ., p. 62.

89.   Particularly noticeable in the USA: see H. Giaretto, 'Humanistic Treatment of Father-Daughter Incest' in R. Helfer and C. H. Kempe (eds), *Child Abuse and Neglect*, Cambridge, Mass., Ballinger, 1976, ch. 8; as to England see BASPCAN, *Sexual Abuse of Children*, Rochdale, BASPCAN, 1981.

90.   S. F. Appleton, 'Growing Up with Goldstein, Freud and Solnit', *Texas Law Review*, 58 (1980), p. 1343.

91. Goldstein *et al., Before The Best Interests. . .*, p. 64.
92. See, to like effect, K. D. Katz, 'When In Doubt, The Parents Win Out', *Albany Law Review*, 45 (1981), pp. 525, 529.
93. See, e.g. J. Holt, *Escape from Childhood*, Harmondsworth, Penguin, 1975, p. 206.
94. Goldstein *et al., Before The Best Interests. . .*, p. 72.
95. Idem.
96. Ibid, p. 73.
97. See, e.g. the work of the Park Hospital in Oxford described by M. Lynch, 'Family Unit In a Child's Psychiatric Hospital', *British Medical Journal*, 2 (1975), p. 127, and by M. Lynch and C. Ounsted, 'Residential Therapy — A Place of Safety' in R. Helfer and C. H. Kempe (eds), *Child Abuse and Neglect*, Cambridge, Mass., Ballinger, 1976, p. 206.
98. See E. Elmer, *Fragile Families, Troubled Children: The Aftermath of Infant Trauma*, Pittsburgh, University of Pittsburgh Press, 1977.
99. D. Besharov, in a book review of *Before The Best Interests of The Child*, *Vanderbilt Law Review*, 34 (1981), p. 481, also complains of this fault in the Goldstein *et al.* analysis.
100. Children and Young Persons Act 1933 s.1(7).
101. See R. Bourne and E. H. Newberger, *Critical Perspectives on Child Abuse*, Lexington, Mass., D.C. Heath, 1979.
102. Goldstein *et al., Before The Best Interests. . .*, p. 91.
103. Ibid, p. 92.
104. Idem.
103. Ibid., p. 93.
104. Wardship may be used. See N. Lowe and R.A.H. White, *Wards of Court*, London, Butterworths, 1979, p. 108.
105. See, e.g. the *Green* case (1979) 393 N.E. 2d 836. See also the discussion in *Before The Best Interests of The Child* of the *Hofbauer* case (pp. 250-2).
106. *Hart v. Brown* 289 A. 2d 386 (1972).
107. In Goldstein *et al., Before The Best Interests. . .*, p. 107.
108. Hence the controversies each time a change in the law is mooted. A good discussion of these in the context of the Abortion Act 1967 is V. Greenwood and J. Young *Abortion In Demand*, London, Pluto Press, 1976. On the moral issues more generally see L. W. Sumner, *Abortion and Moral Theory*, Princeton, N.J., Princeton University Press, 1981.
109. In *Re Green* 292 A. 2d 387 (1972).
110. Ibid., p. 329.
111. Ibid., p. 355.
112. *Re Seiferth* 127 N.E. 2d 820 (1955).
113. Goldstein *et al., Before The Best Interests. . .*, p. 105.
114. *Re Seiferth*, p. 823.
115. *Re Sampson* 278 N.E. 2d 918 (1972).
116. Goldstein *et al., Before The Best Interests. . .*, p. 104.
117. Ibid., pp. 104-5.
118. *Re D* [1976] Fam. 185.
119. Ibid., p. 113.
120. Idem.
121. B. Dickens, 'The Modern Function and Limits of Parental Rights', *Law Quarterly Review*, 97 (1981), pp. 462, 474.
122. As to which see G. Calabresi and P. Bobbitt, *Tragic Choices*, New York, W. W. Norton, 1978, and N. Hershey and R. Miller, *Human Experimentation and the Law*, Germantown, Md., Aspen Systems, 1976. There are useful materials in R. Mnookin, *Child, Family and State*, Boston, Little, Brown, 1978, p. 399.
123. Thus the standard text, C. R. A. Martin, *Law Relating to Medical Practice* (Tunbridge Wells, Pitman Medical Books, 1979 (2nd ed.)), makes no reference to the problem.
124. *Re B* [1981] 1 W.L.R. 1421.
125. See I. Kennedy, 'Reflections On The Arthur Trial', *New Society*, 7 January 1982, pp. 13-15.

126. *Re B.*, p. 1423.
127. Ibid., p. 1424.
128. Ibid., p. 1424-5.
129. Goldstein *et al., Before The Best Interests. . .*, p. 97.
130. In Kelsey, 'Shall These Children Live? A Conversation with Dr. Raymond S. Duff', *Reflection*, **72** (1973), pt 4 at p. 7.
131. See, e.g. Richard Brandt, 'Defective Newborns and the Morality of Termination' in Marvin Kohl (ed.), *Infanticide and the Value of Life*, Buffalo, Prometheus Books, 1978.
132. R. Duff and Campbell, 'Moral and Ethical Dilemmas In The Special Care Nursery', *New England Journal of Medicine*, **289** (1973), p. 890.
133. Goldstein *et al., Before The Best Interests. . .*, p. 97.
134. P. Foot, 'Euthanasia', *Philosophy and Public Affairs*, **6** (1977), p. 85.
135. Brandt, 'Defective Newborns. . .', p. 89.
136. But Alexandra has now returned home. See *The Observer*, 5 December 1982.
137. See *The Times*, 19 August 1981.
138. BMA, *Handbook of Medical Ethics*, 1981 edition, paras. 5.11 and 5.12.
139. See *The Times*, 14 September 1981.
140. Claire Tomalin, 'Alexandra: The Cruel Folly', *The Times*, 1 September 1981.
141. Idem.
142. See E. Harbridge, 'Life or Death — Who Decides?', *Community Care*, 19 November 1981, pp. 4-5.
143. J. A. Robertson, 'Involuntary Euthanasia of Defective Newborns', *Stanford Law Review*, **27** (1975), pp. 213, 263.
144. J. Harris, 'Ethical Problems in the Management of Some Severely Handicapped Children', *Journal of Medical Ethics*, **7** (1981), p. 117.
145. Cf. J. A. G. Griffith, *The Politics of the Judiciary*, London, Fontana, 1981 (2nd ed.).
146. See, similarly, I. Kennedy, 'Where Doctors and the Law Can Meet', *The Times*, 8 September 1981.
147. Karen Quinlan, though not a child, is one such example. Her case is reported at (1976) 355 A. 2d 646. The case is discussed by I. Kennedy, 'The Karen Quinlan Case: Problems and Proposals', *Journal of Medical Ethics*, **2** (1977), p. 3. There is also a symposium in *Rutgers Law Review*, **30** (1977), pp. 243-328.
148. D. and M. Brahams, 'The Arthur Case — A Proposal For Legislation', *Journal of Medical Ethics*, **9**(1983), p. 12.
149 A. Holder, *Legal Issues In Pediatrics and Adolescent Medicine*, Chichester, Wiley, 1977, p. 105.
150. *Medico-Legal Aspects of Family Law*, Toronto, Butterworths, 1979, p. 105.
151. *Re P* (1982) 80 L.G.R. 301.
152. Ibid., p. 303.
153. As it could do. See *Re B* [1975] Fam. 36.
154. See Child Care Act 1980 s.10(2). See further as to this, M.D.A. Freeman, 'The Legal Battlefield of Care', *Current Legal Problems*, **35** (1982), p. 117.
155. For a review of the issues see A. Samuels, 'Can a Minor (under 16) Consent to a Medical Operation?', *Family Law*, **13** (1983), p. 30.
156. *Planned Parenthood of Missouri* v. *Danforth* 428 U.S. 52 (1976).
157. *Bellotti* v. *Baird* 443 U.S. 622 (1979).
158. *Carey* v. *Population Services International* 431 U.S. 678 (1977).
159. *Planned Parenthood . . .* v. *Danforth*, p. 75.
160. *Bellotti* v. *Baird*, p. 647.
161. Ibid, p. 648.
162. *Carey* v. *Population. . .*, p. 713.
163. *Bellotti* v. *Baird*, p. 645.
164. *Parham* v. *J.R.* 442 U.S. 584 (1979).
165. Ibid., p. 604.
166. Idem.
167. Ibid., p. 635.

168. J. Goldstein, 'Medical Care For The Child At Risk: On State Supervention of Parental Autonomy', *Yale Law Journal*, **86** (1977), p. 645.

169. *Parham* v. *J.R.*, p. 605.

170. Watson, 'Children, Families. . .', p. 672.

171. Ibid.

172. T. Szasz, 'The Child As Involuntary Mental Patient: The Threat of Child Therapy To The Child's Dignity, Privacy and Self-Esteem', *San Diego Law Review*, **14** (1977), p. 1005.

173. Watson, 'Children, Families . . .', p. 675.

174. E. Goffman, *Asylums*, Garden City, N.Y., Doubleday, 1961.

175. D. A. J. Richards, 'The Individual, The Family, and the Constitution: A Jurisprudential Perspective', *New York University Law Review*, **55** (1980), pp. 1, 60.

176. *Tinker* 393 U.S. 503 (1969) (first amendment rights of free speech extended to public school students protesting Vietnam war).

177. *Goss* v. *Lopez* 419 U.S. 565 (1975) (high school students entitled to hearing before suspension).

178. *Ingraham* v. *Wright* 430 U.S. 651 (1977) (prior procedural protections not required when school children face corporal punishment).

179. Richards, 'The Individual. . .', p. 60.

180. Ibid., p. 61.

181. See Plato's *The Republic*.

182. DHSS, *A Review of The Mental Health Act 1959*, London HMSO Cmnd. 8320.

183. Mental Health (Amendment) Act 1982, (now in Mental Health Act 1983).

184. *Re S* [1978] Q.B. 120, 144.

185. See J. Rawls, *A Theory of Justice*, Cambridge, Mass., Harvard University Press, 1971, p. 92, for a definition of primary social goods. See also p. 440 where 'self-respect' is added to the list.

186. J. Rawls, 'Consent, Representation and Proxy Consent' in W. Gaylin and R. Macklin (eds), *Who Speaks For The Child: The Problems of Proxy Consent*, New York, Plenum Press, 1982, p. 191 at p. 205. This book came to hand too late for much account to be taken of it.

187. *Wisconsin* v. *Yoder* 406 U.S. 205 (1972).

188. Ibid., p. 232.

189. Ibid., pp. 244-5.

190. Ibid., p. 247.

191. *Re Snyder* 532 P. 2d 278 (1975).

192. Ibid., p. 281.

193. See *The Sunday Times*, 3 August 1980, *The Sunday Times* (Colour Supplement) 15 March 1981, *The Sunday Times*, 17 January 1982 and *The Times*, 27 January 1982.

194. Quoted in *The Sunday Times*, 3 August 1980.

195. Quoted in *The Sunday Times*, 17 January 1982.

196. Which is sixteen for the purpose of this case.

197. *Re B* [1981] 1 W.L.R. 1421.

198. *Re D* [1976] Fam. 185.

199. Representation is a complex concept. See H. Pitkin, *Representation*, New York, Atherton, 1969.

200. Dworkin, 'Consent, Representation . . .', p. 205.

201. *Re Green* 292 A. 2d 387 (1972).

CONCLUSION

It is not intended in this brief conclusion to summarise the contents of the book. Nor is this intended as a recapitulation of the proposals for reform contained within individual chapters. Instead I offer a brief coda in which I ask where thinking about children has reached and where it is to go from here.

We are now three years on from the International Year of the Child. The logo has disappeared and most of the events of the year are now a distant memory. The media have new concerns: nuclear warfare and the peace movement, law and order and the police. The country has witnessed riots in the inner city and has been embroiled in war. Besides events such as these, the problems of separated children or handicapped school-leavers appear insignificant. IYC brought the plight of children to our living-rooms, but was our concern more than a temporary infatuation? Have policies towards or concerning children changed?

There have been some changes. Penal policies towards children who offend have become increasingly punitive. A characteristic recent phrase is the 'short, sharp shock'[1]: punishment meted out in glasshouse-style detention centres. The residential care order has also arrived.[2] Fifteen years ago we talked of 'children in trouble': now the talk is of 'young offenders'.[3] The change of rhetoric is symptomatic of a change in ideology. It might be welcomed, for it is a move away from treatment and an acceptance that there is a distinction between delinquent youth and endangered children, if rights were to accompany responsiblity. But there is little hope of that.

The recent past has also seen increasing disquiet over the powers which local authorities exercise over children in their care and their parents. As a result of pressure, not least from the Children's Legal Centre,[4] some controls have now been placed on the powers of local authorities to put children in care into secure units.[5] The injustice of local authorities divesting parents of their rights and duties by an administrative mechanism has been brought to the attention of Parliament.[6] So have a number of cases in which access to children in care has been denied, but legislation has now imposed some constraints on a local authority's discretion.[7]

Attention has also been focused on matters relating to children which seem to have had little impact in the media, and therefore on the public, until the immediate past: lead pollution,[8] incest[9] and the problems children encounter on their parents' divorce[10] have all been thought about, researched and publicised in the early 1980s to a greater extent than before. What impact this activity will have on public policy remains to be seen. An opportunity to acknowledge the existence of sexual abuse was missed by the DHSS in its most recent circular on child abuse.[11] The Law Commission, however, in its thinking on the economic consequences of divorce, has given priority to the needs of children and this is likely to be reflected in future legislation.[12] It has also recently proposed that all remaining disabilities suffered by illegitimate children be removed.[13]

Generally, though, policies towards children have changed little in the last three years. Child poverty is worse,[14] youth unemployment greater, more children are locked up than in 1979. Many of the issues remain the same. The debate about corporal punishment has got no further.[15] Indeed, a recent court decision[16] may have taken a backwards step since it appears to hold that local education authorities may not take the initiative in abolishing corporal punishment in schools. This may seem surprising coming in the same year the European Court of Human Rights condemned the British practice.[17] But that should not surprise us for even within policies taken totally within this country there is little coherence when matters relating to children are considered. But why should there be? What is the state of our thinking about children?

Children's rights, as I have indicated, have been embraced enthusiastically by writers, commissions, legislatures and judges. But only the most cursory thought has been given to what is meant by the phrase, and what the implications of children's rights are. It is not difficult or rare to find proponents and opponents of a measure both using children's rights arguments or at least rhetoric.[18] Did the Children Act of 1975 advance children's rights or frustrate them? One lobby sees the legislation as a 'children's charter' (nearly all children's legislation has been so characterised by its entrepreneurs): another interprets the Act as a measure which legitimated inequalities in the child care system. These arguments (unfortunately they are rarely debates) often reside in a vacuum. Thinking about children's rights has concentrated on policies, not principles. This is doubly unfortunate for moral and political theory has so much to offer. There are exceptions, of course, like Michael Wald and David Richards (as discussed in Chapter 2) but in general the impact of contemporary moral and political thinking on those concerned with children's rights has been minimal (in just the same way, one may add in parenthesis, as the sociology of deviancy has almost passed by those concerned with juvenile justice; they, oblivious to the advances of the newer discipline, still work happily within positivistic criminology).[19] One result has been that discussions about children's rights tend to end up as 'protection versus autonomy', expressed in pat phrases like 'protecting children or their rights'.[20] These dichotomies are false, as I have demonstrated in Chapter 2.

If thinking about children's rights has not got very far, concrete policies have not progressed very far either. In part they are piecemeal and lack coherence because an overarching philosophy is lacking. But I believe the deficiencies lie not merely in thinking but also in implementation. To put it bluntly: who speaks for children? There are, it is true, a number of pressure groups, the Child Poverty Action Group, the National Association of Young People in Care, Justice for Children, the Family Rights Group etc., and they have some impact. But no one is directly responsible for policies relating to children. Not only is there no ministry of children but decisions relating to children are spread across a number of departments, the DHSS, the Home Office, the Lord Chancellor's Department, the Department of Education and Science etc. There have been calls for legislation to be accompanied by a family impact statement.[21] The idea has made little headway in this country. I believe its adoption to be important. It is also important for the actual effects of legislation to be regularly monitored. There is a precedent for this in the Children Act 1975.[22] But it is not just legislation which should be examined in these ways. The policies and practices of local institutions, education authorities, social services departments and others which directly affect the lives of families, particularly children, and those of government departments should be similarly scrutinised.

We need to create a new institutional framework to promote children's rights. I have a number of suggestions. First, there should be a member of the cabinet with direct responsibility for matters concerned with children. He would be answerable in Parliament and he would be responsible for legislation concerning children and for preparing statements about the impact of other legislation on children.[23]

Secondly, we should establish an institution which combines the roles of an ombudsman and a commission like the Commission for Racial Equality or the Equal Opportunities Commission. We need an institution to which complaints about the treatment of children can go and which would have the same or similar investigative powers as the CRE or EOC. We need an agency committed to the welfare of children with wide-ranging investigative powers, the ability to hold inquiries and to take institutions, like local authorities, to court. If bad practices exist, and ample evidence of this has been provided in this book (see especially Chapter 5), they cannot be eradicated within a framework of private law. A case-by-case approach nibbles at the edges. It adjusts disagreements that arise within an established order.[24] It does not provide leverage for change. Just as the elimination of racial discrimination, particularly indirect discrimination, requires the extensive use of public law remedies[25] (a fact recognised in the 1976 Race Relations Act), so does the eradication of bad practices in an area like that relating to children in care, or those within a local educational authority. Valuable as the jurisdiction of local commissioners for administration is, something with bigger teeth and a greater bite is called for.

Thirdly, important though a Ministry and a Commission are, a network of institutions at grassroots level is also imperative. We need a network of local children's legal centres to educate, to advise and assist and to stimulate action on behalf of children in their areas. Rights remain dormant if those who have them do not assert them. It is in part absence of 'legal competence',[26] failure to mobilise the law on one's own behalf, which has led, as Galanter[27] put it in a justly famous article, 'the "haves" to win out'. If children's rights are to be more than a political slogan, then children must demand them and must be encouraged and educated to do so. Access to people, lawyers and others, with an expertise and a commitment will enable the young to develop the sort of claims consciousness which is part of a rational autonomy.

Notes

1. The phrase was coined by W. S. Gilbert (in *The Mikado*). Its contemporary use dates from a speech of William Whitelaw at the Conservative Party Conference (see *The Guardian*, 11 October 1979).
2. See Criminal Justice Act 1982 s.22.
3. The title of the most recent White Paper on the subject (London, HMSO, 1980, Cmnd. 3601).
4. *Locked Up In Care*, London, Children's Legal Centre, 1982.
5. Criminal Justice Act 1982 s.25.
6. See *Against Natural Justice — A Study of The Procedures Used by Local Authorities in Taking Parental Rights Resolutions Over Children in Voluntary Care*, London, National Council of One Parent Families, 1982. There have been a number of abortive attempts to alter the situation. One unconvincing but rather typical defence of the status quo is M. Hawker, 'Children Have Rights Too', *Community Care*, 6 January 1983, p. 14.
7. See J. Tunnard, 'No Access For Parents', *New Society*, 63, no. 1053, 20 January 1983, p. 100. See now Health Act 1983 s.6 and Schedule 1.
8. See R. Rogers, *Lead Poison*, London, New Statesman Publications, 1982.
9. See F. Rush, *The Best Kept Secret — Sexual Abuse of Children*, New York, McGraw Hill, 1980; BASPCAN, *Child Sexual Abuse*, Rochdale, BASPCAN, 1981.
10. See J. S. Wallerstein and J. B. Kelly, *Surviving The Break-Up*, New York, Basic Books, 1980.
11. *Child Abuse: Central Register System*, LASSL (80) 4, August 1980.
12. *The Financial Consequences of Divorce*, Law Com. No. 112, London, HMSO, H.C. 68, 1981.
13. *Illegitimacy*, Law Com. No. 118, London, HMSO, H.C.98, 1982.
14. Child Poverty Action Group, *Poverty — What Poverty?*, London, CPAG, 1982.
15. Society of Teachers Opposed to Physical Punishment, *The Truth About Public School Beatings*, London, STOPP, 1982.
16. R v. *Greater Manchester L.E.A.*, *The Times*, 29 October 1982.
17. Council of Europe, European Court of Human Rights, Case of Campbell and Cosans, Strasbourg, 25 February 1982.
18. See L. Fox, 'Two Value Positions In Recent Child Care Law and Practice', *British Journal of Social Work*, 12 (1982), p. 265.
19. For agreement see H. Parker and H. Giller, 'More And Less The Same: British Delinquency Research Since The Sixties', *British Journal of Criminology*, 21 (1981), p. 230.

20. The phrase is Farson's. See R. Farson, *Birthrights*, Harmondsworth, Penguin, 1978, p. 9.
21. See also F. Field, *Fair Shares For Families: The Need For A Family Impact Statement*, London, Study Commission on the Family, 1980, p. 6 *et seq*.
22. Section 105.
23. See B. Jackson and S. Jackson, *Childminder*, Harmondsworth, Penguin, 1981, ch. 15.
24. Cf. L. Mayhew, *Law and Equal Opportunity*, Cambridge, Mass., Harvard University Press, 1968, pp. 272–3.
25. See L. Lustgarten, *Legal Control of Racial Discrimination*, London, Macmillan, 1980.
26. See J. Carlin *et al.*, 'Legal Representation and Class Justice', *University of California Los Angeles Law Review*, **12** (1965), p. 381.
27. M.Galanter, 'Why The "Haves" Come Out Ahead: Speculations on The Limits of Legal Change', *Law and Sociology Review*, **9** (1974), p. 95.

APPENDIX

United Nations Declaration of the Rights of the Child

Preamble

Whereas the peoples of the United Nations have, in the Charter, reaffirmed their faith in fundamental human rights, and in the dignity and worth of the human person, and have determined to promote social progress and better standards of life in larger freedom.

Whereas the United Nations has, in the Universal Declaration of Human Rights, proclaimed that everyone is entitled to all the rights and freedoms set forth therein, without distinction of any kind, such as race, colour, sex, language, religion, political or other opinion, national or social origin, property, birth or other status.

Whereas the child, by reason of his physical and mental immaturity, needs special safeguards and care, including appropriate legal protection, before as well as after birth.

Whereas the need for such special safeguards has been stated in the Geneva Declaration of the Rights of the Child of 1924, and recognized in the Universal Declaration of Human Rights and in the statutes of specialized agencies and international organizations concerned with the welfare of children.

Whereas mankind owes to the child the best it has to give.

Now therefore, the General Assembly proclaims this Declaration of the Rights of the Child to the end that he may have a happy childhood and enjoy for his own good and for the good of society the rights and freedoms herein set forth, and calls upon parents, upon men and women as individuals and upon voluntary organizations, local authorities and national governments to recognize these rights and strive for their observance by legislative and other measures progressively taken in accordance with the following principles:

Principle I

The child shall enjoy all the rights set forth in this Declaration. All children, without any exception whatsoever, shall be entitled to these rights, without distinction or discrimination on account of race, colour, sex, language, religion,

283

political or other opinion, national or social origin, property, birth or other status, whether of himself or of his family.

Principle 2

The child shall enjoy special protection, and shall be given opportunities and facilities, by law and by other means, to enable him to develop physically, mentally, morally, spiritually and socially in a healthy and normal manner and in conditions of freedom and dignity. In the enactment of laws for this purpose the best interests of the child shall be the paramount consideration.

Principle 3

The child shall be entitled from his birth to a name and a nationality.

Principle 4

The child shall enjoy the benefits of social security. He shall be entitled to grow and develop in health; to this end special care and protection shall be provided both to him and to his mother, including adequate pre-natal and post-natal care. The child shall have the right to adequate nutrition, housing, recreation and medical services.

Principle 5

The child who is physically, mentally or socially handicapped shall be given the special treatment, education and care required by his particular condition.

Principle 6

The child, for the full and harmonious development of his personality, needs love and understanding. He shall, wherever possible, grow up in the care and under the responsibility of his parents, and in any case in an atmosphere of affection and of moral and material security; a child of tender years shall not, save in exceptional circumstances, be separated from his mother. Society and the public authorities shall have the duty to extend particular care to children without a family and to those without adequate means of support. Payment of state and other assistance toward the maintenance of children of large families is desirable.

Principle 7

The child is entitled to receive education, which shall be free and compulsory, at least in the elementary stages. He shall be given an education which will promote his general culture, and enable him on a basis of equal opportunity to develop his abilities, his individual judgment, and his sense of moral and social responsibility, and to become a useful member of society.

The best interests of the child shall be the guiding principle of those responsible for his education and guidance; that responsibility lies in the first place with his parents.

The child shall have full opportunity for play and recreation, which should be directed towards the same purposes as education; society and the public authorities shall endeavour to promote the enjoyment of this right.

Principle 8

The child shall in all circumstances be among the first to receive protection and relief.

Principle 9

The child shall be protected against all forms of neglect, cruelty and exploitation. He shall not be the subject of traffic, in any form.

The child shall not be admitted to employment before an appropriate minimum age; he shall in no case be caused or permitted to engage in any occupation or employment which would prejudice his health or education, or interfere with his physical, mental or moral development.

Principle 10

The child shall be protected from practices which may foster racial, religious and any other form of discrimination. He shall be brought up in a spirit of understanding, tolerance, friendship among peoples, peace and universal brotherhood and in full consciousness that his energy and talents should be devoted to the service of his fellow men.

TABLE OF CASES

INDEX